A Century of Greco-Roman Philology

Featuring the American Philological Association
and the Society of Biblical Literature

SOCIETY OF BIBLICAL LITERATURE
BIBLICAL SCHOLARSHIP IN NORTH AMERICA

Kent Harold Richards, Editor

Frank Chamberlain Porter: Pioneer in American Biblical Interpretation — Roy A. Harrisville

Benjamin Wisner Bacon: Pioneer in American Biblical Criticism — Roy A. Harrisville

A Fragile Craft: The Work of Amos Niven Wilder — John Dominic Crossan

Edgar Johnson Goodspeed: Articulate Scholar — James I. Cook

Shirley Jackson Case and the Chicago School: The Socio-Historical Method — William J. Hynes

Humanizing America's Iconic Book: Society of Biblical Literature Centennial Addresses 1980 — Gene M. Tucker and Douglas A. Knight, editors

A History of Biblical Studies in Canada: A Sense of Proportion — John S. Moir

Searching the Scriptures: A History of the Society of Biblical Literature, 1880-1980 — Ernest W. Saunders

Horace Bushnell: On the Vitality of Biblical Language — James O. Duke

Feminist Perspectives on Biblical Scholarship — Adela Yarboro Collins, editor

Erwin Ramsdell Goodenough: A Personal Pilgrimage — Robert S. Eccles

The Pennsylvania Tradition of Semitics — Cyrus H. Gordon

The Bible and the University: The Messianic Vision of William Rainey Harper — James P. Wind

Max Leopold Margolis: A Scholar's Scholar — Leonard Greenspoon

A Century of Greco-Roman Philology — Frederick William Danker

Moses Stuart — John H. Giltner

A Century of Greco-Roman Philology

Featuring the American Philological Association
and the Society of Biblical Literature

by

Frederick W. Danker

With the Assistance of
Jennifer Gadd, Deborah Holton,
Richard Krenning, Joan La Fournaise,
and
Lois Danker, Technical Advisor

Scholars Press
Atlanta, Georgia

SOCIETY OF BIBLICAL LITERATURE
CENTENNIAL PUBLICATIONS

Editorial Board

The Society of Biblical Literature gratefully acknowledges a grant from the National Endowment for the Humanities to underwrite certain editorial and research expenses of the Centennial Publications Series. Published results and interpretations do not necessarily represent the view of the Endowment.

Library of Congress Cataloging-in-Publication Data

Danker, Frederick W.
A century of Greco-Roman philology.

(Biblical scholarship in North America; no. 12)
Bibliography: p.
I. Classical philology — History. 2. Learning and scholarship — United States — History. 3. Bible — Criticism, interpretation, etc. — United States — History.
I. Title. II. Series.
PA70.U6D36   1987   938'.007'073   85-30412
ISBN: 0-89130-985-3
ISBN: 0-89130-986-1 (pbk.)

In the beginning was the Word.
St. John

Crescat scientia, vita excolatur.
Paul Shorey

CONTENTS

PROLOGUE ix

PART I. GREECE AND ROME 1

    Chapter 1. Contextuality 3
    Chapter 2. Hellenistic Judaism 13
    Chapter 3. Exegetical Exhibits and Formal Features 17

PART II. BASIC INTERPRETIVE WORK 27

    Chapter 4. Concordances and Word Indexes 29
    Chapter 5. Lexicography 43
    Chapter 6. Grammar 57
    Chapter 7. Epigraphy 91
    Chapter 8. Papyrology 115

PART III. A CENTURY OF SELF-DISCIPLINE 129

    Chapter 9. Mudwashing and Whitewashing 131
    Chapter 10. Philological Voodoo or Pseudorthodoxy 143
    Chapter 11. Assorted Philological Aberrations and Ailments 159
    Chapter 12. Research with Responsibility 167
    Chapter 13. Arts and Hazards of Reviewing 189

PART IV. LITERARY PHILOLOGY 197

ABBREVIATIONS 223

BIBLIOGRAPHY 225

EPILOGUE 299

Prologue

A Harvard University Catalog for the year 1906–1907 indicates that the word philology was used to cover everything from Vedic noun inflections to literary criticism and the Epistles of St. Paul.

Any attempt, then, to record in one small volume an inventory of a century of American philological inquiry, even with special reference to the Greco-Roman world, would certainly be interpreted as an exercise in futility, nourished by hybris. Much less would it be possible to write a scientific history, if indeed there be such a species, in so small a compass and within the brief space of time envisaged for a centennial assignment. Even such a valued piece as Ulrich von Wilamowitz-Moellendorf's *History of Classical Scholarship* is vitiated by its provincial approach.[1]

In the matter of American scholarship much of the problem is related to a fundamental deficiency in theoretical subject matter. Friedrich August Wolf built on foundations laid by Christian Gottlob Heyne and introduced what he thought was the science of classical philology on 8 April 1777. Many of his conclusions, especially those relating to Homer, are no longer considered worthy of inclusion in fame's eternal register.

Despite the fact that with the passage of time it has proved increasingly difficult, if not impossible, to reach the Parnassian peak of a perspective that would help one grasp the basic rationale of what is embraced by *Altertumswissenschaft*, Wolf's achievement dare not be trivialized. As Adolf Harnack observed, Wolf did succeed in bringing classical studies out of the "vestibule of theology." And it was Wolf's pioneering spirit that provided the initial stimulus for creation of scientific academies, for publications of inscriptions, for editions of classical and patristic authors and of Byzantine historians, to mention but a few, and without which biblical scholars would have been far more limited to scholastic debates. The development of *Thesaurus Linguae Graecae*, whose canon of Greek authors as listed by Luci Berkowitz (1977) forms a part of that continuity, is in effect a bicentennial tribute to Wolf. Ironically it puts much of the total available written expression of the

---

[1] For pre-20th century developments in classical study, see Ulrich von Wilamowitz-Moellendorf, *History of Classical Scholarship* (tr. Alan Harris; Baltimore: Johns Hopkins, 1982; 1st German ed. 1921). Hugh Lloyd Jones updates in an introduction, pp. v-xxxii, with the observation that the German scholar snubbed American scholarship, especially by omitting reference to Basil Gildersleeve, whose contributions fell within Wilamowitz's temporal framework.

Greco-Roman world at the touch of a key, but at the same time suggests that the attainment of a comprehensive discipline will, like the expectations of the figures on Keat's Grecian urn, ever elude the grasp.[2]

Yet the very lack of a discipline, in the strict sense of the term, constitutes strength of possibility for celebration of a centennial of philological effort. To invite the presence of all who engaged over a hundred years in *Altertumswissenschaft* was of course impossible. Such topics as Greco-Roman philosophy, political and military institutions and legal procedures, prosopography, theatrical productions, metrics, metrology, numismatics, and a host of ancient sciences that are part of the biblical world called for attention, but their treatment would have expanded the bulk of the SBL Centennial Series beyond the boundaries of time and space envisaged by the editors. Needed was a work that would assist classicists and students of the Greek Bible in recognizing their common base of interest and of problems.

Near the end of the century biblical students who discovered that the Greek Bible was part of the vast network of Greco-Roman, as well as of Semitic culture, were rushing to Rome and Athens for contextual data, but some were not aware of the complexities involved in such research and others were ignorant of significant work done long before they strolled from the Temple to the Stoa. Classical scholars increasingly appreciated what Clifford Moore stated in 1911, that "antiquity must be studied in all its manifestations and that consequently the New Testament and the writings of the Church Fathers belong to the classical philologist as much as to the theologian." (509) It was becoming steadily apparent to classicists that the documents of the New Testament provided them with precisely the kind of literary expression and dramatis personae that were generally lacking as dominant factors in the so-called Classics, whose canon took shape in higher literary circles and appealed to audiences and readers with especially refined taste.[3]

To assist scholars on both sides of the street to develop further acqaintance in the agora of mutual interest is, therefore, one of the objectives in the composition of this centennial volume. To that end it appeared advantageous to select representative areas in which philological inquiry came to expression, with special reference to basic inquiries and resources necessary for appreciation of the ancient languages and to the processes whereby the ancient texts become a part of humanity's total self-expression and its quest for understanding the rationale of existence. In effect this meant a charting of philological oscillation. On the one hand, there is the claim of the older philology, with its diachronic emphasis on determination of sources, literary forms, grammatical and lexical history, verifiability of ancient data, and

---

[2] On the difficulty in establishing a distinction between linguistics and philology see, among others, Shorey, 1906a, 1906b; Kelsey, 1908; Sturtevant-Kent, 1928; Garvin, 1974. Nida's (1972) discussion of the implications of linguistic theory for biblical scholarship is a model of clarity.

[3] Cf. Copley, 1952:201.

related matters. On the other, there is the synchronic interest that sees the ancient documents as part and parcel of the present insofar as those documents give expression to what is perennially human.

These extremes display the basic shift that has taken place in terminology. Whereas philology once included in its embrace the older linguistics, the study of basic elements of utterance, with a strong emphasis on comparative analysis, as exhibited by the inclusion of studies in Sanskrit, Iroquois, and Algonquin in early issues of *TAPA*, development in the twentieth century was in the direction of a separation of such linguistic science from what can well be classified as literary philology, which is interested primarily in the study of documents, either as sources for data other than the linguistic or as aesthetic phenomena, or both. The incorporation in *TAPA* 19 (1888) of J. Ernest Whitney's discussion of "Continued Allegory" in Edmund Spenser's *Faery Queene*, was a sign of the times; thereafter, a broader interest in literary work as totalities, in themes, plots, and cultural phenomena made itself felt in that annual. This approach was in marked contrast to the work of many critics after Albrecht Ritschl, who received this epitaph from Wilamowitz: "The last idea they had was to enter into another man's mind. They could hardly spare the time to acquaint themselves with their author's diction before they began correcting it."[4]

Linguistics in turn underwent a crisis when Ferdinand de Saussure gave it a fresh direction with his investigation of basic structures that underlie human communication.[5] Reductionalistically put, all this ferment, much of it going on without a clearly established theoretical framework in which it might be understood, has been mirrored in the conflict between the sponsors of what some have viewed as atomistic trivialization and the champions of abiding things of the spirit. Defenders of Matthew Arnold's holistic perception ask whether a dominant interest in minutiae was consonant with the intrinsic values of classical and biblical literature in the cultural and religious history of humanity. As Paul Shorey put it in "structural" terms, one needs to "know the thoughts of the ancients in their true perspective and proportion, in their right relation to one another, and to the modern world" (Shorey, 1906a: 195). The on-going battle over the Homeric poems exhibits the depth of scholars' commitment to their views. Charges of heresy, uncompromising stance against the "infidel," retrenchment to arguments that were as unconvincing as the worst efforts of their opponents, with inevitable declination of the original faith as old difficulties were rediscovered — all this appears to be a description of entrenched biblical scholars, but is in fact ascribed by the British classicist Eric Robertson Dodds to "naive" Homeric Unitarians in

---

[4] Wilamowitz, *History of Scholarship* (see note 1), p. 136.

[5] On this and later developments, see the overview by Spivak, 1976, of Jacques Derrida, *Of Grammatology*. For a general discussion of linguistics, see Davis, 1973.

their battle against sectarian Analysts.[6] Dodds depicts John Scott (1921), America's chief exponent for the unity of Homer as a "skillful if unscupulous controversialist," who "succeeded by a careful choice of examples in conveying the suggestion that the greatest scholars of Germany were not only pedants but fools."[7] Moreover, chides the British scholar, "Analysts and Unitarians are slow to learn from each other, and sometimes give the impression of not having troubled to read each other's work."[8]

This latter-day Homeric war is one of the extreme forms of the recurring conflict, with counterpart at some points on the field of biblical scholarship. And just as the "wrath of Achilles" has offered to some Homeric scholars a strain of thematic unity for the *Iliad,* so the philological struggle in many of its various phases suggested itself as a cohesive force for discussion of a century of philological effort. Whether in epic, in works designed for the theater, or in historical form, Greeks displayed a special interest in the theme of conflict, and this centennial volume gives image to that fact.

The American Philological Association

The American Philological Association (APA) and the Society of Biblical Literature (SBL), originally known as the Society of Biblical Literature and Exegesis, provided the basic locale within which the character of the action could be perceived; and their chief publications, *Transactions of the American Philological Association* and *Journal of Biblical Literature,* supplied much of the dialogue. APA and SBL are therefore the siderial features in this centennial work.[9]

Stimulated by the establishment of the American Association for the Advancement of Science, as well as by organization of the American Oriental Society, a group of more than fifty scholars met in New York City on 13 November 1868 to develop plans for organized encouragement of philological study. In the course of the exploratory session, George Comfort, professor at Allegheny College and later at Syracuse University, outlined the need for such collegial enterprise, with stress on openness of membership to "all professors of language of respectable standing in our colleges, universities, theological seminaries, and other schools of high education, and to others interested in the promotion of philological studies" (Shero, 1963:xi).

---

[6] Cf. E. R. Dodds, "Homer and the Unitarians," in *Fifty Years (and Twelve) of Classical Scholarship, Revised with Appendices,* with various articles by British scholars (Oxford: Blackwell, 1968; 1st edition, 1954), p. 11.

[7] Ibid., 9–10.

[8] Ibid., 12.

[9] For review of the first fifty years of *TAPA* and the APA see F. Moore, 1919; Shorey, 1919; Bloomfield, 1919. Centennial update by Shero, 1963. For the seventy-fifth anniversary of *AJP,* see Rowell, 1954.

As determined by the committee on arrangements, the constituting convention met in Poughkeepsie, New York, on 27 July 1869. Professor William D. Whitney was elected president; Benjamin W. Dwight and Albert Harkness, vice-presidents; and Comfort, secretary. At noon on July 29, the American Philological Association became a legal identity.

In the sessions that followed, the members exhibited their breadth of interest, with discussion ranging from the place of modern languages in the curriculum to linguistic phenomena in American Indian languages. But there were clear signals that such delicacies as Algonquin and Iroquois would be apportioned to other sects in the philological world. Whitney's rhetoric in the opening address was not couched in Salian terms. "The classics," he proclaimed, "will occupy the leading place; that department will be most strongly represented, and will least need fostering, while it will call for most careful criticism" (Shero:xvi). And in a paper delivered at one of the sessions, Professor Comfort, observing that "only medicine, law, theology, and some branches of natural science, were being taught in postgraduate schools," pointed out the need for postgraduate instruction in language.

Such pleas for specialization in the humanities were bound to hasten the end of the intimate philological ecumenism practiced in the early years of APA, and within a brief span of time the classical elect exercised a dominant role. Sensitive to the future, proponents of the study of English and other modern languages made their departure in 1883 and formed the Modern Language Association of America. A symbolic by-product of the separation was the battle that developed, as noted earlier, between Homeric Universalists and Homeric Separatists. This is not to suggest that classicists are any more snobbish than, say, their collegues in the field of biblical studies. It is simply in the nature of circumstances that scholars, qua scholars, must play the role of tragic heroes. One primary demonstration of tension illustrates the point. Throughout the history of SBL and APA, presidents of these organizations have with prophetic voice deplored a narrow perspective that precludes the larger vision of ultimate responsibility to humanity as earth's chief enterprise. Ironically, the rush toward specialization brought with it an isolation that would in later decades be remedied somewhat by recognition of the need of wider-ranging contact in a world enlarged by developments in linguistics.

Meanwhile, as partial antidote to the hazard of introversion, the APA very early maintained contact with allied groups. In 1881 the membership linked arms with the American Association for the Advancement of Science in deprecating the practice of awarding the Ph.D. as an honorary degree. Dissatisfied with the broad sweep of *TAPA* and the fact that it appeared only annually, Basil Gildersleeve helped bring the *American Journal of Philology* into being. Soon there was a division of the house, and philological inquiry in the narrower sense of grammatical and lexical study siphoned the interests of those who were interested in the basic elements that constitute human utterance, apart from semantic determination. Articles on such topics as the origin of languages, phonetic alteration, sonants and surds, aphasia, dissimulated gemination, sonant fricative consonants, assimilative forms, and vowel mutation began to take less and less space in *TAPA*, being rerouted to the journals of specialized linguistics that were coming into being.

The Society of Biblical Literature

Originally incorporated as the Society of Biblical Literature and Exegesis, the origins of this association are recited in detail by Ernest Saunders, *Searching the Scriptures: A History of the Society of Biblical Literature 1880–1980*. Published by the Society in 1982, this work chronicles the origins of the Society at a meeting held in Philip Schaff's study in New York City on 2 January 1880. A year later the Society's *Journal of Biblical Literature and Exegesis* began publication. Philology in its Teutonic form of stress on source-critical aspects soon became evident, and interest in literary criticism as practiced in classical circles remained relatively rare until the century of publication neared its end. Many of the issues of *JBL* therefore have the appearance of recycling problems that engage the attention of German scholars to this day.

Although the Society was firmly behind archeological exploration in the last decades of the 19th century, very little study of epigraphic material made its way into the pages of *JBL*. In 1941 Julius Morgenstern called for the ringing of the death-knell for Teutonically dominated research, with an invitation to peer into a future made possible by developments in archeological and folklore research. Not until the 1960s did such criticisms begin to bear a bountiful harvest. In the year 1967 the society was introduced to group research, and under the dynamic leadership of Robert Funk developments were swift. In 1971 the Society began in earnest to publish scholarly works and studies produced by its members. "Since that time," writes Saunders, "the trickle has swelled to a torrent as the Society has set the pace for other professional guilds" (Saunders:61). In contrast to the welcome accorded women for decades in APA, as evidenced by their numerous articles in *TAPA* and other classical journals, SBL relied on males for research, a phenomenon that was formally terminated in 1979 with the formation of the Women's Caucus.

Signalling the end of dominance of historical-critical exegesis was the publication of *Semeia*, an experimental journal that was wafted from the very beginning in 1974 by the spirit of Ferdinand de Saussure and of other pioneers in literary criticism. SBL had come of age. In its maturity it displayed ability to profit from the accumulation of criticism. With awareness of contextuality blossoming, the Society was in the 1980s fully engaged in exploration of much of the terrain that had long been explored by classicists and associates in the fields of *Religionsgeschichte* and anthropology. Biblical scholars were crossing the street in greater numbers than ever before. Once Germany had done all the exporting. Now there was a balance of trade.

Conclusion

A primary advantage in using APA and SBL as the stars in this centennial volume was the opportunity to give expression to the performance of many philologists whose contributions do not at first sight seem to merit recognition from historians but nevertheless are little hinges on which the many doors of history swing. Alas, too often historians describe the richly decorated salons and ignore the entrance chambers. The present work, therefore, proposes to supply data and some analysis that will make possible a more precise appraisal by some historian who approaches from a broader perspective, and with a view to theoretical embracement, what was done in America in these last hundred years. Hence the text moves from a consideration of cultural contextuality (Part I) through a series of concerns for minutiae that are traditionally viewed as the proper province of philological research (Part II), and after a survey of methodological approaches (Part III) terminates with a discussion of contemporary instruments for attaining meaningful access to ancient documents (Part IV).

Some readers will miss references to certain categories of publications. Little account is taken, for example, of the manufacture of commentaries; but such as make a special mark in history, as does *The Beginnings of Christianity,* do receive notice. It was impossible, within the time assigned, to research the specific philological contributions of commentaries, both classical and biblical, that might be construed as staking an advance in the interpretation of the texts they purport to explain. Commentaries such as those of Theodore Woolsey on the *Medea* and *Alkestis,* or the one on Pindar by Basil Gildersleeve, mark a stage in American independence of judgment and are rare. Most of those on the market recycle continental debates. It simply must be granted that, during most of the century, for the study of ancient documents American philological contributions have been strongest in grammar, papyrology, and epigraphy, and in these areas they display the scientific expertise that qualifies their work as products of scientific inquiry worthy of the name.

Through references to discussions of specific topics, such as those in Part I, biblical students especially are alerted to the resources available in the vast reservoirs of learning filled by their colleagues in the classical field. Indeed, the many references to specialized studies are designed to open avenues for informed research by those who aim to engage in interdisciplinary study. Through the bibliographies cited in the run of *TAPA* alone, students can find entry to most of the secondary literature that is worth reading.

Literary philology, that is the explication of texts, is the dominating subject in this volume. References to works on archeology are, therefore, limited primarily to those publications that exhibit data relating to papyri and epigraphs. One or the other publication may not at first sight appear to pay dividends for study of the New Testament. Studies on Athenian fiscal matters by Benjamin Meritt, for example, might seem to offer little promise for elucidation of St. Paul's writings. Yet no one seriously engaged in sociological study of material relating to Greece can ignore Meritt's discussions, and his careful scientific methodology will more than repay a reasonable investment of effort.

Since Eldon Epp has been encouraged to discuss the history of textual criticism in America, there was no need to clutter this volume with material that comes with better grace from his expert hand.

Besides endeavoring to display the depth of commitment to philological investigation that was manifested by biblical and classical scholars, this book reflects the human qualities that have penetrated their work. Indeed, one of the delights in preparing this centennial study was encounter with so many who knew how to lighten the heavy cast of thought. Of acrimonious critique there was little. The really great among those who enriched a century were not unduly impressed by their own egos. Nor were they intimidated by those of others. And the spirit of an Aristophanes was no stranger to them. If, therefore, there sounds at times, as especially in Part III, a jocular, or even what may appear to some a frivolous note, those who hear it will correctly interpret it as an expression of a barrage of influences that would not be denied. In keeping with this concern to reflect the breadth of culture and *humanitas* that characterized so many of America's finest scholars, Part III serves to balance the two tedious portions that precede and the one that follows it. Thus the composition mirrors the delightful diversity that characterized a century of scholarly activity. For as their published works and the memorials expressed in appreciation of their efforts attest, many of the scholars who are mentioned in this study did not invite their students to slumber.

Those who are familiar with the New Testament and the literatures of Greece and Rome will also recognize that this book could not fail to embody or adapt many of the forms and motifs found in ancient authors, with alternation of thetical and anecdotal style. Among the more obvious is the Theophrastian-Galenic tone in Part III, with its parodying of neologistic tendencies. Thus the genuine humanity of scholars points to the literatures, and these in turn take on new life in the descriptions of scholarly exchange.

A word remains to be said about the mode of notation and orthography. The bibliography cites works that are, in the main, products of American scholarship. These are indicated in the text by a liberal use of date in association with author. In those cases where the book itself is the "star," for example, collections of papyri or of epigraphs, the bibliography offers a short title and date. Details about foreign publications, except for standard reference works, are provided in the endnotes. But some Europeans who have practically taken out research citizenship in America also appear in the bibliography. One or another Ausländer may also have slipped in. May such return the hospitality with a revision of President John Kennedy's boast in Berlin and say, "Ich bin auch ein Amerikaner." In accordance with century-old practice in American classical philology, Greek names are generally transliterated. Instead of the Latinized forms that came into vogue when discussion of things Greek took place in Latin, we now have Aischylos, Sophokles, Polybios, and Themistokles returned to their homeland. But until the end of the next century one must, for want of courage, reluctantly settle for the form Thukydides, which is only slightly less barbaric than Thucydides, but appears to some less outlandish than Thoukydides. And since the entire English-speaking world refers to the great Athenian dialectician as Plato, it would be pedantic to undo the apocopation of that revered name.

With the help of a Distinguished Service Fellowship Award conferred by the Aid Association for Lutherans this book was able to enjoy an earlier completion than was originally anticipated. For this display of beneficence and for other contributions of this organization to the advancement of research the entire American philological community owes a debt of gratitude.

Part I
Greece and Rome

I am a part of all that I have met.
Tennyson, *Ulysses*

1

CONTEXTUALITY

Consideration of historical setting is an important methodological aspect of a comprehensive literary-philological approach to NT documents. Early issues of the *Journal of Biblical Literature* contained a number of articles that took account of the Greco-Roman context for numerous NT documents.[1] After about a decade, other philological interests began to dominate the Journal and for many years major contributions relating to Greece and Rome were relatively rare.

The 1950s saw reversal of a trend toward recycling of nineteenth century debates and SBL's journal began to reflect renewed interest in a broader philological outreach that included exploration of Greece and Rome. May it "presage a renaissance of student interest in *Religionsgeschichte* in America," wrote Harold Willoughby (1954) in praise of Frederick Grant's *Hellenistic Religions* and in echo of Donald Riddle's (1947) plea in *The Study of the Bible Today and Tomorrow.*

At about the same time, a Swedish scholar was minimizing Hellenistic influence on the New Testament,[2] and less than two decades later F. Grant (1969) observed that "the whole swing of classical and theological (i.e., biblical) study is moving toward the hellenistic period in both Hellenism and Judaism, and not least in NT studies."[3] The trickle became a stream and at the end of SBL's first century numerous publications by members of the Society of Biblical Literature, the Catholic Biblical Association, and other scholarly groups devoted to religious studies became a major resource for insight into the spirit of ancient Greece and Rome, with some fresh methodological approaches for understanding early Christian communities and their documents.

---

[1] See, for example, Abbott, 1890, with scrutiny of the Classics and the Septuagint.

[2] Bertil Gaertner, *The Areopagus Speech and Natural Revelation* (Lund: Gleerup, 1955).

[3] See also Talbert's (1975) criticism of a German scholar's publication. From *The Bible in Modern Scholarship* (1965) one could not infer that much of significance for biblical scholars was going on in classical studies. Neither Koester's (1965) nor Cohen's (1965) essays in this volume offset a suggestion of provincialism.

Historical Context

America's biblical scholars might for a time have spared themselves some embarrassment had they paid more attention to studies that emanated from what came to be known as the "Chicago School." A quarter-century before Grant had noted that America's exegetes were beginning to recognize anew how much more there was to exegesis than the reworking of European-sponsored puzzles, Harold Willoughby (1922) observed a heightened historical interest in the social context of early Christianity. Its Jewish background had been carefully studied, but Hellenistic environmental factors, he lamented, still awaited adequate investigation.[4] Major contributions in the latter direction came from Willoughby, and associates Shirley Case (whose "criticism by social environment" became the trademark of the so-called "Chicago School") and Donald Riddle.[5] Willoughby succinctly positioned the movement: "In place of the historico-literary interest of 1900 that was concentrated on early Christian documents, and in place of the religio-historical interest of 1914 that was diffused over wide environmental areas, there has developed the socio-historical interest of 1926 that is focused on the religious living of early Christians in the social milieu of the first century" (1927:66).

In a work entitled *The Social Origins of Christianity,* Case (1923:32) succinctly defined the procedure:

In short, New Testament study as socially conceived begins with emphasis upon the actual experience of the people who composed the Christian societies in New Testament times. The student seeks to orient himself amid the vital activities of the Christians both in relation to their environment and within their own communities as they are found scattered about the Mediterranean in the last half of the first century. In this way he hopes to acquire a point of view and an insight into the meaning of the several New Testament writings that will be in accordance with the design of their authors and the understanding of their original readers. Furthermore, in tracing the subsequent history of the New Testament books one recognizes the necessity for a like social emphasis. In order to understand the fundamental causes that led to their use in the churches and resulted in their preservation, assembly into a collection, and elevation to a position of canonical authority, one must give attention primarily to the interests and activities of the Christian groups within which the process of canonization was carried through to completion.

In this study Case develops the thesis that he advanced in *The Evolution of Early Christianity* (1914), in which the origin of Christianity is viewed as response to natural forces that reside in the environment. From Case's

---

[4] See also Willoughby, 1927:61–62.
[5] On the Chicago School and Case's socio-historical contributions, see Hynes, 1981.

perspective, such approach removed the New Testament from exhibition "as a mummy . . . in a museum of antiquities or as a corpse over which one held an autopsy" (Case, 1923:31). His right to make pronouncements was established through severe discipline. According to Colwell (1960:202), Case, thoroughly drilled in "word study, source analysis and all the philological skills and arts that distinguished the previous generation," had transcribed and translated every line of Aramaic then extant so as to familiarize himself with the Palestinian background of the New Testament.

Through his *Evolution* and his *Experience with the Supernatural in Early Christian Times* (1929) Case offered a digest of European *Religionsgeschichte*, and these two publications serve as a basic English-language text for all succeeding American discussions of the Greco-Roman context for the rise and development of Christianity.[6]

Contact with classicists at the University of Chicago helped stimulate the kind of research undertaken by Case. A study such as that by Edwin Rankin (1907) on the role of cooks in ancient Greece, with a chapter on their social status (11–36), was a sign of things to come. And during the same period that Case was redirecting scholars' sights, Mikhail Rostovtzeff, a victim of Eastern European social change, was running Greco-Roman history through the sieve of his aristocratically oriented perceptions, with the result that his study of imperial Rome, *The Social and Economic History of the Roman Empire* (1926), shows less interest in a broad array of environmental data than with the problem of Rome's decline and fall. Replaced as a study edition by a German edition in 1931 and by an Italian edition in 1933, a second English-language edition was needed, and P. M. Fraser supplied this in 1957 on the basis of the additions and modifications present in the Italian edition, but with numerous corrections and additions of his own. Rostovtzeff's *Social and Economic History of the Hellenistic World* (1941) suffers a handicap of thetical priority similar to the earlier work, but together with that publication provides all students of the Greco-Roman world with an extraordinary amount of archeological data—much of which is enclosed in notes that in a number of cases are in effect monographs of enduring quality—for more comprehensive social description and analysis. During the same period, Tenney Frank (1930) lectured on the development of the literature of the Roman Republic as a native product in its political and social context.

A decade after Rostovtzeff's work on the Hellenistic world, Paul Coleman-Norton, assisted by Frank Bourne and John Fine, published a significant addition to socio-historical investigation under the title *Studies in*

---

[6] Case, 1914, is fuller in documentation than Case, 1929. For a survey of general socio-environmental interest displayed at the time in the study of early Christianity, see Willoughby, 1927, esp. pp. 58–69.

Roman Economic and Social History in Honor of Allan Chester Johnson (Johnson Festschrift, 1951). Ten years later, Coleman-Norton and Bourne collaborated with Johnson in the translation and annotation of 321 Roman legal documents, under the title *Ancient Roman Statutes* (1961). A number of these documents relate to rights and privileges of the Jewish populace.

When biblical scholars interacted with classicists, the fruits of such labors frequently were of enduring quality. Enriched with contributions by Kirsopp Lake, Henry Cadbury, Silva New, Robert Casey, Lily Taylor, and Thomas Broughton, the fifth volume, edited by Frederick Foakes Jackson and Kirsopp Lake, of *Beginnings of Christianity* (1933), contains a network of information-packed veins that pulsate with the very life of Greece and Rome.[7]

Colleagues at the University of Chicago encouraged the trend and helped students build an elementary philological base for Hellenistic studies through selections from a broad range of Koine texts. Edgar Goodspeed and Ernest Colwell (1935) published 82 texts with brief introduction and notes, accompanied by a vocabulary. Goodspeed's broad acquaintance with first century Greek writers finds expression in an article entitled "The Possible Aramaic Gospel" (1942). Three years later, Colwell and Julius Mantey published *A Hellenistic Greek Reader* (1939). This last work lacked illustration of the "Asian" style, a deficiency that was soon remedied by Allen Wikgren and his collaborators, Colwell and Ralph Marcus, through inclusion of an inscription by Antiochos of Kommagene in *Hellenistic Greek Texts* (Wikgren et al., 1947).

Reciprocity and Cult

Of prime importance for interpretation of Greco-Roman documents is awareness of the role that status played in Greco-Roman society. Integrally connected is the presupposition that reciprocity constitutes a basic structural element for a well-ordered society. A thorough history of Greco-Roman reciprocity remains to be written, and the immensity of the task will require the resources of an international team of scholars. In 1927 Joseph Hewitt supplemented Otto Loew's discussion of *Charis* with an article on "The Terminology of 'Gratitude' in Greek."[8] But apart from a few European publications that had dealt with special aspects of the subject no major effort to relate Greco-Roman views of personal excellence and reciprocity to study of the New Testament was registered until Charles Mott (1971) engaged in a

---

[7] Lake and Cadbury, 1933. See Enslin, 1933, for recognition of the importance of *The Beginnings of Christianity*. James Hardy Ropes provided *The Text of Acts* as vol. 3 in the series. Published in 1926, it was lauded in an obituary for Ropes in *HTR* 26 (1933) as "the model of a critical edition." Sherman Johnson (1958:9) cited *Beginnings* as a notable exception to the sparse use of the new material in Asia Minor by New Testament scholars.

[8] O. Loew, *Charis* (Marburg Dissertation, 1908).

study of ethical terminology in the Pastorals, with special reference to Philo, under the title *The Greek Benefactor and Deliverance from Moral Distress*.[9] As the first installment of a two-part work, Frederick Danker's *Benefactor* (1982) endeavors to shore up a demonstration of New Testament usage of the reciprocity model with detailed analysis of terms and phrases in Greco-Roman epigraphs.[10] Contracts and reciprocity are the principal themes in J. Paul Sampley's *Pauline Partnership in Christ* (1980) and in Hans Betz's discussion of Second Corinthians 8–9 in the "Hermeneia" series (1985).

Since Greco-Roman views of excellence are intertwined with environmental, social, and civic considerations, it is to be expected that deities and heads of state receive a major share of recognition as benefactors.[11] Devotees and subjects reciprocate the services with appropriate responses designed for perpetual remembrance, and philology cannot ignore the form whereby public and privately expressed appreciation finds expression. In the case of statues, the material that is chosen serves as a paralinguistic feature. Kenneth Scott (1931) illustrates this fact in an article entitled, "The Significance of Statues in Precious Metals in Emperor Worship." From such and other expressions of adoration and gratitude scholars derive much data relating to Greco-Roman religion and theology.

As Case well documented in *The Evolution of Christianity* (Case 1914, 195–238), a major component of the Greco-Roman reciprocity system is the imperial cult. Dominating the scene is Alexander the Great, whose mystique captured the imagination of the entire Mediterranean world.[12] Lionel Pearson (1954) sought to lift the veil in "The Diary and the Letters of Alexander the Great," and Charles Robinson (1943) concluded that Alexander promoted his own apotheosis. Three decades earlier, William Prentice (1923) supported Kallisthenes as the original historian of Alexander. The celestial ascent of Demetrios Poliorketes, the Rommel of antiquity, receives documentation from Kenneth Scott (1928) in "The Deification of Demetrius Poliorcetes."[13]

Replete with information on the rise of Roman imperial cult is Augustus Merriam's (1883) "The Caesareum and the Worship of Augustus at Alexandria." Allan Ball (1909) concludes in "The Theological Utility of the Caesar Cult" that the emperor was a "concrete illustration of the principle of a worldwide Providence."[14] But more comprehensively composed is the first

---

[9] See Danker, 1982:49–50.

[10] Editions of the Greek texts underlying the translations in Danker, 1982, were to follow.

[11] Nock (1944) discusses the cult of heroes, an important factor in consideration of other Greco-Roman cultic phenomena. On reaction of early Christian apologists to ancient ruler cult see Inez, 1946.

[12] Perrin (1895) discussed the legend of Batis and passages in Greco-Roman writers who present Alexander as an avenging Achilles.

[13] Compare the divine honors accorded to Philip II, see Fredricksmeyer, 1979.

[14] An abstract of Ball's paper appeared in *PAPA* 40 (1909):xvii-xviii. As Mark Clark (1983)

Philological Monograph of the American Philological Association, *The Divinity of the Roman Emperor*, by Lily Taylor (1931).[15] Directing attention to ancient literary sources, K. Scott discusses "Emperor Worship in Ovid" (1930) and "Plutarch and the Ruler Cult" (1929).[16]

According to Duncan Fishwick (1972), Vespasian advanced imperial cultic interests by enhancing the prestigious character of the provincial priesthood. To sketch the progress of imperial cult in Spain was the object of George Fiske's "Notes on the Worship of the Roman Emperors in Spain" (1900).[17]

Nero's reputation is so enveloped in myth and fancy that Russel Geer's (1931) promise, "I shall not try to interpret facts" but wish "merely to ascertain them," while scarcely adequate as a statement of historical methodology, at least prescribes an antidote to schoolish gossip. There is no indisputable evidence that Nero identified himself with Sol, challenges J. Rufus Fears (1976).[18] Refuting some of the negativism, Theresa Roper concluded in a study of Nero, Seneca, and Tigellinus that Nero was not nearly the rascal that is generally assumed, nor was he the nemesis of Seneca. "The tendency to divide Nero's reign into good and bad halves," she says, "must be abandoned" (1979:357). And after fresh perusal of *Sibylline Oracles* 4. 119–124, Paul Gallivan (1973) concludes that the oracular passage does not refer to the first of three imposters who appeared before 96 C.E.

Aretalogy and Demonology

Closely associated with recognition of imperial prestige and beneficence is awareness of and response to divine powers. In 1914 Case had alerted Americans to the importance of the subject, but not until the second half of the twentieth century did classical and biblical scholars begin to share in earnest the Chicago School's interest in Greco-Roman approaches to the trancendent in such areas as aretalogy, demonology, and miraculous healing. As Morton Smith's bibliographical data in "Prolegomena to a Discussion of Aretalogies, Divine Men, the Gospels and Jesus" (1971) indicate, these areas of study had been for the most part preempted in the first quarter of the twentieth century by German scholars.

A suggestion that it was time for more vigorous exploration of the territory by members of SBL came in 1932 in the form of an article by Selby

---

demonstrates, Romans are a people of hope, and they find in imperial virtue the warrant for domestic blessing.

[15] See also Taylor, 1920.

[16] For a broad transcultural grasp, see Frankfort, 1948. On "The Political Philosophy of Hellenistic Kingship," see Goodenough, 1928.

[17] For a discussion of "Imperial Mysteries" see Pleket, 1965.

[18] See also Fears, 1977.

McCasland, "Portents in Josephus and in the Gospels."[19] McCasland here echoed Case's work[20] in the years that followed he made significant contributions to the study of thaumaturgy.[21]

Further encouragement for renewed interest in *Religionsgeschichte* came in the pages of *JBL* from a European, Ernst von Dobschuetz (1944), under the title "Christianity and Hellenism." From the Grants came both discussions and source books. Robert published *Miracle and Natural Law in Graeco-Roman and Early Christian Thought* (1952), but without evident reference to Case, who had been interred only five years earlier. In two contributions to "The Library of Religion," Frederick Grant (1953, 1957) introduced students to numerous facets of Greco-Roman religion with translations of selected texts from "literary" and "non-literary" sources.

Much discussion, especially of the Gospel of Mark, relates to the role of the so-called "Divine Person" or *theios aner*. Wilfred Knox, of Cambridge, England, called attention to Greco-Roman data that related especially to the role of Herakles in ancient perceptions of the divine hero.[22] Otto Betz (1972) treated the concept in connection with Mark's Christology, and Carl Holladay (1977) called for re-examination of use of the category "divine man" in the study of New Testament Christology.[23]

Alice Walton's *The Cult of Asklepios* (1894) called attention to a major recipient of devotion in the ancient world. And the Edelsteins, Emma and Ludwig, filled out the portrait with their *Asclepius: A Collection and Interpretation of the Testimonies* (1945), which received a major review from Gregory Vlastos (1948). McCasland (1939) did his part by plotting cults of Asklepios at Hammath (Emmaus near Tiberius), at a locale near Gadara, at Nablus, and at Ascalon. In 1980 Andrew Hill drew on Carl Roebuck's (1951) exhibits of votive offerings discovered at the temple of Asklepios beside the Spring Lerna at Corinth for exposition of 1 Cor 12:14–25.[24] As at Ste Anne

[19] See esp. Josephus, *J.W.* 6:288–309. Cf. Barton, 1924, on signals of divine appointment in Philo.

[20] On portents, see Case, 1929:67–76.

[21] See McCasland, 1951 and 1957. Anitra Kolenkow (1980) discusses miracle as part of a spectrum of divine powers that also included prophecy.

[22] Wilfred Knox, "The 'Divine Hero' Christology in the New Testament," *HTR* 41 (1948) 229–71.

[23] More serviceable may be the broader genus of "Recital of Excellence" or "Aretalogy," of which recitals about a "divine person" constitute but one species; for all contributors to the welfare of humanity are people or deities of excellence and qualify for recognition under the reciprocity system, but not all excellent beings are "divine persons" or perform all the things ascribed to divine persons; see Danker, 1982, *passim*, and cf. Hadas, 1959:170–81. See also Jonathan Z. Smith's (1975) challenge of traditional presuppositions, but supplement his discussion of Philostratos with Gildersleeve's treatment (1890:251–96). Much use is made of Greco-Roman authors by Remus, 1982.

[24] Numerous photographs of votive offerings in Mabel Lang, 1977, are derived from Roebuck's work. For detailed bibliography and archeological data relating to Corinth see Murphy-O'Connor, 1983.

de Beaupre near Quebec City, where hundreds of crutches and other mementos of St. Anne's therapeutic influence are exhibited, grateful beneficiaries of Asklepios's healing powers left memorials to his concern for them at his shrines.[25]

A number of New Testament recitals have to do with expulsion of demons. Hippokrates wrote on what he called "The Sacred Disease," but Wesley Smith (1965) claims that there is a gulf between the phenomenon Hippokrates describes and the demonological perspective of New Testament writers.[26]

Religious Life, the Mysteries, and Hermetica

Since Gaston Boissier's *La religion romaine d' Auguste aux Antonins*, little had been done, and much of that from a limited perspective, to define the religious life of ordinary Romans during the period of the early Empire.[27] In "The Pagani among the Contemporaries of the First Christians," Harold Weiss (1967) argues that there was a strong religious fervor among these civilians, whose designation as *pagani*, or members of a territorial division known as a *pagus*, is the source of the derogatory derivative "pagan."[28]

Much important information about Hellenistic mystery religions finds summation in Case's works[29] and in Arthur Nock's article on the "Mysteries" in *Encyclopedia of the Social Sciences* (11. 1942: 172–74). Willoughby (1929) provided an interpretation of their ceremonials and sacraments in a study entitled, *Pagan Regeneration*. At the end of the nineteenth century Benjamin Wheeler (1899) discussed the cult of Dionysos, with special reference to the hope of immortality.

---

[25] See also Vlastos, 1948:280. On the healing cults in general, see Jayne, 1925; and for Asklepios, esp. pp. 240–306. For additional discussion and bibliography, see Danker, 1982:192–196, and Achtemeier, 1972. Achtemeier's perplexity (1975) over St. Luke's method of treating Old Testament tradition is readily dispelled by consideration of Asklepios's function as philanthropic savior.

[26] See also the list of Anitra Kolenkow's various contributions to the study of demonism in the ancient world (1980:1505–06). On the power of exorcists, see Bonner, 1943.

[27] Gaston Boissier, *La religion romaine d' Auguste aux Antonins* (Paris: Librairie Hachette, 1892). The pioneer study of religious and social development and their interaction is, of course, Numa Denis Fustel de Coulanges, *La cité antique: étude sur le culte, le droit, les institutions de la Gréce et de Rome* (3d ed., Paris: Hachette, 1870).

[28] See also A. J. Festugière, *Personal Religion among the Greeks* (Berkeley: University of California, 1954). An informative series of essays is contained in Neusner, 1968. Youtie, 1944b, declares that "systematic study of papyrus materials" is "useful for gauging the reality and intensity of personal religious sentiment," and that such study "would add considerable vitality to the history of the later paganism" (121, n. 9). He calls attention to *PPrinc.* 111.167 and *PMich.* III.213, both from the third century.

[29] See Case, 1914:284–330 and Case, 1929: esp. 226–28, 250–58, 282–85.

Specialists explored the Old and the New Testament for data that might be viewed in relation to gentile mystery cults. Julius Bewer (1926) in a presidential address before the Society of Biblical Literature expressed skepticism over Rudolf Kittel's claim that Judaism had "decisively" influenced Alexandrian mystery religion.[30] Stimulated by the work of Willoughby and others, Elbert Russel (1932) thought that he had found three stages of mystery cult experience in the major Johannine writings. A half-century later such ingenuity might have been garbed in depth-structural and folklorist jargon and have met with more conviction. But as a product of objective historical investigation it fell into the category of over-zealous attempts to link biblical patterns of belief to gentile cult, and in a presidential address before SBL it came under the omnibus censure of William Hatch (1939). Hatch proclaimed that salvation loomed larger than immortality of the soul as a factor in the success of Christianity.[31]

For exhibition of the Hermetic writings, in which Greek ideas mingle with themes found in Eastern religions, students were early indebted to Willoughby's *Pagan Regeneration* (1929:196–224) and to the labors of Arthur Nock and A. Festugiere (1946–1954), who respectively prepared a critical edition of the text and a translation. R. Grant provides samples in *Gnosticism* (1961). William Grese (1979), the first American to have a full-length monograph included in the series *Corpus Hellenisticum Novi Testamenti*, related Hermetic data to the New Testament and other Early Christian literature.[32] Four decades earlier, Mary Lyman (1930) pointed to numerous differences between the Hermetica and the Johannine writings.

Christianity's Feud with the Gentile World

Shirley Case thought he had found the answer to the secret of Christianity's success in ultimately displacing traditional Greco-Roman religion, but, as Donald Winslow candidly admits in *Catacombs and the Colosseum* (1971:248–51), the question continues to baffle historians.[33] Yet it is beyond dispute that one of the reasons for Christianity's early growth was the general tolerance that Rome displayed toward her subject peoples and their ancestral customs.

At various times in the early centuries of Christian experience Rome moved with force against what seemed to be a threat against her cherished

---

[30] Rudolf Kittel, *Die Hellenistische Mysterienreligion und das Alte Testament* (Stuttgart, 1924).

[31] Compare Minear, 1941.

[32] On the work of the American Branch of *CHNT* see the quarterly bulletins of The Institute for Antiquity and Christianity published at Claremont Graduate School, Claremont, California 91711. On the interpretive principles used by Hermetic authors see Shanahan, 1982. For formal aspects in Hermetic writings see Nock, 1925.

[33] Walter Woodburn Hyde, *Paganism to Christianity in the Roman Empire* (Philadelphia: University of Pennsylvania, 1946), does not offer a satisfactory solution.

institutions. In fairness to Rome it must be noted that Christians had already in the first century fostered misunderstanding by failing to clarify statements about unworldliness,[34] and it is probable that the move of Christian groups away from adherence to Jewish traditions encouraged doubts about their entitlement to special consideration.[35]

After Constantine's institutionalization of the Christian movement, some of those who espoused faith in the Nazarene did not return the favor of Rome's traditional toleration of a variety of religious practices. At the time of the complete triumph of the church in Rome, Augustus' *Arca Pacis* met destruction through decree. And who can forget the brilliant and beautiful Hypatia, one of the world's most distinguished Philosophers, master of Neoplatonic thought, of impeccable reputation, and highly esteemed by Synesios? Torn from her chariot—probably during the season of Lent, in 415—by alleged Christians who apparently bore allegiance to Cyril, bishop of Alexandria, she was dragged to the Caesareum, divested on the church steps, and done to death with oyster shells.[36] Those who have stomach for more can read Elmer Merrill, "The Church in the Fourth Century" (1919), and Clifford Moore (1919), "The Pagan Reaction in the Late Fourth Century."[37]

As someone summed the matter, bishops "proved their doctrine orthodox by apostolic blows and knocks." And Ernest Sihler wrote the epitaph for *agape*: "Strong were the imperial decrees against heretics and for the Nicene creed" (1908:358).

[34] See, e.g., John 12:25; Matt 13:40–49; 16:26; Mark 8:36; Luke 9:25; Rom 12:2; 1 Cor 1:20; 2:6–12; 3:18–19; 7:31; 8:4.

[35] See, e.g., Krodel, 1971:260–61; Benko, 1980. It is also probable that St. Luke's references in Luke 1 to the ancient roots of Christianity; his references to converts from higher social levels, as in Acts 17; and his reference to attack from uncultured elements, as in Acts 17:5, suggest an apologetic front against the type of criticism made by Tacitus *Annals* 15.44. Luke's adoption of Septuagintal style for narration in his Gospel and for recital of early events in Acts would convey an antique flavor and thereby suggest a venerable and respected heritage as antidote to assumptions of alleged religious novelty.

[36] Standard discussions include Richard Hocke, "Hypatia, die Tochter Theons," *Philologus* 15 (1860):435–74, and Karl Praechter, "Hypatia," in PW 17 (1914):242–49. Edward Gibbon deserts the boundaries of historical responsibility with questionable detail in his description of Hypatia's death (*The History of the Decline and Fall of the Roman Empire*, ed. J. Bury, 5 [London, 1911], ch. 47, p. 117). In addition to Charles Kingsley's romanticized version see T. T. Phrangkopoulos, *Hypatia* (Bucharest, 1971), written in Greek.

[37] See also McGiffert, 1909; Pease, 1919; Laistner, 1951; Swift, 1965; R. Grant, 1970. For critique by St. Paul's contemporaries, see M. Smith, 1980.

2

HELLENISTIC JUDAISM

In his last report as editor of *Journal of Biblical Literature* Erwin Goodenough complained about the state of NT scholarship and suggested that unless the NT Book Review section included more studies in contemporary Judaism and Greco-Roman religion and philosophy it should appear only occasionally. "Not at any time for a century and a half was so little of importance being written," he exclaimed (1943:xi). It was an invitation to end an era.

Anxious to demonstrate the superiority of ecclesiastically sanctioned values over those of other traditions, scholars of Christian persuasion had over the centuries purchased esteem for Christian qualities at the expense of Greco-Roman values. Hand in hand with such acquisition went demonstrations of Judaism's inferiority.[1]

After World War I, noticeable moves toward larger appreciation of Jewish contributions to the history of religion, especially in the Hellenistic period, became apparent in American scholarship from both Jewish and non-Jewish directions. Goodenough took the lead by setting forth his views on symbolism in Hellenistic Jewish art (1937a,b), which ultimately culminated in a multi-volume work entitled *Jewish Symbols* (1953), whose deficiencies as well as epoch-making contributions are set forth in detail by Morton Smith (1967) and Arthur Nock (1955, 1957, 1960). Also among the chief stewards was Ralph Marcus, whose "Selected Bibliography (1920–45) of the Jews in the Hellenistic-Roman Period" (1946–47) and his references to special topics in vols. 6 and 7 of his translation of Josephus in the *Loeb Classical Library* constitute impressive witness to creative features in ancient Jewish life and thought. George Moore set much of the record straight with his three-volume *Judaism in the First Centuries of the Christian Era* (1927–30). And in a contribution to the Monograph Series of *JBL,* Norman Johnson (1948) discussed "the Jewish concept of God."

Under the tutelage of Robert Pfeiffer (1949) and Charles Cutler Torrey (1945) American scholars became more intimately acquainted with the

---

[1] See Levy, 1947, esp. pp. 88–89.

rationale and characteristics of intertestamental Jewish literature.[2] Torrey also championed study of Aramaic as a prerequisite for philological work on biblical texts written in Greek; and Carl Purinton (1928) explored the Wisdom of Solomon for translation symptoms.[3]

Frank Porter (1908) looked for Greek views of pre-existence of the soul in the Book of Wisdom,[4] and three decades later Stella Lange renewed the search (1936). Still later, James Reese (1970) concluded that Isis serves as a model for the writer of the Book of Wisdom.[5]

According to Eisig Silberschlag (1933), the earliest records of Jews in Asia Minor derive from Klearchos, one of Aristotle's disciples, and other Greek writers.[6] Debate goes on about attitudes toward Jews in ancient times. The geographer Strabo entertained a high opinion of Moses.[7] Louis Feldman (1950) found sympathizers of the Jews in classical literature and inscriptions, whereas Adalbert Polacek (1981) focused on Flaccus' actions in 38 C.E. and argued that they were paradigmatic for the events of 1938. As is clear from Jerry Daniel's study, "Anti-Semitism in the Hellenistic-Roman Period" (1979), race and religion are easily confused, and xenophobia was a persistent drain on Roman administrative policy. To do justice, then, to ancient Roman views, it appears more accurate to think in terms of specific anti-Jewishness rather than general anti-Semitism, especially since Romans dealt in their farflung empire with many groups of Semites.[8] Moroever, one minimizes the enormity of the modern crime against Jews by archaizing it in terms of ancient hostility that lacked the primary ingredients of Nazism's ultimate obscenity.[9]

---

[2] On Jewish production of Greek literature see, e.g, Wacholder, 1974.

[3] On translation Greek see Rife, 1933, and other literature cited by Mussies, 1976:1062. For discussion of Greek loan words, see Liebermann, 1942 and 1950, and M. Smith, 1951: chap. 1.

[4] F. Porter, 1908:1.207–69. For developments in Septuagintal research consult *Bulletin of the International Organization for Septuagint and Cognate Studies* and the references *passim* in Klein, 1974.

[5] For contributions in the first half of the twentieth century on the Maccabean literature, the Greek text of Enoch, and the Sibylline Oracles, see, e.g., Torrey, 1902 and 1942; Tracy, 1928; G. Zuntz, 1942 and 1944; Youtie, 1944. During the third-quarter of the century, George Nicklesburg was among those who made substantial contributions to the study of Intertestamental Literature; see esp. Nickelsburg, 1972 and 1984:89–156.

[6] On Klearchos see also Stern 1974:143 and 1976:1110–11; for the treatment of Jews in Greek and Latin literature, see Stern, 1976.

[7] Strabo *Geography* 16.2.35–37. On the treatment of Moses in the Greco-Roman world, see Gager, 1972.

[8] One of the objections to Jewish life was its isolationist pattern; see bibliography in Feldman, 1970:164 n. 49.

[9] Stern (1976:1145) writes concerning Cicero, that "even if we cannot call Cicero an outright anti-Semite, his attitude towards the Jews was different from that of his contemporary . . . Varro (116–27 B.C.E.)." On the same page Stern uses the expression "anti-Jewish" in reference to a part of Cicero's *Pro Flacco*. In his discussion of Tacitus, Stern is fair to the Roman point of view: Eastern religions and Egyptian religion were suspect; and in reference to Tacitus's description of the riots in the time of Cumanus and Felix, Stern points out that Tacitus holds the procurators,

Philo and Josephus

Two ancient Jewish writers, Philo and Josephus, offered considerable stimulation to American research. Francis Colson, George Whitaker, and Ralph Marcus produced the Loeb edition of Philo's works (Loeb *Philo* 1929–62).[10] With better grasp of classical philosophy than of Philo's spirit, Harry Austryn Wolfson (1947) published two volumes on Philo in 1947.[11]

Hermeneutical issues in connection with Philo's work found scrutiny in Montgomery Schroyer's study of Alexandrian literalists (1936). A formal feature came in for analysis in an article by Curtis Larson (1946) entitled "Prayer of Petition in Philo."[12] Burton Easton (1932) worked Philo's allegorization of Cain and Abel into a presidential address on ethical lists in the New Testament. Erwin Goodenough (1935) endeavored to connect Hellenistic philosophical strains in Jewish thought, and in 1936 he discussed Philo's views of immortality. Willoughby (1929, 225–62) provides a brief introduction to Philo's mysticism. Efforts to draw lines of connection from Philo to the author of Hebrews were made periodically. Sidney Sowers (1965) discussed the hermeneutics of both Philo and the author of Hebrews. Four decades earlier, George Barton (1924) had made much use of Philo in a discussion of divine appointment of certain people born of divine promise.[13]

Among the outstanding American contributions to Hellenistic Jewish studies was the completion of the Loeb Classical Library volumes devoted to Josephus. Ralph Marcus was involved in the production of vols. 5–8 and Louis Feldman did the ninth volume and the general index to the entire set (1926–1965). Marcus worked also with Henry Thackeray during the years 1930–55 in the production of the first four parts (Alpha to Epsilon) of a lexicon to the works of the Jewish historian.

Endeavoring to refute Robert Eisler's defense of the authenticity of passages relating to John the Baptist and Jesus in the Slavonic version of

---

not the Jews, responsible (1976:1156–57). Harry Leon (1960:45) views the policy of the Roman emperors, especially under Tiberius, Claudius, and Domitian, as "consistently friendly and tolerant," apart from "ephemeral exceptions."

[10] The two supplementary volumes, containing respectively "Questions and Answers of Genesis" and "Questions and Answers of Exodus" (1953), are Marcus's chief contribution in this edition.

[11] See review article by Goodenough (1948), and an earlier essay on method (1939), which was followed by an introduction to Philo (1940), with emphasis on Philo's Hellenistic orientation. An earlier work on Philo's politics (Goodenough, 1938) includes an extensive bibliography, edited by Goodenough and H. L. Goodhart. Near the end of the Centennial, Samuel Sandmel published an introduction to Philo (1979). For detailed bibliography for the years 1935–81, see Hilgert, 1984.

[12] See also Attridge, 1979.

[13] On Philo and the Oral Law, see Belkin, 1940.

Josephus,[14] Solomon Zeitlin wrote *Josephus on Jesus* (1931) and even disclaimed the authenticity of the corresponding passages in the Greek text.

Through the work of Frederick Foakes Jackson, Americans had an opportunity to see more of the "historical" Josephus (1930). A half-century later, Harold Attridge (1976) showed that Josephus had followed Thukydides and Polybios for discussion of contemporary affairs in the *War* and that for the *Antiquities* he preferred the method of Dionysios of Halikarnassos. Eva Sanford (1935) on her part noted a strange development. Whereas Josephus had written the *War* as propaganda in favor of Roman rule, later generations used the work to "stir up rebellion against secular authority and imperial power," to "convert Jews to Christianity," or to "convert Christians to complete or modified Judaism." In the Middle Ages, Sanford observes, Josephus was used as authority on most subjects for which classical authors were commonly consulted, as well as for the background he offered in Jewish matters (127).[15]

In Louis Feldman's (1968) study of Josephus's apologetic technique, Abraham can be seen portrayed as a "typical national hero, such as was popular in Hellenistic times, with emphasis on his qualities as a philosopher and scientist, and no less . . . on his qualities as a general and as a romantic hero" (156).[16]

---

[14] Robert Eisler, *The Messiah Jesus and John the Baptist* (ed. in English by Alexander Krappe; New York: L. MacVeagh, Dial Press, 1931).

[15] On Jewish nationalism in the Greco-Roman period, see Farmer, 1956.

[16] On Josephus and the Essenes, see Strugnell, 1958. Feldmann's (1984) annotated bibliography of books and articles published during the period 1937–80 on Josephus and his works is a tribute to the ancient Jewish historian's potential for arousing interest. Supplement Feldman with treatments of both Philo and Josephus, by Harold Attridge and P. Borgen, in *Jewish Writings* 1984:185–282.

3

EXEGETICAL EXHIBITS
AND FORMAL FEATURES

It is not easy to mark the line that divides parallelomaniacs and cultural contextualists. Yet the effort must be made, especially by New Testament exegetes, who deal with documents that are written in Greek and therefore could be expected to receive a hearing from auditors who decoded them variously in terms of their Greco-Roman exposure. Display of the following exegetical exhibits, presented for the most part seriatim according to the New Testament canonical order, is not a signal for pan-Greco-Romanism, but an expression of appreciation for the many contributions made by American students of Greco-Roman matters for potential enrichment of biblical studies. Only a sampling from the bulging storehouse of America's scholarly inquiry can be offered here, and this in keeping with Korinna's advice to the youthful Pindar, to sow with the hand and not with the sack.

Despite Eduard Norden's disclaimer that Paul had no first-hand acquaintance with Greek literature,[1] attempts are made from time to time to demonstrate direct or indirect dependence not only of the Apostle's writings but of other New Testament documents on classical literature.

Direct Influence?

Written about 75 C. E., Dio Cassius *History* 65.15, contains an account of the flogging of Diogenes and the beheading of Heras. Benjamin Bacon (1923) thought he saw influence of this account on Mark's recital of the execution of John the Baptist. William Oldfather (1932) determined to know whether Menander was cited in the Pastorals. William Heidel suggests a line of thought extending from Plato's *Euthyphro* to Paul on the subject of righteousness (1900). And Joseph Callaway (1948) saw a connection between *Lysis* 209–10 and Gal 3–4.[2] Of a different order are the claim of Rosamond Sprague (1967), that Paul was arguing against descendants of Parmenides in

---

[1] Eduard Norden, *Die Antike Kunstprosa*, 2 (Leipzig: Teubner, 1918) 158.
[2] For other Platonic parallels alleged for the New Testament, see Murley, 1930.

1 Corinthians 12, and Abraham J. Malherbe's (1968) suggestion that 1 Cor 15:32 contains an anti-Epicurean strain.[3]

Network

More fruitful than search for direct influence of the Classics on the New Testament is the use of Greco-Roman data as part of a network of linguistic patterns, customs, symbols and imagery, and modes of thought to aid in its contextual elucidation. Alert biblical scholars can redirect classicists' streams of thought and clean their own expository lenses for clearer perception of a text. Diachronic method here blends with synchronic, and the random specimens that follow suggest a wealth of possibilities.

All interpretation of New Testament documents requires awareness that they were in the first instance written to be heard by people who knew Greek. Assumption of Aramaic association or reflection of Semitic patterns is, therefore, subordinate to awareness of the Hellenistic texture of a New Testament document. For example, the paratactic structure of 1 Thess 5:19–22 may strike one as tortured Greek, but the fact is that paratactic structure is common in Homeric epic (Notopoulos, 1949)[4] and in lyric poetry from Archilochos to Pindar. A debate between Erwin Goodenough (1945) and Robert Casey (1945) illustrates aspects of the problem faced by scholars in bridging the diachronic and the synchronic. In an article entitled "John: A Primitive Gospel" (1945), Goodenough urged more emphasis on the relation of early Christianity to Hellenistic Judaism. Casey (1945) responded that Goodenough accorded too much respect to "lost sources."

New Testament Writings

A brief glance at some of the secondary literature suggests the importance of contextual considerations for understanding specific items of the New Testament.

The Synoptists

Commentators on the New Testament ought not bypass Herbert Youtie's article on "publicans and sinners" (1936). A discerning piece by Roger Pack (1955) on Artemidoros suggests how Jesus mingled sympathy with judgment in the classification of publicans with whores and sinners (288–89).[5] In this

---

[3] For other alleged polemical approaches see, for example, Karris (1973), opting for anti-Sophist polemic in the Pastorals; and Neyrey (1980), with an anti-Epicurean polemic in 2 Pet.

[4] Cf. Bruno Gentili (of the University of Urbino), "The Interpreting of the Greek Lyric Poets in Our Time: Synchronism and Diachronism in the Study of an Oral Culture," *Contemporary Literary Hermeneutics* (1981) 114.

[5] Cf. Ernst Badian, *Publicans and Sinners: Private Enterprise in the Service of the Roman Republic* (Ithaca, NY: Cornell University, 1972).

same study Pack (283 n.9) observed that "thoughts of crucifixion seem to have caused nightmares even for those who ran no risk of such punishment." The story in Matthew 27:19 about the disturbing dream of Pilate's wife belongs to humanity's experience, as does Boswell's tossing in the night after witnessing an execution.[6]

One may discount obsolete features of psychological probing in a study by Benjamin Robinson (1904) of "elements of forcefulness" in the sayings of Jesus, but his references to classical literature are worth scrutiny.

In a transcultural study entitled "Proverbs, Maxims, and the Historical Jesus," Charles Carlston (1980) took students over Greco-Roman and rabbinic terrain. Similarly Robert Pfeiffer (1937) had shown that Hebrews and Greeks drew on cultural elements that were featured in the Mediterranean world.

As for the subject of Greco-Roman thaumaturgy relative to the Gospels, it is difficult to find a more comprehensive collection of references than those in Morton Smith's *Clement of Alexandria and a Secret Gospel of Mark* (1973b).[7]

Luke-Acts

One need spend only a little time in Greco-Roman literature and in specialized study of the Hellenistic era to sense St. Luke's broad acquaintance with the culture of his time.

Henry Cadbury's *The Style and Literary Method of Luke* (1920) and *The Making of Luke-Acts* (1927) have demonstrated their durability, with much of it owed to his broad acquaintance with Greco-Roman documents of various literary levels and to his integrity in dealing with evidence. These works, together with Cadbury's five installments on lexical matters relating to Luke-Acts (1925–33) offer students an impressive array of perceptive analysis and comment.

Most of what is worth saying about the census referred to in Luke 2:1–3 has been stated by Lily Taylor (1933), the first woman to hold the Jane K. Sather lectureship at Berkeley.[8]

An important contribution to prosopography came to the attention of biblical scholars through an article by Jerry Vardaman (1962). An inscription, discovered by an Italian archeological team and first published by Antonio Frova, refers to the Roman administrator as a "prefect." Once again St. Luke's general accuracy in Roman bureaucratic matters received endorsement.

References to extraordinary displeasure, as found for example in Luke 19:27,[9] receive illumination from the kind of data cited by Robert Rogers in

[6] For further evidence of the popularity of Matthew's Gospel where Greek was in use, see Hans Dieter Betz, *Essays on the Sermon on the Mount* (Philadelphia: Fortress, 1985).

[7] For critique of M. Smith, 1973a,b, see p. 164–65.

[8] Against Taylor's view see Horst Braunert, "Der römische Provinzialzensus und der Schätzungsbericht des Lukas-Evangelium," *Historia* 6 (1957) 192–214.

[9] Cf. Matt 25:30, 1 Thess 2:16, and Rev 22:15.

"The Emperor's Displeasure—*amicitiam renuntiare*" (1959).

A striking social symbol in the Roman Empire was the golden ring. Meyer Reinhold's (1971:esp. 279) discussion of Roman interest in status suggests why Luke 15:22 allots special significance to the receipt of a ring by the returning wastrel. The same author calls attention to ancient critique of luxury consumption in a way that immediately brings the story of Dives and Lazarus in Luke 16:19–31 to mind.[10] As William Greene observed in *Moira* (1944), reversal is a dominant note in much of Greek literature, and Luke makes his work a part of the data base for this recurring theme.[11]

Even though his Christian auditors would reorient themselves to the narratives in Luke 24 and Acts 8, the writer of Luke-Acts knew well the interest that some of them undoubtedly had shown in stories of heroes who travelled magically, and of adventurers who returned home incognito. Gerald K. Gresseth discusses both types of story in "*The Odyssey* and the *NALOPĀKHYĀNA*" (1979:69).[12]

Was Paul a failure at Athens? J. M. English (1898) did not think so, for he found numerous persuasive features that must have appealed to the Apostle's audience on the Hill of Ares.

St. Luke's masterful account of St. Paul's perilous journey to Rome, as recorded in Acts 27–28, received appropriate contextual recognition from Vernon Robbins (1978) in a study of Luke's "We-passages." Underlying the four major works of Lionel Casson cited by Robbins are several publications in *TAPA* that will reward scrutiny in exposition of Acts 27–28.[13]

That the Third Evangelist's frequent references to embassies of two would be readily understood by auditors acquainted with Greco-Roman practice can be readily determined from Derek Mosley's information concerning the size of ancient Hellenic embassies (1965).

St. John's Gospel

A study of the expression *eraunate tas graphas* ("you search the Scriptures") in John 5:39 brought the French scholar M.-E. Boismard, dedicated to the older philological methodology, to the conclusion that the text reflects two textual traditions that stem from an Aramaic original.[14] Four decades

---

[10] See Reinhold, 1971:284 on luxury consumption, and bibliography; cf. 1 Pet 3:3 and Martial's indictment of conspicuous consumption, *Epigrams* 4:61; 5. 39; 9. 59; 10. 87; 12. 69.

[11] Greene (1944:34–35) accounts for the popularity of the theme in Archilochos; see also Hesiod *Works and Days;* Pindar *Isthmian* 4:33 and 5:52.

[12] In the same issue, see Nortwick, 1979.

[13] See Casson, 1950, who introduces data from Acts 27, with photograph showing the *parasēmon*. On Paul and Acts, see Casson, 1951:144 n. 35. Isserlin (1955) states that we must in the light of evidence of later sailing achievements admit more latitude of choices than does Casson.

[14] M. E. Boismard, "A propos de Jean v. 39: Essai de critique textuelle," *RB* 55 (1948) 5–34.

earlier, Joseph Harry (1901) brought the New Testament passage into the orbit of Aischylos *Prometheus* 119 by confirming assignment of the indicative to the Aischylean passage.[15]

Increased appreciation of the impact made by John 1:1 on Greco-Roman auditors of the Fourth Gospel can be derived from H. D. Cameron's study (1970), "The Power of Words in the *Seven Against Thebes*."

St. Paul and the Author of Hebrews

Sensitivity to St. Paul's semantic contacts with the Greco-Roman world pays exegetical dividends, and students of the New Testament continue to be rewarded for close scrutiny of Arthur Nock's numerous and durable works relating to Paul's world.[16]

Whether Paul had the express intention of associating his language about faith with the *fidei commissum* of Roman law can never be determined with certainty. But Greer Taylor (1966) makes a strong case for Paul's modular use of this legal datum in the phrase "faith of Christ" in the Letter to the Galatians.

Greco-Romans were quite satisfied with the reflecting qualities of their mirrors, and Samuel Bassett (1928) thought so too when he interpreted 1 Cor 13:12 as a reference to the reflecting function of mirrors rather than to technological deficiencies. Translators of the New Testament were slow to incorporate what should never have become a discovery. The *New English Bible* sees "puzzling reflections," and *Good News* follows *Revised Standard Version* with a reference to dimness.[17] In connection with the same epistle, J. W. Nott used his knowledge of the Homeric epics and Theokritos to grasp the active sense present in the passive form of the verb *egēgertai* in 1 Corinthians 15. Paul emphasizes Christ's rising not as a past phenomenon but as an ongoing reality (Nott, 1888).

As indicated in chapter 1,[18] portents and prophecy played a large role in the Greco-Roman world. In an essay entitled "The Apocalypse of Ezra," Phillips Barry (1913) makes generous use of Greco-Roman material relating to interest in prophecy. And expositors of 1 Corinthians 11 will find

---

[15] Apart from a seventeenth-century theologian (Robert Barclay), Harry refers to Hartung as one of the minority reports for the indicative. Overlooked is the testimony of R. Potter, who in a translation of the drama (*Tragedies of Aeschylus* [London, 1819]) rendered: "Ye see me bound, a wretched god, abhorr'd/By Jove, . . ." Harry included this reminder: "That errors are often perpetuated simply because the writer, or teacher, will not think for himself might be shown by numerous examples" (1901:65).

[16] See, e.g., Nock, 1933, 1938, 1964.

[17] Bassett's view is shared in the main by Norbert Hugede (*La métaphore du miroir dans les epîtres de saint Paul aux Corinthiens* (Neuchâtel: Delachaux, 1957) and by David H. Gill ("Through a Glass Darkly: A Note on 1 Corinthians 13, 12," *CBQ* 25 [1963] 427–29), who was unaware that Hugede (p. 128) had taken note of Plutarch *Moralia* 382A (*Isis and Osiris* 76).

[18] See p. 8–9.

interesting the procedure followed in the cult of Apollo Deiradiotes in which two male promanties appear to interpret a female promantis.[19] For ancient views of female decorum one does well to note the data cited by Leonard Woodbury (1978:279–98 n. 35).

To the literature on the history of ancient publishing procedures Evan Sage (1919) added a study on the fortunes of Martial's poems. Sage's essay is worth reading in conjunction with Edgar Goodspeed's hypothesis concerning the publication of St. Paul's correspondence.[20]

The commercial imagery in Philippians reflects a mode of thinking explored by Paula Nassen in connection with Pindar *Olympian* 10.[21]

Ephesians 6 is heavy with military imagery. Consideration of the subject of early Christian attitudes towards the Roman military can profit from studies by Henry Cadbury (1918) and by Meyer Reinhold (1971). Service in the military was generally limited to Roman citizens, and usurpation of citizenship carried severe penalties. Reinhold notes that slaves could on occasion be called to arms, but only rarely, and under desperate circumstances (295–98).

James Thompson (1975) saw an association with Platonic metaphysics in Heb 12:27. Some may not agree with his conclusions, but they will probably thank him for an instructive lecture.[22]

Epistle of James

Genealogical sin, as portrayed in James 1:5, might well have been understood by some readers as a counterpart of genealogies of ethical concepts. D. Herbert Abel (1943) explored the latter in a range of literature from Hesiod to Bacchylides.

The Apocalypse

Among early efforts to relate classical data to biblical apocalyptic is Grace Macurdy's (1910) study of Platonic eschatological myth in St. John's apocalypse and in the Book of Enoch. An interesting correlation of data in an inscription (apparently from 93 C.E.) and of references to famine in the Book of Revelation is made by David Robinson (1924). For religio-historical understanding of the Apocalypse see Betz, 1969.

---

[19] See Kadletz, 1978:95. Neither Barry nor Kadletz is noted in David Aune's (1983) well-stocked repository for prophetic data. To Aune's bibliography, add Talbert, 1980.

[20] See esp. Goodspeed, 1933 and related titles by Goodspeed cited in Cook, 1981.

[21] For more detailed exhibition of the exegetical potential in the study of Greek commercial terminology see Danker, 1972.

[22] See also Thompson, 1979 and cf. Yerkes, 1952.

Pseudoparallelism

Pseudoparallelism is a constant hazard. Martial 6.7 contains a jeer at a Tellesina who married for the tenth time and thereby committed legalized adultery. If one seeks a general Mediterranean context, it will be discovered that numerous Greco-Roman epigrams containing references to henomagomy — eschewing a second marriage out of commitment to one's deceased spouse — are more appropriate for understanding the admonition in 1 Tim 3:2 about having "one wife." On the other hand, Martial 1. 84, which calls attention to the use of female slaves to produce sons,[23] may be indirect testimony to the probability that 1 Pet 3:7 is dealing delicately with the problem of Christian masters in their relation to female slaves.

Sociological Study

Backgrounding, the principal feature in most of the studies sketched above, is grist for socio-historical study. And as indicated earlier, the Chicago School encouraged biblical students to develop a sharper socio-historical understanding to undergird exegetical discipline. Deficient in sociological theory, Shirley Case conceived of first-century Christianity basically in functional terms, as response to social needs.[24] But one of his sentences in an essay entitled "The Life of Jesus" (1927) conveys a rumble of the future: "The context of a document, as indicative of the social experiences out of which it arose, is more determinative than even a knowledge of the literary relations to one another, or any hypothesis as to an original Aramaic background." His sentence merely rephrased what Cornelius Felton wrote in 1836 about the "necessity to build up anew in our imagination the structure of Athenian society, if we would enter fully into the spirit of the raciest portion of their literature," namely Attic comedy (372). It remained for a later generation to tap sociologists for information on "characteristic human motivations and activities" (Hynes, 1981:82) that would supply historians with basic ingredients for synthesis, and exegetes with fresh resources for entry into the world of the text.

A half-century after Case had begun his work, members of SBL, stimulated by the German scholar Gerd Theissen, began to apply sociological theory in a probe of documents for clues as to the social stratification of the communities and the societal structures presupposed by the kinds of statements that find expression in the documents.[25] Setting the

---

[23] See Sullivan, 1981:221.

[24] Case, 1927:41. On Case's theoretical deficiencies see Meeks, 1983:3.

[25] Gerd Theissen, *Sociology of Early Palestinian Christianity* (tr. John Bowden; Philadelphia: Fortress, 1978) and *The Social Setting of Pauline Christianity: Essays on Corinth* (tr. with an introduction by John H. Schuetz; Philadelphia: Fortress, 1982). Especially significant is the increased awareness of the importance of small groups in the formation of Christian society. Filson (1939) gave some indication of what could be done in this area of inquiry, and Herbert

pace in America was John Gager, whose name became associated with "study of the social world of early Christianity" through his *Kingdom and Community* (1975). Especially important are numerous contributions by Abraham Malherbe and Wayne Meeks,[26] and the application of theoretical principles by Elisabeth Schuessler Fiorenza (1984) to a reconstruction of "early Christian history as women's history."[27] In *The Revolt of the Widows*, Stevan Davies (1980) explores women's piety in the world that generated the Apocryphal Acts. One of the most enterprising introductions to theoretical aspects of sociological interpretation, together with practical application to a specific document of the New Testament, is John Elliott's *A Home for the Homeless* (1981).[28]

Accurate sociological analysis is close companion to knowledge of the political and cultural profile of cities and larger geographical areas. Important for understanding of Paul's contacts at Neopolis is Stephen Mitchell's (1979) challenge of William Ramsay's assignment of colonial status for Iconium to the time of Hadrian. According to Mitchell, "Iconium at least from the reign of Claudius was ostensibly a double community," that is, both a polis and a colony. From Moses Hadas (1931) one learns that Gadara could boast of Menippus, the satirist; of Meleager, noted for his epigrams; and of Philodemos, who stocked his shelves at Herculaneum with mostly his own dull works. Much of Galilee was "*not* Hellenized," argues Sean Freyne in *Galilee from Alexander the Great to Hadrian* (1980). And according to S. Thomas Parker (1975), the Dekapolis is simply a "convenient appellation," not a league or confederation.

Mayer (1979) traces the development of the small-group concept in Christian circles.

[26] See Malherbe, 1968, 1977b; and bibliography of his work in Meeks, 1983:266; for Meeks's contributions, see Meeks, 1983:267; cf. Nock, 1925.

[27] Fiorenza's work closes a gap that developed after Helen Spurrell, of England, began the study of Hebrew in her fifties and in 1885 published *A New Translation of the Old Testament Scriptures from the Original Hebrew* (London: James Nisbet), and after Elizabeth Cady Stanton published *The Woman's Bible* in 1895. In answer to criticism of her interpretation of the Old Testament, Stanton asked why it was "more audacious to review Moses than Blackstone." According to Nancy A. Hardesty, Stanton believed that " 'whatever the Bible may be made to do in Hebrew or Greek, in plain English it does not exalt and dignify woman' " ("Elizabeth Cady Stanton," in *American Women Writers* (ed. Lina Mainiero, vol. 4 [New York: Ungar, 1982] 152). See also Gretchen Buenger Leppke, *Feminist Critique of the Interpretations of Created Female in the Image of God* (STM dissertation, Lutheran School of Theology at Chicago, 1983).

[28] See esp. Elliott, 1981:1–20. The seed-plot for Elliott's *Home for the Homeless* is *The Elect and the Holy* (1966), one of the most thorough and instructive philological presentations on any New Testament writing to be produced by an American. See also Malina, 1981, Gottwald, 1983, and the bibliography in Meeks, 1983, to which add Murphy-O'Connor, 1983 (on Corinth) and Stowers, 1984 (on Paul's preaching activity). On St. Paul's trade see Hock, 1978 and 1980. Knowledge of Greek clubs and associations is essential for inquiry into ancient social structures. Overlooked at times is the important study by Forbes (1933) on associations of the *Neoi*. See also Ferguson, 1944.

Formal Features

American biblical scholars were generally more interested than their classical colleagues in formal features of documents,[29] but production in this area was not especially heavy until the last decades of the twentieth century, when reconsideration of Greco-Roman documents was responsible for a rash of publications on Greco-Roman formal phenomena.[30]

Given the form of many New Testament documents, it is no surprise that epistolography became a favored province of research.[31] In a study of Arethusa's letter to Lycotas (Propertius 4.3), James Dee calls attention to German work which traces the origin of the epistle as a literary genre to the spurious collection of letters attributed to Alexander and others. Taking account of Rom 16:1–2, Clinton Keyes (1935) explored the Greek letter of introduction.[32] Paul Schubert's study of the Pauline thanksgiving (1935) set the titular form that would appear in many later productions. The 1960s and 1970s blossomed with studies that were confined in the main to papyrological data.[33] What Martin Stirewalt (1974) noted about the absence of inscriptional evidence in a book by Chan-Hie Kim on the Letter of Recommendation was generally true of American study of ancient epistolography.[34] The one brilliant exception, Charles Welles, whose *Royal Correspondence in the Hellenistic Period* (1934) will still be celebrated at the end of the next centennial, and with renewed attention having been paid to the light that can be shed on New Testament epistolary content through study of letters on ancient stone.

A major contribution to recognition of the diatribe form was Edward O'Neil's edition of Teles (1977).[35]

---

[29] But see, e.g., Parry, 1940, on the moral formula attached to Aisopic fables, which ought to be examined further for application to passages in the NT; see esp. Luke 12:21; 15:7, 10; 17:10; 21:31; Rom 6:4, 11, 19; 1 Cor 4:1; 9:24; Jas 2:12. Important is Ingalls's (1979) discussion, "Formular Density in the Similes of the *Iliad*," which offers some remedy for omission in the work of Parry and others.

[30] Cadbury (1923) was among the first American scholars to call more than casual attention to the continental form-critical approach. Paul Minear's form-critical study in 1942 (on the "needle's eye") was a rarity in *JBL* prior to the 1950s.

[31] Francis Exler (1923) remained for decades America's prime contributor to the study of Greek epistolography as exhibited in the papyri.

[32] Kim (1972) discusses the species in detail.

[33] Among the publications were Funk, 1966: 250–74 ("The Letter: Form and Style"); Sanders, 1962 and a follow-up article by White, 1971; O'Brien, 1977; Mullins, 1968 (on the greeting); Doty, 1973 (a brief general discussion); White, 1972a (on the official petition); and White, 1972b (on the body of the Greek letter).

[34] Formal features have a long life, and late productions may permit tracing of deep roots. It is prudent, therefore, to be aware of Mathisen 1981 (a look at Late Roman Gaul), with bibliography on Gallic letters for 420–520 C.E. See also Sherk, 1969.

[35] See Malherbe, 1978 and Stowers, 1981 for additional bibliography and discussion, and cf. Nock, 1925.

Of other categories, interest was displayed in the Farewell Speech Form;[36] the "Topos";[37] liturgical forms;[38] aretalogies;[39] the riddle as a popular form of entertainment;[40] the decretal form;[41] the gospel form;[42] and rhetoric in general.[43]

[36] Budesheim, 1976; Richard, 1979.

[37] Bradley, 1953 (in Pauline exhortation); Sandy, 1970 (sympotic usage, esp. 471 n. 15); and Mullins, 1980 (the New Testament form).

[38] Mowry, 1952; Sanders, 1971; Horning, 1983.

[39] M. Smith, 1971.

[40] Reckford, 1977:288 n. 5.

[41] Householder, 1940; Danker, 1982.

[42] Talbert, 1977; cf. Talbert, 1978.

[43] Kennedy, 1980.

Part II
Basic Interpretive Work

Common decency requires that we recognize those
who have advanced our own achievements.
Pliny the Elder

4

CONCORDANCES AND WORD INDEXES

Before the Computer Age, the making of concordances and indexes required such an incredible amount of time and sheer industry, divorced from broader literary-cultural interest, that some scholars raised questions about such investment. Someone has termed it "a form of self-inflicted torture which vies in monotony with the task of the Danaids." Yet the philological potential of concordance usage cannot be denied, and in this chapter recognition is especially accorded to those who labored through the long day before computers came to shorten the hours. In technical usage the term concordance is reserved for books that cite the key word in its context (Kwic). A word index ordinarily lists only the location for each word cited. Usage has been fluid, but since 1965 it has been customary in computer circles to distinguish the Kwic type from those that cite only key word and text reference.[1]

Concordances and the Computer

One of the earliest manufacturers of concordances to make historical impact is Hugh of St. Cher, who directed preparation of an index to the Vulgate between 1230 and 1238. Confronted with the same type of problem faced by modern lemmatizers, Hugh had to find divisions for his text. In lieu of verse divisions he divided each chapter into seven equal parts, which he marked with letters of the alphabet. The work was of limited serviceability because it listed merely references (the so-called "tokens" of a word index) rather than relevant quotations of text. Three English Dominicans remedied this in 1250–52.[2]

The first concordance to a part of the Bible in English is the work of Thomas Gibson, who in 1535 published in London *The concordance of the New Testament most necessary to be had in the handes of all soche, as desire the communicacion of any place contayned in the new testament.*[3]

---

[1] See Burton, 1981b: esp. 92 and 1981a:5–6.

[2] On the general history of concordances, see Danker, 1970:1–10; on Hugh, ibid. 1–2; Burton, 1981a:6.

[3] Title cited as recorded in *DNB* 7:1163.

Sharing the historical limelight with with these pioneers are Vannevar Bush, an American, and Roberto Busa, an Italian scholar. Prior to World War II, Bush had designed at the Massachusetts Institute of Technology a device to scan microfilm and select desired segments of text for reproduction. Not long thereafter Busa observed certain automatic equipment at work in various applications at IBM in New York, the R.C.A. laboratories in Princeton, the Library of Congress, and the Department of Agriculture in the United States Capital.[4]

In the course of his observations Busa experienced the equivalent of a vision, an "intuition." A few years later he was able to state that intuition had become "acquired fact; the punched card machines carry out all the material part of the work of (making a concordance)." These words appear in his Introduction to *Sancti Thomae Aquinatis humanorum ritualium varia specimina concordantiarum,* published in 1951, which according to Dolores Burton, "inaugurated the history of the automatic production of concordances and word indexes."[5]

Busa's first concordance was based on four hymns ascribed to Thomas Aquinas. Since the texts chosen were brief, Busa included them and then presented the concordance in six parts: "an alphabetical list of words with their frequency and an index to their lemmas, a reverse index with frequencies, a list of word forms with their frequencies arranged under their lemmas, a list of the relevant lemmas, an *index locorum,* and a concordance with verse line context for each word in the hymns."[6]

Apart from Moses, Jesus Christ, or Muhammed, only a person of the historical stature of Aquinas could have commanded the devotion that ultimately in 1974 produced *Index Thomisticus: Sancti Thomae Aquinatis Operum Omnium.* In 1951 Busa had estimated that this concordance, if done manually, would have taken a half-century to produce, and four years if done by machine. The estimate failed to take into sufficient account the time that would actually be spent in putting the Corpus Thomisticum on punched cards, pretesting an IBM 750 in the production of an index and concordance of the Qumran Scrolls, and then transferring the Corpus Thomisticum from cards to magnetic tape with all the proofreading demanded by the operation. By 1974, when the first volumes appeared, Busa and associates had invested "roughly one million man hours" and the "10,600,000 words of input required 110 reels of magnetic tape" that eventually filled "sixty photocomposed folio volumes" (Burton, 1981a:3).

[4] Burton, 1981a:1.

[5] Much of this and the following information on the use of computers in the production of concordances is derived from three articles by Dolores M. Burton (1981a,b,c).

[6] Burton, 1981a:2; for details on the problems surmounted by Busa in the eggshell stage of the technology, see 2–3.

John Marbeck nearly merited a heretic's death for producing a concordance on the entire English Bible in 1550. But John Ellison, following Busa's lead, became a celebrity for piloting production in 1957 of *Nelson's Complete Concordance of the Revised Standard Version of the Bible* (Ellison, 1957).[7] According to Howard Aiken, of the Harvard Computation Laboratory, Ellison was the "first humanist to walk into the . . . Laboratory with a specific problem wanting to use the computer."[8]

Ellison's achievement set Stephen Parrish's mind to work at Cornell University, where Lane Cooper had laid foundations for concordance production. In May 1913, Cooper planned *A Concordance to the Works of Horace*. He finished the work in spring of 1914.[9] Such speed of production owed much to Cooper's managerial ingenuity. A few years before work began on Horace, Cooper had gathered a corps of graduate students and Cornell homemakers, who helped him construct a concordance to Wordsworth out of eight printed copies of a standard Wordsworth text that were cut into snippets, which were then pasted one each to a card. In the work on Horace, for which he used eighteen collaborators and cut up fourteen copies of F. Vollmer's 1910 editio minor of Horace,[10] he refers to a set of instructions that he made available to scholars for preparing slips, and the greatly modified computerized procedure at Cornell's concordance-producing center is to this day called "Method Cooper."[11] Without detracting from Cooper's achievement, it must be observed that Alexander Cruden began work on a "complete" concordance of the entire Bible in 1736 and presented it to his Queen on 3 November 1737. History does not record that he depended on helpers. Nor is his alleged lunacy to be ascribed to this extraordinary display of devotion.[12]

[7] In contrast to the unesthetic appearance of early computerized productions, Nelson's Concordance to the Revised Standard Version of the Bible had a more bookish cast, simply because the company was willing to spend $65,000 extra to set the book in type (Burton, 1981c:143). *A Concordance to the Apocrypha/Deuterocanonical Books of the Revised Standard Version*, derived from the Bible Data Bank of the Centre Informatique et Bible (Abbey of Maredsous) appeared in 1983 (Grand Rapids: Eerdmans).

[8] Burton, 1981a:6. The publishers admitted that Univac's analytical genius could stand some developing and that it still had courses to take in Hebrew and in Greek. Also, the day would come when Univac or some offspring could distinguish the adverb "well," for example, from its homonym for "cistern." The acclaimed accuracy of the computing was not offset by minor typographical errors, such as on pages 299 (1 Thess 4:16) and 585 (John 20:27).

[9] The publisher (Carnegie Institution of Washington) accepted it on 21 May 1914; it was published in 1916.

[10] Variants from Vollmer's 1912 edition were included in the final stages of editing. The names of Cooper's collaborators, including professors and homemakers, are cited on p. ix of Cooper's Preface.

[11] Burton, 1981a:7.

[12] Cruden corrected his own work, *A Complete Concordance to the Holy Scriptures of the Old and New Testament: In Two Parts* (London, 1738) in the course of several editions, and his level of accuracy set an enviable record; but his claim to completeness was based on an idiosyncratic view of the translated biblical text. His original publication included "A Concordance to the

Under the general editorship of Parrish, who enjoyed the technical collaboration of James Painter, Cornell's computer packaged in succession Matthew Arnold (1959, no punctuation, only hyphens, processing time 38 hours), William Butler Yeats (1963, with punctuation, print remains upper case, and with a "Programmer's Preface" by Painter, 12 hours), Emily Dickinson (1964, first computerized variorum concordance, 10 hours), William Blake (two and one third hours), and Jean Racine (1968, representing a variety of progressive techniques, including such items as accents, identification of speaker of each line of verse, high-frequency words counts).[13]

In 1959 Hans Peter Luhn made a major advance in the manufacture of concordances when he developed a program that was capable of putting key words into a fixed position within a specific count of spaces for context.[14]

After such ground-breaking, "The Computer Bible" began production in 1969 with *A Critical Concordance to the Synoptic Gospels*, edited by J. Arthur Baird (1969a),[15] "the first such application of the computer to content analysis of the Bible."[16]

Baird (1969b:29) describes the relationship:

> The basic tool that has given wings to my study is a concordancelike printout where every word of the text, every time it is used, is arranged alphabetically; and opposite each usage in parallel columns are listed the reference, the speaker-audience relationship, the historic point, the source, and the form appropriate for that word. As a result, patterns of various kinds have become immediately apparent: patterns, I might add, that are the result of such an exhaustive cross section that they would not be observable in any other way. With this tool, the Synoptics have become a new world for one who thought he knew something about them. With this new technique, there is a possibility of Synoptic analysis achieving a measure of scientific accuracy. The work to follow in this book has been thoroughly informed by this computerized synopsis.[17]

Books, Called Apocrypha," and a preface that is replete with information about concordances. Some reprints of Cruden's concordance do not do justice to the thoroughness of his work.

[13] Burton, 1981a:8.

[14] See Burton, 1981a:13 for bibliography of Luhn's work.

[15] A revised edition appeared in 1971 under the copyright of Biblical Research Associates Inc., whose general editors for the Computer Bible at the time were Baird and David Noel Freedman.

[16] Baird, 1969a:1; see also Baird, 1969b:28, and for additional history, 198 n. 22.

[17] The work of Baird is based on Albert Huck, *Synopsis of the First Three Gospels* (9th ed.; Oxford, 1949). On other concordances in the "Computer Bible" series, see Burton 1981b:87. As his contribution to the Computer Bible, A. Q. Morton, of Scotland, prepared a computerized version of the Greek New Testament. For Morton's autobiographical recital of "prehistoric" computer times, see A. G. Morton, "The Annals of Computing: The Greek New Testament," *Computers and the Humanities* 14 (1980):197–99. Those who are more skeptical of the newer technology may find support in the fact that p. 197 cites Morton's middle initial in the byline as "G." and in the biographical note at the bottom of the page correctly as "O." In Burton, 1981c:142, we have an "O." Computers do indeed have a way of eliciting respect for mystery; and

In 1973 Lloyd Gaston added the word *Electronicae* to John Hawkins's title *Horae Synopticae* (Oxford, 1909) in an avowed effort to improve on the British publication by subjecting the vocabulary of Matthew, Mark, and Luke to analysis by computer. Richard Edwards followed in 1975 with a concordance to "Q," the material common to Matthew and Luke, but not found in Mark.

Classicists joined biblical scholars in use of the new technology. David Packard (1968) saved $7500 by writing his own program for the production process involving a concordance to Livy, and four massive volumes that would have cost $300,000 to typeset came from the press at considerably reduced cost in the new Kwic format. Once the text had been proofread after being punched onto about 65,000 cards and then copied onto magnetic tape, the concordance was produced in about three hours on an IBM 7094 computer. "Some men, intent upon greater things, have thought little on sounds and derivations," wrote Samuel Johnson in defense of his concern for orthography in the preparation of his Dictionary.[18] And some might consider it pedantic to include a conjunction such as *et*,[19] but Packard covers every word written by Livy, while at the same time emphasizing that it was not considered a wise investment of time to attempt lexical classification. "Repeated instances of the same word are subalphabetized according to the words which follow in the context . . ." (1968:v). This procedure immediately alerts the user to parallel phraseology. The spelling of the Oxford Classical Text is followed through book 35, and the Teubner edition is used for the remainder. Since new critical editions were in progress at the time, no effort was made to index manuscript readings.

About the time that Packard was working on Livy, Louis Roberts had an IBM 7094 alphabetize and sort in seventy minutes time the material that had been keypunched for his Concordance of Lucretius (1968).[20] And in 1972 the Boston Theological Institute announced that it had begun the publication of a series entitled "Concordances to Patristic and Late Classical Texts," produced and typeset by computer.[21] To keep themselves abreast of the use

---

one of the values of a centennial volume is relief of future scholars from fruitless prosopographical research. For further information on Morton's contributions to the "Computer Bible" see Burton 1981b:87.

[18] Samuel Johnson, *A Dictionary of the English Language*, ed. by H. J. Todd, vol. 1 (London: Longman, 1827) 2.

[19] James T. Allen wrote in his Introduction to *A Concordance to Euripides* that citation of "every instance in an author's works of *de, kai,* and the like . . . is wasteful pedantry" (Allen, 1954:vii). Developments in linguistics have demonstrated the fallacy in such foreclosure of exposure to basic data, and computer technology has invalidated a pejorative judgment that may have borne some validity in days of manual production.

[20] The text for the concordance is Cyril Bailey, *Titi Lucreti Cari, De Rerum Natura* (Oxford, 1963).

[21] See "Announcements," *JBL* 91 (1972) 586.

of computers in humanistic applications, scholars maintained contact with the information carried in the journal *Computers and the Humanities,* which offers direction to other periodicals and literature.[22] In his *The Emerging Technology,* R. E. Levien (1972) pointed the way to ground-floor inquirers. Of further special importance in the early 1980s were *A Guide to Computer Applications in the Humanities,* by Susan Hockey (1980), and *Computing in the Humanities,* ed. by Peter Patton and Renee Holoien (1981).

The Patton-Holoien publication offers information on the various projects at the University of Minnesota's Computer Center in the fields of linguistics, lexicography, literature, archeology, language instruction, musicology, and art. As the history of production of grammars indicates, syntax has always been the trouble-center for grammarians. But just when grammarians seemed to be developing a theoretic grasp of sentence structures, the importance of taking into account larger language units, in terms of which the more circumscribed units might be understood, thrust itself forward with insistent impact. In this respect technology patterned afresh the age-old conflict between atomistic and holistic interpretive procedures.

Dorothy Clay (1958–60) made a major contribution with her manually produced dissertation on the vocabularies of the three great Greek tragedians. Clay divides words first of all into two broad categories: derived and underived items. These are then arranged according to parts of speech. The derived items are further classified according to type of derivation, such as suffixed words and compounds. Thus it is possible to determine, for example, all suffixed compound adjectives in *-tos* or nouns derived from verbs with or without ablaut variation. The Fribergs, Timothy and Barbara, worked along similar lines and discovered that the discourse structure of the Koine, and therefore of the Greek New Testament, had been relatively unexplored. In a chapter of Patton-Holoien entitled "A Computer-Assisted Analysis of the Greek New Testament Text" (Fribergs, 1981a:15–51) they point out the unscientific character in much of traditional literary-critical approach to the Greek New Testament and question the narrow literary base on which computerized statistical analyses relative to authorship of biblical documents are based.[23] It is not enough to know the variables: one must be familiar with the constants. Besides lexical items, it is incumbent on the philologist to focus on grammatical items, such as case, tense, mood, voice, gender, person, and number.

John Beekman, of Wycliffe Bible Translators, endeavored to move the discussion beyond the semantic phase to the development of a theory that could accommodate both syntax and semantics. But the narrow base of

[22] On early developments in the use of computers for classical research see McDonough, 1967; Waite, 1970 and 1972.

[23] The Fribergs have in mind especially W. C. Wake, A. Q. Morton, and S. Michaelson, whose publications are noted in Fribergs 1981a:47.

analysis of individual New Testament documents hampered construction for demonstration of his hypothesis. The Fribergs aimed to remedy this defect by developing a text of the entire Greek New Testament combined with a tagged grammatical analysis of every word. The work bears the title *Analytical Greek New Testament* (Fribergs, 1981b).[24] This combined text provides a "new tool for translation theory, which seeks to identify the ingredients crucial to the process of saying meaningfully in one language what is meaningful in another." (Fribergs 1981a, 21.) It also opens the door to newer types of concordances that will make fresh reading of ancient texts possible. Once universal discourse structures are determined, it will be feasible to enunciate a typology of discourse, and even more accurate translation from one language to another will be possible.[25]

Other chapters in Patton-Holoien offer an historical base for understanding development in application of computers to the study of Roman prosopography and the teaching of Greek and Latin language skills.

Pre-Computer Indexes and Concordances

Preeminent among the American pre-computer-age concordance manufacturers was William Oldfather of the University of Illinois. Born of missionary parentage, at Urumiah, Persia, on 23 October 1880, Oldfather received his doctorate at the University of Munich and in 1909 began teaching the classics at the University of Illinois, where he worked indefatigably until his death, 27 May 1945, in a canoeing accident.[26] Just as Lane Cooper had done for concordances, Oldfather interpreted his experience in compilation of word indexes as protection of posterity from wasted labor and frustration. His advice appeared under the title "Suggestions for Guidance in the Preparation of a Critical *Index Verborum* for Latin and Greek Authors" (Oldfather, 1937).

After producing indexes of Seneca's dramas (1918) and of the works of Apuleius (1934), Oldfather and Howard Canter used material gathered by Monroe Wetmore and Alfred Dame, and together with Kenneth Abbott

---

[24] For example, the mnemonic tag VPPANM-S means that the following information is contained in the word: Verb, Participial in form, Present tense, Active voice, Nominative case, Masculine gender, and Singular number. The hyphen is not fundamental to the analysis, but marks the place where the identification of the person of a verbal form—first, second, or third—is indicated.

[25] For prophecy of developments in computer usage that would make traditional types of concordances obsolete, see *Research Tools for the Classics* (1980:14). On the design of a complete computerized data bank of Greek literature and documents written before 700 C.E., entitled *Thesaurus Linguae Graecae (TLG)*, directed by Theodore F. Brunner, see *Research Tools for the Classics*, p. 37 and the introductory pages in Berkowitz, 1977.

[26] For references to Oldfather's numerous publications, see Pease, 1945; cf. memorial notice in *CJ* 41 (1945–46) 9–11.

edited an index of Cicero's Epistles (1938), with the plea that editors of prose works mark their text in smaller sections of not more than five lines each.

The same team (1964) edited an index of Cicero's writings on rhetoric including the *ad Herennium,* of unknown authorship. Ellison's recruits appear to have been more reliable than Oldfather's assistants drawn from the ranks of the National Youth Administration student helpers in the 1930s, for at least one half of the cards for this index had to be rewritten to make them at all usable. Only one of the editors, Kenneth Abbott, survived to complete the work.

The Deferrari Productions

A conversation that Roy Deferrari of the Catholic University of America once had with Lane Cooper in the course of reading proof for Cooper's concordance of Boethius led to the founding of what was to become in all appearance a concordance syndicate.

The illustrious fourth century Latin poet Aurelius Clemens Prudentius of Spain, whose text was edited by Johannes Bergman in 1926, moved into further prominence with the publication of a concordance by Deferrari and James Campbell (1932). Together with Maria Fanning and Anne Sullivan, Deferrari produced A *Concordance of Lucan* (1940), based on Alfred E. Housman's text of 1927. This concordance was to supplant George Mooney's index to Lucan's *Bellum Civile.*[27]

After getting Maria Eagan to join his syndicate, Deferrari produced a concordance of Statius (1943). Instead of using A. Klotz and R. Jahnke's text in the Teubner series, Deferrari worked out of J. S. Phillimore's and H. W. Garrod's texts in *OCT,* both of which have a number of misprints that are carried over into the concordance.

Ovid received his due in a combined concordance and index verborum published by Deferrari, Maria Barry, and Martin McGuire in 1939.

Other Classical Concordances

Henrietta Holm Warwick used the technical assistance of Richard L. Hotchkiss for the compilation of a concordance to Vergil in the Kwic format, including *Eclogues, Georgics,* and *Aeneid* (1975). The concordance is based on the *OCT* text of R. A. B. Mynors.

Iowa State marshalled the words of Terence and C. Valerius Flaccus. Virginia Henderson (1930) produced an index to Terence in typescript, based

---

[27] George W. Mooney, *Index to the "Pharsalia" of Lucan,* in the "First Supplemental Volume" of *Hermathena* 44 (1927) 5–310. The title *Pharsalia* is less accurate than the broader term *Bellum Civile.* Mooney's Index is based on Heitland's text in the *Corpus Poetarum Latinorum* (ed. Postgate:1900, vol. 2. Deferrari and company aimed to correct Mooney's text, but users of their concordance are advised to note the long list of corrections made by Richard Bruère (1941).

on R. Kauer's and W. M. Lindsay's text in *OCT,* but without reference to variants. In 1932 Edgar Jenkins observed, without reference to Henderson's work, that "no completely satisfactory index of the vocabulary of Terence seems ever to have been published." One is inclined to ask whether any work is ever "completely satisfactory," but Jenkins did endeavor to offer "a complete alphabetical list of all references to every word (including enclitics) in the plays of Terence" (Jenkins, 1932:v). As in Henderson's work, the basic text is Kauer and Lindsay, but Jenkins includes variants from other texts and statistics of usage.

After completion of an index to C. Valerius Flaccus's *Argonautica,* William Schulte received his degree in 1931 from the State University of Iowa. Schulte's Index is based on various texts, including that of Otto Kramer,[28] and was published in 1935 as the third volume of "Iowa Studies in Classical Philology." When one considers the fact that Valerius averages about one commentary per century—an average that Gildersleeve would have considered too many—this index was an unexpected contribution to the quest for philological trivia. But one scholar's trivium may prove to be another's Via ad Parnassum, and Gildersleeve's prejudice against compilation of indexes, on the ground that young degree candidates ought to develop holistic appreciation of the classics as monuments of mind and soul, did not deter Norma Young from making her index of Silius Italicus the eighth volume of "Iowa Studies in Classical Philology" (1939).[29]

At New Haven, Monroe Wetmore (1911) contributed an index to Vergil and explained all in a subtitle: "Complete word-index to the acknowledged works of Vergil, the *Eclogues,* the *Georgics* and the *Aeneid* and to the poems usually included in the Appendix Vergiliana." Wetmore based his work on Otto Ribbeck's text edition of 1895, but with variants from Ribbeck's critical edition of 1894 and from other editions. After each word Wetmore indicates its number of occurrences. Until the publication of a concordance of Vergil in the Kwic format by Henrietta Warwick, referred to earlier, the only competitor was Christian Heyne's *Index,* published in his edition of Vergil (Leipzig, 1787–89). Originally Wetmore had planned to produce a complete lexicon for Vergil's works, and had made international inquiry to determine whether anyone else had such a work in mind. Receiving no replies to that effect, he proceeded with his research. After about a thousand pages were ready for the press, in 1909 he received word that Hugo Merguet, to whom

---

[28] Teubner text, 1913.

[29] Lane Cooper appears to have had Gildersleeve in mind when he complained that the value of concordances "sometimes is questioned by persons who might, if well-disposed, be influential in advancing their publication in America . . ." In support of his plea for more enlightened consideration, he cited the French Academy's expression of esteem for Livet's *Lexique de la Langue de Moliere* (3 vols.; Paris, 1895–97); see Cooper 1916:vi. For further affirmation of the value of concordances, see Schulte 1937.

he had sent information four years earlier, was engaged in the same type of project, with the result that Wetmore turned his data into the Index that bears his name.[30]

A year after his first edition of the Index to Vergil, Wetmore contributed a complete word index to Catullus (1912) based on R. Ellis' *OCT* edition of 1904, with variants from other editions. It held the field for sixty-five years until the editorial expertise of Vincent McCarren (1977) combined with the computering skills of William Tajibnapis. The latter work uses the Kwic technique developed by Packard in his concordance to Livy.

Cornell's reputation for classical scholarship was enhanced with the publication of a complete index to Antiphon, prepared by Frank Van Cleef (1895). Less than four decades later, James Mountford and Joseph Schultz contributed a combined index of Servius's commentary on Vergil (1930). Schultz uses G. Thilo's and H. Hagen's editions for Servius and Paul Wessner's edition of Donatus's commentary on Terence.[31] Superseding Adolf Brinck's index for Hiller's edition of the Tibullan corpus is Edward O'Neill's *Concordance* (1963), a model of clarity, which prints the key word in italics, with the line number placed ahead of the context, thus permitting the list to function both as index and concordance.

At the end of the nineteenth century, Xenophon's *Anabasis* was a standard resource for students beginning the study of Greek, and John White and Morris Morgan (1891) provided them with an illustrated dictionary that grouped words in Xenophon's book etymologically.

To assist students of Enoch, Campbell Bonner and Herbert Youtie added an index to *The Last Chapters of Enoch in Greek* (1937). Bonner (1940) also incorporated an index to his edition of Melito's Homily on the Passion of Jesus.

Edgar Goodspeed, assisted by willing students, supplied indexes to the Apostolic Fathers (1907) and to the Apologists of the second century (1912). In keeping with increased awareness of the Hellenistic context for understanding of the New Testament, St. Luke's works received a great deal of attention in the closing decades of the twentieth century, and James Yoder's *Concordance to the Distinctive Greek Text of Codex Bezae* (1961) made data more accessible for reconsideration of some of the problems connected with this unusual textual witness. Of special interest would be the implications of this textual tradition for sociological study of the communities that helped shape it.

Thanks to the University of California Press, a concordance to Euripides appeared in 1954. Forty-three years had elapsed before James Allen, with assistance from Gabriel Italie, completed the manuscript. During the earlier

---

[30] Hugo Merguet, *Lexikon zu Vergilius mit Angabe sämtlicher Stellen* (Leipzig, 1912; reprint Hildesheim, 1960).

[31] Servius derived much of his material from Donatus, hence the combined index.

periods of its preparation, Allen drew on the skills of assistants, who helped him, on his own admission, play "philological solitaire" with a pack of 250,000 cards or slips. In 1938 Italie announced his completion of a collection of material for a Euripides lexicon, on which he had been working for thirteen years. Unlike Merguet, who ignored an American invitation to collegial enterprise,[32] Italie responded to Allen's request for assistance in preparation of the concordance Allen had in mind. Each was to do half. Hazards of war prevented full cooperation, and Italie contributed material only for *lambda, mu, nu,* and *omikron.* Allen died on 29 September 1948, before arrangements for publication could be completed. Nevertheless, his manuscript was spared the fate of a concordance that had been completed in 1866 by another devotee of Euripides, a Dr. Korioth, whose largely illegible manuscript fell into unpublished repose in the archives of the University of California Library. But editorial readers at Berkeley and Oxford, England, evidently experienced no eyestrain in bringing Allen's project to an elegant conclusion.

Biblical Concordances

Until computers became popular, American biblical scholars were dependent in the nineteenth century and through much of the twentieth on European import of concordances that took consideration of the Greek text. Ezra Abbot (1870), highly esteeemed in his time as a textual critic, completed *A Critical Greek and English Concordance of the New Testament,* which had been begun by Charles Hudson under the direction of Horace Hastings. Hudson, a printing expert, almost brought it to completion without ever reducing it totally to writing, but did not live to see it through the final stages of publication. The book was published in Boston in 1870 by the Scriptural Tract Repository.[33] Later editions incorporated William Greenfield's *A Greek Lexicon to the New Testament* (Boston: H. L. Hastings, 1882),[34] which was revised by Thomas Sheldon Green under the title *A Greek-English Lexicon to the NT* in an eighth edition of the concordance (Boston: H. L. Hastings, 1891). Abbot's concordance was designed as "a traveling companion," and in contrast to a bulkier British work[35] classifies the passages in which each Greek word occurs and exhibits the numerous ways in which it is translated. The ingenious cross-referencing system makes it accessible also to those who lack Greek. Since mere citation of chapter and verse is made for the use of each term, the work is more properly classified as an index. The revisers of

---

[32] See above on Wetmore, 1911.
[33] A second rev. ed. of Abbot, 1870 appeared in 1871 (Boston: H. L. Hastings).
[34] The number of this edition is not indicated.
[35] George Vecesimus Wigram, *The Englishman's Greek Concordance of the New Testament* (London: Central Tract Depot, 1839).

the King James Version found it useful in the preparation of their work, which appeared in 1881.[36]

Jacob Smith declared independence with his *Greek-English Concordance to the New Testament* (1955). This work lists the Greek vocabulary of the New Testament in a total of 5,524 words, and tabulates each according to its various renderings, together with the number of times each rendering occurs in the King James Version.[37]

Working along different lines, John Stegenga (1963) retired from an active business career and spent ten years in the production of *The Greek-English Analytical Concordance of the Greek-English New Testament*. Besides citing every vocabulary item in sequence, this concordance uses the root-word-family approach, and a cross-referencing system enables the student to locate any word that forms part of a group of related words, thus helping the student avoid the common mistake of ignoring cognates in word study. It is regrettable that Frans Neirynck and Frans van Segbroeck failed to take note of this massive effort in their supplement to several concordances of the New Testament.[38] But deplorable is the fact that Stegenga invested 36,000 hours of his personal life in a production whose value is somewhat vitiated through unscientific features in the compiler's classification by root. Perhaps a centennial volume of the present kind and periodic invitations by editors of learned journals for assistance in the execution of certain specialized types of tasks, such as Cooper's helpers rendered, could minimize much waste of capable talent, not to speak of treasure. A testimony to more enlightened zeal was the industry displayed by John Recks. Dissatisfied with the inaccuracies in the British Moulton-Geden *Concordance to the Greek Testament*, he took great pains while still in seminary to help the publishers ensure a more reliable edition.[39]

Near the turn of the nineteenth century, American users of the King James Version could boast a notable domestic product in the form of James Strong's *The Exhaustive Concordance of the Bible* (1894). Strong lists every word of the KJV, takes account of the Revised Version, and gives the underlying Hebrew and Greek term for the English renderings.[40] Strong himself never trained for the clergy, but as professor of exegetical theology at Drew University, from 1867 until his death in 1894, he exercised a profound

---

[36] See Danker, 1970:8.

[37] This type of concordance facilitates comparative statistical analysis. For such possibilities see Holly 1983, who makes a detailed comparative study of Nestle-Aland 25th and 26th editions of *Novum Testamentum Graece*.

[38] Frans Neirynck and Frans van Segbroeck, *New Testament Vocabulary: A Comparative Volume to the Concordance* (Leuven: Leuven University, 1984).

[39] Harold K. Moulton acknowledges Recks's "valuable list of corrections" in the preface to his fourth edition of *A Concordance to the Greek Testament* (Edinburgh: T. and T. Clark, 1963).

[40] This work was copyrighted in 1890, but according to information in an edition printed in 1944 (New York, Abingdon-Cokesbury), the first edition was printed "April, 1894."

influence on the shape of a substantial portion of America's ministerium. Besides his Concordance, Strong wrote on a variety of subjects and was largely responsible for successful completion of the *Cyclopaedia of Biblical, Theological, and Ecclesiastical Literature.*[42] Only three volumes had been completed when Strong's colleague M'Clintock died. Strong finished the work and added two supplementary volumes (1885–86).

Basil Gildersleeve may have thought that the manufacture of concordances had little to do with appreciation of the classics as literature and that their production furnished ammunition for the anti-classics rhetoric of besilvered materialists. Paul Shorey took the stand for the defense: the "compiler of an index indeed has a better chance of immortality than many a more pretentious author. Successive generations of scholars rise up and call him blessed, and his reputation does not wax with theories that come and go."[43] It was another theory for which time had its refutation, when modern technology shifted the eschatological advantage to computers.

[41] Robert Young's *Analytical Concordance to the Bible* is a British production. Its publishers have been careless in presenting their facts of publication. The first edition appears to have been published in 1879, in Edinburgh, by G. A. Young and Co. The 7th ed. (New York: Funk and Wagnalls, 1899) was "revised throughout" by Wm. B. Stevenson of Edinburgh. All editions have carried essays, by various authors, on Palestinian geography and antiquities. For the 20th American edition, 1936, William F. Albright contributed "Recent Discoveries in Bible Lands."

[42] John M'Clintock and James Strong, *Cyclopaedia of Biblical, Theological, and Ecclesiastical Literature* (10 vols.; New York: Harper, 1867–81).

[43] Paul Shorey, *CP* 27 (1932) 208.

5

LEXICOGRAPHY

Latin has always enjoyed a natural advantage, not only because it became an international language for theological, scientific, and literary communication, but in view of its potential as a linguistic pony for those aspiring to mastery of Romance languages and the jargon that has penetrated the English language. As for Greek, it may elicit more unadulterated affection for its intrinsic qualities and for the larger bulk of superior ancient classics that it has generated, but it does not invite the broad range of interest secured by Latin, and its struggle for survival in the schools compels extraction of an even larger measure of commitment.

With the publication of Charles Yonge's *An English-Greek Lexicon,* edited by Henry Drisler (1870), teachers of Greek developed renewed respect for publishers who kept their options open in the face of mounting demands for works of a "practical" nature. In the course of the struggle of survival for Greek, instructors had pondered afresh the importance of Greek composition in the learning of classical or Koine Greek. Undeniably, a faculty for syntactical and lexical discrimination can be developed through the writing of Greek sentences, and a major instrument for attaining such an objective is Yonge's work. But, as anyone who has used a multilingual dictionary for letter-writing knows, the end-product can swell with risibility factors if the dictionary offers no guidance in contextual idiom. Similarly, a composition that was made up of words or phrases drawn at random from Homer, Herodotos, Pindar, Plato, or Theokritos would be a linguistic hash, not a literary communication.

A dictionary ought to give some indication of the literary history of a given term. If it is not purely poetic, what is its range of usage? Attic, Hellenistic, or both? Recognized or inferior writers? Yonge's work was the first of its kind to take systematic account of such questions by assigning authorities for every Greek word or phrase admitted into the lexicon.

It is necessary, of course, to keep in mind a given author's literary motivation for the use of a specific term, but Yonge's method does provide a student with some breadth of choice for intelligent decision. The American editor, Henry Drisler, adhered to Yonge's principle in the additions and modifications that he incorporated in Yonge's work, which was published in England in 1849, with a second edition in 1856. These additions amount to about 15 % of the work. They include Greek equivalents for "a" or "an"; specialized ecclesiastical and cultic vocabulary, such as abbey, abbot, anathema, ascension; grammatical terms, such as ablative, accentuation, accusative apposition, augment; words of natural science, medicine, and other arts, such as abdomen, afterbirth, aquarius, asbestos, axis; and words of a miscellaneous nature, such as abbreviation, academic, acrostic, ah, aha, almanac. For words without Greek equivalents the student is referred to other English words of similar meaning, to wit, the entries abstinent, abstract (as a substantive) admittance, affiliation. Additional account is taken of range of usage of English terms; for example, Drisler includes usage of the term "absolution" in reference to sins, and "abuse" in the sense of wrong use. Correspondingly, Drisler adds Greek expressions to lists of equivalencies. There are Greek terms for France, Spain, Mt. Jura, or the Harz mountains, to cite but a few. Want your name in Greek? Drisler obliges with "A List of some of the more important Greek Proper Names." Why he did not think William was important we will probably never know. But he did not miss *Erres*. In 1949 Greeks used an alternate spelling for Henry by rendering President Truman's first name *Charre*. Charles Short's prefixed essay "The Order of Words in Attic Greek Prose" is a tidy contribution of a hundred double-column pages and an ornament to American scholarship. Fifteen thousand pieces of evidence are here arranged, as an early reviewer pointed out, with exceptional sense of order.[1] This essay and the appended treatise on Greek Synonyms, translated from the French of Alexander Pillon, remain abiding storehouses of information not only for composers of Greek verse or prose, but also for interpreters of the ancient documents.

As is apparent from the recurring references to nineteenth century American scholars, one does well to take account of their critical methodology, which is often more penetrating in comparison to much of what is practiced in the twentieth century precisely because the fog of traditional philological dogmas was thicker. There is not much to add, for example, to the very thorough critique of Richard Trench, *Synonyms of the New Testament*, by a reviewer in 1872, who went under the initials "E.A." Especially instructive is the discussion of the verbs *erōtaō* and *aiteō*. Trench argued for "ask" in John 16:23; E.A. for "request."[2]

---

[1] See *North American Review*, 111 (1870) 211–17.

[2] See ibid. 114 (1872) 171–89; the review is based on the 7th revised and enlarged edition of Trench's *Synonyms of the New Testament* (London: Macmillan, 1871); on *erotaō-aiteō*, see esp. 187–89. George Berry (1897) made a modest attempt to update Archbishop Trench's discussion of synonyms in the Greek New Testament. To cite but one example of misleading philology in Berry's work, the entry "To Love" (section 31), asserts that "*agapaō*, and not *phileō*, is the word used of God's love to men. . . ." Apart from the fact that John 16:27 explictly affirms that God loves (*philei*) those addressed at the moment by Jesus, Jas 2:23 identifies Abraham as a "friend of God" (*philos theou*). Nouns are not to be isolated semantically from their cognate verbs, and

To make Homer more accessible to students in the twentieth century, William Owen and Edgar Goodpseed compiled *Homeric Vocabularies* (1906). For a revised and enlarged edition, Clyde Pharr (Norman: University of Oklahoma, 1969) brought together the Greek words and their English meanings, which had been listed separately in the earlier printings. The lists are in terms of relative occurrences.[3] For sheer monumental proportions there is probably no philological work comparable to the performance exhibited in the first ten fascicles of *Lexikon des frühgriechischen Epos*, which Liselotte Solmsen helped launch in 1955.[4]

Onomastics received enrichment from Demetrius Georgacas (1971) through his work on place names in Asia Minor.

Among the more illuminating articles on general developments in the area of lexicography is Georgacas's study, "The Present State of Lexicography and Zagustas' *Manual of Lexicography*." (1976).[5] His quotation from James Root Hulbert's *Dictionaries British and American* (New York: Philosophical Library, 1955), "I know of no more enjoyable activity than working on a dictionary," contrasts with that of another who said, "Whom the gods hate they make lexicographers."

Greece itself made possible a major American lexicographic production in the 1800s. In Thessalian Magnesia there is a mountain of over 5,300 feet, called Pelion. Together with Ossa, which towers a thousand feet higher, it forms a wall that shuts off the interior of Thessaly from the sea. Born at the foot of Pelion in 1807, Evangelinus Apostolides Sophocles spent his early youth near the legendary home of Achilles. Beginning in 1837, he taught Greek at Yale University and from 1840 to 1883 at Harvard, where he brought his lexical and grammatical studies to published fruition. In 1870 he published his *Greek Lexicon of the Roman and Byzantine Periods (From B.C. 146 to A.D. 1100)*.[6] The introduction to Sophocles's extraordinary assemblage of

---

principles of transformational grammar are to be taken into account. If the editor of the Supplement to Berry's work had in mind humanity in general, as distinct from a select circle, he took no pains to clarify the point. Cf. also Louw, 1982.

[3] The University of Oklahoma Press also reissued Richard John Cunliffe, *A Lexicon of the Homeric Dialect* (London: Blackie and Son Limited, 1924), but apparently unaltered by American editorial hands.

[4] The tenth fascicle brought the work through *Dione*. At that pace it would not have seen completion until the next centennial of SBL. Perhaps it was also recognized that Greek was being outbid by other disciplines at a steadily increasing rate. In any case, German *Gründlichkeit* had to make some adjustments to reality. By altering the original conception, G. Patzig thought that completion would be possible around the year 2000.

[5] For an introduction to Georgacas's *Modern Greek-English Dictionary*, see "Modern Greek-English Dictionary: A Section of Edited Entries: *akontiō-akourastos*," *Orbis* 22, 2 (1973) 389–403.

[6] Much of Sophocles's earlier work, *A Glossary of Later and Byzantine Greek*, which forms vol. 7 (new series) of the Memoirs of the American Academy (Cambridge, England, 1860), is

data on the Koine and its development includes a who's who of secular and ecclesiastical writers, most of whose names students may find as memorable as those of past United States vice presidents or secretaries of state.

Apart from Sophocles's work, America has produced no lexicon of any major segment of Greek literature comparable to those published on the Continent. In a co-operative endeavor with Europeans, Basil Gildersleeve, together with William Goodwin and Henry Drisler, assisted the British lexicographer Henry Liddell in the preparation of the seventh edition of *A Greek-English Lexicon* (Oxford, 1882). Their contributions related especially to discussion of particles and technical terms of Attic Law. A century later, Robert Renehan (1982) made vocabulary entries that were "either inadequately documented or non-existent" in the revised ninth edition.

The Greek Old Testament has long looked for a systematic and comprehensive treatment of its lexical features that would improve on the work of Johann Schleusner's five-volume work (Leipzig, 1820–21). In 1972 Robert Kraft, in concert with John W. Wevers, Charles T. Fritsch, John Edward Gates, and other members of an SBL Lexicography Seminar, edited an exploratory volume entitled *Septuagintal Lexicography.* And in 1983, J. A. A. Lee made a welcome study of the Greek version of the Pentateuch. But as the end of the century drew near, students still were left with Schleusner's work in Latin.

The delicate balance that scholarly Jewish leaders endeavored to maintain between their obligations to ancestral practice and their interest in non-Jewish culture comes to revealing expression with some little-known lexicographical information in Saul Liebermann, *Greek in Jewish Palestine* (1942).

New Testament Lexicography

In no area of biblical scholarship does the story of American philological study come through with so noticeable a German accent as in New Testament lexicography.

Early in the nineteenth century there was some indication of potential for independent production. In 1825 Edward Robinson published a revision and translation of Christian Abraham Wahl's *Clavis Novi Testamenti Philologica* (Leipzig, 1822). The entire edition of 1500 copies was sold within four years. But Robinson's own researches and such publications as Johann Winer's work on grammar and Franz Passow's on lexicography suggested to

---

incorporated in the Lexicon. The third printing (1887) of the latter is termed a "memorial edition," which was authorized by the president and fellows of Harvard College and edited by Joseph Henry Thayer; it includes a number of corrections of the second impression of 1870. The firm of Frederick Ungar, New York, reprinted the memorial edition in 1957. *Research Tools for the Classics* (1980:57) calls attention to an expansion of Sophocles' Lexicon undertaken by Anastasius C. Bandy.

Robinson (1836) that he call no man master, and he proceeded to prepare an independent work, "adapted," as he puts it in the Preface to his lexicon, "to the wants of students in our own country" (U.S.A.). In the manner of ancient historians, who were wont to celebrate the maculae of their predecessors, Robinson further states in his preface that he "found occasion on every page" of Johann Schleusner, Karl Bretschneider, and Wahl, "to distrust their judgment and accuracy," and to turn from them habitually to the original authorities (iv). Robinson's sensitivity to the direction that philological inquiry would ultimately take is apparent in his method of citation of secular authors; preference is given to authors of the later dialect as opposed to sponsors of the Attic epoch. The sure touch of a master is apparent on every page, with unerring grasp of what is essential to assist students in their probing of the original text. Few lexicons exhibit evidence so clearly marshalled. And it is regrettable that North American academia failed to capitalize on the vouchers issued by Robinson. Apart from G. Abbott Smith's *A Manual Greek Lexicon of the New Testament* (1921), designed to "serve as a table companion . . . for the average" person, America's New Testament lexical energies were to be exhibited in repackaged Teutonic philology.

Thanks to Joseph Thayer's indefatigable industry,[7] the English-speaking world gained access to the best that was available in Europe during the last quarter of the nineteenth century. Karl Grimm had put Christian Wilke's *Clavis Novi Testamenti philologica*[8] under contribution in his *Lexicon Graeco-Latinum in libros Novi Testamenti* (Leipzig, 1862), and in 1886 Thayer published a translation of the Wilke and Grimm second edition of 1879. Thayer's adoption of comparative philological methodology, with stress on etymology, contrasts with developments at the turn of the century, and even the publication of a corrected edition in 1889 could not disperse the pall of obsolescence that had settled on Thayer's work even before its publication.

Even while Thayer was busy converting scholarly currency at the older rates of exchange, a German scholar was feverishly fomenting a philological revolution that would require an entirely new issue of grammatical and lexical notes. In 1895, Gustav Adolf Deissmann published *Bibelstudien*, a book that encouraged biblical students to sharpen their exegetical expertise through acquaintance with a vast body of newly-discovered data that could relieve deficits in New Testament research. Mediterranean stones had long exposed peculiarities of Greek dialects; but now papyrus, a medium available to Everyperson in the Greco-Roman world for recording business and personal matters, revealed semantic features that could prove a vehicle for revised understanding of New Testament idiom. Yet Deissmann had to ask himself what it might be that mesmerized biblical students even in Aufklärungsland to be dedicated to denial of the future.

---

[7] On Thayer's literary production, see Ropes, 1902.

[8] Dresden and Leipzig, 1839; 2d ed., 2 vols., 1851.

But Germany's awakening did come. While Americans were reclining at ease with Thayer and spending most of their time recycling source-critical problems inherited from a pre-Deissmann period, Germany maintained a lexical production that would later make it mandatory for Americans to stamp another major lexical effort: "First made in Germany." Erwin Preuschen made the first serious move toward a post-Deissmann philological hall of fame. Unfortunately, like many of his peers he had no nose for history and almost guaranteed himself oblivion with his *Vollständiges griechisch-deutsches Handwörterbuch* (Giessen, 1910). It was not "vollständig," and was unique primarily in the balance of the title: *zu den Schriften des neuen Testaments und der übrigen urchristlichen Literatur.* Inclusion of data from the Apostolic Fathers was indeed a new phenomenon in a lexicon of the New Testament, but papyri and inscriptions still went begging for recognition. After Preuschen's death in 1920, Walter Bauer of Göttingen tried to rescue the project with a second edition (1928), but then set himself the task of publishing a completely revised edition, which appeared in 1937. So many were the changes and so numerous the new entries that the work became known simply as Bauer's Lexicon.

Less than a decade later, F. Wilbur Gingrich, of Reading, Pennsylvania, alerted American scholars to their "poverty" in reference to New Testament lexicography.[9] Except for essays on isolated terms and a series of lexical notes by Henry Cadbury,[10] members of the biblical studies guild had showed little interest in lexicography as a discipline. This state of affairs, the Reading scholar wrote, "is well illustrated by the fact that the English-speaking world has no definitive unabridged lexicon of the Greek New Testament which takes into account the rapid strides which the science has made since 1890. We have introductions and commentaries by the dozen but the great lexicon still goes begging" (Gingrich, 1945:179). In 1954 he spelled out the rationale for fresh lexicographical work on the New Testament. The Greek New Testament is itself a "landmark in the course of semantic change."

In 1949, Gingrich, together with William Arndt, who had found food for philological thought during his graduate study of Polybios, set out to improve conditions for America's biblical student,[11] but not without first encountering

---

[9] As early as 1933 Gingrich engaged in criticism of Bauer's work. In 1927 he had shown promise in an M.A. thesis (*The Terms Heart and Conscience*) at the University of Chicago; and in 1932 he produced "Paul's Ethical Vocabulary," a part of his Ph.D. thesis, published in a "Private Edition, distributed by the University of Chicago Libraries."

[10] Samples of Cadbury's lexical interest are displayed in *JBL* 44 (1925) 214–27; 45 (1926) 190–209; 305–22; 48 (1929) 412–25; and 52 (1933) 55–65. See also C. Umhau Wolf, "Concerning the Vocabulary of Paul," *JBL* 67 (1948) 331–38.

[11] Arndt's Ph.D dissertation bears the title: *The Participle in Polybius and in St. Paul* (Washington University, St. Louis, 1935). F. H. Allen had produced a related dissertation (University of Chicago) in 1907: *The Use of the Infinitive in Biblical Greek.*

economic reality. The management of the University of Chicago Press, which had been approached for participation in the project, did not see appreciably more interest in advanced Greek and Latin philology than in Assyrian and Babylonian at America's universities. Not anticipating more than a few thousand sales in the Semitic category, and at the same time displaying publishers' surprising ability to underestimate the pace of the public pulse, the Press was reluctant to embark on a new lexical venture without substantial subsidy, which was finally secured by Arndt's colleague, Martin Scharlemann. Thereupon, in 1950, Arndt and Gingrich accepted the hospitality of the University of Chicago, and enjoyed the collegial atmosphere of that university's distinguished lexicographical resources, including especially the erudition of its chief lexicographer, Mitford M. Matthews.

Bauer's fourth edition began to come out in fascicles in 1949, and the two American editors kept pace with the German product, which was completed in 1952. After writing out 24,000 slips of paper, Arndt and Gingrich filed their work with the Press in January, 1955. In the spring of the same year, England's Cambridge University Press, which had agreed to cooperate in the venture, began setting type. Publication took place in Cambridge on 25 January 1957, and two days later in Chicago, under the title *A Greek-English Lexicon of the New Testament and Other Early Christian Literature: A translation and adaptation of the fourth revised and augmented edition of Walter Bauer's Griechisch-Deutsches Wörterbuch zu den Schriften des Neuen Testaments und der übrigen urchristlichen Literatur.* In distinction from its later revised form (BAGD) this edition bears the acronym BAG. It is unfair to Bauer, whose investment of toil was prodigious, to make reference to this work in bibliographies without inclusion of the subtitle.[12] On the other hand, since the American product includes modifications of Bauer, it is important that references to the work do not simply read "Bauer."

Whereas Bauer was already at work on a fifth edition even while the English translation was in production, arrangements had to be made for an American revision. After Arndt's death, 25 February 1957, Frederick Danker was assigned to share the task with Gingrich. The revisers took account of new biblical papyri, especially the Bodmer collection, and on the basis of fresh reading of much of the ancient literature entered numerous corrections and additions of their own. Theirs and Bauer's modifications accounted for more than 20% increase in the text of the new English-language edition, thus making it the most modern New Testament lexicon in 1979, the year of its publication. A large measure of credit for the success of this venture is to be accorded Lorman M. Petersen for his negotiations with the German

---

[12] Bauer had reread most of the ancient Greek literature in preparation for his task. His stress on Hellenistic features was evident, and W. D. Davies, in a review of BAG (see *JBL* 77 [1958]:365–67) thought that Bauer had shortchanged the Semitic undertone of the NT.

interests.[13] The acronym of the revised edition is BAGD.

To serve biblical students who initially required less than Bauer provided, the University of Chicago Press asked Gingrich to compose an abridgement of the larger lexicon. It appeared in 1965 under the title *Shorter Lexicon of the Greek New Testament.* The publication of BAGD required a revision of this work, and after Gingrich's retirement Danker was asked to prepare the copy. Besides being the first lexicon to emphasize the use of gender-inclusive language, this revision, published in 1983 (Chicago: University of Chicago), was based on Nestle's 26th edition of the Greek New Testament, and further reading of ancient texts led to modification of a number of interpretations in BAGD, together with correction of some of its content.

A major source of frustration for the lexicographers connected with BAGD was the rapidity of development in the science of linguistics. Admittedly, BAGD was obsolete even when it was born, yet it was to be the only lexicon of its kind available for many decades, a fate shared by most specialized lexicons of the period. No editors could enjoy more cooperation than that which was extended by the staff of the University of Chicago Press, but other resources for production of the kind of lexicon that the editors would like to have created were lacking. It was not feasible to entertain the kind of thorough revision that was suggested, for example, by Lane McGaughy's outline of the use of the verb *eimi* (1933:150–51). BAGD was therefore a holding effort, and only a cooperative endeavor on an international scale, with translations of a joint product appearing simultaneously, could ever see the work revised with tolerable adequacy.

Lexical aids in a less technical format have appeared from time to time. Thayer supervised Wallace N. Stearns (1896) in the preparation of a supplement to *A Greek-English Lexicon to the New Testament,* which had originally been prepared by William Greenfield of England and revised by Thomas Sheldon Green as a brief guide to the vocabulary of the Greek New Testament.[14] The Supplement includes *"new words and forms"* that are not found in the Textus Receptus but are taken from editions of the Greek New Testament by Lachmann, Tischendorf, Tregelles, Westcott and Hort, and the Westminster Revised.

A year later, George Berry (1897) claimed to fill a need for a small New Testament lexicon that would at the same time offer more morphological data than its prototypes. A supplementary chapter provided basic information on selected synonyms.

Periodically effort is made to form a linguistic yoke that will make lighter the burden of learning New Testament Greek. Ozora Davis (1893) developed a miniature version of the type of work associated years later with the name of Morgenthaler. Her statistical study groups words for the most part under

---

[13] For further details see Danker, 1970:124–27.

[14] H. L. Hastings, editor of *The Christian,* wrote the preface for this edition.

roots, with a table showing distribution for a given term in four major categories: (1) Matthew, Mark, Luke-Acts; (2) Hebrews, James, the Petrines, and Jude; (3) Johannine writings; (4) Paul's Letters. The words that are used more than ten times total 898. An appendix lists a central meaning for each numbered item. Four years earlier, Charles Bradley and Charles Horswell published *New Testament Word Lists*. The first part lists the Greek words that appear ten times or more, to a total of 1067, along with their numerical distribution. The second part offers a general meaning for each term.

Along the same lines as Davis's work is *A Comparative Lexicon of New Testament Greek* by Leslie Elliott (1945), who brings together in a column many of the NT words that are "built on the same root or stem," and the English meaning is given briefly opposite each word. Elliott hoped that by observing the similarities students would increase their mastery of the vocabulary. Bruce Metzger (1946) followed with a two-part list, one consisting of words occurring ten times or more and the other classifying these and other words of less frequency by root. But, as Eugene Goetchius (1968) pointed out in response to a publication by Thomas Rogers (1968), the "root" approach is linguistically hazardous. It is to some extent helpful in collection of compounds, as in *aggel*-formations, but not for conglomerates cited under such headings as, for example, *ag, agel, agr, agon, axi,* or *ege* that are to be found in lists more detailed than is the one supplied by Rogers.

Designed especially for users of the English Bible is Marvin Vincent's *Word Studies* (1887–1900). The author "aims to put the reader of the English Bible nearer to the standpoint of the Greek scholar, by opening to him the native force of the separate words of the New Testament in their lexical sense, their etymology, their history, their inflection, and the peculiarities of their usage by different evangelists and apostles" (vol. 1, p. v).

Among the important explorations in specific semantic domains is Ernest Burton's *Spirit, soul, and flesh* (1918). A quarter-century earlier, the role of Semitic words in Greek and Latin received attention from William Muss-Arnolt (1896).

An instructive exchange on the hazards connected with determining the focus of a term is to be found in *JBL* for the years 1904–1905. Phillips Barry (1904) argued that *symphōnia* in Luke 15:25 means "bagpipe," as rendered by Wycliffe.[15] George Moore (1905) agreed that Luke does indeed refer to a musical instrument, but that Barry had no grounds for his specific identification, especially since Dan 3:5, a key passage for Barry, does not refer to a bagpipe. Undaunted, Barry came back in 1908, citing more evidence for the ancient history of bagpipes than most Scots will ever want to know.

Other examples of references to Greek and Roman literature in early issues of *JBL* include an antidote to the Nero-redivivus myth in Milton Terry's (1894) proposal that the term "Babylon" in the Apocalypse encodes a referent

---

[15] Barry (1904) makes much use of Polybios (31.4) and Latin authors.

that includes Jerusalem;[16] and Henry Nash's (1902) discussion of the relation of Logos and Law in the Apostolic period.

Late in the century, Moises Silva (1983) offered an introduction to lexical semantics in *Biblical Words and their Meaning*,[17] with emphasis on the importance of distinguishing language and theology.

Latin Lexicography

The name "Andrews" became a trademark for the most well known of the American lexicons of classical Latin. Like its counterparts in the Greek sector, it bore the continental stamp.

Ethan Allen Andrews's *Latin-English Lexicon* appeared in 1850.[18] It is a translation of a work produced by Wilhelm Freund of Germany. Joseph Esmond Riddle of Oxford had previously supplied the English-speaking world with a translation of a shorter lexicon that Freund had published. The title page of Andrews's work does not accurately describe the burden of production. The Preface credits Rennselaer David Chanceford Robbins with translating A-C inclusive, and William W. Turner for the translation of D-Z. Theodore D. Woolsey translated the Author's Preface, originally written by Wilhelm Freund,[19] whose preface is dated "Breslau, January 8, 1834." Freund's statement of lexicographical obligation summarizes the philological perspective of the period: the lexicographer ought to (1) give the history of every single word; (2) note any unusual forms; (3) give etymology; (4) give distinct and peculiar meanings of words (the "exegetical element of lexicography"); (5) provide synonyms; (6) state the rhetorical aspect of a term (registration); and (7) provide statistical information (rare or frequent usage).

A British revision and reprint of "Andrews'" Dictionary was made by William Smith, whose name appears on numerous compilations of Greek

---

[16] Compare Minear, 1968. Jerusalem, he writes, "had become in prophetic terms all cities — Sodom, Tyre, Egypt, Babylon, Nineveh, Rome. . . ." (102). Minear does not appear to mention Terry's article.

[17] Danker (1982) exemplifies semantic field study with stress on cultural perspective. David Aune (*Interpretation* 38 [1984] 423) roots his critique of such approach in the older philology and fails to take account of expanded linguistic considerations, such as those described by Silva (1983). See also the constellation sketched by Garvin, 1974. As does Aune, Matthys Klemm displays some of the older word-study approach in *"EIRENE" im neutestamentlichen Sprachsystem* (Bonn: Linguistica Biblica, 1977). For a systematic description of the function of a lexicon as a source for reference information, see Gates, 1972.

[18] The complete title reads: *A Copious and Critical Latin-English Lexicon, founded on the larger Latin-German lexicon of Dr. William Freund: with additions from the lexicons of Gesner, Facciolati, Scheller, Georges, etc.* (New York: Harper, 1850).

[19] In this instance we know who the real producers were. But like anemones beneath the water, many a scholar — such as Karl Junack, a major force behind the production of the Nestle-Aland edition of the Greek New Testament and accompanying Synopsis — have made substantial contributions to the success of a work and then are given brief mention in a prefatory note, frequently without adequate description of the scope of their contribution.

and Roman antiquities, biography, and geography. More extensive alterations were made by Oxonians John T. White and Riddle, who published their work under the title *A Latin-English Dictionary* (London: Longman, 1862). Freund himself corrected the Andrews translation for this edition, with special attention paid to etymologies, and added Sanskrit analogies and new lemmata. Riddle then made alterations and additions after comparison with the German original. White, in turn, took the corrected copy, rearranged and rewrote a number of articles, and incorporated additional material to such an extent that the British version became one third larger than the American, an outcome that prompted White to boast that it was "entitled to the character of a new work."

"All these Dictionaries," an anonymous critic of the White-Riddle edition wrote in *North American Review*, "have one feature in common. They are manufactured works. The editors have revised them, corrected them, and added to them; but they have not fairly mastered their subject, gone back to the fountain-head, and drawn again at first hand from the ancient sources. They are manufactured works, Mr. White's as well as the rest."[20] The reviewer thought that the inclusion of words from patristic literature would have been more appropriate for a thesaurus than for a manual. Subsequent to citing numerous omissions of substantives, adjectives, adverbs, and verbs, the reviewer criticized retention of antiquated etymological theories, which rest on "the old confusion between literatures and languages, the old error that, because the Latin literature is later than the Greek, the forms of the language must likewise be so. As well might we say that *eleēmosynē* is a lengthened form of the English word *alms,* or that the German *Natter* was formed from the English *adder* with an *n* prefixed."[21] After exposing numerous instances of errors in reference, the reviewer concludes that White's industry was "misdirected," for he began with "no elevated or well-defined theory of what was needed in Latin lexicography; and in carrying out his plan, such as it was, he has groped his way along mechanically, amidst the darkness of corrupt texts and second or third-hand citations. We sincerely hope that this may be the last of the manufactured lexicons. A critical dictionary founded on the best texts, exhibiting all characteristic or anomalous forms of words that occur, and with a plenty of trustworthy citations, is a great want. It will be long before this want is met."[22]

As indicated above, the Andrews tradition goes back to Riddle, who was the first to put a smaller dictionary by Freund into English. Four years after the White-Riddle publication, a minister named P. Bullions published *A Copious and Critical Latin-English Dictionary: Abridged and Re-arranged*

---

[20] *North American Review* 96 (1863) 496–502; see p. 496. The searching criticism in this review is in accord with that which was advanced by Lane (1859) against Freund's work.

[21] Ibid., 96:497–98.

[22] Ibid., 502.

*from Riddle's Latin-English Lexicon, Founded on the German-Latin Dictio-
naries of Dr. William Freund with a Brief Comparison and Illustration of the
Most Important Synonyms, Compiled and Abridged Chiefly from the works of
Dusmenil, Ramshorn, Doederlein, and Hill* (New York: Sheldon, 1866). The
chain remained unbroken.

Dissatisfaction with the current Latin lexicographical resources did not
diminish. Harper and Brothers wished to proceed with what appeared to be
a mere face-lifting of Andrews and handed to the prospective editor, Henry
Drisler, the revisions, corrections, and additions that Freund had supplied to
the publishers. Drisler advised the company that "a reconstruction of the
work was desirable," but "such as he could not command leisure to make."[23]
The publisher then turned Freund's work over to Charles Short and Charlton
Lewis. Besides possessing competence in the classics, Lewis was an editor
of the *New York Evening Post*, from 1868–71, and was active in public affairs,
including prison reform. Short was recognized for his painstaking
philological work on the Classics, as exhibited, for example, in his study on
Greek word order in Yonge's *Greek-English Lexicon*. He was also a valued
member of the committee for the revision of the English Authorized Version
of the Bible.[24] Short worked on the letter A (pp. 1–216) and Lewis on the
remainder (pp. 217–2019) in the production of *Harper's Latin Dictionary*
(Lewis and Short, 1879). After more than a hundred years of service its place
was taken by the *Oxford Latin Dictionary*, which was conceived in 1933, with
fascicles appearing from 1968–82.[25] Oxford's content exceeds that of
Harper's by one-third.

In 1879, Harper asked Lewis to abridge the large lexicon, but Lewis
thought it would be preferable to compile an independent dictionary that
would "include all that a student needs, after acquiring the elements of
Grammar."[26] The result was *A Latin Dictionary for Schools* (1888). This work
is not a dictionary of the Latin language. It is designed with specific reference
to the books read in Latin courses, including the entire works of Terence,
Caesar, Cicero, Livy, Nepos, Vergil, Horace, Ovid, Juvenal, Phaedrus, Curtius, Sallust's *Catiline* and *Jugurtha*, and Tacitus's *Germania* and *Agricola*.

The dean of Germany's philologists, Friedrich August Wolf, had visions
of a lexicon that would be more complete and better arranged than those of
Gesner and Forcellini. The year 1900 began to endow the dream with

---

[23] "Publisher's Advertisement" to *Harper's Latin Dictionary* (1879), iii.
[24] Charles Short, "The New Revision of King James' Revision of the New Testament. 1. Some
account of the Previous English Revisions and of the State and Treatment of the Greek text,"
AJP 2 (1881) 149–80; II–V. "An Examination of the Revision of S. Matthew," 3 (1882) 139–69; 4
(1883) 253–82; 5 (1884) 417–53; 7 (1886) 283–309.
[25] Peter Geoffrey William Glare, ed., *Oxford Latin Dictionary* (Oxford: Clarendon, 1968–82),
defines classical Latin from its beginnings to the second century of the present era.
[26] Lewis, 1888:v.

substance. At that time there appeared the first fascicle of *Thesaurus Linguae Latinae*, a joint effort of five German universities and known as TLL (Leipzig: Teubner). Various American scholars were instrumental in helping to maintain the high quality of this immense work. By 1930, the editors could announce that work had progressed through letter C. In 1983 scholars were able to scrutinize entries under P. Many of those who had reached the age of fifty had been born after signal developments had taken place in linguistics. They could sense some of the antique flavor of parts of a work that had been pyramiding for almost a century. Many of them probably would not see the final period put after the entry *zythum* (or whatever the last word might be), and most of them would not be able to afford the completed work. But nothing will soon take the place of TLL for specialists in Latin.

Lexicons do not comprise the most exciting genre of philological production, and those who compile them can judge whether these words from Samuel Johnson's preface to his Dictionary are an appropriate appraisal of their own efforts:

> It is the fate of those, who toil at the lower employments of life, to be rather driven by the fear of evil, than attracted by the prospect of good; to be exposed to censure, without hope of praise; to be disgraced by miscarriage, or punished for neglect, where success would have been without applause, and diligence without reward.
>
> Among these unhappy mortals is the writer of dictionaries; whom mankind have considered, not as the pupil but the slave of science, the pioneer of literature, doomed only to remove rubbish and clear obstructions from the paths, through which Learning and Genius press forward to conquest and glory, without bestowing a smile on the humble drudge that facilitates their progress. Every other author may aspire to praise; the lexicographer can only hope to escape reproach, and even this negative recompense has been yet granted to very few.[27]

---

[27] Samuel Johnson, *A Dictionary of the English Language*, ed. by H. J. Todd, vol. 1 (London: Longman, 1827) 1.

6

GRAMMAR

During the early decades of the eighteenth century, German scholarship dominated American study of Greek Grammar. The very title of Charles Anthon's chief work, *A Grammar of the Greek Language, Principally from the Greek of Kuehner, with Selections from Matthiae, Buttmann, Thiersch, and Rost, for the Use of Schools and Colleges,* as late as 1854, blatantly commemorates the dependence.[1] This work is at the same time an enlargement of an earlier grammar by Anthon, who underwrites his European indebtedness with the assurance that it now includes more paradigmatic, declensional, and conjugational forms, with frequent reference to Sanksrit and "other cognate languages."

Even up to the time of Archibald Robertson (1914), biblical scholars saw their grammatical holdings stamped "Made in Germany." Not so American classicists. While Anthon's work was coming off the press, more Americanized productions were bidding for the future, and their prodigy made such strong claim on it that Paul Shorey in his survey of half a centennial was able to declare in 1919 that American "grammars and annotated school and college texts" were "rather better on the whole than those of Europe" (Shorey, 1919:49). A number of the exhibits cited in the following paragraphs overlap Shorey's canon.

Early Introductory Classical Greek Grammars

Among the earliest American grammars of ancient Greek is Benjamin Fisk's (1831) *A Grammar of the Greek Language.* The motto on the title page signaled basic awareness: *Syn myriois ta kala ponois.* ("No success without pain.")[2] The Preface in this edition reflects the depth structure that generated numerous prologues in the works of ancient historians. Fisk has read "all the more popular Greek authors, most of them many times" and he has used

---

[1] Anthon's work was published in New York by Harper. On Anthon's academic integrity and philological acumen see Hullinger, 1980:78–94. In 1909, the only Americans mentioned by Samuel Angus in a review of current philological contributions are E. D. Burton, J. H. Thayer, and A. T. Robertson.

[2] Euripides, *Fragments* 236.

the work of his predecessors, but declares that he is putting in more syntax, a feature that would eventually outweigh any other aspect in determining the longevity of succeeding grammatical publications.

Alphaeus Crosby (1844) received such a good reception for *A Grammar of the Greek Language* that a thirty-eighth edition appeared in 1870.[3] In 1849 Crosby combined grammar, reading selections, and exercises in *Greek Lessons*.[4] The notes on the lessons, which are from Xenophon, refer to Crosby's Grammar. Crosby considered the pedagogical importance of the recognition factor and took all selections from one Greek author, so that the student might not be distracted by diversities of style.

James Hadley founded *A Greek Grammar for Schools and Colleges* (1860) on Georg Curtius's *Griechische Schulgrammatik* of 1852. Hadley pushes Attic to the front, but gives dialectical forms in smaller type so as to show relationships. To simplify students' work, for which posterity would reward his *Grammar* with renewed longevity, he reduced the entire mass of verbs into nine classes. William D. Whitney, professor of comparative philology at Yale University, lauded Hadley as "America's best and soundest philologist."[5] Specific indication of Hadley's sound judgment can be derived from his rejoinders to Ludwig Ross, of Halle, who asserted that, "amid the wreck of letters and the crush of words," one thing displayed permanent continuity, and that was the pronunciation of Modern Greek. "I consider it," Ross said, with the finality of an auctioneer banging his gavel, "as being from the time of Inachos, or whatever else may be more ancient than Inachos, the only correct pronunciation." "All honor to courageous faith!" retorted Hadley. "It is something, as the world goes to believe in the historic reality of Inachos, a millennium earlier than the earliest known monument of the Greek language." In rebuttal of Ross he went on to make the point, that it is questionable whether Latin is really corrupt Greek. Unable to conceal his glee in expressing a theme for which Basil Gildersleeve and Paul Shorey preserved some of their purplest prose, Hadley wrote: "We will not confess here—we are ashamed to own it even to ourselves—a certain secret satisfaction in finding that Germany—before which we hide our diminished heads,

[3] A revised edition appeared in 1871 under the title *A Grammar of the Greek Language. For the Use of Schools and Colleges* (N.Y.: Chicago, Woolworth, Ainsworth). The motto on the title page is taken from Aischylos *Persians* 824: *mimnesth Athenon Hellados te* ("Be mindful of Athens and Hellas").

[4] The edition of 1854 is copyrighted 1849, with the title: *Greek Lessons, Consisting of Selections from Xenophon's Anabasis, with Directions for the Study of the Grammar, Notes, Exercises in Translation from English into Greek, and a Vocabulary* (Boston: Phillips, Sampson). The motto, *Archē de toi hēmisy pantos* ("Underway is halfway"), an allusion to Hesiod, appears under an outline of the Parthenon, an enduring trademark of the Crosby series. *An Introduction to Greek*, by Henry Lamar Crosby and John Nevin Schaeffer (Boston: Allyn and Bacon, 1928) shows the Parthenon on the cover, but no motto. A new edition of Crosby's *Greek Lessons* was published in 1871 (New York: Potter, Ainsworth).

[5] Sandys, 1908, 3:463.

acknowledging her to be first without second in philological studies — can send out from the high places of her universities specimens of fantastic absurdity scarcely equalled on this side of the Atlantic. . . . If at times we grow weary of the twilight in which we still move, and sigh with despairing hope for the Perfect day, it may be well that a Professor Ross should come, and open for us a glimpse into the darkness visible, the realm of chaos and old night, which we have left behind us, as we trust, finally and forever."[6] Hadley made every effort to exploit technological resources whereby students might "come in Latin or in Greek" and hold the line against the onrush of anti-classical materialism. By using differences in type in his *Grammar* he endeavored to distinguish "those leading facts and principles which should engage the first attention of the learner." But others desired an abridged form on the ground that it was more suitable for beginners, and in 1869 *Elements of the Greek Language Taken from the Greek Grammar* was published to meet such need. Hadley's *Grammar* was largely rewritten and published by Frederic Allen in 1884.

To help students maintain continuity in their beginning Greek course, Edward Coy wrote an exercise book to the Hadley-Allen Greek Grammar (1890). Students never were happy over juggling separate books for rules and their application, not to speak of a lexicon. To ease their burden, Albert Harkness (1861) had written a *First Greek Book*, which supported basic grammatical instruction with an introductory reader, including notes and vocabulary. Among the Greek selections are fourteen "jests." Since the tolerance level of readers of a centennial volume has not been certified, two examples of the genre may even be deemed a surcharge on patience. A scholar encountered a colleague and said, "I heard you had died." "Gracious, no!" said the other. "You can see I'm very much alive." "Well," said the first "my informant is far more credible than you." —Another scholar wished to cross a river, so he entered a boat on horseback. Queried, he replied, "I was in a hurry."

For an antidote one can turn to Latin and read Quintilian's brief essay on humor (6.3), which includes such jests as the following: Augustus wanted proper decorum observed at the Games. He caught a Roman knight drinking and sent him word, saying, "When I wish to dine, I do it at home." The knight replied: "Yes, but you don't have to worry about losing your seat." Anxious to curry the favor of Augustus, the people of Tarraco notified the Emperor that a palm had started to grow on an altar they had dedicated to him. Augustus asked, "How many fires have you kindled on it lately?"

Alston Chase (1941) refurbished the Harkness-type format some decades later, but the time between was filled with production of works by

---

[6] Hadley, 1873:167 and see esp. pp. 161–67. These essays were published by Hadley's family and friends, with a preface by W. D. Whitney.

numerous teachers of Greek who struggled, as do ministers in preparing instructional material for adult classes, to develop suitable textbooks and supplementary exercises. Indeed, the history of grammars, Greek and Latin, from the latter part of the nineteenth century well on into the twentieth is the story of a search for a golden mean between grammatical information and the cultivation of interpretive skills through exposure to authors and through compositional exercises.

In the judgment of William Harper and William Waters, deductive approaches appeared to induce lack of interest and small results. The two educators therefore produced *An Inductive Greek Method* (1888) consisting of seventy-two lessons, based on portions of Xenophon's *Anabasis*.[7] In answer to pleas from teachers of Greek, Harper invited Clarence Castle to assist him in the production of an even simpler work, which appeared under the title *An Inductive Greek Primer* (1893) The lessons are shorter and call to the pupils' aid their knowledge of Latin. After the 103 lessons comes the text of *Anabasis* 1. 1–8, followed by a word-for-word parallel rendering of chapters 1–2, and a "free translation" of chapter 1. An appendix, with its summary of grammatical categories, constitutes a mini-grammar. Twenty-one "Suggestions to Teachers" remain a welcome contribution from master educators.[8]

In their *Beginner's Greek Book* (1906), Allen Benner and Herbert Smyth follow the trend of using the *Anabasis* as a base for understanding Greek as a medium for literary expression and not as a mere excuse for the learning of oppressive paradigms. *Elementary Greek*, by Theodore Burgess and Robert Bonner (1907), functions as an exercise book and like Benner-Smyth's work concentrates on the *Anabasis*.[9]

On the assumption that students were receiving far less Greek in the twentieth century than did their peers in the nineteenth, Alston Chase and Henry Phillips developed *A New Introduction to Greek* (1941). Originally pitched between *Greek Through English* (London: J. M. Dent, 1926) by Great Britain's Arthur Way, and John White's *The First Greek Book* (1896), the revised edition of this grammar as printed in 1974 (Cambridge: Harvard University) is designed for one semester of college work, three times a week, and loses no time in acquainting students with such authors as Demosthenes, Plato, Thukydides, and Herodotos. Guidance in the choice of vocabulary was supplied by John Cheadle, author of *Basic Greek Vocabulary* (1939). The striking illustrations and captions were provided by Sterling Dow, Hudson Professor of Archeology at Harvard.[10]

---

[7] An edition of *An Inductive Greek Method* was published in the same year by Ivison, Blakeman.

[8] Harper and Castle also produced *Exercises in Greek Prose Composition, Based on Xenophon's Anabasis, Books I-IV* (New York: American Book Co., 1893).

[9] Burgess also authored *Epideictic Literature* (Chicago: University of Chicago, 1902).

[10] On the importance of an attractive page in textbooks, see Dow, 1951.

Reference Grammars

Reference grammars that could be used throughout a student's acquisition of the ancient Greek language have been sparse, and specialists have had to rely in the main on German productions. But three American scholars brought some remedy for students who lacked German.

James Aloysius Kleist and "Kaegi"

Among the numerous resources for the promotion of classical study in the first half of the twentieth century was *The Classical Bulletin*, a publication of St. Louis University unofficially and officially since the first issue of two pages in February 1925. This publication owed its persistent growth to the efforts of James Kleist, who entered the Society of Jesus, 8 April 1891, four days after his eighteenth birthday, and began teaching the Classics at St. Louis University in 1928. In addition to his untiring efforts on behalf of the advancement of classical studies, he produced one of the more informed commentaries on the Greek text of the Gospel of Mark (1936). Lending structure to his numerous interpretations of classical and New Testament Greek was his refined grammatical sensitivity that found expression in his translation and adaptation of one of Adolf Kaegi's grammatical works under the title *A Short Grammar of Classical Greek, With Tables for Repetition* (1902).[11] Because of its clear exhibition of the basics of Greek grammar, including a summary list of 93 "Chief Rules of Syntax," Kleist's elementary reference grammar, known generally simply as "Kaegi," became a fixture especially in schools that followed the German Gymnasium.

William Watson Goodwin

Among the most distinguished names of the older American classical scholars is William Goodwin, born in 1831 at Concord, Massachusetts. After graduating from Harvard College he spent two years in private teaching and study and then attended various German universities, among them Goettingen, where he received his doctorate in 1855.[12] When Cornelius Felton was chosen president of Harvard University in 1860, Goodwin was elected his successor in the Eliot professorship of Greek literature, a post that he held as self-styled "guardian of the gate" (to ensure the survival of Greek) until his retirement in 1901.

---

[11] Adolf Kaegi published his *Griechische Schulgrammatik* in 1884 (Berlin: Weidmann); and *Kurzgefasste Griechische Schulgrammatik*, the basis for Kleist's adaptation, appeared in October, 1892. For details on Kleist, see Richard Arnold's Introduction, with bibliography, in *Classical Essays Presented to James A. Kleist, S.J.* (St. Louis: Classical Bulletin, St. Louis University, 1946) ix-xx.

[12] Goodin's dissertation is entitled, *De potentiae veterum gentium maritimae epochis apud Eusebium.*

From his student days Goodwin was interested in archeology and was the natural choice for the first directorship of the American School of Classical Studies upon its founding in 1881. His keen interest in the fortunes of Greece won him the Knight of the Greek Order of the Redeemer. National and international honors came his way. Among those who conferred honorary degrees at home were Amherst College and the Universities of Columbia, Yale, Chicago, and Harvard. Recognition abroad came from Cambridge, Oxford, and Edinburgh; and fifty years after his promotion to the doctorate, Goettingen gracefully renewed his degree. He served as president of the American Philological Association in 1871 and in 1884, and headed the American Academy of Arts and Sciences in 1903. On 15 June 1912 Professor Goodwin went to his "long home." In an editorial memorial tribute, Clifford Moore said of him: "Pretence, display, and all insincerity he detested. Kindliness, gracious dignity, and a natural nobility marked him all his life. . . . Few men have been more loved, and few have so deserved men's affection" (1912: 4).

To meet the need of a reference grammar that would provide well for school use and that could be used as a stepping-stone to college work and beyond, Goodwin developed *An Elementary Greek Grammar* (1870), a book of 235 pages. Dissatisfaction with "the old-fashioned method of forming the cases of the nouns from the nominative, and the various verbal forms from the present indicative" induced Goodwin to adopt "formation from the nominal or verbal stem" in this work, which also signalled an emphasis that was to become Goodwin's badge of grammatical achievement — syntax.[13]

Goodwin's Grammar was more detailed than "Kaegi" and through the services of Goodwin's worthy successor, Charles Gulick, secured its hold in 1930 on further generations of students.[14] "I have entirely rewritten Parts I and II (Phonology and Inflection)," writes Gulick, "and to a great extent Part III (Formation of Words). . . ." Inasmuch as Goodwin had aimed at a descriptive rather than an historical grammar, Gulick claims that he sought to confine himself largely to explanation of the Greek language on "its own soil," in preference to much "inclusion of its pre-history or of Indo-European

[13] For an early evaluation see Anonymous, 1871. A revised and enlarged edition of this grammar came out in 1879, containing 393 pages, and a new edition of 451 pages followed in 1892 under the title *A Greek Grammar* (Boston: Ginn.) A reprint of this edition appeared in 1963 (New York: St. Martin's), with the preface dated "August 1894." This preface is the same in wording as the one dated "June 30, 1892" in the "Revised and Enlarged" edition of 1892. Except for the inclusion of the "Errata" cited in the edition of 1892, the edition of 1963 appears to he identical, even to the pagination, and it is ungracious on the part of Macmillan to ignore on the verso of the title page the edition of 1892 and make reference to a printing in 1894 as a *"New edition."* Because of many careless, and often non-existent, references to older editions and printings, it is practically impossible to write a history of production of grammars and lexicons. The preliminary information in the pages of the University of Chicago's publications of New Testament Greek grammars are models that all publishers might well emulate.

[14] Goodwin's (1930) preface refers to this Grammar as a "third edition."

forms." Yet he could not refrain from introducing historical matter, some of which caused a darkening of counsel.[15] Among the features of the revision is the reduction of the classes of verbs from eight to five. In keeping with linguistic developments the verbs *eimi* and *phēmi* do not appear as grammatical pariahs in a category marked "irregular or anomolous," but receive treatment with other *-mi* verbs. An effort is made to use contemporary idiom in translations, and citations from later authors and the New Testament help make this grammar live up to its title. Acknowledgment of Basil Gildersleeve's numerous contributions to the advancement of knowledge of Greek grammar receives due recognition.

A reviewer lamented the fact that "all too few students" were using Goodwin's Grammar. "What has become" he queried, "of the Greek classes which used to spring up every year in every school deserving to be called a place of education?" And staying for his own answer, he spoke in mournful numbers, "Gone, alas, gone perhaps irrevocably." Nor could he resist a sigh over the change from the black-gold-red binding of the two earlier editions to a jaunty blue with silver lettering: "somewhat *infra dignitatem*."[16]

Herbert Weir Smyth

Between Goodwin-Gulick and a massive reference grammar such as Eduard Schwyzer's *Griechische Grammatik*[17] is the work of Herbert Smyth, who demonstrated his qualifications in a study of the Greek Melic Poets (1900) and of the Ionic dialect (1894). In *A Greek Grammar for Colleges* (1920), which follows the same plan as his *A Greek Grammar for Schools and Colleges*, published in 1916 (New York: American Book Co.), Smyth aimed to "set forth the essential forms of Attic speech, and of the other dialects, as far as they appear in literature; to devote greater attention to the Formation of Words and to the Particles than is usually given to these subjects except in much more extensive works; and to supplement the statement of the principles of Syntax with information that will prove of service to the student as his knowledge widens and deepens" (Smyth, 1920:v). He expresses his indebtedness to William Hale's discussion of Greek deliberative constructions (1893); to two articles by Joseph Harry, one on the omission of the article in Greek (1898) and the other on modal features (1905); and to Basil Gildersleeve for articles in *AJP* and *TAPA*.[18]

Despite the recognition that Smyth received, also from Schwyzer, for some of his grammatical studies, his linguistics was still that of the Neo-

---

[15] See list of samples cited by Kent, 1932.

[16] Ibid., 384.

[17] Eduard Schwyzer, *Griechische Grammatik*, 3 vols. (Munich: Beck, 1950–53).

[18] Gildersleeve (1916:210) chastised Smyth for departing from Goodwin, 1889 (rev. ed. of *Greek Moods and Tenses*) in favor of Madvig's doctrine on *hopōs* and *hopōs an*, §1345, in the 1915 ed. of Smyth's Grammar.

grammarians and therefore pre-Ferdinand de Saussure and Louis Hjelmslev. Moreover, knowledge of ancient Greek moved at such a rapid pace, thanks especially to the work of epigraphists, that a revised edition became imperative. Harvard University's Department of Classics succeeded in acquiring the plates of the 1920 edition, and Gordon Messing proceeded with a revision, which took account of Proto-Indo-European Tocharian and Hittite texts.[19] These had been undergoing systematic decipherment since 1915, with significant contributions from Edgar Sturtevant and Emma Adelaide Hahn. Sterling Dow gave revised copy for paragraph 348, on the Greek system of notation; and for 350d, on dating. Since Smyth's original and more elementary *A Greek Grammar for Schools and Colleges* was out of print, and since it was necessary to dissociate *A Greek Grammar for Colleges* from the elementary work, the revision was entitled simply *Greek Grammar*.

Students who wish to develop competence in deciphering philosophical texts can learn the language through Francis Fobes's *Philosophical Greek, an Introduction* (1957).

Syntax

"Where two or three words are gathered together, there is syntax amongst them, whether you like it or not." Long before John Sinclair made this comment (1968:215), Goodwin had "begun in the enthusiasm of youth as an ephemeral production" what was to become a standard resource known as *Syntax of the Moods and Tenses of the Greek Verb* (1860), which would for more than a century help pilot students of the classics without stranding them on some barren linguistic coast shrouded in theoretical fog.

The first edition of this work, whose publication costs were paid out of Goodwin's own pocket, appeared in 1860, followed by a somewhat enlarged publication in 1865, which one reviewer (1866) adjudged to be "greatly superior" to works by Baumlein and Aken in Germany.[20] In the Preface to this second edition Goodwin observed that "many scholars" tend "to treat Greek syntax metaphysically rather than by the light of common sense," under whose "dominion" Greek syntax was finally restored by Madvig. To sharpen the point, he cited Hermann's application of Kant's *Categories of Meaning*. The result, he said, is "discovery of hidden meanings which no Greek writer

---

[19] On Tocharian and Hittite texts, see Sturtevant 1933, who makes repeated reference to Greek and Latin. A revised edition appeared in 1951, with E. Adelaide Hahn as co-editor. In 1931 Sturtevant provided *A Hittite Glossary: Words of Known or Conjectural Meaning with Sumerian and Akkadian Words Occurring in Hittite Texts* (Baltimore: Johns Hopkins) (2d ed.; Philadelphia: University of Pennsylvania, 1936). For bibliography on early study of Hittite, see Albrecht Goetze, "The Present State of Anatolian and Hittite Studies," *Haverford Symposium* 1938:136–57.

[20] Anonymous review of W. Goodwin, *Syntax of the Moods and Tenses of the Greek Verb* in *North American Review* 102 (1866) 301–6.

ever dreamed of, but more especially in the invention of nice distinctions between similar or even precisely equivalent expressions." It was a lesson that interpreters of St. John's Gospel, to cite but one, would be long in learning. After numerous reprintings of the second edition, a "rewritten and enlarged" edition appeared in 1889. A half-century later, E. Adelaide Hahn (1953) included in her study of subjunctives and optatives a summary of Continental and American work on syntactical problems and expressed herself in substantial agreement with Goodwin's views on the two grammatical moods (1953:8–10).

When Paul Shorey (1919) assessed the accomplishments of American philologists at a semi-centennial meeting of the Philological Association of America, he adjudged that America's classical grammars were "rather better on the whole than those of Europe" (49), and as one of his pieces of evidence cited Goodwin's *Moods and Tenses*. Some of Goodwin's success derived from judicious respect for the syntactical sensitivity expressed by the first editor of the *American Journal of Philology*, and Goodwin gladly signed the debenture.[21]

Basil Lanneau Gildersleeve

Basil Gildersleeve, son of Benjamin and Louisa (Lanneau) Gildersleeve, was born in Charleston, South Carolina, 23 October 1831. After securing his Ph.D. at the University of Göttingen (15 March 1853),[22] he returned to the United States and spent three years in study, writing, and tutoring. In 1856 he received appointment to the Chair of Greek at the University of Virginia and served in that capacity for twenty years, with double duty as Latinist from 1861–66. During summer months of his tenure he served at the front in the Confederate Army. Struck by a Spencer bullet, he lay on his back for months and left action with a permanent limp, but with heightened feeling for Greek idiom and syntax derived from reading the bare texts of the orators during his tour of duty.[23] He was married to Eliza Fisher Colston of Virginia, and had two children: Raleigh Colston and Emma Louise.

After publication of various books designed for students of Latin, he received an appointment in 1875 to the professorship of Greek at Johns Hopkins University, which opened its doors to students in autumn of 1876. He forthwith began his thirty-nine year tenure of vaccinating classical students against all manner of grammatical viruses.[24]

No lover of atomic theorists, Gildersleeve proceeded to display his keen perception of Hellenic resources for expression of thought in Greek. In 1876

---

21 Preface to Goodwin, 1889:viii-ix.
22 Gildersleeve's dissertation bears the title: *De Porpyrii studiis Homericis capitum trias.*
23 Shorey, 1919:39.
24 Biographical details in Gildersleeve, 1930:xxiii-xxiv. See also the addresses, with bibliography, by John Scott (1925) and Charles Miller (1925).

he read a paper at the annual meeting of the American Philological Association on *ei* with the future indicative and *ean* with the subjunctive in the tragic poets. No respector of persons, in the following year Gildersleeve found Justin Martyr's *Apology* a useful repository for his rapidly developing inventory of syntactical formulae. At the meeting of APA in 1878 he read a paper on syntax and delivered the presidential address.

Goaded by syntactical fever and exacerbated by the vandalism committed in various quarters against the lights of Greece and Rome, Gildersleeve launched, in 1880, the *American Journal of Philology,* a quarterly magazine devoted to publication and research in the general field of philology and classics. About forty volumes appeared under his direction, and it is questionable whether any learned periodical has ever seen editing done with such verve and breadth of culture. Crying aloud and sparing not, Gildersleeve instructed, regaled, confounded, and not infrequently distressed an international public with his farrago of Horatian wit, philological precision, and cutesy journalism. *Caveat lector* was his motto. One "must beware of the American Journal of Philology, in which he will find recorded from time to time the sins of those who occupy the chief seats," he wrote in his allusive manner and with customary candor (1930:349).

Concerning the conception of the Journal he wrote that there was need of "stimulating production" that "would make the establishment of a medium of philological intercommunication a more urgent necessity than it is felt to be now. The want of such a medium is admitted in some languid way, but there seems as yet to be no acute sense of the privation, and it certainly betokens great supineness on the part of our scholars that a country which boasts a Journal of Speculative Philosophy should not have even a solitary periodical devoted to a science which counts its professional votaries by hundreds, if not by thousands, and that our professors and teachers should be satisfied with consigning an occasional paper to the slow current of a volume of transactions, or exposing a stray lucubration to struggle for notice amidst the miscellaneous matter of a review or the odds and ends of an educational magazine" (1890b:98).

Pindar's epinician odes were Gildersleeve's first love, and the romance flowered in 1885 with a masterful discussion of the Olympian and Pythian Odes. "My Pindar," he wrote, "is the only book I ever made as a labor of love: and though I recognized the fact that others knew Pindar better than I could ever hope to know him, and though my philological training bade me study all the great interpreters, still I dared to face what seemed to me the vital problems independently" (1930:149). Typical is his first sentence in the preface to *Pindar.* "The Text of this edition . . . has been constituted according to my best judgment and that best judgment has excluded all emendations of my own."

Apart from the intrinsic value of an introduction to Pindar through a scholar who combined empathy with professional integrity, the commentary in Gildersleeve's *Pindar* is filled with striking descriptions of syntactical and poetic realities. A persistent foe of unimaginative pedantry, Gildersleeve celebrates Pindar's transformation of maritime vessels, which dash against rocks of narrative, into bees that hie from flower to flower (*Pythian* 10.53): "Pindar lives himself into a metaphor, as if it were no metaphor; hence metaphor within metaphor. No mixed, only telescoped, metaphor" (1890a:355). The temptation is great to cite example upon example of Gildersleeve's precise appraisal of his author's meaning, such as the capital interpretation of the plural *en phonais* in *Pythian* 11.37: "Notice the effect of the plural," he exhorts: " 'Weltering in his gore' " (361). But there is more, much more to record of Gildersleeve's accomplishments.

After years of collecting material on Greek syntax, he finally brought out in 1900 the first part of his major contribution on the subject. In his preface he acknowledges the valued services of his pupil, colleague, and friend, Professor Charles Miller (Gildersleeve and Miller, 1900–1911). "Taking the Attic Orators as the standard of conventional Greek," he wrote, "we have worked backward through philosophy and history to tragic, lyric, and epic poetry, comedy being the bridge which spans the syntax of the agora and the syntax of Parnassus. Individual syntax we have not been able to set forth with any fulness, but the different departments have been represented to the best of our ability and judgment. The plan has saved us from giving the usual medley of examples, it has forced us to rely largely on our own collections and to examine the texts for ourselves, and it will enable those who come after us to fill up these outlines with greater ease" (Part 1, iv). Gildersleeve did not have much good to say about Robert Browning. A "perverse writer spits in your face, and such an one is Browning" (1930:238). But Gildersleeve appears to have underwritten Browning's estimate of the grammarian who was "dead from the waist down." He was determined not to be semicadaverous, and throughout his *Syntax*, which is a mine of good things happily expressed, Gildersleeve never deserts high dedication to elucidation of literary forms.

Originally, Gildersleeve had hoped to include in his study of Greek syntax full catenae of examples from Homer to Demosthenes, but the long hope outmatched the space of life that would be brief even for him, and in the preface to the second part of his *Syntax* he announced the dissolution of his partnership with Miller with this expression of gratitude: "I desire that all credit be given to him for the value of this segment of the work as a repository of fact" (Part 2, iii).

In clearly-outlined no-nonsense prose that anticipates the style of a Wall Street newsletter, Gildersleeve and Miller exhibited the bountiful resources of classical Greek. To a close relative of the historical present, and to the dismay of many stodgy continental scholars for whom humor and readability spelled negation of science, he gave the name "Note-Book Present" (*Syntax*

1, 86).[25] "The aorist is the shorthand of the perfect" (89). The aorist in general: "Upshot Aorist." The "Ingressive Aorist" he nicknamed "Outset Aorist" (104). In connection with remarks on the future tense, he cautioned: ". . . Whenever we translate the Greek future by *shall* or *will*, we make an analysis for which the Greek language is not responsible" (265). Sapir and company would not do much better than that. And Charles Baudelaire had expressed only slightly more ecstasy over the charms of grammar in general,[26] but Gildersleeve did it without entering the underworld of hashish. The future, preached Gildersleeve, was originally a mood, and the "periphrasis that comes nearest to the modal future is *mellō* with the infinitive" (115). "The subjunctive mood is the mood of anticipation," he wrote, and then added in one of his rare excursions into fine print in the first volume: "Anticipation and expectation are not to be confounded. Anticipation treats the future as if it were present. Expectation postpones the realization. To anticipate payment and to expect payment are by no means the same thing even in popular parlance, and grammarians should be at least as exact as the ungrammatical herd" (147 n. 1.)[27] As though he were interviewing some ancient Julia Childs, he recalls in another context the cooking scene in the *Acharnians* (lines 1005–07) of Aristophanes under the rubric: "The present imperative often produces the effect of an action that is watched" (160). It is sad that Browning's Grammarian lacked such vision.

In one of the issues of "Brief Mention," America's Nestor of grammar demythologized Greek case structure in strains that compete with John Keat's *Ode to a Grecian Urn:* "The nominative then is the point of departure, the positive pole. The genitive is the door, the Daleth of the Semites, the delta of the Greeks, the deep well of love, the place within which, the place from within which emerges the tide of life. The dative is that which gives and takes (Pindar *Olympian* 13. 29). The accusative is the resultant, the other pole of activity." "The accusative is not a whither case. It is simply the result of an action," as in the phrase "To make port" (1930:319–20). Oversimplification? Gildersleeve, the soaring eagle, was not intimidated by the rhetoric of cawking daws, and scores of graduate students taught by Gildersleeve were never charged with debasing the currency of literary Greek.

A few minutes of exposure to Gildersleeve's approach to the sexuality of syntax were enough to convince some department heads that students of Beginning Greek ought not to be abandoned to the unimaginative and inexperienced mercies of graduate students or tenured pedants. Informed

---

[25] All references to Gildersleeve's *Syntax* are to page, not section.

[26] "La grammaire, l'aride grammaire elle-même, devient quelque chose comme une sorcellerie évocatoire; les mots ressuscitent revêtus de chair et d'os, le substantif, dans sa majesté substantielle, l'adjectif, vetement transparent qui l'habille et le colore comme un glacis, et le verbe, ange du mouvement, qui donne le branle à la phrase." *Le Poeme du haschisch* in *Les Paradis Artificiels* (Paris: Louis Conard, 1928) 50.

[27] Gildersleeve refers the reader to *AJP* 15 (1894) 399 and 523; Justin Martyr, *Apol.* 1.2.4.

and vivacious pedagogical method was Gildersleeve's antidote to *rigor mortis* in the realm of Greek and Latin studies. Introduction of such a fine language as Greek was to be left to those who can handle the occasion with a sensitive finesse that draws on comprehensive acquaintance with the ancient literature.

To give some semblance of cohesion to his total syntactical output, Gildersleeve drew up an index of his syntactical articles, notes, and observations that had been printed over the years, under the title: "Indiculus Syntacticus" (1915), which he then published in lieu of his regular "Brief Mention," and—in view of his reputation for levity—with a colleague's admonition as motto: *nec ut soles, dabis iocos.*

As indicated above in connection with the publication of *Pindar,* Gildersleeve was a master in the interpretation of Greek style and had little appreciation for fuzziness in scholarly inquiry. It was not sufficient that a critic make declarations about the style of an author; he or she is obligated "to point out the facts that made it so" (Gildersleeve 1930:xxx). Minute and painstaking research was Gildersleeve's method for arriving at a conclusion. A stylist himself, even his annotations and his translations of proof passages make interesting and instructive reading.[28]

Gildersleeve was responsible, perhaps more than any other American philologist, for awakening local pride in scholarly production. Echoing Perikles's Epitaphion, he proclaimed in 1909, in a presidential address before the American Philological Association, that America's philologists had at last compelled Germans to read English. But provincialism is highly resistant, and in 1912 a second edition of Hermann Hirt's *Handbuch der griechischen Laut- und Formenlehre* showed no knowledge of American work on Greek dialects and it made no mention of *Classical Philology* in its list of "Zeitschriften."

Gildersleeve's One-Liners

Impatient with posturing, Gildersleeve unleashed numerous one-line descriptions of pedants, ancient or contemporary, and some of these vignettes do a better job of summarizing than is to be had in major encyclopedia articles. And it mattered not who held the "chief seat in the synagogue."[29]

Justin Martyr: "Incondite writer" (115).

Persius: "Hopeless prig" (115).

Aelian: "An utterly untrustworthy scribbler" (*Pindar,* x.)

---

[28] One of Gildersleeve's self-styled "best essays" is prefixed to Henry Cary's translation of *The Histories of Herodotus* (New York: D. Appleton, 1899.)

[29] All page references are to Gildersleeve, 1930, unless otherwise specified.

Marcion: "A rat from Pontus who gnaws away at the Gospels."

Strauss: He "evaporated the Glad Tidings of Great Joy" (*Essays*, 358).

Professor Shorey: "An exceptional man, and my judgment is open to suspicion because I am a Hellenist" (118).

Demosthenes: "Outswears all the Attic orators" (124).

Polybios: "He is scrupulous in the avoidance of hiatus, but there is one hiatus that he cannot escape, the yawn in the face of his reader" (209).

Herakleitos: "Surrounds his ripe fruit with a protective envelope, so that it may not fall into the hands of unworthy nibblers" (80).

Polyanthea, or Parallelomania: Frequently "the appositeness of the citations is by no means in keeping with their number" (210).

Dissertations: "Long endurance guarantees the toughness and large charity the amplitude" (153).

Plutarch: "Philosophic washerwoman of Chaeronea" (*Essays*, 300).

Aristophanes: "Spoiled darling of the Muses" (239).

Swinburne: A case of "moral leprosy" (*Essays*, 203).[30]

Jebb: "A man of admirable poise, of wonderful insight, of flawless style, a scholar whose renderings made all others seem coarse or crude" (149).

Constantine the Great: "A sorry Christian in theory and practice" (*Essays*, 363).

Antoninus: "Introspective keeper of a pathological peepshow" (*Essays*, 300).

The Kappadocian St. George: "A fraudulent pork-commisary as a layman, a truculent tyrant as a prelate, he deserves more attention than he has received at the hands of his unconscious imitators in these latter days" (*Essays*, 356).

Lucian: "No hope, no love. No good God for him but good Greek" (*Essays*, 351).

Use of Scriptural language: Soon to be put "in the category of recondite allusions" (220).

---

[30] Gildersleeve described Swinburne's *Laus Veneris* as "A museum of morbid moral anatomy" (1890:203). His basic objections echo an evaluation by a reviewer in *North American Review* (104 [1867]:287–92) of Algernon Charles Swinburne's *Laus Veneris, and Other Poems and Ballads* (New York: Carleton, 1867). The reviewer's critical perspective and estimate of Swinburne received their summary in these words: "All which disgusts is prohibited" to art (p. 289). What revision in his rhetoric would Gildersleeve have made had he undertaken the kind of study made by J. Henderson (1975) of obscene language in Attic comedy? Yet even in this linguistic variety modern script writers could offer lessons to Aristophanes and his guild.

Double entendre in contemporary authors like Browning: "There is nothing more obscene than an obscene conundrum, and erotic and skatologic riddles play an important part in that region of folklore" (215).

On the position of Pindar's *ariston men hydor* in Gildersleeve's almanac of commonplaces: "It goes under Aquarius" (237).

Slit-skirt: "Bequest from those *phainomerides*, the Spartan belles" (289).

Many grammarians: They are "like Renan's Eastern sage, whose name being interpreted means *hou to sperma eis tēn kephalēn anebē . . ."* (320).

The Greek language: "The cases made havoc with compounds. Syntax killed synthesis" (355).

Herodotos: "One of the most fascinating, large-minded, artistic and lovable natures in the whole world of classical literature" (38).

Interpreters with little time for grammar: One "who does not know the syntax of Thukydides does not know the mind of Thukydides" (146).

Gildersleeve: If he "were to edit Pindar again, even the ghost of the digamma would disappear" (157).

Thus did Gildersleeve "intersperse with verdure and flowers the dusty deserts of barren philology."

On 9 January 1924, Gildersleeve paid his fee to Charon, and went on to the study of ultimate grammar. As though he were sacrificing a cock to Asklepios, he had earlier practiced the translator's art on a poem by August von Platen, and in a manner that previewed Ezra Pound's later admonition, "Make it New."

Death of Pindar

When I depart on God's appointed day,
Quick and unconscious passage be my lot,
Like stars' that quit the sky and tarry not,
Swift as the comet's train which fades away.

Such was the end of Pindaros, they say:
The theatre at Argos holds the spot
Where, heedless of the play's soul-stirring plot,
The weary bard in peaceful slumber lay.

A perfect image of serene repose,
His grey head resting on his favourite's knee;
His sleep grew deeper as the play went on;

The play was o'er, the audience rustling rose,
The boy essayed to wake him tenderly—
In vain, for Pindar to the gods was gone.[31]

(1930:396)

Paul Shorey

Associated with Gildersleeve in the task of awakening America to the importance of the legacy of Greece and Rome was Paul Shorey. He was admitted to the Illinois bar in 1880, but preferred to study the Classics. After obtaining his doctorate at the University of Munich in 1884, he began his teaching career at Bryn Mawr College in 1885, and in 1892 became Professor of Greek at the University of Chicago, where he taught beyond his age of retirement and almost until his death on 24 April 1934.[32] The bibliography of his writings is lengthy, and had he not labored so diligently to answer Cicero's question, "What is the life of humanity, if the memory of things past is not woven with the texture of the future?" he could have left an even larger legacy of monuments to his sensitivity for the nuances of the ancient writers, including especially Plato.[33]

Anxious to see American scholars rise up from prostrate worship of the Baal of German *Wissenschaft,* Shorey was frequently misunderstood as anti-Teutonic. But even a casual perusal of European books and periodicals at the turn of the twentieth century reveals a number that must be assessed on a scale ranging from unwitting provincialism to arrogant disdain.

Shorey found his chief antagonist in Berlin University's Professor Wilhelm Wilamowitz-Moellendorf. Despite the fact that Shorey had been invited to name his own topic for the course of study he was to offer as Roosevelt exchange professor for 1913 at Berlin, Wilamowitz objected to presentation of Plato's *Republic* as well as to lectures on the odes of Pindar, on the ground that these subjects were well taken care of at the University. Translation: Wilamowitz had led courses on Pindar, had written at length on Pindar, and was engaged in a work on Plato. Shorey's response to pettiness was Aristotle's *De anima.*

A decade before his experience at Berlin, Shorey (1906b:382) had praised the "great revival of classical scholarship" as "one of Germany's chief

---

[31] Gildersleeve, 1930:396. On Platen, who in Gildersleeve's phrase, clothed "modern thought with the purple light of antiquity," see Gildersleeve, 1890:401–50.

[32] Shorey expresses his passion for Hellenism especially in publications 1906b, 1910, 1917, 1919, 1921, 1925b, 1926, and 1927. His assessment (1925a) of Henry Arthur Jones, British dramatist, displays Shorey's firm resistance to intellectual fraud. Many shared Shorey's enthusiasm. In *Value of the Classics,* edited by Andrew F. West (1917), appear testimonies from leaders in all walks of life as to the benefits of a classical education.

[33] An extensive sampling of Shorey's philological contributions, especially in the form of articles and book reviews, is available in Tarán, 1980.

gifts to the modern world." Lessing, Winckelmann, Herder, Goethe, Schiller, Heyne, Wolf, Hermann — all received Shorey's undiluted adulation. But Shorey was not wont to sacrifice his own critical responsibility in exchange for a fraudulent academic peace, and in the same context he chided Wilamowitz for "naively" styling as "ewige Poesie" an "entire lost Hesiodic epic from seven lines of fragments and a few remarks of the scholiast on Pindar (374). At the same time he ranked Wilamowitz along with Jebb and Gildersleeve as one of the preeminent classical scholars in the five decades that preceded. But he thought that Wilamowitz should have cultivated better manners and ought to have refrained from defining any one who did not share his own opinions as a person who had no right "mitzureden" (1919:59).

Shorey's lack of patience with the pyramiding of hypothetical construction on a narrow data base broke out in a rash of wit at the fiftieth observance of the founding of the American Philological Association. "The German philological mind, like the German political mind," he declaimed, "is fertile and ingenious in the multiplication of arguments for a chosen thesis or a foregone conclusion. It cannot be trusted to weigh them. Few recent German scholars have taken to heart Ritschl's commandment: 'Thou shalt not believe that ten bad reasons equal one good one.' And the leaders of the present generation too often forgot the solemn admonition of Niebuhr: 'Above all things, in every branch of literature and science, ought we to preserve our truth so pure, as utterly to shun all false show; *so as never to assert anything, however slight, for certain of which we are not thoroughly convinced; so as to take the utmost pains when we are expressing a conjecture to make the degree of unbelief apparent'* " (Shorey, 1919:44). His end notes in *What Plato Said* (1933) offer ample testimony to his concern for "what is so" and the crushing of specious error. In this passion he emulated Howard Crosby (1880), who expressed regret that the committee responsible for the revision of the King James Version was not doing a thorough-going job of modernization: "The truth is what we desire," and we must be prepared to "sacrifice style to sense."

For exhibition of German provincialism Shorey cited Kroll's *Altertumswissenschaft im letzten Vierteljahrhundert,* which was not designed in principle, as is the present volume, to celebrate scholarly production in a specific geographical area. Kroll's chapter on Greek grammar made no mention of Gildersleeve or Goodwin. We are used to that, shrugged Shorey. "Karl Lamprecht lectured on nineteenth century historiography at St. Louis and named a score or so of German historians, but not one French, English, or American name." Why take a back seat for American productions, asked Shorey. Wilamowitz did not teach Greek metric in 1913 any more effectively than was done at Bryn Mawr in 1886. Then he cited one of Leo's howlers in quoting Alexander Pope: "the proper study of mankind's man." Christ, he charged, "uses the roughly anapaestic 'Erlkoenig' as an example of weighty trochees and light tripping dactyls. Endeavoring to deflate continental pomposity, Shorey asked, why any American who possesses an ear should worry about their theories of meter. Our native product, which shall be nameless, of mare's nests in that kind is amply sufficient." Of one book praised by Kroll he chirped, "No one who knows Greek and is familiar with Plato could possibly praise Lutoslawski's book if he had read it." Kroll's judgments, Shorey went on to say, "are perfunctory, not critical. We hear of *bahnbrech-enden Untersuchungen* and of a dozen or so of masterly volumes. But it is rarely possible to put your finger on any definite acquisition of new truth, and there is no hint that many of the masterly books were evidently written in haste from first impressions of texts that the writers had read up as they wrote, and that nearly all of them need to be recomposed, abbreviated, and weeded of the errors that make them unsafe guides for all but the most cautious students" (1919:47–48).

After surveying the scene and taking the measure of England's production, Shorey concluded that America at least ran a close second to Germany, but that Americans did not know what they had on the home front. His comment on Thomas Day Seymour summarizes his respect for American scholarship. In Seymour's books, he said, "you will conveniently find . . . more things about Homer that are so than you will easily discover elsewhere. If you can get inspiration only from the things that are not so, then I recommend the *Homerische Untersuchungen* and the *Rise of the Greek Epic*, though Cauer's *Grundfragen* runs them close" (Shorey, 1919:55).[34]

Of that part of Shorey which can be termed grammarian it cannot be said that "he decided not to Live but Know." He was too deeply saturated with Hellas to lose touch with the whole. Precisely for this reason his grammatical contributions reward attention. They are for the most part scattered in his books on Plato and also in *Classical Philology*, where he expressed himself frequently both as author and reviewer. Biblical studies could have been spared a huge deposit of "things that are not so" had scholars bothered to "walk across the street" to see how this expert in classical philology practiced the exegetical trade. Besides being a part of all that he had met, Shorey, who did not share the view that "it is more blessed to gush than to construe," performed his work superbly well. And the deed can still be done.

While many in the land were chanting, "Let dollars grow from more to more and so be all accounts enriched," Shorey endeavored to save their souls from the corruptive rust of barbarism. Blending phrases from Tennyson's *In Memoriam* and Vergil's *Aeneid* (6.663), Shorey came up with the following motto for the University of Chicago: *Crescat scientia, vita excolatur:* Let knowledge grow from more to more, and so be human life enriched.[35]

---

[34] Funk's (1976) appraisal of American lag in independent biblical research contrasts with Shorey's celebration of emancipation for classical scholars.

[35] T. W. Goodspeed, 1925:467–68; Leon Kass, "Modern Science and Ethics: Time for a Re-Examination," *University of Chicago Magazine* (Summer, 1984) 26. For an estimate of Shorey's

Other Grammatical Studies of Ancient Greek

Especially remembered as a philological pontifex is Evangelinus Aposolides Sophocles, who helped American classicists and biblical students appreciate the importance of a knowledge of modern Greek for study of the ancient aspects of the language. In *A Romaic Grammar* (1842), Sophocles exploded an Aeolic-Doric origin of modern Greek and explained that the term Romaic refers to the modern Greek language as spoken "by the mass of the people." Byzantine Greek is "the last stage of the Common Attic" and has Romaic as its "legitimate offspring." It is termed Romaic "because Greeks, long before the fall of the Graeco-Roman empire called themselves *Romaioi,* because there was more glory attached to the name." Sophocles goes on to observe that "at this very day, many a devout monk thinks" that the term *Hellenes* is "a horrible appelation," to be equated with *eidololatrai,* and "not fit for a Christian nation."[36]

An expanded form of Sophocles's grammatical discussion, but without the chrestomathy and vocabulary, appeared under the title *Romaic or, Modern Greek Grammar* (1857) and carried the information that "with Theophanes (A.D. 758–816) we enter the confines of Modern Greek."[37] In 1847 Sophocles published *A Greek Grammar, for the Use of Schools and*

---

legacy and his stature as a human being see *Classical Philology* 29 (1934) 185–91, and Bonner, 1934. Shorey's dissertation on Plato's theory of rational processes, *De Platonis idearum doctrina atque mentis humanae notionibus commentatio* (Munich: Theodor Ackermann, 1884; reprinted in Tarán, 1980:253–313), was an impressive promise of such works as *The Unity of Plato's Thought* (Chicago: University of Chicago, 1903), the two-volume translation of Plato's *Republic* in the Loeb Classical Series (1930–1935), and *What Plato Said* (Chicago: University of Chicago, 1933).

[36] Sophocles traces Romaic to the time of Theodoros Ptochoprodromos (or simply Prodromos, fl. 1150), the author of two Romaic poems addressed to Emperor Manuel Comnenus.

[37] On Byzantine literature, see Karl Krumbacher, *Geschichte der Byzantinischen Literatur von Justinian bis zum Ende des Oströmischen Reiches (527–1453)* (2d ed. by A. Ehrhard and H. Gelzer; Munich, 1897). On literature in Romaic, see Krumbacher, "Vulgärgriechische Litteratur," 787–853. On Theodoros, see Krumbacher, pp. 804–6; Herbert Hunger, *Die hochsprachliche profane Literatur der Byzantiner* (Munich: Beck, 1978) 1.135. Krumbacher terms "wichtig" (p. 806) the commentary on Theodoros's poems by Adamantios Korais (1748–1833), Atakta . . ., text, pp. 1–37 (Book 1, lines 1–396; Book 2, lines 1–655); commentary, pp. 39–331 [Paris, 1828]). Korais reproaches Theodoros for writing poor Romaic, but misses the point of Theodoros's use of Byzantine Greek as framework for his profane Greek.

Sophocles's interest in the promotion of classical Greek studies is reflected in his *Greek Exercises, Followed by an English and Greek Vocabulary Containing About Seven Thousand Three Hundred Words* (Hartford: H. Huntington, 1841). The basic tactic in this work is a columnar list of English sentences adjoining a list of Greek words that need to be put in the proper grammatical form: Example: "Doors made of palmtree"; *thyra phoinix poieō* (per. pas. par.)."

For work in progress on Byzantine literature, see *Research Tools in Progress* (1980) 57–58., also Jan Pinborg "Classical Antiquity: Greece," in *Current Trends in Linguistics,* ed. Thomas A. Sebeok, vol. 13 (The Hague: Mouton, 1975) 121.

Colleges,[38] of which Goodwin said that Sophocles "recognized the same principles" as did Madvig (whose Grammar was also published in 1847) on the meaning of the aorist optative and the infinitive and the construction of *hoti* and *hos* in oratio obliqua.[39]

American contributions to the grammatical study of papyri and inscriptions are cited below, chapter 8. Of special interest here is the publication by Carl Buck (1933) of *Comparative Grammar of Greek and Latin*.[40] In 1937 he acknowledged the help of Professors Kent, Lane, and Whatmough in the preparation of corrections for a new printing. Unlike Gildersleeve, Buck had a self-confessed "lesser interest" in the field of syntax.

German scholars thought they knew how to pronounce ancient Greek and Latin. Edgar Sturtevant, who later held a post in linguistics at Yale, was equally certain that there was still something to be learned about the subject and in 1920 revealed his findings in *Pronunciation of Greek and Latin*.

Grammatical Study of Biblical Greek

The prevailing hermeneutical climate in Germany during the eighteenth century suggested the need for more accuracy in establishing interpretations of New Testament passages. Grammatical study, it was thought, could prove a primary instrument for controlling subjective and arbitrary exegesis. Among the principal contributions were the the works of Johann G. B. Winer and Alexander Buttmann.

In the preface to the sixth edition of his Grammar,[41] Winer chastised expositors for approaching New Testament Greek as though it had no relation to ordinary discourse. As early as 1859, a Professor Edward Masson of Edinburgh had stated in his translation of the sixth edition of Winer's grammar: "Apart from Hebraisms—the number of which has been grossly exaggerated—the New Testament may be considered as exhibiting the only genuine *fac-simile* of the colloquial diction employed by *unsophisticated* Grecian gentlemen of the first century, who spoke without pedantry—as *idiotai*, and not as *sophistai*."[42] Although his eyesight began to falter so badly that he had to depend on the eyes and hands of others to complete the work,

---

[38] A revised ed. of *A Greek Grammar* appeared in 1867 (Hartford: William Y. Hamersly).

[39] Goodwin, 1882:ii.

[40] There had been nothing to speak of in English since John Edward King and Christopher Cookon, *The Principles of Sound and Inflexion as Illustrated in the Greek and Latin Languages* (Oxford: Clarendon, 1888), and Victor Henry, *A Short Comparative Grammar of Greek and Latin for Schools and Colleges*, tr. by R. T. Elliott (London: Sonnenschein, 1890).

[41] J. G. B. Winer, *Grammatik des neutestamentlichen Sprachidioms* (6th rev. ed.; Leipzig: Vogel, 1855).

[42] The quotation is from *A Grammar of the New Testament Diction by Dr George Benedict Winer*; translation from the 6th enlarged and improved edition of the original, by Edward Masson, 2d ed. (Edinburgh, 1860) viii.

Winer labored to the very end of his life in preparation for a seventh edition, whose finishing touches were left to Gottlieb Luenemann. The three translations of previous editions of Winer's Grammar had already appeared when Joseph Thayer was asked to undertake the translation of the seventh edition, which is "substantially a revision of Professor Masson's translation."[43]

Thayer's reasoning behind such acceptance of a very demanding assignment finds expression in the translation he made a few years later of a grammar by Alexander Buttmann (1873). In its preface he deplored "the somewhat indiscriminate depreciation of the study of the dead languages at the present day," declaring that it was "not without injurious influence upon those who are preparing themselves to be expounders of the Divine Word" (Buttmann and Thayer, 1873:v). In Buttmann's Grammar, Thayer recognized less subjective and at the same time more scientific, accounting of biblical data than in the work of Winer, who in his zeal to defend the New Testament writers against the charge of exotic Greek emphasized classical parallels and did not do justice to the role of the Septuagint in the diction and syntax of the New Testament. To make Buttmann's work even more useful for American students, Thayer incorporated references to the standard school grammars used in the United States and England (p. vii), to the more specialized treatments of moods and tenses by W. W. Goodwin, and to Prof. Short's "Essay on the Order of Words in Attic Greek Prose."[44] The Greek New Testament text generally used in this translation of Buttmann's work is that of Lachmann's larger edition of 1842, with readings from Codex Sinaiticus.

Archibald Thomas Robertson

About the same time that Thayer was completing his translation of Buttmann's grammar, a home near Chatham, Pennsylvania County, Virginia, heard on 6 November 1863 the first syntax of one who would in a few decades run a race with the British and the Germans for the honor of displaying the new grammatical treasures that were soon to be exposed in amazing quantity by alert sifters of the sands of Egypt.

In the winter of 1879, a few weeks after he had been licensed to preach, a somewhat shy Archibald Thomas Robertson began his studies at Wake Forest College, where he soon developed a reputation as a formidable debater. Between chores during his first vacation on the family farm, he read the first book of Xenophon's Anabasis, "so as to be well up in Greek" (Gill, 1943:40). During his last year at Wake Forest he trained, with all the dedication of an Olympic athlete, for the school's coveted Greek Medal. Homer, Herodotos, Aischylos, Euripides, Demosthenes, Lysias, Plato, and Xenophon—he wrestled them all into surrender of their syntax. But the

---

[43] See Winer and Thayer, 1869:xi.
[44] Short's Essay is prefixed to Drisler's edition of Yonge, 1870.

referee had the last word. Thirty years later he adverted in writing to the adverse decision with the note: "I have never regretted the work I did for the Greek medal. Without knowing it I was laying the foundation for my future life-work" (Gill, 1943:49).

After completing his preparation for the ministry at Louisville Seminary, Robertson was invited to serve as one of its instructors, and on 25 May 1895 succeeded his homiletics teacher, John A. Broadus, as full professor of Greek.

About the year 1886, Robertson determined to write a detailed grammar of the Greek New Testament. Broadus thought that he and Robertson should update Winer, but after writing about a hundred pages of the proposed revision Robertson was convinced that the task was hopeless. The great progress made in comparative and historical grammar had hopelessly antiquated Winer's work. Grammarians had been accustomed to think in terms of rules. Any data that did not square with the rules were classified as exceptions. In the course of time exceptions soon outweighed what was considered regular. Fortunately the ancients had taken no thought of grammarians' concerns and yet managed to produce interesting literature. And Robertson was determined to help the world learn more of the facts about Greek, which was in his judgment the most perfect organ of human speech (Gill, 1943:156). Paul Schmiedel, of Germany, had also caught the vision, but died in the middle of a sentence.[45] Only one other scholar, James Moulton, appeared to be in the running and capable of completing within the near future so formidable a task. The friendly race was on. Cambridge, England versus Louisville, U.S.A. And the professor from Munich, Germany, who had announced in 1909 that not a single American scholar had produced on an extensive scale a work of the slightest scientific value, would soon have the opportunity to update his priggish judgment of American academia (Gill, 163), which was rapidly moving out, as Gildersleeve and Shorey were wont to repeat, from under the "German yoke."

Robertson's grammar kept increasing in bulk and, in his own words, "struck him with terror" (Gill:164). Finally, about the middle of February, 1912, Robertson completed his task—all in longhand. Since his Short Grammar, published in 1908,[46] had been so popular, he anticipated at least a moderate welcome of the larger work. Inasmuch as some publishers have not been generally noted for sensing the pulse of the public, especially when it has to do with books of a technical nature whose time has come, a portion of the reply of George H. Doran, publisher of Robertson's Short Grammar, deserves to be quoted in recognition of such prophetic vision: "If I am judging aright, this new work, because of its having full advantage of study and research down to the present date, will supersede all previous work along the line of the Grammar of the Greek New Testament. . . . It will be revolutionary

---

[45] See Danker, 1970:121.
[46] See below, p. 83.

in that you recognize the colloquial Greek of the untutored Apostles and have departed entirely from the purely classical forms of all present works on the Greek New Testament. The importance of such a radical step cannot be over-stated, and such a work should be internationally published. Indeed, I am sure that it must have the heartiest cooperation of publishers and scholars on both sides of the Atlantic. With information before me I would then like to submit the entire matter to the consideration of Messrs. Hodder and Stoughton and Sir William Robertson Nicoll; for the magnitude and importance of the undertaking demands the most careful preliminary investigation" (Gill, 172–73).

Doran's historical perspicacity ran into a plea of conflict of interest at the firm of Hodder and Stoughton, who were under contract to publish Moulton's projected grammar. After receiving Doran's regrets, Robertson shipped his mammoth manuscript to Scribner's, which also turned it down. In the meantime Doran had second thoughts and persuaded Hodder and Stoughton to consider a cooperative venture. The Grammar—later Robertson referred to his manuscript as "It," in somewhat the tone of a Pavarotti referring to "The Voice"—appeared to be saved, but Robertson's numerous annotations, combined with his longhand, suggested to the publishers an invitation to bankruptcy after paying off blinded typesetters. The publishers urged that the entire manuscript be typewritten, double spaced. Robertson shuddered at such a mountainous task, not to speak of eating soup, alphabet that is, warmed over ten times. To satisfy the publishers, who wished to retain their solvency and at the same time hold the price within reach of anticipated consumers, Robertson poured his family's savings into the venture. Finally, with Robertson on the verge of bankruptcy, the Board of Trustees of the Louisville Seminary authorized a revolving Faculty Publishing Fund.

Whether the typesetters worked harder on decipherment of Robertson's handwriting than did the grammmarian on understanding the mysteries of New Testament Greek will never be determined. In any event, on 12 June 1914 the mammoth classification of data came off the press and in nine years went through four editions.[47] Moulton never lived to complete his own grammar. A footnote in the second volume of his A Grammar of New Testament Greek reads as an epitaph: "Dr. Moulton's MS ends with paragraph 130."[48] A victim of Germany's submarine campaign in the Mediterranean, Moulton died in April, 1917, before he could complete the treatment of suffixes, which is contributed by W. F. Howard, editor of the second volume.

From the extravagant praise recorded by Robertson's biographer, Everett Gill, one might assume that the Big Grammar was the last word in

---

[47] Second ed., 1915; 3d ed. rev. and enlarged, 1919; 4th ed., with correction of a few *errata*, 1923. A fifth edition appeared in 1931, published by Harper.
[48] James Hope Moulton and Wilbert Francis Howard, *A Grammar of New Testament Greek*, vol. 2 (Edinburgh: T. and T. Clark, 1920) 332 n. 2.

New Testament grammatical research. For his recognition of the importance of papyrology and epigraphy in elucidation of New Testament data Robertson receives high marks. With the help of comparative grammatical analysis he clarifies much that is often obscured by rote recitation of grammarians' rules, but his syntactical doctrine is so attached to a belief in the persistence of root meanings that major adjustments must be made with the help of more modern linguistic studies. Pre-critical dogmatism comes through blatantly in such statements as: "If the devil used Aramaic, then we have Christ's own translation of it or that of the Evangelist (Luke)" (Robertson, 1931:1009). "Peter clearly spoke in Greek on the Day of Pentecost, . . ." (28). Such comments tend to dilute some of the confidence evoked by much analysis that is otherwise marked by sobriety of judgment. Also, it is simply not true, for example, that bilingual ability necessarily implies competence in both oral and written expression, as is suggested by the comment about the Epistle of James: "The incongruity of such a smooth piece of Greek as this Epistle being written by a Palestinian Jew like James vanishes when we consider the bilingual character of the people of Palestine" (123). Assuming that the letter is not pseudonymous, Robertson was bound, at a minimum, to grapple with the question of the relative probability of James' literary training. Waiters may be able to speak five or more languages, but not produce an acceptable manuscript on a given subject. For that matter, publishers are convinced that scholars on the whole do not know how to write.

Oddly, it was the Germans who had the reputation of being mountains in labor, with the value of some of their progeny in grave doubt. Robertson's *Grammar,* devoted to a book of very slight dimensions, contained a total of 1454 pages in the fourth edition, but its author had not generated a minuscule *mus.* With immense analytical and descriptive power Robertson had compelled the European philological world to revise its estimate of America's biblical scholars' ability to produce a major scientific work. And the fact remains that no American classical scholar has equalled this type of achievement. Robertson noted in his preface that the appearance of his Grammar marked the four hundredth anniversary of the first printed Greek New Testament (1931:xv).[49] It was an appropriate observation and made with justifiable pride upon the completion of what Robertson himself termed an "almost impossible task" (1931:xiv).

As a quick general reference work Robertson's large *Grammar* proved unwieldly, and its theological idiosyncracies depreciated some of its value as a resource for objective study of the Greek New Testament. In addition, its

---

[49] The first printing of the Greek New Testament, as edited by Diego Lopez de Stunica, for Cardinal Francisco Ximines' Complutensian Polyglot, was completed on 10 January 1514, but not officially published until 22 March 1520. Erasmus rushed into print with his own edition, which issued from the press on 1 March 1516.

expansive prose proved too expensive for the average student. More helpful in meeting the practical needs of theologians, philologists, linguists, pastors and scholars, and students of varying acquaintance with New Testament Greek was the German work of Friedrich Blass, especially as revised by Albert Debrunner, and later translated by Robert Funk (BDF) (1961).

Other Grammatical Study of Biblical Greek

The University of Chicago Press, which had undertaken the publishing of a translation of Walter Bauer's Lexicon of the Greek New Testament (BAGD) agreed that a rendering of Blass-Debrunner into English would make an ideal companion volume. Robert Funk, whose dissertation on the syntax of the Greek article displayed in-depth acquaintance with modern linguistic developments, proved eminently qualified for the assignment, which was to involve some revision of the German grammar, especially to overcome vestiges of the parochialism that it shared with many continental scientific works (BDF, 1961, xiii-xiv). In his preface to the translation of Blass-Debrunner, Funk explains why a fresh work was not feasible at the time: "The choice of Blass-Debrunner as the vehicle for an advanced grammar in English was obvious once it had been determined that a wholly new work was not a practical option; for such a work, if undertaken afresh, would be many years in the making and it is not at all certain that the present situation in philological and NT studies would support such an undertaking" (xiii).[50] The passage of a decade would reveal that Funk was neither indolent nor negligent of ultimate responsibility to the scholarly world.

With Americans' need for a concise advanced grammar in their own language satisfied, Funk could proceed to find a pedagogical outlet for his increasing interest in basic hermeneutical inquiry. There was no dearth of beginners grammars of NT. The bridgework — that was the challenge. Robertson and Davis thought they had solved it with their *Shorter Grammar*. In terms of practical experience it was no solution. Some beginners could profit from features in the intermediate grammar, but it was awkward to juggle two books. Funk's resolution of the problem is clearly exhibited in the title of his own work: *A Beginning-Intermediate Grammar of Hellenistic Greek* (Funk, 1973). The title is to some extent a misnomer, for this Grammar introduces the student to the more restricted usage of the New Testament and the Apostolic Fathers, with emphasis on the New Testament. Presumably the title was designed to ensure reception of the study of New Testament Greek within non-sectarian precincts. Be that as it may, this *Grammar* incorporates major linguistic advances. What Eugene Nida and others were endeavoring to tell translators is here applied to the learning of a language whose basic

[50] The dearth was chronic. In 1938 Clarence Craig reported that he had found only two articles on grammatical problems in seven journals for the years 1932–37.

structures are exhibited without entombment in grammarian's graveyards.[51] And flexibility is a prime feature of this highly instructive pedagogical instrument.

Corresponding to Goodwin's work on moods and tenses is Ernest Burton's *Syntax of the Moods and Tenses in New Testament Greek* ([1888] 1898).[52] In contrast to historical grammar, which deals with development of form and function through the various periods of the history of a language, Burton's work specializes in exegetical grammar, which "takes the forms as it finds them, and defines the functions which at a given period each form discharged, and does this from the point of view of the interpreter, for the purpose of enabling him to reproduce the thought conveyed by the form" (2). Burton's disclaimer of emphasis on historical aspects does not mean that he ignores historical features. His frequent comparisons of classical and New Testament usage, for example, contribute to appreciation of nuances that might otherwise escape the student. Also helpful are Burton's numerous illustrations of English usage to clarify points under discussion. Some estimate of the esteem in which Burton's work is to be held can be garnered from Ernest Colwell's lament that "philological expertise died with Burton."[53] Colwell is of course well known for his study (1933), now known as Colwell's Rule, on the use of the article with predicate nouns.[54]

A degree of exegetical befuddlement could be dissipated were more attention paid to the factor of colloquial syntax in both classical and New Testament documents. Caleb Harding made a forceful plea in 1925 in an essay entitled "Greek Grammar Illustrated from the Morning Newspaper"[55]

---

[51] See, e.g. Nida, 1964 and 1969.

[52] Burton's *Syntax* first appeared in pamphlet form (44 pages) and was printed for private circulation, in 1888. A second and enlarged edition was published in 1893. The third edition corrects errors that came to Burton's attention and makes a "few alterations of statement which the use of the book" convinced him were "desirable" (Burton, 1898:viii). Burton's keen knowledge of syntax is further apparent in his discussion "Syntax of the Article," in *Notes on New Testament Grammar* (Chicago, 1904), which stimulated Arthur Wakefield Slaten's *Qualitative Nouns in the Pauline Epistles and Their Translation in the Revised Version* (Historical and Linguistic Studies, 2d series, 4 (Chicago: University of Chicago, 1918). On the use of the article in the NT, see also Colwell, 1933.

[53] Funk, 1976:18. A reprint of Burton's work was published in Edinburgh, 1955, but is less up to date than Johannes de Zwaan's Dutch translation and revision, *Syntaxis der Wijzen en Tijden in het Grieksche Nieuwe Testament* (Harlem, 1906), which adds much explanatory material, more references to classical usage, and takes account of papyrological data.

[54] On Colwell's "rule," see McGaughy, 1970:72–79. James Denney had called attention to the problem of rendering John 1:1 with "Jesus is God" (*Letters of Principal James Denney to W. Robertson Nicoll 1893–1917* [London: Hodder and Stoughton, preface dated 1 October 1920] 121).

[55] Caleb R. Harding, "Greek Grammar Illustrated from the Morning Newspaper," *PAPA* 56 (1925) xxxiv.

and reinforced related observations expressed a decade earlier by Paul Shorey (1916).[56]

Intermediate and Introductory Grammars of the New Testament

One of the offshoots of Robertson's preparation for his main work was *A Short Grammar of the Greek New Testament* (Robertson, 1908). This grammar was designed to serve as a bridge between grammars for beginners in the study of New Testament Greek and the large grammar that was in production. So successfully did it do its work that it quickly found its way into Italian in 1910; French and German in 1911;[57] and Dutch in 1912. A ninth edition (Robertson and Davis, 1931) incorporated colleague W. H. Davis' revision of the section on Accidence.[58] In accord with developments at the end of the nineteenth century, Davis bracketed forms not actually used in the New Testament.[59] This eminently sane and merciful decision endorsed other philologists' complaints about loading students down with philological baggage that has no actual literary existence.

During graduate study at Johns Hopkins University, in 1901, a student named John Gresham Machen came to appreciate Gildersleeve's distinctive personality and breadth of philological scholarship. A few years later, while serving as instructor at Princeton Seminary, Machen showed that he had absorbed some of his illustrious teacher's passion for Greek grammar. While struggling with the pedagogical deficiencies in John Homer Huddilston's *Essentials of New Testament Greek* (New York:Macmillan, 1895), Machen determined to write his own grammar, which appeared in 1923.[60] Intended primarily for students without any knowledge of Greek, this grammar concentrates on New Testament usage without reference to Attic prose. Participial usage, a dominant Greek phenomenon, is broached at the eighteenth of thirty-five lessons. Exercises include Greek and English sentences, which are for the most part not taken verbatim from the New Testament. Whether

---

[56] In *Republic* 10.598c, Shorey notes, Plato writes *technōn* instead of *technitōn*. In Sophokles, *Philoktetes* 1057, Odysseus says to Philoktetes, " 'We don't need you with the bow, for we have Teucer, a master of this art.' " A bit of illogicality, avers Shorey, as in a guest's reply to a waiter's question, "How do you want your eggs?" "Two fried eggs, one fried on one side and the other on the other." (Shorey, 1916:207–8). For an additional example from Plato, see Rose, 1938. Students of the New Testament might well begin their exploration with the first chapter of John.

[57] The German edition, edited by Hermann Stocks (Leipzig: Hinrichs, 1911) was a revision rather than a translation and incorporated quotations from the LXX (including the Apocrypha, Josephus, and other writings in the Koine).

[58] A tenth edition appeared in 1933 with corrections of *errata* "made in the text where practicable" and a list of *corrigenda*.

[59] See, for example, Lane and Morgan, 1898.

[60] See Ned B. Stonehouse, *J. Gresham Machen: A Biographical Memoir* (Grand Rapids: Eerdmans, 1954) 174.

Machen's rationale—students' alleged intimate acquaintance with the English Bible—still applies is subject to debate.

Efforts to meet the challenge of students' various philological backgrounds did not slacken. *A Manual Grammar of the Greek New Testament*, by Harvey Dana and Julius Mantey (1927) whose pages exhale Robertson's inspiration, endeavors to grapple with the "average" student's need for "an accurate and comprehensive compendium."[61]

Signalling developments in linguistics is *The Language of the New Testament*, by Eugene Goetchius (1965), who uses linguistic analysis to help beginners acquire a knowledge of NT Greek in sixty lessons. Emphasis is placed on recognition of basic differences in the structures of Greek and English. Funk's three-volume work cited above expands on the linguistic principles.

Sakae Kubo's *A Beginner's New Testament Greek Grammar* (1979) takes college students through 123 lessons. The first fifty-three present grammar, and the reading of John begins with lesson fifty-four. James Walther (1966) used the same gospel for inductive study of New Testament Greek. Adopting a similar approach for beginners, William LaSor, assisted by Peter Hintzoglou and Eric Jacobsen, centered on the Book of Acts (1973).[62]

Under no illusions as to the amount of time spent by ministers in the use of a Greek New Testament, and fully aware that knowledge of English grammar is an endangered species, Ernest Colwell and Ernest Tune (1965) collaborated in a record-breaking minimalist production: *A Beginner's Reader-Grammar for New Testament Greek*. Immediately after brief exposure to the alphabet and the pronunciation of Greek words, students look at biblical texts and proceed to develop skills in tracing a word they encounter to its appropriate lexical entry. A syntactic morphological presentation facilitates the process.

Generous exposure to New Testament examples of syntactical usage is available in Carlton Winsbey's *Syntax of New Testament Greek* (1979).

Latin Grammar

As did their contemporaries in connection with the Greek language, mid-nineteenth century grammars of Latin began to show signs of independence from European domination. An anonymous reviewer noted in 1864 that *A Latin Grammar for Schools and Colleges*, by Albert Harkness (1864)[63] was no mere reflection of German work, and would dislodge the

---

[61] Mantey (1951) had a strong conviction that *eis* was at times used causally in the New Testament. Marcus (1951) corrected him on alleged examples in non-biblical Greek.

[62] Vol. 2 contains the Grammar, and vol. 1 reading lessons keyed to the Grammar.

[63] See *North American Review* 99 (1864) 617–19.

manual of Andrews and Stoddard.[64] One of the virtues of the book is the attention paid to syntax.

When fire destroyed, along with the plates, much of the edition of Gustavus Fischer's *Latin Grammar* (1876) many potential consumers of this product were deprived of the fruits of the author's dedicated effort to assist students to understand what was actually *happening* as they moved from one grammatical phenomenon to another. Fischer, who resigned his chair of Latin at Rutgers University to devote full time to the production of the *Grammar*, aimed at having students not merely think in Latin, but to think grammatically. The *Grammar* was designed to meet the needs of both beginning and advanced students. The First Part is specifically directed to study in preparatory and grammar schools. Part Two was designed to meet the needs of "higher college courses."

Attempts at the end of the nineteenth century and in the early decades of the twentieth to revive interest in Latin found partial expression in production of a variety of grammars. Prodded into pedagogical ingenuity by the constant erosion of interest in the classics, a number of teachers of Latin approached publishers with the latest antidote to cultural blight. So numerous were the productions that their recognition would require a monograph. But there were four that put in an especially strong bid for sustained attention.

In 1872, Joseph Henry Allen and James Greenough developed a Grammar founded on comparative theory, with emphasis on inflection by stem.[65] The book was an immediate success and went through numerous revisions. A revised edition was published in 1877 with slight alteration of title.[66] A further change of title was made in 1889, when the book was named *Allen and Greenough's Latin Grammar for Schools and Colleges, Founded on Comparative Grammar.*[67] Professor Greenough projected further revisions, which were completed by George Kittredge, Albert Howard, and Benjamin D'Ooge. The title now read: *Allen and Greenough's New Latin Grammar for Schools and Colleges, Founded on Comparative Grammar* (Boston: Ginn, 1903). In acordance with general practice, the editors include a set of

---

[64] The 18th ed. of Ethan Allen Andrews and Solomon Stoddard, *A Grammar of the Latin Language for the Use of Schools and Colleges,* appeared in 1849, with an advertisement lamenting the death of Stoddard.

[65] Greenough's co-editor is not to be confused with William F. Allen, who was co-editor with Joseph H. Allen of *Manual of Latin Grammar,* which appeared in 1868 (Boston: Edwin Ginn, Woolworth, Ainsworth, 1868) and was reviewed in *The New Englander* 28 (1869), with the observation that it was singularly deficient in clarity and quality. The establishment of *HSCP* owed much to Greenough's efforts; see Kittredge, 1903.

[66] J. H. Allen and J. B. Greenough, *A Latin Grammar, Founded on Comparative Grammar,* rev. ed. (Boston: Ginn and Heath, 1877).

[67] The work of revision for this edition was done by Greenough, assisted by George L. Kittredge.

"Important Rules of Syntax," ninety-one in number.[68]

To meet the needs of high school pupils and college undergraduates for a resource grammar less technical than Allen-Greenough, D'Ooge wrote *Concise Latin Grammar* (Boston: Ginn, 1921). A similar resource grammar, composed to guide students through their college courses, was designed earlier by Harry Edwin Burton (1911).

Despite the excellencies of Allen-Greenough, the touch of Gildersleeve was enough to ensure the durability of what became known as *Gildersleeve's Latin Grammar*, which came out in a third edition in 1894, co-edited by Gonzales Lodge, and enjoyed numerous reprintings. Gildersleeve concentrated on syntax for this edition. Lodge was responsible for nearly everything else that pertained to the history of usage. But for all deviations from the theory of the old grammar they bore joint responsibility, and until Lane's grammar appeared their work was the only American production that in Sihler's (1902) judgment could be called scientific. The brief summary definitions of what constitutes, for example, the "genitive," and the 138 "Principal Rules of Syntax" (pp. 437–44) represent but a fraction of the power of this *Grammar* to attract the interest of advanced students of Latin.[69]

Prudent measuring of life's short taper prompted George Lane to request Morris Morgan to complete about 120 pages that remained in first draft form for a projected resource grammar. Lane died on 30 June 1897, and Morgan brought the work to press under the title, *A Latin Grammar for Schools and Colleges* (1898). Lane endorsed a developing policy of admitting no form in the "principal parts" unless it was actually represented in the authors.[70] Under the editorship of Morgan, a revised edition of Lane's Grammar appeared in 1903. Hanns Oertel, convinced that phonology should play a subordinate role in school grammars, contributed revision material for the chapter on "Sound" (paragraphs 16–179).[71]

A working textbook for high school students was certain to find a warm welcome at the turn of the twentieth century, and William Hale and Carl Buck were confident that they had the answer in *A Latin Grammar* (1903), which, they emphasize, does not purchase the historical aspect of Latin at the expense of the descriptive. A few years after the publication of this *Grammar*, Hale (1906) delivered a paper entitled, "A Century of Metaphysical Syntax" before the Congress of Arts and Science, held in 1904 at St. Louis,

---

[68] D'Ooge emphasized development of a proper regard for Latin word order in his own *Latin for Beginners* (Boston: Ginn, 1909). Exercises in Latin and in English are there associated with each lesson.

[69] Gildersleeve's earlier *A Latin Grammar* appears to have been first published in 1867 and revised in 1872.

[70] Morgan accepted responsibility for the polishing of Lane and Morgan, 303–73, 387–436.

[71] A reprint of the revised edition of 1903 was published in New York by the Greenwood Press (1968).

Missouri, and blew the whistle on the entrenched practice of classifying syntactical phenomena on the basis of Kantian categories of thought. Hale's ability to reduce the customary apprehension experienced by first-term high school students is well reflected in his *A First Latin Book* (1907). Teachers of any generation can profit from the consummate clarity of presentation in this book.

For decades, teachers of Latin tried everything but giving away trading stamps with each lesson in the textbook. Indeed, no group of learners outmatched classical students in receipt of pedagogical beneficence. Even the titles of grammars diminished in syllables, and Herbert Elmer's choice of the irreducible title *Latin Grammar* (1928) signalled simplicity itself. In keeping with Cornell University's tradition of bearing a large share of responsibility for perpetuation of an endangered species, he chastised numerous grammarians, not excluding Charles Bennett, for making life unnecessarily miserable for students of Latin. But Latin syntax is not quite so tractable as Elmer advertised it, and the Gildersleeve-Lodge, Allen-Greenough, and Hale-Buck grammars overpowered Elmer's reductionism.[72]

What Goodwin and Gildersleeve endeavored to do for Greek, Charles Bennett strove to accomplish for Latin in *Syntax of Early Latin* (Bennett 1910–14.) Paul Shorey evaluated this work as one of the important declarations of American independence from the dominance of German scholarship (1919:49).

Postscript

Even from what has been so briefly sketched here it is apparent that concern for the triumph of the life of the spirit over the deadness of the letter penetrates also the history of grammatical studies. Benjamin Wheeler, president of the University of California and author of a Strassburg dissertation on *Der griechische Nominalaccent* (1885), described the study of grammar at its worst: "Grammar is to the average healthy human being the driest and deathliest of all the disciplines. Except as it serves a temporary practical purpose of offering a first approach to the acquisition of a language, or of presenting to maturer study a convenient tentative and artificial classification of certain facts, it brings spiritual atrophy and death to him who gives and him who takes" (Wheeler 1899:462).[73] Gildersleeve replied that not even Boeckh "would have sanctioned the crusade against the feeble folk who insist on knowing what the letter means before they let themselves be carried away by the spirit" (1930:114).[74]

---

[72] See John A. Scott's (1930) critique.
[73] Bloomfield, 1888, deals in detail with Wheeler's views.
[74] See also Gildersleeve, 1902:1–2.

As exhibited by the foregoing exchange, there is at some depth level of the scientific impetus a generative force that surfaces periodically in a variety of dramatic encounters. Two primeval urges, diachronic and synchronic, appear to be dominant, and scarcely anywhere more apparent than in the ongoing production of grammatical works. Traditional descriptions of grammatical features struggle for survival in the face of periodic attacks such as the bombardment by Hermann Fraenkel of standard categorizations, in "Three Talks on Grammar" (1975).

Doctrines worth the name ought to have universal validity, but Fraenkel, in the spirit of Hale's blast at Kantian tyranny over grammar (1906), demonstrates that the validity of even basic axioms concerning the verb are subject to serious question. Fraenkel carries his heresy to the point of questioning the propriety of the nomenclature "third person," and calls Sanskrit, once considered doctrinally pure, in support of his contention.

As Fraenkel sees it, pseudorthodoxy conceives bad categories and brings to birth "pseudosingulars" and "pseudo-Active Voice" and all other grammatical shame and vice. One wonders, reading Fraenkel's strictures, how anyone manages at all to speak a language, but that is strictly a grammarian's viewpoint. Users of their own language do very well without the "rules," and they handle the multifarious irregularities with tremendous glee over the discomfiture of pedantic grammarians. In fact, avers Fraenkel, his simplified approach releases users of a language from the perdition of "manifold provisos and illogical exceptions, its underhand maneuvers, and papered-over pitfalls." For the benefit of the obdurate he adds these words of consolation: "The difficulty for us in switching to an unfamiliar theory is not in any complexity of what is to be learned afresh but in the task of unlearning what is all too firmly ingrained in our minds."

Just as Reimarus, Semler, Strauss, Baur and company found the amount of unsubstantiated viewpoints that centuries of recitation of doctrinaire shibboleth had heaped over the Bible an intolerable affront to minds intent on arriving at an accurate perspective of historical circumstances, so Fraenkel was appalled to discover that "more than 2000 years ago, grammatical theory and speculation took a wrong move, arming itself with one set formula or another, and as time went by, assuming the awesome powers of authoritative tradition, so as to succeed in messing things up thoroughly and for good." As though he were reciting problems of the Society of Biblical Literature or pleading for a return to the Apostolic *Zeitalter*, he went on to say: "Our task would be lightened immensely if we could start from a blank slate, a *tabula rasa*. Instead, we are burdened with the unpleasant labor of unlearning while we would prefer merely to learn. On our way, we shall be saddled with the business of some destructive criticism and some amount of unraveling gratuitous tangles" (Fraenkel, 1975:130.) But Fraenkel is no anarchist, and just before directing his aries toward pronominal bastions, he pleaded, with Pauline intonation, for an amicable resolution: "Let us then go to work and sift; let us sort out what seems true and useful and discard what was mistaken and is useless" (131).

The truce endures but for a moment. Fraenkel's rhetoric renews momentum. In opposition to "preposterous" pronominal theory, Fraenkel suggests a more inclusive category that would include also the "where" and "there" stuff of daily speech. To meet the categorical need he mints the word "luma," which has the scientific advantage of having had no meaning. (Something akin to the first words of St. John, "The Word was made Flesh," which must have sent linguistic shock waves through the Mediterranean world.) Aware of the spirit of Masada that permeates hardshell grammarians, Fraenkel adopts an irenic tone: "As you see, what I am explaining now is no absolute novelty, but was recognized by some people at least long ago. Only it has not permeated public consciousness; it has not been applied systematically, and has not yet percolated into 'popular grammar,' which persists, and is likely to persist for a rather indefinite amount of time, to believe in 'a pronoun standing for a noun' " (137).

How to account for nihilism is Fraenkel's final concern. As are the imprecatory psalms to theologians, so is the negative to grammarians. Theoretically it ought not exist, for when we use one we stare at a black and empty hole" (143). As Duns Scotus put it in another context, the problem with theology is that there is no subject matter. Thanks to Fraenkel's willingness to journey forth, dreadful Hades gives up some of its prey, and his final conclusion is certain to provoke inquiry as to its ultimate validity: "A final verb form never takes an *un*-prefix as long as that prefix expresses a denial," such as in the hypothetical expression *unsaw*. What Fraenkel tacitly generates here is, that a poet may say, "I uncame, I unsaw, I unconquered," but Caesar will not be undone. All which things are, of course, an allegory.[75]

---

[75] Critics anxious for the fray will think of *unlocked, uncovered, undid,* and the like, but these terms do not refer to the failure of an event to materialize. They do not deny that the original event took place but merely indicate the reversal of a process. One can erase a person from one's mind, but one cannot undo, except in a transferred sense, the seeing of the person. Yet precisely this role of metaphor and its manifestations in the alteration of the normal contours of language constitutes a major problem.

7

EPIGRAPHY

Historians since the days of Herodotos have, except for periodic eclipses, recognized the value of epigraphy as a fruitful source of enlightenment. To Philochoros, third century B.C.E., goes the honor of bringing together what may have been the first *Corpus Inscriptionum*.[1]

Odysseus had set a record for world traveling and remained instrumental in developing Greece's appetite for guide books. Delphi, at the beginning of the second century B.C.E., gained further renown under the pen of Polemon. An honorary citizen of Athens and of other states, Polemon indirectly encouraged tourist trade by writing about the Delphic treasures. But the most famous of the Baedekers was Pausanias. Scarcely a shrine in Greece was denied his curiosity-ridden eye. Inscriptions were an important source of information for him, and some of the monuments that epigraphists are able to read after him are found quite accurately copied in his *Description of Greece*. After Pausanias comes the first major eclipse, until Cola di Rienzi (1313–54) took the road to Rome, and Ciriaco de' Pizzicolli (1391–ca. 1455) to Greece, in search for inscriptions. But not until August Boeckh, of Germany, and his production of the *Corpus Inscriptionum Graecarum* did Greek epigraphy become a discipline in its own right.[2]

Because of their primary documentary character, epigraphs offer a generally reliable check on other ancient sources of information. If Pausanias receives high marks, Herodotos must settle for a little less. Herodotos is a better writer of the story of history than recorder of its bruta facta, according to O. Kimball Armayor (1978), who concludes from epigraphic data that the Father of History is not among our best authorities on Ancient East ethnography.

So beset with possibilities for falsification of history are the literary sources for the life of Alexander that increasing attention is being paid to epigraphic witness to his career. In *Alexander the Great and the Greeks*,

---

[1] Herodotos 5.77; on epigraphic interest in Antiquity, see Wilhelm Larfeld, *Handbuch der griechischen Epigraphik*, vol. 1 (Leizig: Reisland, 1907) 16–25.

[2] Cf. Grady, 1931. The third of Boeckh's four-volume effort (Berlin, 1825–77) was produced with the collaboration of J. Franz; the fourth by E. Curtius and A. Kirchhoff.

A. J. Heisserer (1980) endeavored to edit "the most accurate text for each fragment or stele, to determine as precisely as possible the right date for each inscription, and to arrive at the proper historical context from an analysis of the content of the inscriptions combined with the ancient literary sources." He states that "all surviving documents represent various types of communication between the king and the city-states, such as a treaty, a letter, a judicial injunction to be decreed by local law, or a direct order" (p. xi). Heisserer argues that Alexander began his reign with the intention of developing politico-legal relationships with the city-states, but gradually became more autocratic. Scrutiny of the inscriptions suggests that the literary sources do not appear to have had a "strong and direct relationship to archival records contemporary with the era itself" (237).

In the Beginning

It was said of Charles Norton of Harvard University, that "there was scarcely a worthy cause during his long life that did not elicit his sympathy" (Lord, 1947, 2). Owing to his zeal, The American School of Classical Studies at Athens, founded in 1881, opened on 2 October 1882, with admittance based on academic standing and without consideration of gender. The first director of the School (1882–83) was William Watson Goodwin, and among the first enrollees was John Sterrett, who had received his degree from the University of Munich. No American appreciated more than did Sterrett the importance of inscriptional evidence, and his indefatigable zeal in search for new material earned the esteem of the American School's governing board. His reports, "Inscriptions of Assos" and "Inscriptions of Tralleis" dominate the first volume of *Papers of the American School of Classical Studies at Athens, 1882–1883.* Among the inscriptions from Assos is a decree (no. 26) voted on the accession of Gaius in 37 C.E., in words that express traditional anticipation of a New Age. The second volume of the School's Papers (1883–84) incorporates Sterrett's "An Epigraphical Journey in Asia Minor," but publication was delayed until mid-1888 because of Sterrett's difficulty in understanding the Managing Committee's reluctance to accept for publication some of the immoderate language in which he had "denounced certain French scholars" (Lord: 17–18). This delay gave precedence in publication to the third volume of the School's Papers (1884–85).[3]

After the Parthenon with its Doric order, the Erechtheum receives just praise for its Ionic perfection. For knowledge of the history of this ornament of the Athenian Acropolis all students of architecture and epigraphy are most

---

[3] Vol. 3 of the Papers was published in the spring of 1884 and contains "The Wolfe Expedition to Asia Minor" (1–432) and "The Wolfe Expedition to Babylon" (433–48). The expedition was so named after Catherine Lorillard Wolfe, who defrayed the expenses. Inscriptions Nos. 339–42 published in vol. 3 of the Papers, are of interest for their reference to astragalomancy, which was much in vogue throughout southern Asia Minor.

of all indebted to the work initiated by Theodore W. Heermance, early director of the American School at Athens. Greek authorities entrusted with the
preservation of ancient monuments had adopted a plan for thorough
reconstruction of the North Portico of the Erechtheum, and in the autumn
of 1903 Heermance suggested to Professor James Wheeler, Chair of the
Managing Committee, that the government's plan offered an opportunity for
thorough architectural study of the structure. Heermance's request for
funding led to the appointment of Gorham Stevens as the first Fellow in
Architecture of the School. Stevens completed his study of the building in
July 1905, but the death of Heermance in September of the same year altered
plans for publication of the projected studies. World War I complicated
matters still further, and the ultimate publication, *The Erechtheum* (Paton,
1927), lists four names, whose work is represented in the book either by
virtue of pioneer research or editorial dexterity in the reworking and blending of other scholars' material. Besides the names of Stevens, Lacey Caskey,
Harold Fowler, and James Paton, who are cited on the title page, credit goes
to Bert Hill, Director of the School, for exercising his own critical and correc-
tive hand in the production of the volume.[4] The epigraphic showpiece of this
volume is the text of a block of white marble that was found in two pieces,
but without much loss of text.[5] The heading indicates that the main portion
of the inscription is a report (409–8 B.C.E.) made by the commissioners of
the temple. Nothing escaped their notice. Column by column, block by
block, they inform the People of Athens about the progress and the quality
of the work, what is finished, what remains to be done.[6]

Among the most distinguished alumni of the School in Athens (1920–22)
was Benjamin Dean Meritt, who became Professor at Princeton University's
Institute for Advanced Study in 1935. In his *Epigraphica Attica* (1940) Meritt
endeavored to show that the physical properties of a stone need to be taken
into consideration when studying inscriptions. William Ferguson baptized
the method "architectural epigraphy." According to Donald Bradeen and
Malcolm McGregor, editors of *PHOROS* (1974), a volume of tribute to Meritt,
"this book remains the best introduction for the ambitious epigraphist who
seeks guidance in method, as the titles of the chapters accurately promise:
Readings, Reconstruction, Lettering, Restoration" (Bradeen and McGregor,
1974: 6). In a vein related to the emphasis made by Meritt, Harold Hastings
(1912) called attention to the relation between inscriptions and sculptured
representations on pre-Roman tombstones of Attica.

Appropriate inventory of the philological contributions of American
epigraphic research would require considerably more space than can be
allotted in a survey of diverse scholarly activity. Only some of the chief sites,

---

[4] For information on the editorial process, see Paton 1927:vii-ix.
[5] The dimensions of the block are 1.08 m. high, 0.505 m. wide, 0.09 m. thick.
[6] On the inscription, see Paton, 283–84; text and translation, 286–97.

beginning with Asia Minor, can be visited. Bureaucracy and commemoration are among the principal topics. The journey will end with a visit to American repositories of epigraphic treasure.[7]

Sardis

Epigraphic remains at Sardis received principal attention from William Buckler and David Robinson in the seventh volume of *Sardis*, which contains, together with the inscriptions discovered at the ancient city during the American excavations of 1910–14 and 1922, all other inscriptions previously published from that site. These inscriptions permit tracing of the cultural and political affiliations of Sardis, which was a center of imperial cult. The earliest of the 231 inscriptions collected in the volume dates from the fifth century B.C.E. A finely preserved decree (No. 4), commemorates the faithful service rendered by a keeper of the king's treasury (ca. 155 B.C.E.). Number 8 is a collection of documents, including a letter of Augustus, about 1 July 5 B.C.E., to the Sardinians. Imperial cost-consciousness is the dominant note in no. 16, which conveys instructions on trimming the cost of gladiatorial shows. And no. 18 is a declaration by a guild of building artisans concerning mutual obligations of employers and employees. Interpreters of the Apocalypse ascribed to St. John can here find much to enrich their understanding of the Epistle to Sardis (*Sardis*, 1932). The Graeco-Lydian and Lydo-Aramaic inscriptions cited in volume six of *Sardis* (1916) clarify points of Lydian grammar and vocabulary. Buckler and Robinson provided earlier access to numerous inscriptions recorded in *Sardis* through articles in *AJA*.[8]

Dura-Europos

Dura-Europos gave up to persistent searchers an inventory of secrets long kept from epigraphists and papyrologists. Systematic exploration of the site began in 1927, with Yale University and the French Academy of Inscriptions and Letters cooperating in the effort. According to Yale's President James R. Angell, the University had chosen to invest in the effort at Dura a large part of the funds that the General Education Board had allotted to Yale for the promotion of humanistic studies.[9] The Yale report on Dura-Europos spans the years 1929–47. The very first volume (1929) is a preliminary report of the first season of excavations, conducted in the spring of 1928 by Yale University in association with the French Academy of Inscriptions and

---

[7] For further details on the various sites, see *Princeton Encyclopedia of Classical Sites*.

[8] See *AJA*, "Greek Inscriptions from Sardes," part 1, 16 (1912) 11–82; part 2, 17 (1913) 29–52; part 3, 17 (1913) 353–70; part 4, 18 (1914) 35–74; part 5, 18 (1914) 321–62. For bibliography on Sardis, see Hanfmann, 1983:xvii–xxvi.

[9] The French Academy of Inscriptions participated in the expedition. The Yale staff included Paul Baur, Alfred Bellinger, Clark Hopkins, Mikhail Rostovtzeff, and Charles Welles.

Letters and includes a remarkable set of inscriptions recorded on the Palmyrene gate in Greek, Latin, and Palmyrene. These proved of importance for establishing the date of the structure and the surrounding fortifications (*Dura-Europos*, 1929)[10] A preliminary report, by the same two editors, of the second season of work, October 1928 to April 1929, demonstrated the importance of even very small fragments for better understanding of details relating to the Roman occupation of the ancient city (*Dura-Europos*, 1931).

Of special interest to students of the history of religions is the mention of a deity named Zeus Betylos in the report of the fourth season of work (*Dura-Europos*, 1933). *Betylos*, say the editors, "is a Greek transcription of the Semitic compound *bethel*, that means *house of El*, and was used in ancient Semitic worship to describe the cult-stone in which El was considered as being present."[11]

Inscriptions from the Dura Mithraeum found in the seventh and eighth seasons of work at Dura-Europos give some idea of the type of menu enjoyed there by banqueters of sorts. Among the numerous documents in the volume is a long parchment in Greek concerning division of property acquired by inheritance (*Dura-Europos*, 1939, 427–32).

After Mithras, Dolichenus was the most popular deity in large areas of the Near East, with a cult that had penetrated deeply the Roman army in the second and third centuries of our era. Part Three of the Dura-Europos report for 1935–36 includes inscriptions found in the Palace and in the Dolicheneum. Documents in the latter refer to Jupiter and Zeus as Dolichenus, who was the most popular of the Oriental deities next to Mithras (*Dura-Europos*, 1952).[12]

Antioch

The very first document in the third volume of Princeton University's report of excavations at the Antioch located on the Orontes River is of

[10] *Dura Europos* (1929) includes a preface by James Agnell, source of the information cited above. Baur was Curator of Classical Archaeology in Yale University and his colleague, Rostovtzeff, was Professor of Ancient History and Classical Archaeology.

[11] *Dura-Europos*, 1933:69, No. 168. For the Greek inscriptions see Nos. 168–371, pp. 56–178. On 5 March 1933, in the course of the sixth season of work (see *Dura-Europos*, 1936), fourteen fragmentary lines of the hitherto unknown Greek text of Tatian's *Diatessaron* bridged sixteen centuries and were destined to give the quietus to some theories while generating others. Written on parchment, the fragment mentions Salome and relates that the wives of Jesus' followers beheld "the Crucified One," after which Joseph of Arimathea receives mention. Tatian's Diatessaron is ordinarily dated around 170 C.E.

[12] For the Palace inscriptions in *Dura-Europos*, 1952, see pp. 27–57; for the inscriptions in The Dolicheneum, pp. 107–24. For reference to Jupiter and Zeus, see Nos. 970 (in Latin) and 971 (in Greek).

interest to students who desire further information on the industry of innkeeping in the ancient world (*Antioch On-the-Orontes*, 1941:83–115).[13]

Gerasa

Fallen into oblivion since the days of the Crusades, the ruins of ancient Gerasa regained the attention of the Western world in the first half of the nineteenth century, chiefly through descriptions of travels to the site by Ulrich Setzen, J. L. Burckhardt, J. S. Buckingham, and others. After their publications, numerous conservation efforts were undertaken, and from 1928–34 Yale University and the British School of Archaeology sponsored a joint expedition. The American director was Benjamin Bacon, who had become interested in the site as the result of a visit made in 1906 while he was director of the American School of Oriental Research in Jerusalem. In charge of field operations was J. W. Crawford, Director of the British School.

As editor of *Gerasa: City of the Decapolis*, Carl Kraeling (1938) drew on the expertise of numerous colleagues to present the report of the excavations in historical perspective. Among the contributors are William F. Stinespring, Clarence Fisher, Albert Detweiler, Chester McCown, Charles Welles, Alfred Bellinger, and Paul Baur. The dominant feature of the volume is Welles's edition and discussion of a complete corpus of all texts from Gerasa known at the time. Cited in two parts, the texts cover the period from Tiberius to Constantine, and from Julian to the city's demise. The word *theatrizō* appears in one of the most extensive inscriptions (No. 192) found at Gerasa. Its presence in this agonistic document, inscribed in honor of Titus Flavius Gerrenus, president of the annual contest, prompted Henry Cadbury (1930) to declassify the word as a New Testament hapaxlegomenon.

Roman Administrative Policy

Ancient Mediterranean civic life offers an unceasingly fertile field for study, nourished as it is by a constant flow of epigraphic information. A major contribution to the subject of Rome's attitude toward the provinces, including those of Asia Minor, is *Municipal Administration in the Roman Empire* by Frank Abbott, noted for his research in Roman politics and history, and Allan Johnson, recognized for his Greek epigraphic acumen (Abbott and Johnson, 1926). The authors first discuss the differences in status of various tributary cities, the development of Roman policy towards them, and the circumstances that led to their decline and ultimately to the decline of the Roman

---

[13] Inscription No. 111, pp. 83–84, includes what appears to be an innkeeper's greeting. The editor's commentary includes literature on innkeeping. Princeton's excavations at Antioch were begun in 1932 by George W. Elderkin and Richard Stillwell, under the general supervision of Charles Rufus Morey; see "A Community of Scholars," by Taylor, 1947:42–43. See also C. R. Morey, *The Excavations of Antioch-on the-Orontes* (Baltimore: Museum of Art, 1937).

Empire. The second major portion consists of municipal documents in Greek and Latin from Italy and the provinces, along with numerous items that derive from Egypt. From the bibliographical entries it is apparent that Abbott and Johnson eschewed the insularity so characteristic of numerous European publications in their time. David Magie mined their resources for his masterful two-volume treatise, *Roman Rule in Asia Minor to the End of the Third Century after Christ* (Magie, 1950).[14]

Hellenistic ruins are the source of numerous pieces of official correspondence that were chiseled on stone. In 1934 the French epigraphist Louis Robert suggested that scholars cease production of general selections of sylloge and concentrate on publication of corpora relating to a specific field.[15] Before Robert's ink was dry, Charles Welles had already put away the pen with which he wrote *Royal Correspondence in the Hellenistic Period* (1934). In this work, a standard practically from the day of its publication, Welles gives text and translation of seventy-five pieces of imperial correspondence, from Antigonos (311 B.C.E.) to Artaban III (21 C.E.). An introduction of one hundred pages discusses the use of letters in Hellenistic diplomacy, their composition, style, and language. An appendix discusses in alphabetical order a number of words that call for special exegetical attention in these documents. Welles has several items not included by F. Schroeter in his discussion of letters,[16] such as the letter (no. 45) of Seleukos IV to Seleukia, in Pieria; and no. 75, of Artabanos III of Parthia, to Susa.[17]

Greece

Bureaucratic, calendaric, and economic data are prime epigraphic evidence that have contributed so much to the detailed knowledge historians now possess concerning ancient Hellas. Of special significance is the role played by discovery of the names of archons for precision in chronology.

Kydenor, an Athenian Archon of 243–42 B.C.E, probably never meant to cause trouble, least of all to earn a distinguished place in history as disturber of the peace. In 1923 the first inscription to bear his name shook the foundations of Athenian epigraphicdom. All archon lists compiled up to 1923, including the one by William Ferguson (1899),[18] were out of alignment,

[14] For documentation of Roman policy in proconsular Africa, see Nostrand, 1925.

[15] Louis Robert, in *Revue de Philologie* 8 (1934) 406–8.

[16] F. Schroeter, *De Regum Hellenisticorum Epistulis in Lapidibus Servatis Quaestiones Stilisticae* (Dissertation, Leipzig, 1931).

[17] Letter No. 45 first appeared for publication in *Syria* 13 (1932) 255–58. No. 75 was discovered in the winter of 1931–32, and is now in the Louvre Museum; it was first edited by Franz Cumont, *Comptes Rendu de l'Academie des Inscr. et Belles-Lettres* (Paris, 1931:238–59). On Welles's personal qualities, see memorial notice by Anna Swiderek, *JJP* (1974) 7–8, and the editorial notice in *BASP* 6 (December 1969) 60. For bibliography of Welles's work, see Rigsby, 1966.

[18] See also W. Ferguson, 1907.

and a second inscription with his name, discovered in 1938, was only part of a substantial increase in epigraphic evidence that, amid the welter of conflicting opinions, necessitated overhaul of eight years of work intervening between William Dinsmoor's *The Archons of Athens in the Hellenistic Age* (1931), which was dedicated to Ferguson, and Dinsmoor's *The Athenian Archon List in the Light of Recent Discoveries* (Dinsmoor, 1939.) In *The Archons of Athens in the Hellenistic Age* Dinsmoor made what Ferguson termed a "sustained effort" to determine the calendar that was actually in use at Athens during the 323 years between the epoch-making reform of Meton in 432 B.C.E. and the completion of his seventeenth cycle in 109 B.C.E. (Ferguson, 1932, 3). Besides Ferguson, who laid to heart the dictum *dies diem docet* and through his methods exercised an enduring fascination on Dinsmoor, the only other American to engage in serious investigation of the subject was Allan Johnson.

In the preface to his publication of 1939, Dinsmoor acknowledges the debt he owed to Benjamin D. Meritt. After securing his degree from Princeton University, Meritt "began his epigraphic life" at The American School of Classical Studies at Athens (1920–22), where he became associated with Allen West. The two scholars focused on documents relating to the Athenian Empire. In 1928 Meritt published a study that was to be basic for all subsequent work on the Athenian calendar. Entitled *The Athenian Calendar in the Fifth Century Based on a Study of the Detailed Accounts of Money Borrowed by the Athenian State, I.G. I 324* (Cambridge: Harvard University, 1928), the book made such a profound impression that at the age of 30 Meritt became a full professor at the University of Michigan. Shortly thereafter, Meritt accepted responsibility for the publication of epigraphic materials found in the excavations of the Athenian Agora that were conducted by the American School of Classical Studies in 1931 (Meritt, 1933).[19]

Dinsmoor praised Meritt's "unfailing zeal and generosity" that had kept Dinsmoor in touch with epigraphic developments in the Agora of Athens, with the result that Dinsmoor was able to adjust his own exposition to new discoveries.[20] Ferguson had aired his further investigations of Athenian chronology in *Athenian Tribal Cycles in the Hellenistic Age* (1932). Meritt, together with William Pritchett, pursued the matter in *The Chronology of Hellenistic Athens* (1940). The greater part of this book deals with the years before 200 B.C.E. and features information about tribal cycles gathered from

---

[19] The ten numbered items in Meritt (1933) range from the 6th century B.C.E. (a small dedicatory piece) to 2d C.E. (a letter to Athens from the joint emperors Marcus Aurelius and Commodus). Of interest to epistolographers is the comparatively elaborate greeting in this latter document (No. 10). The remaining documents are chiefly decretal, in honor of ephebes, taxiarchs, and official boards.

[20] Excavations of the ancient Athenian Agora were begun in 1930 with a dig planned by T. Leslie Shear of Princeton.

the inventories of the priests of Asklepios. Carefully protecting the scholarly world from rash assumptions that are frequently a hotbed for conclusions that must inevitably wilt under the heat of future-dispensed fact, the authors admit that they remain in the dark about a phenomenon of "double-dating" by civil months in the second century, and they refuse to pontificate about a break in the cycle, which in their judgment can be firmly established for the year 247, but must await further study for elucidation. The authors also express the hope that any strictures concerning their findings might not be the product of thetical disagreement but be controlled by appeal to original sources, especially as found "in *Hesperia* and the Berlin *Corpus*." They further state, with Shoreyan accent, that they have endeavored to avoid provinciality, but German publications have "frequently" been "of such character that any discussion of views now long untenable would seem to give them greater importance than they deserve." Especially do they lament Kircher's persistent refusal to see a lambda instead of an alpha, or less probably delta, as the initial letter of the secretary's demotic in the year of Diomedon, with the result that so much is made to depend on the "beginning with a false premise."[21]

The advantage of inscriptional material over so-called literary sources in calendaric discussion found renewed endorsement in Sterling Dow and Robert F. Healey's *A Sacred Calendar of Eleusis* (Dow and Healey, 1965). Literature, the editors observe in this study of IG 2.1363, affords insight into worshipers' feelings.[22] But inscriptions tell us more precisely what actually went on. Unfortunately they are less well known; and inscribed sacred calendars, or "piety in catalogue form," are among the least known of all.

Alan E. Samuel must have felt the spell of the contemporaneity, the factual precision, and the non-tendentious character of bureaucratic-calendaric lists, for he became a devoted partner in what Dinsmore once referred to as a budding popular pastime, and spent over forty-two pages in *Greek and Roman Chronology: Calendars and Years in Classical Antiquity* to provide his readers with a convenient means for determining locations of evidence for the Athenian archon list. Besides presenting developments in astronomical knowledge and its connection with calendaric theory, Samuel's book is an inviting source of information on Greek local calendars and lists of months, the multitudinous variety of whose names can wear down the hardiest of budding epigraphists (Samuel 1972).

---

[21] Meritt and Pritchett, 1940: Preface. The difficulty is pointed out in singular fashion by Robinson, who observed in connection with one of Calder's readings of a stone: "The break on the stone is a very old one and Calder probably mistook the restoration of the name in question for actually preserved letters" (1926:231). For further discussion of calendaric matters by Meritt, and especially his later debate with Pritchett, see Meritt (1964), who restates his commitment to the highest principles of scholarly inquiry (259–60).

[22] For the list of consular fasti, see Samuel: 256–76.

Monetary data are an integral element of research relating to bureaucracy, and Meritt, who had established himself as an authority in the field of ancient Greek fiscal documents, developed the point in *Athenian Financial Documents of the Fifth Century* (Meritt, 1932). In this work Meritt tried to drive home the lesson that evidence must be systematically established before the historian is privileged to use it. In his spare time Meritt had been engaged with Allen West in reconstructing the stele on which the Athenians had recorded the great assessment of the Empire undertaken in 425 B.C.E. (Meritt and West, 1934). Meritt considered his succeeding study, *Documents on Athenian Tribute* (1937), a preparatory work for a comprehensive study of the physical evidence for the history of the Athenian Empire.

So massive was the challenge that he associated himself after West's death in 1936 with Henry Wade-Gery and Malcolm McGregor in a long-range four-volume production program, under the title *The Athenian Tribute Lists* (Wade-Gery and McGregor, 1936). With the help of this work, which covers the period 454–406 B.C.E., one can follow the growth and decline of the Athenian Empire and learn something about its management from year to year.[23]

From the time of Kleisthenes, Athens was accustomed to expedite its official business through a committee of the whole whose members were known as the *prytaneis*. The *prytaneis* controlled the agenda for both the Council (*boulē*) and the Popular Assembly (*ekklēsia*). Sterling Dow (1937) put this political phenomenon under renewed scrutiny of epigraphic evidence in *Prytaneis*.

Michael B. Walbank does not appear to leave one stone unturned in his documentation of that venerable and civilized practice of Greek interstate relations known as proxeny (Walbank, 1978). *Proxenoi* served as hosts or intermediaries for foreigners visiting their city. Since each state had its own legal systems and cultic practices, strangers could find themselves in stressful situations. To break the barrier of alien status an influential person in Athens, for example, might offer services to visitors from Rhodes. Athens in turn would have friendly Rhodians who would render service to Athenians who came to Rhodes. In gratitude for the services rendered, the visitors on return to their city might encourage passage of a decree recognizing a patron as *proxenos* and benefactor of their city, with the proviso that said *proxenos* enjoy such rights as choice seating at the national contests, relief from imposts, and freedom from the customary bureaucratic harassment that a foreigner might experience. Walbank projects two volumes beyond this study

---

[23] The work by Wade-Gery and McGregor includes: Vol. 1, testimonies, 571–92; vol. 2, literary and inscriptional testimonies, 88–121; vol. 3, studies of the text and financial history of the Confederacy and Empire; vol. 4, general index, 1–134; a Greek index, 135–234; and a bibliography (235–78), which is practically a canon of epigraphical work, beginning with an item from London in the 19th century to a contribution by Meritt in 1953.

and therefore limits himself to presentation and discussion of ninety-four proxenies that survive from the fifth century prior to the collapse of the Athenian Empire at the end of the Second Peloponnesian War in 404 B.C.E. The second volume is to incorporate material relating to the fourth century, and a third is to include an analysis of the office of *proxenos* throughout its history as an Athenian institution, with a comparison of Athenian practice and that of other Greek states.

As one of the lecturers in the University of Cincinnati's series held in honor of Louis Taft Semple, a benefactor of the University, Meritt entered the debate that has waged over the genuineness of a decree of Themistokles ever since its discovery in Troizen in 1959 by Michael Jameson.[24] His lecture is entitled *Greek Historical Studies* (1962) and includes a translation of a portion of the Themistoklean text with a summary of the balance (Meritt, 1962: 22–23). An annotated bibliography on just this one inscription would constitute a sizeable monograph.[25] Meritt opts for genuineness, and biblical scholars who at every turn face a similar problem of determining authenticity will do well to review their own methodology in the light of Meritt's careful use of evidence in this lecture and in all his writings.

Land tenure in ancient Athens is the subject of a study entitled *Horoi*, by John van Antwerp Fine (1951). *Horos* stones served as boundary markers and were used in connection with leasing of property, or helped to publicize liens on real estate. The so-called mortgage stones functioned under the last category, and Fine edits thirty-five new specimens. Important information on artists and sculptors is contained in the "Archaeological Summary" by Antony Raubitschek and Lilian Jeffery in their study of dedications on the Acropolis.[26]

In addition to his other achievements, Benjamin Meritt made a significant contribution to our knowledge of Corinth with his edition of *Greek Inscriptions 1896–1927* (Meritt, 1931). To students of the history of the pronunciation of Greek, the Byzantine inscriptions in this volume are of special interest. A number of them come from the hands of illiterate persons who preserve in unconventional spelling the sounds they hear in the spoken language, such as *ukoumenēs* for *oikoumenēs* and *himas* for *hēmas*.[27] John Kent (1966) continued the work of Meritt and of Allen West (1931).

---

[24] See the editio princeps in *Hesperia* 29 (1960) 198–223, 418.

[25] For a starter, see Meritt, 1962:23 n. 30.

[26] See Raubitschek and Jeffery, 1949:479–525. They dedicated the work to Meritt.

[27] Excavations of Corinth were begun by the American School of Classical Studies at Athens in 1896 and were continued nearly every year until 1916, but no adequate provision was made for publication of the results. The School began again in 1925 to control the excavations under the hand of Director Bert Hodge Hill. Together with Richard Stillwell, then Assistant Director of the School, Harold Fowler brought out in 1932 the belated first volume of the *Corinth* series: *Introduction, Topography, Architecture*.

Numerous inscriptions relating to the healing ministrations at Corinth's Asklepieion are available in translation in Mabel Lang's *Cure and Cult in Ancient Corinth* (1977).

Because of its popularity as the central shrine of Greece, Delphi had no lack of inscriptions and at the turn of the 19th century became an epigraphist's paradise. In an endeavor to cover the history of Delphi's influence in the development of inter-Greek relations, Eleanor Grady (1931) incorporated the fruits of many epigraphists' labors in a Columbia University dissertation entitled *Epigraphic Sources of the Delphic Amphictyony.*[28]

Commemorative and other Epigraphs

A large proportion of epigraphs are commemorative, either in praise of the living or in memory of the dead. Most of those that fall in the class of epitaphs and frequently in the form of epigrams owe their origin to private devotion. Those that formulate public recognition of various manifestations of excellence in character or performance are ordinarily formulated as decrees and may emanate either from civic groups or private clubs and societies. Occasionally individuals may extol their own virtues.

Versification on stone received special attention from Frederic Allen, in volume four of *Papers of the American School of Classical Studies at Athens, 1885–1886.* Allen's discussion covers the period from the fourth to the second century B.C.E. Sixty years later, Paul Friedlander and Herbert Hoffleit (1948) covered the earliest period down to the Persian Wars. Epitaphs and funereal stelae or pillars offer a constant stimulation to scholarly inquiry. In a report of one of his earliest travels in Asia Minor, John Sterrett wrote, with special reference to inhabitants in the general vicinity of Iconium: "The people . . . seem to have had little interest in the affairs of the world, and spent their surplus energy in preparing tombs and epitaphs for themselves" (Sterrett, 1885:15). In 1933, James Oliver thought he had made a convincing case for his reconstruction of a monument that had been erected in honor of the valiant Greek warriors at Marathon. The two epigrams contained on it had, he argued, come one each from the hand of Simonides and Aischylos (Oliver, 1933). One of Germany's foremost epigraphists disagreed, but Oliver held his ground.[29]

Important not only to philologists but also to students of the evolution of Christian art are the better than two hundred plus stelae recovered by University of Michigan excavators working from February to April, 1935, at a site called Kom Abou Billou, in Egypt. At the suggestion of Arthur Boak, distinguished papyrologist, Finley Hooper studied the 194 stelae that went

---

[28] In her introduction (1–7) Grady succinctly sketches the history of epigaphic research, with special reference to Delphi.

[29] See especially Oliver, 1933: No. 11, pp. 480–94.

to the University's Kelsey Museum of Archaeology. Hooper determined that the stelae "belong to the last centuries of paganism in Egypt, centuries characterized by economic decline and artistic stagnation" and serve to bridge the mummy portraits of the first and second centuries and the Coptic period. In some respects they point ahead to the Christian art that followed (Hooper, 1961:1). Devotion to children, spouse, and friends is mentioned frequently.

To judge from inscriptions found in catacombs, Greek was the language preferred by Jews in Rome. Harry Leon (1960) cites a goodly number from Jean-Baptiste Frey, *Corpus Inscriptionum Iudaicarum.*

Of special interest for the study of Montanism are the epigraphs collected by Elsa Gibson (1978) in *The "Christians for Christians" Inscriptions of Phrygia.*

Used with caution, epitaphs can be a valuable source of vital statistics. On the basis of a study of 168 ages reported on stones from Kom Abou Billou, Hooper determined an average age of 32.88 at death, with a distribution of 28.49 for women and 36.89 for men, with scarcely any account taken of the infant mortality rate (Hooper, 1956). Two decades earlier, Bessie Richardson (1933) had explored the subject of old age as portrayed in Greek literature and inscriptions, with lines from Henry Longfellow's *Morituri Salutamus* framing her study:

> For age is opportunity no less
> Than youth itself, 'tho in another dress,
> And as the evening twilight fades away
> The sky is filled with stars, invisible by day.

Richardson examined the sepulchral inscriptions of 2022 persons, and in an appendix provided a catalogue of the evidence. Finley's study has the advantage of methodological concentration, but both his and Richardson's are victims of the undisciplined arbitrariness of fate that leaves the past with tempting ambiguity on the doorstep of the present. Richardson's labors simplified some of Richmond Lattimore's work of organization of thematic strains in Graeco-Roman epitaphs. His University of Illinois dissertation, *Ideas of Afterlife in the Latin Verse Inscriptions* (1935), led to the publication in 1942 of *Themes in Greek and Latin Epitaphs.* Lattimore manifests broad acquaintance with the secondary literature, but notes that William Hartke's inaugural piece, *"Sit tibi terra levis" formulae quae fuerint fata* (Bonn: Georgi), was not available to him.[30] On maledictions, a common theme in sepulchral epigraphs, one does well to consult Nock, 1941.

Most inscriptions record acknowledgment of male contributions to the body politic. Admittedly, Helen McClees assumed a challenging task when she investigated the subject of recognition from civic assemblies for public

---

[30] Lattimore, 1962:65 n. 237.

service rendered by women, under the title A *Study of Women in Attic Inscriptions* (McClees, 1920). Of special interest to biblical students is her conclusion that Christianity, at least as mediated by Asiatics, may have proved beneficial to the poor and to slaves, but actually lowered the quality of status enjoyed by women.[31]

Irene Ringwood pursued the matter of public recognition of women at Greek festivals. In her Columbia University dissertation, Ringwood endeavored to reconstruct from inscriptions a composite of the non-Attic festivals of the mainland and most of the islands that are adjacent. Athletic competitions at first dominated the contests, but the passage of time saw the inclusion of musical and dramatic performances, prosodia, eulogies of the emperor, bull fights, and horse and chariot racing. One of the most unusual prizes was a dish of honey and suet given to the winner in the Lacaonian Syrmaea Festival (Ringwood, 1927).

Since very little is available in English on the ancient Hellenistic custom of awarding crowns for distinguished service or outstanding performance of various kinds, the essay by George Hussey (1892), "Greek Sculptured Crowns and Crown Inscriptions," with tables of inscriptional evidence, continues to render service on the subject.[32]

Two Egoists

Opramoas

Standing peerless among financial wizards of antiquity is Opramoas, whose most productive period spanned the years 114–152 or 153. This tycoon from Lycia was determined to evade oblivion by covering the walls of his mausoleum with one of the longest inscriptions on record. Recorded are the numerous crowns and awards that he received for distinguished service; and some recital of his ultimate survival in the memory of humanity may serve as tribute to a voracious appetite for immortality that preserved so much for latter-day philology.

Credit for the discovery of his lengthy claim to fame goes to three Englishmen, Lieutenant Thomas Spratt, of the Mediterranean Hydrographical Survey; Edward Forbes, a naturalist of King's College, London; and a clergyperson, E. T. Daniell. The three sailed in 1842 on the surveying ship *Beacon*. All three were drafters and aimed to produce a monograph on the history, civil and natural, of Lycia. Spratt was to document the geographical data, Forbes was responsible for the natural history, and

[31] A representative collection of texts in translation is available in Lefkowitz and Fant, 1982, an amplification of their publication of 1977. See also Pomeroy, 1975.

[32] For the inscriptions, see Hussey, 1892:135–61. For bibliography on the subject of bestowal of crowns, see Danker, 1982:483 n. 163, and add Michael Blech, *Studien zum Kranz bei den Griechen* (Berlin: de Gruyter, 1982).

Daniell was to focus on antiquities and to work up the manuscript. In the spring of 1842 the explorers wrote in their journal:

> *April 10th.*—Yesterday and today have been spent among the ruins of Rhodiapolis, sketching and copying manuscripts. Among them is the longest that we have met with in Lycia; so long, that after giving as much time as we could spare to the task, all three of us dividing the labor, we could carry away not more than a third of it; It is carved on a monument standing in front of the theatre, and was apparently dedicated to a citizen in commemoration of his virtues and good services. The letters are well cut and well preserved, especially those on blocks which formed the basement.[33]

The scholarly world never saw their record of this long inscription. Daniell died of malaria at Adalia and the other two explorers had to be content with what they confessed was an "imperfect narrative" of their entire exploration in Lycia. The Rev. Mr. W. Hechler placed in *The London Times* of 2 August 1894 a request for further information concerning their discovery of the Opramoas inscription, but without success. Fortunately Samuel Birch had copied, albeit imperfectly, some of Daniell's material. Otto Benndorff used Birch's manuscript, now in the possession of the British Museum, for work on the inscription. Benndorff's editorial work was in turn put under contribution by E. Loewy, one of a team of Austrian scholars who in 1881 and 1882 investigated afresh the ruins of Lycia. When Loewy found the inscription it was in a heap. A pine tree soared high above the rubble of letters. It took him from the evening of 28 to 30 May 1882 to copy the incisions on thirty of the stones. On a second visit to the site, June 17–21 of the same year, Loewy worked with Eugene Petersen in copying Opramoas's record of his philanthropy, expressed on more than a hundred of the squared stones.[34]

The few references by American scholars in the first half of the twentieth century to this Rockefeller-Mellon-Carnegie of ancient history, who made a specialty out of *euergesia* or public philanthropy, made no impression on biblical scholars, nor on most classical students, whose chief source of information on ancient philanthropy is Seneca's work *On Benefits*. David Magie (1950) had called repeated attention to Opramoas in his *Roman Rule in Asia Minor to the End of the Third Century after Christ*, published in two volumes, one consisting of text and the other of notes.[35] In 1957 Jacob Larsen also extended an invitation to learn about this extraordinary gentleman and at the

[33] Quoted in Danker, 1982:104.

[34] Danker, 1982:104–5. Details concerning the loss of Daniell's material are here cited in the hope that some scholar may be alert to unexpected opportunity. Ancient inscriptions have been recovered from washboards in modern houses; and it is possible that Daniell's notes are either awaiting discovery or announcement thereof. For literature concerning this inscription, see pp. 104–6 and passim 141–51.

[35] For references to Opramoas, see Magie 1950:2, Index, s.v. "Opramoas."

same time develop more in-depth acquaintance with political and social realities of the Greco-Roman world. The invitation went largely unheeded, but the first translation in English of all that remains of Opramoas's own record of his entitlement to immortality, as recorded on the walls of his mausoleum in Rhodiapolis, may suggest to a larger percentage of American scholars the importance of the historical and cultural data in this unique document.[36] Apart from material for sociological study, especially significant are its contributions to prosopography and to knowledge of imperial rescripts, a species of document too often ignored by biblical scholars in discussions of epistolography.

Antiochos I of Kommagene

In the northern part of Syria lay what once was known as the district of Kommagene. Its reigning king at the time of the Battle of Tiranocerta was Antiochos I, a son of king Mithradates Kallinikos and Queen Laodike. Antiochos mastered the art of political survival in dealing with Lucullus, Pompey, and Antony, and aimed at historical survival by building an impressive mausoleum, inscribed with details for perpetual cultic observance. To double his chances for immortality, Antiochos had two copies recorded, one on the east side and the other on the west side of his burial structure.[37]

About the middle of the first century B.C.E. Antiochos's thirst for glory prompted him to chisel to his father's health. He repeated much of the former inscription on the mausoleum that Mithradates Kallinikos had built for himself, but with numerous additions and modifications that make his second inscription especially attractive to biblical scholars engaged in ascertaining more precisely the cultic and theological contexts within which Christianity developed. Ignored for centuries by practically everyone but the populace of Nemrud-Dagh, this second inscription elicited wide-spread attention after local residents had, in 1951, alerted Friedrich Karl Dorner, of Germany, to its existence. Antiochos was not so garrulous as Opramoas, but Doerner recognized that the extensive remains would require more investment of time and energy than he could muster at the moment. In 1953 he associated himself with an American epigraphist, Theresa Goell, and the two

---

[36] See Danker, 1982:110–51 for translation and commentary. For additional information on Opramoas published since Danker's *Benefactor*, see especially André Balland, *Fouilles de Xanthos VII. Inscriptions d'époque imperiale du Letoon* (Paris: Klincksieck, 1981) 173–224, with discussion of two newly-discovered texts, which may well have been composed by Opramoas himself.

[37] The *editio princeps* of the long inscription was edited by Karl Humann and Otto Puchstein, *Reisen in Kleinasien und Nordsyrien. Pt. 2: Reisen nach dem Nemrud-dagh, 1882–1883* (Berlin: Dietrich Reimer, 1890). For references to epigraphic corpora and secondary literature, see Danker, 1982:238.

published their findings in 1963 under the title *Arsameia Am Nymphaios* (Goell and Dorner, 1963).[38]

The first of Antiochos's two inscriptions prompted Eduard Norden to define its Attic style as "bacchantic dithyrambic prose."[39] He would, in all probability, have been even more impressed with the flights of rhetoric taken in the memorial to Antiochos's father. From such perspective of literary assessment at least one conclusion of a methodological nature can be drawn: The traditional classification of epigraphs into literary and non-literary texts scarcely does scientific justice to the variety of extant data. Who would trade a piece like this from Antiochos's memorial to his father for a comparable portion of lines from certain so-called "classical" authors who survive only because they happen to have written in Latin or in Greek but have not seen a translator in a hundred years?

> I, in accordance with the will of the Gods, have consecrated the sacred law and have had it engraved on inviolable monuments, and this law shall be binding and shall be held inviolable by all generations of humanity that unending time shall, through the lot of each, bring in succession to this land; for they must know how terrible is the avenging wrath of the royal *manes* and that it pursues impiety no less than it does negligence and arrogance; for when the law of consecrated heroes is despised it brings on penalties no prayers can redress. As for holy deeds, they are no burden to the doer, but impiety inexorably brings within its wake a load of misery. My voice proclaimed this law; its ratification came from the mind of the Gods.

Or this, concerning the impious?

> Pierced in his base heart, the root of his wicked life, by the unfailing arrows of Apollo and Herakles, let bitter gain possess him in the depths of his being that is so hateful of the good; and through the wrath of Hera let him discover how heavenly justice imposes the penalty that brooks no unrighteousness and undeterred by flattery renders its service as bitterest avenger of impious intention and struck by the lightning bolts of Zeus Oramasdes, let all his relations, who share his evil blood, and all his house, which defiles God's land by opening hospitable doors to impiety, let them all glow with hostile flame.[40]

Psalmists might approximate such awefully magnificent oaths. The Mayor of Casterbridge did not come close.

Amateurs and Museums

A few words need to be recorded in recognition of certain amateurs and benefactors, without whose efforts some of America's museums and seats of learning would not have been able to offer the kind of stimulation that

---

[38] See Danker, 1982: No. 42, for translation of the inscription.
[39] See Danker, 1982:237–8.
[40] The translations are taken from Danker, 1982: No. 42, lines 80–94 and 231–37.

arouses the curiosity and interest of budding scholars.

Among the treasures of the Brooklyn Museum are a number of classical inscriptions, many of which belong to what is known as the Wilbour Collection. Charles Edwin Wilbour, born at Little Compton, Rhode Island, in 1833, was known for his proficiency in Greek at Brown University. After joining the staff of the *New York Tribune* in 1854, he was admitted to the bar in 1859, but neither of these professional activities satisfied him so much as did the culture of ancient Egypt. Wilbour studied with Gaston Maspero in Paris, and nothing delighted him more than wintering on the Nile studying, writing, collecting inscriptions, papyri, ostraka, sculpture, and other objects. In a study of the Brooklyn Museum's epigraphic holdings, Kevin Herbert (1972) credits him with being "an especially able philologist," with "a sharp eye for the inscription that was linguistically unusual, historically important, or culturally significant"; and numerous items in the collection attest his careful judgment. So absorbed was Wilbour in his hobby that he never published his findings and left no instructions for the disposition of his notebooks and antiquities. After his death, Mrs. Wilbour arranged to have part of his possessions set aside for the Brooklyn Museum, and the heirs of the estate carried out her wishes. A famous papyrus of Ramesses V is now known as the Wilbour Papyrus. With the Wilbour Collection as a nucleus, the Brooklyn Museum experienced little difficulty in building an enviable collection of Egyptian antiquities.[41]

Boston's Museum of Fine Arts is worth a visit by biblical and classical students because of Edward Perry Warren's (1860–1928) interest in classical antiquities. Thanks to his efforts, Bowdoin College has one of the finest collections of ancient art in America. And thousands of ancient coins, known as the Wulfing Collection, were given in 1928 to Washington University by John Max Wulfing (1859–1929), a St. Louis businessperson.

At Berkeley, the University of California's Robert H. Lowlie Museum of Anthropology contains a substantial collection of classical antiquities, provided through the generosity of Phoebe Apperson Hearst. Of the inscriptions edited by Robert Smutny (1966), eighteen comprise a part of Hearst's contribution. Only 6 of the 21 items included in Smutny's text had been, so far as he knew, previously published.

The strong appeal that Egyptian and Classical antiquities held for the American public at the beginning of the twentieth century can be gauged from the fact that a popular work by Camden Cobern on archeology went into a second edition six months after its first publication (Cobern 1917). Cobern's book draws primarily from secondary sources and was designed

---

[41] Jean Capart (1936) edited Wilbour's correspondence. The astonishing extent of Wilbour's fascination with Egyptian antiquities can be gauged from William Cook's compilation (1924). For further data on Wilbour and other contributors to the cultural assets of America, see Herbert, 1972.

especially to meet the needs of Bible teachers and ministers. Unfortunately the author's unmethodical use of sources itself constituted a source of frustration to those among them who wished to investigate further the data submitted by Cobern.

Oddly, the popular interest in antiquities was not paralleled in the pages of *JBL*. And even as late as 1962, the *Interpreter's Dictionary of the Bible* carried only a few lines on Greek epigraphy in an article entitled "Inscriptions"; nor was the deficiency remedied in the supplementary volume published in 1976. The first article on epigraphy to appear in *JBL* was written by Warren Moulton (22 [1903] 195–200). William Hatch was the first to make use of ancient non-Christian and non-Jewish inscriptions (27 [1908] 134–46). And in his article "Erastus of Corinth," Henry Cadbury (1931) displays acquaintance with principal epigraphic publications and produces a model study for determination of social status; inscriptional material cited by Peter Landvogt, but long ignored by commentators and writers of Bible dictionaries, finds inclusion in this article.[42] Cadbury (1939) also reviewed Carl Kraeling's *Gerasa*.[43]

Special Studies

Studies of special aspects of vocabulary and grammar in inscriptions have appeared from time to time. Philologists have not hesitated to acknowledge indebtedness to Helen Searles (1898), author of *A Lexicographical Study of the Greek Inscriptions.* Searles had projected a Lexicon of the Greek dialect inscriptions, but as most scholars have discovered, the more one learns about the area of one's expertise, the greater is the possibility that neither time nor publisher will be impressed.[44] To avoid the possibility of extinction of her work, Searles decided on a preliminary paper and concentrated in her *Lexicographical Study* on new and rare words in Attic and other dialects. In some respects her study is, as she admits, similar to that of Stephanos Ath. Koumanoudes, *Synagogē lexeōn athesauristōn en tois hellēnikois lexiois* (Athens: Koromela, 1883), but she does not reject a term that is found in the *Thesaurus* or in the Liddell-Scott *Lexicon.* In this way she hopes to provide additional lexicographical help. Except for a few exceptions, she does not take account of material from Christian inscriptions, as Koumanoudes had done with Late Roman and Byzantine data.

---

[42] See also Cadbury, 1934; cf. 1 Cor 10:25.

[43] At the end of the century, various American scholars contributed to a series begun by The Ancient History Documentary Research Centre at Macquarie University, Australia. The first volume, *New Documents Illustrating Early Christianity: A Review of the Greek Inscriptions and Papyri Published in 1976*, by G. H. R. Horsley, was published by the Centre in 1981.

[44] Theophile Homolle, who delayed the publication of inscriptions from Delphi because of his desire to "study all the material himself," finally had to admit his limitations and obtained the assistance of younger French archeologists; see Grady, 1931:5–6.

One of the few American scholars to associate a primary study of inscriptions with interpretation of a selected field of diction in the New Testament is William Ferguson. His study, published in 1913, is entitled *The Legal and Governmental Terms Common to the Macedonian Greek Inscriptions and the New Testament.*

In 1905, Edith Claflin moved grammatical discussion of Greek dialects from a stress on morphology to firmer consideration of syntax with her publication of a Bryn Mawr dissertation, *The Syntax of the Boeotian Dialect Inscriptions.* About three decades later Columbia University encouraged Henry Standerwick to augment European work with *Etymological Studies in the Greek Dialect-inscriptions* (1932).

It is easy to lose one's way in the world of Greco-Roman bureaucracy. Carl Buck blocked at least one source of embarrassment, when he explained that in the case of treaties when the parties differ in native dialect, "the dialect employed is the one appropriate to that party in whose territory the text was found, so far as its provenance is actually known. That is, we have the home versions in the home dialect." As respects honorary decrees, only in a "few exceptional cases" is an honorary decree composed in the dialect of the recipient instead of in that of the issuing agent" (Buck, 1913).

As is apparent from *The Greek Dialects,* published in 1955, Buck was impressed with Searles's work discussed above. Buck's study of 1955 is a "complete revision and expansion" of his *Introduction to the Study of the Greek Dialects, published in 1910.*[45] A primary advantage of basing a study of dialects on inscriptions is the relative absence of corruptions or alterations that one encounters in copies of literary texts. Buck's book does not supersede Friedrich Bechtel's three-volume production[46] but, despite incorporation of less detail, adds material not found in Bechtel. Pages 181–334 of Buck (1955) present dialectical inscriptions.

Epigraphists have long ago beatified Buck for providing them with *A Reverse Index of the Greek Nouns and Adjectives* (Buck and Petersen, 1944). Among other functional features, this work assists scholars in reconstructing fragmentary texts and provides exhaustive material for the history of the formation of Greek nouns and adjectives. Unlike *Rückläufiges Wörterbuch der griechischen Sprache,*[47] Buck's work is not restricted to LSJM, and it includes material from inscriptions, papyri, grammarians, commentators,

---

[45] Ginn and Company supplied four and a half pages of "Corrections and Additions" to purchasers of Buck, 1910.

[46] F. Bechtel, *Die griechischen Dialekte,* 3 vols. (Berlin, 1921–24).

[47] Paul Kretschmer and Ernst Locker, *Rückläufiges Wörterbuch der griechischen Sprache* (Göttingen, Vandenhoeck & Ruprecht, 144; 2d ed., 1963). This German work is a list, with no indication of the position of words in the literature. Buck and Petersen, *Reverse Index,* was set in type in 1939. Petersen's death in the same year and delays in communication because of World War II prevented prompt publication.

patristic writers, scholia, glossaries, and Byzantine Greek. Its potential for probing of deep formal features in texts, including the New Testament, was not exploited for decades.

With expressions of thanks to Professors Duncan Fishwick, John Wilson, and Andy Dyck, epigraphist-grammarian Kweku Arku Garbrah (1977) sent out to the world *A Grammar of the Ionic Inscriptions from Erythrae: Phonology and Morphology*.[48]

David Magie provided researchers with a basic tool for identification of Greek equivalencies for Roman bureaucratic and cultic vocabulary, *De Romanorum iuris publici sacrique vocabulis sollemnibus in Graecum sermonem conversis* (Magie, 1905). One of the principal drawbacks in Magie's book is traceable to the linguistic orientation of his study. It is one thing to learn, as in Magie, that *tamias* is the correspondent of *quaestor*, that *kouaistor* is used as its transcription, and *zētētēs* as its translation; it is another to know which of the three is the standard term used by Greeks in both inscriptions and in formal literature. In this case, *tamias* is the regular word, *kouaistor* occurs in a few scattered inscriptions, and *zētētēs* is met only as a gloss in a lexicon. "Such information is not easy to find in Magie," writes Hugh Mason (1974) in *Greek Terms for Roman Institutions: A Lexicon and Analysis* (ix).

David Robinson and Edward Fluck (1937), in *A Study of the Greek Love-Names Including a Discussion of Paederasty and a Prosopographia*, feature discussion of the *kalos* inscriptions on Attic vases and on art other than vases.

The numerous data that have come to light since Konrad Meisterhans published his inaugural dissertation, *Grammatik der Attischen Inschriften* (Berlin: Weidmann, 1885),[49] encouraged Leslie Threatte to make available a fresh appraisal in what is most assuredly one of the most impressive American epigraphic grammatical discussions: *The Grammar of Attic Inscriptions*.[50]

Latin Inscriptions

Apart from works discussed above that include references to Latin inscriptions, there are a few that elicit attention for their special interest in the Roman tongue.

Lily Taylor (1912), whose dissertation work took her into a study of Latin inscriptions that led to her production of *The Cults of Ostia*, contributed much to the work that lay behind the production of *Latin Inscriptions*

[48] Garbrah's work is vol. 60 of *Beiträge zur klassischen Philologie*, and is based on H. Engelmann and R. Merkelbach, *Die Inschriften von Erythrai und Klazomenai*, 2 vols. (Bonn, 1972–73).

[49] Konrad Meisterhans, *Grammatik der Attischen Inschriften*, rev. ed. 1888., 3d rev. ed. 1900.

[50] Threatte pays due respect to an excellent contribution by a German scholar, W. Lademann, *De titulis atticis quaestiones orthographicae et grammaticae* (Dissertation, 1915). See also the essay by A. S. Henry, "Epigraphica," *Classical Quarterly*, n.s. 14, 2 (1964) 240–48.

1896–1926, edited by Allen West (1931). But other obligations precluded her hand in the preparation of the manuscript and she insisted that her name not appear on the title page. Hence the title page bears the name only of editor Allen West. Of special interest to the history of Roman bureaucracy is document 104, which makes reference to the office of the *argyrotamias,* previously unparalleled in Latin records, but known from Greek inscriptions. The *argyrotamias* was in charge of the productive funds of the community, collected rents and other charges, loaned money, kept appropriate records, and in other ways managed the endowments of the city. The practice of endowing municipalities increased in popularity at the end of the first century C.E. Inscription no. 81, together with its discussion (pages 63–66), is important for the history of the Corinthian Caesarea or Caesarian Games established in honor of Octavian after the Battle of Actium (30 B.C.E.).

Arthur and Joyce Gordon (1958–65) aided historians in their quest of more accurate chronology with the publication of *Album of Dated Latin Inscriptions,* covering the period from Augustus to Nerva. Each of the first three volumes consists of plates and text; the fourth contains indexes. An outgrowth of Part I of their study is *Contributions to the Palaeography of Latin Inscriptions* (1957), which marks an advance on the work of Emil Hubner in the nineteenth century and of the French scholars Jean Mallon and Robert Marichal in the mid-twentieth.

At the Seventh International Congress of Greek and Latin Epigraphy, 9–15 September 1977, James Frank Gilliam introduced the session "Epigraphie et armées" with a number of exhortations to the cohorts for more strenuous work on Roman military districts (Gilliam, 1979, 187–89). He called attention to "the lack of interest in the Roman period, or even parochial disdain, too often found now in archaeologists and archaeological societies active in the Near East." A matter like the recruitment of the army is important for understanding the general social history of the Roman Empire. He went on to sketch the basic business of epigaphists. "They are not interested merely in inscriptions, or in a restricted class of inscriptions. They are interested in problems, developments, institutions, and all the many aspects of antiquity for which inscriptions provide evidence, and their studies require a combination of all relevant and available materials" (189).

The city of Gubbio, Italy, was in ancient times called Iguvium. In 1444 nine bronze tablets were discovered. Two were taken to Venice in 1540, only to be lost; the others remained in Gubbio. There was no dearth of editions of these Tables, which were inscribed in the Umbrian dialect, but students lacked an authoritative English translation. James Poultney (1959) more than made up the deficiency with *The Bronze Tables of Iguvium.* In addition to their linguistic significance, these documents are eminently important for the study of pre-Roman cult. The lexicon in this work accounts for every instance of a word in the Tables. Carl Buck's *A Grammar of Oscan and*

Umbrian (Buck, [1904] 1928) naturally put the Tables under heavy contribution, for they are the primary source for knowledge of Umbrian.[51]

After the publication of his *"Keltika," being Prolegomena to a Study of the
Dialects of Ancient Gaul* (1944), Joshua Whatmough produced a grammar of
the dialects of ancient Gaul (Whatmough, 1963). In this grammar Whatmough included "Addenda" to the Prolegomena, stating that it was not his
aim to "bring up-to-date mere bibliography—that fetish of the timid and
incompetent compiler—but only matters of consequence" (ix). Whatmough's
work, which abounds in citation of inscriptions, contains a wealth of bibliographical detail and was gathered together in a massive posthumous publication: *The Dialects of Ancient Gaul: Prolegomena and Records of the Dialects*
(Whatmough, 1970).[52]

A little-known but pedagogically well constructed aid for understanding
the evolution of Latin is Wallace Lindsay's *Handbook of Latin Inscriptions*
(1897). For example, he cites a very old inscription (*CIL* 14.4123) and then
displays the classical Latin and the English equivalents:

> Manios med fefaked Numasioi
> Manius me fecit Numerio
> "Manius made me for Numerius."

Stephen Omeltchenko's (177) contribution to Latin phonology extends to the
study of quantity and vocalism in documents outside Italy.

In 1888, Charles Bennett, professor of historical theology at Garrett
Biblical Institute, Evanston, Illinois, stimulated interest in early Christian
epigraphy, both Greek and Latin, through his discussion of epitaphs and
graffiti, and of the symbols associated with them.[53] Shortly thereafter, James
Egbert (1896) endeavored to arouse further interest through an introductory
work on Latin inscriptions. His revision in 1923 contains a supplement,
which cites, among other items, collections of Christian inscriptions and
books on the language of inscriptions, with updating of numerous references
to secondary literature.

Epigraphic science boasts numerous examples of heroic devotion that
are deserving of acclaim, but few can claim more than George N. Olcott, who

---

[51] Buck (1928) is a new printing with brief additions and corrections of the first edition, *A
Grammar of Oscan and Umbrian, With a Collection of Inscriptions and a Glossary* (Boston: Ginn,
1904).

[52] Whatmough's *Prolegomena* and *The Dialects* are paginated separately, 1–85 and 1–1376
respectively.

[53] Bennett, 1888:247–71. Graydon Snyder (1985) takes no account of Bennett, but updates the
discussion with emphasis on social factors; see especially his chapter entitled "Inscriptions and
Graffiti," pp. 120–48. A graffito depicting a crucified ass was found in 1856 amid the ruins of the
Imperial Palace in Rome. Snyder's interpretation, pp. 27–28, of this graffito should be checked
against Bennett's (pp. 94–95). Bennett includes references to the earliest discussion of this
famous derogatory cartoon.

said that he felt like a pygmy struggling against a giant when he began *Thesaurus linguae Latinae epigraphicae: A Dictionary of the Latin Inscriptions* (Rome: Loescher, 1904). The giant came in unexpected form, but on 2 March 1912 Olcott was unintimidated as he worked at his table in the library of the American School in Rome. He may have known that Schmiedel of Germany had left a grammar that ended in the middle of a sentence and that Joseph Barber Lightfoot, Bishop of Durham, died pen in hand in an unfinished sentence. Despite the fact that Olcott never saw his publication past the letter A, he had not failed in his task, for what he did he did supremely well, and his work supplements *Thesaurus Linguae Latinae* (see TLL). The American scholar covered ground different from that in Ettore de Ruggiero's *Dizionario epigrafico di antichita romana,* the publication of which began in 1886, with stress on archeological detail. Olcott, on the other hand, concentrated strictly on lexicography, having in mind the compilation of a complete lexicon of more than 200,000 Latin inscriptions dating to 1000 C.E. Besides drawing on the *Corpus Inscriptionum Latinarum,* which at his time contained about 165,000 inscriptions, Olcott included whatever Christian inscriptions he could find, but betrayed intimations of mortality by excusing himself from any attempt at textual criticism. Meanings of words are carefully distinguished and usages classified. For example, a division "III A" s.v. *ara* lists "Arae Sacrae"; and under section "A . . . (a). In Rome" Olcott lists eighteen monumental altars, beginning with "Ara Cereris Matris" through "Vicus Trium Ararum." The entire work was estimated to cover over 4000 pages in eight to ten volumes. Frank Abbott (1907) was out of touch with reality when he reviewed fascicles 5–10 and expressed the hope that the "entire work" would be available "within a reasonable time." At the rate of four fascicles of twenty-four pages each per year, it would have taken over forty years for one person to complete the task. After Olcott's death on 3 March 1912, the Columbia University Council on Research in the Humanities supplied funds for continuance of the project. The second, and last volume to be published, bears the title: *Thesaurus Linguae Latinae Epiraphica: The Olcott Dictionary of the Latin Inscriptions* and treats words from *Asturica* to *Avillinlanus* (Olcott, 1935).[54]

The term Thesaurus is eminently appropriate. In a review of the first volume of the series entitled "Papers of the American School of Classical Studies at Athens," William Longfellow (1885) wrote: "Inscriptions are discoveries capitalized, as it were, and the income of them is only gradually realized."[55]

[54] For work in progress internationally on Greek and Latin epigraphy, see *Research Tools for the Classics,* pp. 46–48.

[55] Longfellow, 1885:203.

8

PAPYROLOGY

A major center of papyrological work in the first half of the twentieth century was the University of Michigan. Professor Francis Kelsey, planner and enterprising fundraiser for the "Humanistic Series" of the *University of Michigan Studies* (first volume, 1904) began the collection of papyri in 1920, and only a decade later the inventory totaled about 5,500 items.[1] In 1921 Kelsey arranged for the joint purchase of papyri by Michigan, Cornell, and Princeton, in conjunction with the British Museum and the University of Geneva. Despite a lack of special funding, Michigan's papyrologists managed to find time outside of their normal academic duties to edit a number of respected contributions. Of Michigan's many publications only a few can be discussed here.[2]

John Winter (1933) called attention to the collection through his "Jerome Lectures," which were published under the title *Life and Letters in the Papyri*.[3] In contrast to the more formal Greco-Roman literature, which generally shows armies on the march and projects the thoughts and actions of leaders in war and peace, Winter's papyri enter into details concerning the life and labor of the multitude. For sociological study Winter's work and others like it are important supplements to, for example, the much more massive but more aristocratically oriented work of Mikhail Rostovtzeff (1926 and 1941). Among the many interesting data in Winter's book is the reminder that papyrological discoveries have given us enriched acquaintance with the mime, a sort of one-act play.[4] Three years later, Winter supervised the editing of the third volume of papyri (*PMich*.III. 1936) in the Michigan collection. Documents 131–221 in this book consist of astrological and mathematical fragments.

[1] See the preface in Johnson and van Hoesen (1931), and the tribute by Sanders (1927).

[2] For further details, see Boak and Bonner, 1931.

[3] Winter's book contains a list of abbreviations used in citing papyrological publications; see pp. 279–85. Further introductory data are available in a work by the British papyrologist Eric Gardiner Turner, *Greek Papyri: An Introduction* (Princeton: Princeton University, 1968), which is written in the manner of W. Schubart's *Einführung in die Papyrusurkunde* (Berlin, 1918).

[4] Winter, 1933:232–37, compares Theokritos 15 and calls attention to Herodas (Herondas) *Miambi*.

A search for biblical fragments ultimately led Henry Sanders, Director of the American School of Classical Studies in 1930, to the publication entitled *A Third-Century Papyrus Codex of the Epistles of Paul*. Campbell Bonner (1934) matched this with *A Papyrus Codex of the Shepherd of Hermas*. In association with Herbert Youtie,[5] Bonner published *The Last Chapters of Enoch in Greek* (1937).

Of the documentary papyri in the Michigan collection, 120 statements of account from the Zenon archive, covering the reigns of Ptolemy II and Ptolemy III, from about 260 B.C.E., were edited in 1931 by Campbell Edgar and constituted "Michigan Papyri I"[6] (*PMich.I* = *PMich. Zen.*). It is well that Zenon, guardian of the collection of documents that bears his name, was not aware that what he had so diligently cared for would one day fall victim to careless hunters of antiquities who would be responsible for the dispersal of his business correspondence, often in fragmentary form, to various research centers in Europe and America. As confidential business manager of Apollonios, a minister of finance under Ptolemy II, Zenon meticulously filed his correspondence and when he transferred his activities from northern Egypt he took his entire mass of obsolescent letters to Philadelphia, a newly settled town in the Fayum, on the edge of the desert, where they survived until their discovery in the Age of Greed. Editor Edgar was quite evidently entranced and impressed by the nature of these documents, for he states (p. 3) that they

> form a wonderful picture of life in Egypt in the very prime of the Alexandrian age. Every rank of society is represented among the correspondents, from the chief minister of the king down to the native swineherd writing from prison. One could fill pages with a list of new and striking details concerning politics, trade, economics, art, manners, and customs. Moreover, though the correspondence is so varied in character, the fact that all the documents relate in some way to Zenon and his circle gives them coherence. Without being a biography, they form a connected series, reflecting his activities from year to year. Viewed against this background they become not only more intelligible, but more real to us.

In its totality this publication is so interesting that one refrains from singling out a preference.

Columbia's share of the Zenon papyri began to appear under the title *Zenon Papyri, Business Papers of the Third Century B.C. Dealing with Palestine and Egypt*, edited with an introduction and notes by William Westermann and Elizabeth Hasenoehrls (*PCol.Zen.I* 1934). Fifty-eight pieces of the Zenon correspondence are included in this volume, and like the texts in the Michigan collection contribute much to our understanding of

---

[5] Youtie, 1973, contains the bulk of articles published after 1930 by the eminent papyrologist.

[6] Edgar states that the papyri included in his edition are part of the University's share of several lots. Other shares had gone to Columbia University and to the British Museum. On others previously published, see *PMich.Zen.* 1931:1–2, note 1.

social and economic conditions in mid-third century B.C.E. From document No. 4 one may conclude that papyrus was fairly cheap in Egypt: sixty rolls, neither size nor quality mentioned, go for three and a half obols each. Number 6, dated early March 257 B.C.E., is a letter to Zenon from Simale, a worried mother. Approximately a year before the writing of the letter, Simale had indentured her young son, Herophantos, into the service of Apollonios under a *paramonē* arrangement.[7] Herophantos apparently came under the direct supervision of a petty official named Olympichos, who was evidently not impressed with the boy's performance. Simale was so distressed at finding her son ill—Olympichos said he was goldbricking and needed a beating to really know what it meant to be sick—that she took Herophantes home with her.

To return to the Michigan Papyri, Nos. 121–28 use all the space in Part One of *Papyri from Tebtunis,* edited by Arthur Boak (*PMich.II.* 1933). The papyri in this volume form a part of the collection of documents from the grapheion or record office of Tebtunis. Part Two of the same title contains Nos. 226–356 and appeared in 1944, through the efforts of Elinor Husselman, A. Boak, and William Edgerton (*PMich. V.* 1944).

Military documents, birth certificates, marriage contracts, a certificate of the assumption of the *toga pura,* and a freedperson's certificate are among the Latin documents (Nos. 167–68 and 429–63) discussed in the seventh volume of the Michigan Papyri, prepared by Henry Sanders and James Dunlap (*PMich.VII.* 1947). Three of the Latin documents (434, 443, and 444) have the names of witnesses signed in Greek. Four others (168, 430, 438, and 463) have additions in Greek. And No. 457 is bilingual. Numbers 167 and 168 of Michigan Papyri III are included because of important revisions that were made.

Karanis provided Michigan with the most numerous group in its inventory. Herbert Youtie and John Winter edited documents 464–521 in the second series of *Papyri and Ostraca from Karanis (PMich.VIII.* 1951). Among the many well-preserved letters in this collection is No. 521, in which a certain Claudianos invokes the full force of the reciprocity system and tells Isidoros that he will cease his benefactions unless Chrestos gives him specified sums of money. In No. 476 a letter writer requests the addressee to communicate a number of greetings, with specific mention of a notary, Didymos. Then follow other types of request (lines 24–29), with the terminal salutation given in lines 30–31. Commentaries on Romans 16 and other portions of St. Paul's correspondence that evidence epistolary "irregularities" are on occasion bloated with pontification that betrays no excursion into the real world of ancient letter writing as exhibited in these documents.

Michigan Papyri I–VIII were all published at Ann Arbor by the University of Michigan as part of its Humanistic Series. After the university's

---

[7] On *paramonē,* see below, pp. 121-22.

discontinuation of this series, E. Adelaide Hahn made a generous bequest to the American Philological Association so that the scope of the Association's monograph series might be broadened. The ninth volume of Michigan Papyri fell under the editorship of Elinor Husselman (*PMich.IX.* 1971) and is No. 29 in the monograph series of the American Philological Association and the third in the series of texts published from the excavations made by the University of Michigan at Karanis. The papyri from this excavation were listed under 2082 inventory numbers, but the number of fragments was actually greater because of groupings of smaller fragments under single inventory numbers. By arrangement with the Egyptian government, the papyri were to be returned to Egypt after study and publication had been completed. The task was so enormous that in 1953 the bulk of the manuscripts, including those that had been published and those on which scholars were not actively working, were returned to Egypt upon request by the Egyptian Department of Antiquities. Husselman's work contains a variety of items, including official documents, contracts, and wills, most of which were selected by the editor during a term as Curator of Manuscripts and Papyri at the library of the University of Michigan.

Michigan's papyri kept finding editors. The very first document in volume 14 of the Michigan Papyri, published in 1980, presents an ingenious argument and plea for release from costly public service. The plaintiff argues that the raising of five children is already a substantial liturgy (*PMich.XIV.* 1980).

Cases of extortion and legal redress are among the topics addressed in the archive of Aurelius Isidorus, a farmer whose business papers, dating from the third century C.E., were edited by Arthur Boak and Herbert Youtie (*PCair.Isid.* 1960).

Apart from their historical interest, two documents from Columbia's papyrological holdings are of special interest because of their display of recycled papyrus. In 1932 William Westermann and Clinton Keyes published the recto side of a roll used for tax records (*PCol. II* = *PCol. I*, Recto). Almost two and a half decades later, verso 1b–1a appeared under the editorial direction of John Day and Clinton Walker Keyes (*PCol. V* = *PCol. I*, Verso [1956]). When the materials on the recto of the rolls had become obsolete, the verso was used but rolled in the opposite direction from that of the original roll. This procedure put the writing of the recto on the outside and the writing of the verso on the inside.

Some explanation needs to be given for the numbering system used in *Columbia Papyri VII. Fourth Century Documents from Karanis,* transcribed by Roger Bagnall and Naphtali Lewis, and edited with translation and commentary by Bagnall (*PCol.VII.* 1979). In 1954, W. L. Westermann edited *Apokrimata. Decisions of Septimius Severus on Legal Matters. Text, Translation, and Historical Analysis* (New York, Columbia University Press, 1954), with a Legal Commentary by A. Arthur Schiller.[8] Although the Westermann-Schiller volume was not a part of Columbia's series, the papyrus published in it was numbered 123, in sequence with the last Zenon text, document 122, which was published as *PCol. IV.* The fifth volume includes the verso of the papyrus whose recto was published in volume 2. The volume entitled *Apokrimata* is therefore frequently referred to as *P.Col.VI*, and the Bagnall-Lewis volume, which begins with document 124, is numbered as the seventh volume. One of the features of the *Apokrimata* is a discussion (pp. 63–70), with extensive bibliography, on women's rights in Roman antiquity, especially relative to economic matters. Plates of documents 124–91, the corpus of the volume, are on microfiche stored at the back cover. Most of the documents, which were found at Karanis, are part of Columbia's holdings in papyrus. Lewis had copied them but lacked the time to edit and publish them. These documents shed light on financial administration between the reign of Diocletian and the 370s C.E.[9]

A portion of Princeton University's holdings in papyri were published in 1931 by Allan Johnson and Henry van Hoesen, *Papyri in the Princeton University Collections (PPrinc.I.* 1931). Edmund Kase received encouragement from Johnson to publish a body of texts which are now numbered 15–107 in vol. 2 of the same title (*PPrinc.II.* 1936).[10] Document 15 (= *P*54 in the list of New Testament papyri) consists of two small fragments of the Epistle of James (recto: 2:16–18, fragment a; and 2:21–23, fragment b; verso: 2:23–25 (fragment a) and 3:2–4 (fragment b). The text on the whole agrees with Vaticanus (B) Sinaiticus (Aleph), and Ephraemi (C), but reads *to stoma* in 3:3, with Alexandrinus (A). It omits *echeis* in 2:18 and *sou* before *chōris* in 2:18. The fragments are not to be confused with *POxy.* 1171 = *P*20 (Gregory-Dobschuetz), which covers 2:19–3:9. The fourteen missing leaves of

---

[8] A re-edited text appears in Youtie-Schiller, 1955. Youtie discusses the text in Section A of the article, and Schiller presents in Section B the legal commentary. A memorial volume entitled *Studies in Roman Law in Memory of A. Arthur Schiller,* edited by Roger S. Bagnall and William V. Harris (Leiden: Brill, 1985) contains articles by Bagnall, Lionel Casson, Naphtali Lewis, Sarah Pomeroy, and others.

[9] William Turpin reopened the subject of *apokrimata* in "Apokrimata, Decreta, and the Roman Legal Procedure," *Bulletin of the American Society of Papyrology* 18, 3–4 (1981) 145–60, with additional bibliography p. 145 nn. 1 and 4. The fact is, he writes, that "an *apokrima* had nothing whatever to do with petitions and their subscriptions. It was an oral decision, given in open court, after the emperor had listened to litigants presenting their case" (p. 146). Turpin uses 2 Cor 1:9 ("sentence of death") in support of his argument.

[10] The Princeton collections consisted of the University's own property and of texts on loan by Robert Garrett; see *PPrinc.II* 1936:v note 1. Kase selected a roll of receipts issued in the years 310–24 for his dissertation, *A Papyrus Roll in the Princeton Collection* (Baltimore, 1933). He sought to clarify problems connected with the dating of the first fifteen-year indiction cycle and the consulship of the Licinii.

document 15 (*PPrinc.II.*, pp. 1–28) would have accommodated the three Letters of John and the opening section of James (1:1–2:16), but it could not have had the two Epistles of Peter plus the missing portion of James. The resulting "arrangement of the Catholic Epistles," writes Kase, "appears to be wholly without precedent." The rest of Kase's volume consists of business documents and correspondence.

Parts of the *Iliad* and of Xenophon *Hellenika;* Isokrates *Antidosis* 16–18; portions of a medical and of a philosophical treatise; official and private documents, including magical papyri, covering the first to the sixth century, are contained in Allan Johnson and Sidney Goodrich, *Papyri in the Princeton University Collections (PPrinc.III.* 1942). As in most American institutions, the collection of Greek papyri at Princeton University owed its inception to the distribution of papyri made by the Egypt Exploration Fund in 1901, 1907, 1914–15, and 1922.

Was Ezek 36:24–38 in the *Vorlage* of the scribe who left a version of the Greek text of Ezek 19:12–37:4 for posterity? Is its text related to those in the Chester Beatty Papyri? Allan Johnson, Henry Gehman, and Edmund Kase express themelves on these questions in *The John H. Scheide Biblical Papyri: Ezekiel (PPrinc.Scheide.* 1938).

Byzantine Egypt: Economic Studies, by Allan Johnson and Louis West, presents an important discussion of the period from 297 C.E. (Johnson and West, 1949).

Yale University's interest in papyrology came into prominence through the efforts of John Oates, Alan Samuel, and Charles Welles, who edited what is now known as *PYale* (1967). The papyri discussed in this volume form part of a collection of papyri housed in Yale's Rare Book and Manuscript Library, which opened in 1963. Edwin J. Beinecke and his family founded the library, and in 1964 Beinecke increased its holdings with a major collection of papyri.[11]

Cornell University asked Columbia to publish some commercial documents, contracts, and census papers. William Westermann and Casper Kraemer did the editing of *Greek Papyri in the Library of Cornell University,* known as *PCorn.* (1926).

New York University invited publisher E. J. Brill to take care of its ancient paper cache from Karanis, as edited by Naphtali Lewis in *Greek Papyri in the Collection of New York University.* Known as *P.NYU* (1967), this collection consists principally of estate documents from the fourth century C.E.

Washington University went to Scholars Press after Verne Schuman edited documents 1–61 of its store under the title *Washington University Papyri* 1. *Non-Literary Texts* (= ASP 17, 1980). Only one item (Inventory 138,

---

[11] On Beinecke's contributions to the study of papyri, see *BASP* 7 (June, 1970):20–22.

known as *P.Wash.U.*Inv. 138) had previously been published.[12] The texts, principally official items and private business documents, range from the first century to the sixth.

A great benefactor of the classical and biblical world receives just adulation through the first volume of American Studies in Papyrology, *Essays in Honor of C. Bradford Welles.* To select one or two of the articles for exhibition would be an injustice to the international group of scholars who show that they know how to honor such a *euergetēs.* Editor Kent Rigsby (1966) must have thought that he was counting the papyri of Zenon when he took fourteen pages to inventory Welles's contributions to posterity.

With funds generously provided by Phoebe A. Hearst, the University of California subsidized the excavations of Bernard P. Grenfell and Arthur S. Hunt in the winter of 1899–1900 at Umm el Baragat, the ancient Tebtunis, in the south of the Fayum. The findings were published over a period of years in a three-volume set under the title *The Tebtunis Papyri* (1902–33). Volume 1 is the first in the series known as "University of California Publications: Graeco-Roman Archaeology," and contains documents 1–264. In addition to Grenfell and Hunt, Edgar Goodspeed, of the University of Chicago, assisted in the production of vol. 2, which is No. 2 in the California series (New York: Oxford University, 1907). This volume contains papyrus documents 265–689 and Ostraca 1–20. The first volume featured papyri found inside the mummies of crocodiles; the second deals with papyri found in the houses of Tebtunis during the first month of the excavations. The first part of the third volume (ed. by Arthur Hunt, J. Gilbart Smyly, Bernard Grenfell, E. Lobel, and Mikhail Rostovtzeff [London: Oxford University, 1933]) covers documents 690–825 and features commentary by Rostovtzeff on No. 703, a copy of a long set of instructions on proper management of various departments of the royal revenues. The document contains 285 lines, and appears to come from the third century B.C.E.

Numerous translations of papyri appear in Allan Johnson's *Roman Egypt to the Reign of Diocletian* (1936), the second volume of *An Economic Survey of Ancient Rome,* edited by Tenney Frank and associates. The documents cover almost every phase of economic and domestic interaction, such as land sales, mortgages, leases, administration of farms, census lists, slavery, marriage and divorce, entertainment, wages and living costs, taxes and imposts.

In a work entitled *Upon Slavery in Ptolemaic Egypt,* William Westermann (1929) demonstrated that Papyrus Columbia Inventory No. 480, from Fayum (about 198–97 B.C.E.) was basic for discussion of slavery in Ptolemaic Egypt. Directing his eyes to the north, he became interested in the term *paramonē* and cognates used in documents of manumission at Delphi. When he wrote an article on the subject, "The Paramone as General Service

---

[12] See Verne B. Schuman, "A Second-Century Treatise on Egyptian Priests and Temples," *HTR* 53 (1960) 159–70.

Contract" (1948), there were more than a thousand slave manumissions from the sacred precinct of Delphi available for study, covering a period roughly from 200 B.C.E. to about 75 C.E. Almost three quarters of the manumissions were outright purchases of freedom. The remaining grants were *paramonē* manumissions. That is, the contract of manumission stipulated that the freedperson had the obligation to "remain with" the manumitter and render such service as might be demanded. To what extent the manumitted person exercised freedom in such a contract became a special object of inquiry in a rejoinder by Alan Samuel (1965). Samuel pointed out that the term is used also in loan and service contracts (297–306). Herbert Youtie pursued the topic in "The Heidelberg Festival Papyrus: A Reinterpretation," a contribution to a Festschrift in honor of Allan Johnson (Johnson Festschrift, 1951). Youtie concluded that the Heidelberg Festival Papyrus did not relate to a *paramonē* but to an apprentice contract.[13]

Owing to the diligence of the American Society of Papyrology (ASP), scholars could be assured that hitherto unpublished inventories would secure editors and that special studies would keep pace with the accumulating wealth of ancient documents. Some of the publications of ASP have already been mentioned. Only a few others can here be mentioned to illustrate the resources that were being made available.

To Naphtali Lewis (1968) we are in debt for the first major contribution on liturgies since Friedrich Oertel's work on the subject. The study is entitled *Inventory of Compulsory Services in Ptolemaic and Roman Egypt.*

Imperial Estates in Roman Egypt, by George M. Parassoglou (1978), updates, with massive bibliography, the discussion of Rome's fiscal presence in Egypt. Identifying document numbers for the papyrological evidence are matched against the list of properties cited in "Appendix Two."

One of the most important documents for study of Roman law and Roman Egypt is *BGU* 1210, the *Gnomon of the Idios Logos.* A great deal of debate relates to the question whether the term is first of all a reference to a privileged royal account or to a title for an official who was in charge of the king's account. The papyrus and Strabo's remarks in his *Geography* (17.1.12) have been responsible for an extensive bibliography on the subject of the *idios logos.* Paul Swarney (1970) reviews the entire matter in *The Ptolemaic and Roman Idios.*

Alan Bowman (1971) gives students an informative summary of matters relating to conciliar action in the third and fourth centuries C.E. in the Mediterranean world, with special emphasis on Egypt, in *The Town Councils of Roman Egypt.*

For those who want to know the difference between an *epikrisis* and an *eiskrisis* (compare Lev 24:12 LXX) *P.Washington University* 134 is among the

---

[13] P. R. Coleman-Norton marshalls a great deal of information about slavery in his portion of the tribute to Johnson, "The Apostle Paul and the Roman Law of Slavery," 155–77.

documents to consult. It receives painstaking study, along with related papyri, from Carroll Nelson (1979), in *Status Declarations in Roman Egypt.*

Chester Beatty Papyri 961 and 962, fourth century C.E., include the Greek text of Gen 9:1–46:33, with parts in very fragmentary condition. Albert Pietersma (1977) subjects them to renewed scrutiny in *Chester Beatty Biblical Papyri IV and V.*

To an outsider the condensed style of writing found in some papyri may be as inscrutable as a page from a German reference work. Kathleen McNamee developed sympathy in the course of research on a dissertation, 1977, at Duke University: "Marginalia and Commentaries in Greek Literary Papyri" and eliminated at least some source of frustration with her publication, in 1981, of *Abbreviations in Greek Literary Papyri and Ostraca.*

Some modal aspects in the documentary papyri are covered by Robert Horn (1926), who expands on Carl Harsing's study of the optative in the papyri (Horn, 1926).[14] Of special interest to students of New Testament Greek is Horn's discussion of *ēn* as a subjunctive form (27–30), and of *hōs an* as an extension of the temporal use of *hōs* (133–36).

Many are the possibilities for error in establishing the text of documentary papyri. Herbert Youtie (1958) helps students cut down the rate with *The Textual Criticism of Documentary Papyri: Prolegomena.*

Edgar Goodspeed and Ernest Colwell had the biblical student in mind when they published *A Greek Papyrus Reader, with Vocabulary* (Chicago: University of Chicago, 1935), but classical students have equally profited from it, especially after reading Winter's book (1933). Along with lists of the Greek numerals and Egyptian months, the *Reader* contains a complete vocabulary for work on the texts. A generous selection of texts, eighty-two in number, illustrates numerous facets of Greco-Roman political, domestic, and religious life (including the role of magic).[15]

In a *Festschrift* for Archibald Robertson, William Davis shows some of the philological and historical bearing of papyri on the literature of the Greek New Testament (Robertson Festschrift, 1933). Included in this congratulatory volume are texts of private letters, invitations, business documents, along with numerous references to grammars. The fact that at the time of its publication some teachers of Greek thought that the translations reduced its value as an introduction to the reading of papyri appears to later generations a risible description of pedagogical Erehwon.

At the International Congress of Papyrology, held in 1970 at the University of Michigan, Francis Gignac announced that he had been working for ten years on a grammar of the papyri of the Roman and Byzantine periods.[16]

---

[14] Carl Harsing, *De optativi in chartis aegyptiis usu* (Bonn, 1910).

[15] A second impression, published in 1936, includes two pages of corrections that were received from F. Wilbur Gingrich, V. B. Schuman, and David Voss.

[16] See Gignac, 1970.

For sheer enormity of the task, his work can he compared to the challenge accepted by Robertson on the grammar of the Greek New Testament. Gignac (1976) informs his readers in the preface to the first volume of *A Grammar of the Greek Papyri of the Roman and Byzantine Periods:*

> The corpus of texts analyzed in this grammar is the total number of the documentary papyri and ostraca from Egypt from the beginning of the Roman period in 30 B.C. to the end of the papyri ca. A.D. 735. The evidence of the magical papyri and astrological texts, inscriptions, and mummy labels from Egypt, and the relatively few Roman and Byzantine papyri from outside Egypt, is included for comparison. Altogether this grammar is based upon an analysis of 15,052 papyri (including documents on parchment, skin, etc.), 7698 ostraca, 2619 minor documents and descriptions, 174 magical papyri and astrological texts, 5687 inscriptions, and 1054 mummmy labels – a total of 32,284 documents.

Gignac's work is a worthy continuation of grammatical study of the papyri beyond the temporal framework of the Ptolemaic period that Edwin Mayser had earlier set for himself, as announced in *Laut- und Wortlehre* (Leipzig, 1906), which was the first installment of Mayser's *Grammatik der griechischen Papyri.* Many phenomena that are too often curtly dismissed by teachers of Greek as "irregularities" receive Gignac's respectful attention and convincing explanation. Liberal use is made of Coptic dialect phonology for elucidation of Egyptian peculiarities, but the non-papyrological items, including thousands of inscriptions, are rarely cited. This grammar resolutely charts the path that leads from Homer through Byzantium to Modern Greek. The bibliography of "Editions of Texts" (5–13) constitutes a basic canon of papyrological editions. For the principal "Reference Works, Periodicals, and Grammatical Literature," see pp. 14–26.

In the late nineteenth century there was discovered a papyrus on whose recto were accounts of receipts and expenditures that are dated in the eleventh year of the reign of Vespasian. On Friday the thirteenth of January 1891, the British Museum published the first edition of this ancient paper. The surface of classical waters was never to be restored to its former calm, for on the verso of the papyrus was a copy of the long-lost *Constitution of Athens.* The title page of the publication, "printed by order of the trustees of the British Museum" reads: *Athenaion Politeia: Aristotle on the Constitution of Athens* (London: 1891), edited by F. G. Kenyon.

Since that celebrated Friday numerous ancient authors, some of whom were principally known by name, took on literary identity. Chief among them is Bakchylides. Recovery of a number of his odes gave scholars opportunity to make fresh assessment of the stature of Pindar.[17] The resurrection of Herondas enlarged conceptions of ancient Greek realism. A papyrus from

---

[17] For a full study of the major odes of Bakchylides see Burnett, 1985. Her introduction recounts the discovery of the poems and inventories early critical reactions.

the fourth century B.C.E. disclosed a large part of Timotheos's *Persians.* Timotheos is said to have influenced Euripides. Largely unknown until the second half of the nineteenth century, recovered speeches of Hyperides (389–22 B.C.E) prompt scholars to second antiquity's favorable judgment of his oratorical ability. Through the Bodmer Papyri more is now known about Menander's strength as a dramatist. As for Sappho, Xenokrates, and all the rest who awaited their turn for time's regenerative deed, one can consult the Oxyrhynchus Papyri. Through the *Bulletin of the American Society of Papyrologists* both biblical and classical students were able to keep abreast of papyrological developments throughout Papyrusland.

Many primary source materials for study of the history of the Jews in Egypt received appropriate treatment both in their edited and typographical format in *Corpus Papyrorum Judaicarum* (1957–64). The first volume of *CPJud* contains a detailed sketch of the historical development of the Jewish people in Egypt during the Hellenistic age; relevant documents of the Early Roman period appear in the second volume; and the third presents papyri from the late Roman and Byzantine period.

Edgar Johnson Goodspeed

Among the chief propagandists for the informational potential of papyrology was Edgar Goodspeed of the University of Chicago. Goodspeed received his inspiration for the study of Greek from James R. Boise, professor of New Testament and Biblical Greek at the old University of Chicago.

It was said that while Boise was a young instructor at Brown University, his president, Francis Wayland, asked him whether he could teach students to pronounce Greek as the ancients did (Goodspeed, 1953:41). Boise said that he could not, and that it was doubtful whether anyone in the country could. Only people in German universities possessed the key. "Then go to Germany and learn to do it!" directed the president. Obedient to his superior, he went to Germany and after his return to the United States Boise taught Greek for a time at the University of Michigan. Disillusioned with the male chauvinism that was manifested there—Michigan first opened its doors to women in 1870—Boise transferred his academic loyalties to the old University of Chicago, whose policies toward women were more characteristic of the liberality for which the university that emerged out of its voluntary demise is also renowned.[18] Under the cajoling of Ernest

---

[18] See Goodspeed, 1953:40–41. Goodspeed's autobiography, *As I Remember,* is one of the delightful narratives of the pre-second-world-war era. His father's story of the University of Chicago (T. Goodspeed, 1925) relates the origins of the University of Chicago. On 8 September 1890, the trustees of the first University of Chicago (which was incorporated 30 January 1857, with classes meeting from September 1858 to 1886) opened the way for the formation of the present University of Chicago by voting a change of name to "The Old University." Two days later the Secretary of State, Illinois, issued a certificate of incorporation to the new institution as "The

Burton,[19] Boise's subliminal influence took effect. It took some doing, for William Harper, who was later to be president of the present University of Chicago, had been pressuring Goodspeed to make Semitics his career. But Goodspeed chose Minerva.

During the summer term of 1895, guest lecturer Caspar René Gregory, an American of French descent and husband of Joseph Thayer's eldest daughter, steered Goodspeed in the direction of manuscript studies with lectures on Greek Paleography and New Testament Textual Criticism. Under Gregory's tutelage Goodspeed became acquainted with his first Greek manuscript—a fifteenth-century copy of the gospels (Goodspeed, 1953:97).

In his last year of graduate study Goodspeed had his first look at papyrus. He writes of the occasion as an astronomer would who sees a new planet swim into his ken. Unfortunately the content had to do with mathematics, which was not Goodspeed's long academic suit. But after conning an international group of scholars to assist him in the decipherment he made his bow into the world of learning. In 1898, Basil Gildersleeve published Goodspeed's glimpse into pre-Euclidean geometry and Egyptian surveying art in the *American Journal of Philology*. Mathematicians showed an interest in it, and in 1903 Goodspeed supplied them with a brief description and translation in *The American Mathematical Monthly*.

After this taste of research, Goodspeed became a papyrus addict. Through his friend James Breasted, of Oriental Institute fame, Goodspeed secured, at the cost of his "modest student savings," two large tin cigarette boxes full of papyrus. He and Breasted took over the kitchen, which was otherwise governed by Goodspeed's mother, and proceeded to steam open the rolls of papyrus. As Goodspeed tells it, they experienced such feelings "as Wordsworth thought the men must have felt who unrolled the charred rolls from the philosopher's house at Herculaneum:

> O ye who patiently explore
> The wreck of Herculaneum lore!
> What rapture, could ye seize
> Some Theban fragment, or unroll
> One precious, tenderhearted scroll
> Of pure Simonides!

Only members of the papyrological craft can understand the depth of emotion stimulated by the equivalent of a store manager's IRS preparation

---

University of Chicago." This new institution bore little resemblance to the old, for its founders were anxious to have it begin with an educational program that could compete with the best in America, and refused to open without secure financial backing. To accomplish this goal, T. W. Goodspeed secured a pledge of $600,000 from John D. Rockefeller, on condition that matching gifts would total $400,000 within the year. Chicago Baptists took only sixty days to raise $200,000. The University opened on 1 October 1892.

[19] On the career of this esteemed interpreter of the NT, see T. Goodspeed, 1926.

and a farmer's grain receipts, with some allowance for "two nice little pieces of Homer, a column of a medical treatise," and "a meager scrap of Isocrates" (Goodspeed, 1953:100–102).

As frequently happens, pieces of papyri from the same batch end up in different hands. Goodspeed was informed that Fritz Krebs, then in charge of the Berlin Greek papyri, possessed forty-three grain receipts similar to those in Goodspeed's hands. A few months later Goodspeed was in Berlin and worked with Krebs on a revision of the texts from his own hoard of ninety-one fragments and later published the 134 pieces in the Chicago Classical Studies.[20]

Another tiny slip of papyrus proved to be a boat ticket:

Ptolemy son of Psenomgeus
Passenger from Karanis
Isidore son of Isidore pilot
    Even full.

Goodspeed showed this ticket at a University affair, and James R. Angell, vice-president at the time, held the time-worn piece up to the light and in the tone of one who has eaten maize exclaimed: "Why, of course it's a boat-ticket! You can see where it's been punched!"

In August of 1909, eight years after his marriage to Elfleda Bond, Goodspeed talked about papyri with a houseguest named George Milligan. Milligan had an addiction similar to Goodspeed's, and one evening the two were discussing an old story about the finding of the first such documents. The year was 1778. And, as monks were wont to do with pages of Sinaiticus at Mt. Sinai, Arabs were said to have burned about fifty scrolls of papyrus "for the aromatic smell they gave forth in burning." Only one roll was saved and it was published as the *Charta Borgiana,* an account of the forced labors of peasants on the Nile embankment at Arsinoe in the year 191–92.[21] It was the first Greek papyrus to be published in Europe.[22] Had the Arabs perhaps thought that they had hit upon a store of tobacco? Goodspeed happened to have some tiny pieces of papyrus without any writing on them and proposed to Milligan that they experiment and see if they possessed any such aromatic qualities. They took the fire shovel that lay near by, lit the papyrus, and sniffed the fumes, which, says Goodspeed, "smelled just like brown paper" (Goodspeed, 1953:124). Years after this preliminary research, Goodspeed made trial of homegrown papyrus in California. His hypothesis blossomed into a discipline. Fortunately for the history of philology and theology, the

[20] See E. Goodspeed, 1953:102–03. Forty-three texts from Karanis are known as *PKar.Goodspeed* (= *PChic.Goodspeed*).

[21] George Milligan, *Here and There Among the Papyri* (London: Hodder and Stoughton, 1922) 10.

[22] Niels Iversen Schow, ed., *Charta papyracea Graece scripta Musei Borgiani Velitris* (Rome, 1788).

Arabs must have discovered that those first fifty Greek scrolls would never make a pipe taste better.

Goodspeed's personal collection of papyri increased steadily. Of the seven papyri featured in *Chicago Literary Papyri* (Goodspeed, 1908), six are republications of papyri owned by the University of Chicago professor. Three of the seven contain fragments of Homer's epics. A fourth, published for the first time, covered sections 9–11 of Isokrates To Nikokles.

Enlightened administrative policies supported Goodspeed in his goal to make his university a proud guardian of manuscript treasures, and not limited to papyri. In an article, "New Manuscript Acquisitions for Chicago" (Goodspeed, 1930), Goodspeed expressed his appreciation for the lessons he learned on the art of extracting money from university authorities. On one occasion the griddle for acquisition of a desirable item was especially hot and he needed money fast. He was advised that Dean Mathews was the one to reach, but he was in Denver at the time. Goodspeed, knowing the ways of deans, did not want to hunt up Mathews a month later in Switzerland or Sweden. So he wired Mathews and received a reply before the day was out, to the effect that all but one hundred dollars would be met. Goodspeed found a donor for the balance, and the University became the owner of "The Prax-apostolos," a parchment manuscript of the Acts and the Epistles written in the 12th or 13th century.

Through his editing of numerous texts Goodspeed contributed to more popular understanding of the contributions of papyri, and through his proposals for resolution of 115 vexed questions of interpretation, which he presented in *Problems of New Testament Translation* (1945), he helped a generation of students recognize the importance of the papyri for up-dated understanding of the New Testament. Two examples illustrate the nature of some of his contributions in *Problems*. Owing to Goodspeed's discussion of papyrological data in connection with the rendering of Matt 6:27, a number of Bible versions that were published after his *Problems* preferred life-span to stature as the referent of *hēlikia* in Matt 6:27. Goodspeed rendered the passage: "But which of you with all his worry can add a single hour to his life?" In Acts 6:2 Luke uses common commercial terminology when he has the apostles state that they do not wish "to keep accounts."[23]

---

[23] For further application of commercial usage in papyri to clarification of passages in the NT, see Danker, 1972:91–114. For work in progress on papyrology, see *Research Tools for the Classics*, ed. R. Bagnall (1980):49–51. For a discussion of Christian documents with special reference to Christians' self-identification on papyri, see Snyder, 1985:149–162.

Part III

A Century of Self-Discipline

If philologians are the most dogmatic of men in their writings, it is not because they are students of the classics, but because they are teachers of the classics, for teaching is an occupation fraught with great danger to that humility and self-distrust which are necessary to the highest intellectual attainments.

Basil Lanneau Gildersleeve

Should you consider this book unworthy of Greek audition, and if, like Aristotle you put truth ahead of friendship, a thick and deep darkness will suppress it, and humanity shall never have a word of it.

Synesios, in a letter to Hypatia

9

MUDWASHING AND WHITEWASHING

To recite a century of literary-philological inquiry without due attention to the critical discipline practiced by biblical and classical scholars would be a gross injustice to all who exposed themselves to correction in the interest of promoting greater excellence. In honor of such sense of discipline, Part 3 includes a variety of methodological considerations that have surfaced either in original presentations or in critique of such presentations.

As will be quickly apparent, no "holders of the chief seats" can expect to be spared by those who will offer their counsel in these pages. And the years to come may reveal that some of the admonitions here recited will have made a lasting impression on those who were entrusted with the future. May it be found that they wore their crowns as lightly, and sometimes even jauntily, as did most of those who here come under review.

Mudwashing and Whitewashing of the Ancients

A primary methodological consideration relates to the manner in which antiquity is approached. Even a cursory review of historical research reveals a constant temptation either to mudwash or to whitewash antiquity.

Mudwashing

Mudwashing the ancients, an academic game that has been played by not a few commentators and social historians, received periodic scrutiny from those who bothered to probe the data more carefully and with a refined sense of historical responsibility. As champions of fairness, American classical scholars proved, on the whole, less prone than biblical specialists to put a moratorium on gentility when dealing with cultures that lie entombed in antique ruin.[1]

---

[1] Some British classicists have nourished the prejudices of biblical interpreters. See, e.g., Edward Selwyn's comments on 1 Pet 4:3–4 (*The First Epistle of St. Peter* [London: Macmillan, 1955]) and his references to the *Companion to Latin Studies* (used in support of allegations of "drunken orgy") and James Adam's (apparently a reference to *The Religious Teachers of Greece*) use of Plato's *Republic* 560E in denigration of the Eleusinian mysteries, which in First Peter's

Those who proceeded from the assumption that Jewish and Christian traditions gave their adherents a moral and spiritual edge over ancient Greeks and Romans found it difficult to avoid engaging in a pattern of subtle or even overt vilification or mudwashing, especially in discussion of Greco-Roman political performance, general morality, and concern for human rights. Only occasionally does one find in the literature any suggestion that on a number of scores gentile antiquity might well put Western culture of a later day under trenchant criticism.[2] Yet, if one is to engage in honest criticism, whether of the Bible or of the Classics, it is necessary that one's own political and cultural experience be placed along with that of others on the scales of historical judgment. If this is not done, the distortion of antiquity will also compound corruption of historical judgment concerning contemporary data.

Ordinarily it is more popular works of the genre of historical novel and television "documentaries" along the lines of *The Flames of Rome*,[3] that entice the public to go slumming in the Soho and Times Square districts of antiquity or to engage in antiquarians' voyeurism, with a dose of ancient equivalents of *The National Enquirer* alleged as "scholarly" guides. Yet even some who might resent the charge of populism may be guilty of encouraging general vilification or disparagement of Greco-Roman culture, and ignore *inter alia* that Tacitus, for example, censured Jews and Christians for what he perceived to be social irresponsibility.

Apart from prejudicial perspective, a subtle contributing factor to the defamation of antiquity is the use of the term "pagan" in scholarly publications to describe anything that is non-Jewish or non-Christian, or both, and in this usage biblical scholars appear to outpoint their classical colleagues. In popular parlance the term "pagan" connotes either idolatry or immorality, or both, or at the very least an inferior religious or moral status. From study pursued in connection with this centennial volume it appears that along with "nigger," "Hymie," "goy," and "heathen," the word "pagan" ought to be jettisoned. In its place numerous scholars have used the word "gentile" in reference to non-Jewish and non-Christian Greco-Roman society. In lower case this term is readily distinguishable from upper case "Gentile." *Mortui etiam sentiunt.*[4]

---

time (a half-millennium later!) were held under the watchful eye of Roman administrators; cf. Johnston 1977:162 n. 3. Even Juvenal (6.50) takes account of the chastity of the participants. "Parallels never meet," cautioned Erwin Goodenough, but Selwyn was not an avid reader of American biblical exposition.

[2] One of the exemplary exceptions to narrower historical awareness may be examined in Forbes, 1936, where attention is called to modern forms of censorship.

[3] Paul L. Maier, *The Flames of Rome: A Documentary Novel* (Garden City, NY: Doubleday, 1981).

[4] Scholars' semantic adjustment is more desirable than insistence on a term which, although

Dependence on traditional failure to read in polemical context a passage such as Romans 1, of which Arthur Nock (1933) wrote that it "possesses precisely the historical value of a mediaeval sermon on ritual murder as practised by Jews" (139), is another contributing factor in depreciation of Greco-Roman morality by biblical interpreters, with side-effects on the general public.

Faced by numerous examples of denigration, many classical scholars have, despite some inconsistencies, endeavored to elicit fair treatment for Greco-Roman society. In an article entitled "Roman Concubinage and Other *De Facto* Marriages" (1974), Beryl Rawson takes Jérôme Carcopino,[5] Ludwig Friedländer,[6] and Hugh Last[7] to task for their allegations of immorality and declares that the "evidence used by Meyer and Plassard can no longer be used to support their sweeping moral conclusions" (304). Rawson declaims: "It is time not only to get the facts straight but also to banish racial, class, and sexual prejudices from Roman social history" (305).

A British scholar, Charles Bullock, chastised Dionysios of Syracuse for his fiscal irresponsibility and self-indulgence.[8] Arthur McKinlay (1939) replied with "The 'Indulgent' Dionysius," charging Bullock with mudwashing Dionysius. Infanticide took place in classical times less frequently than was once thought, concluded La Rue van Hook in 1920;[9] and, as van Hook points out, Aristophanes and Euripides, on whom previous assumptions were based, are not the most reliable of sources.[10] To an article on sex in antiquity,

---

it may be held to be scientifically neutral in the scholarly community, with appeal made to derivation from Latin (bibliographical details in Jacques Poucet, "L'importance du terme 'collis' pour l'étude du developpement urbaine de la Rome archaique," *L'antiquité Classique* 36 [1967]:107–8), is nevertheless understood pejoratively by persons outside the specialists' craft and who need no further stimulation to the prodigious capacity for prejudice that gapes in their midst. The fact is that non-Jewish-non-Christian Japanese, Chinese, and other nationals who do not share Jewish or Christian perspectives feel demeaned by use of the term "pagan" in reference to their religious beliefs, and ancient Romans are entitled to the same courtesy extended to contemporaries. Some extent of the widespread mischief occasioned by scholars' use of the term (and BAGD must plead guilty; see, e.g., under *kosmos*) can be gauged from the rendering of Luke 12:30 in the *Good News Bible* (=TEV, American Bible Society, 1976): "the pagans of this world."

[5] Jérôme Carcopino, *Daily Life in Ancient Rome: The People and the City at the Height of the Empire;* tr. by E. O. Lorimer (New Haven: Yale University, 1940).

[6] Ludwig Friedländer, *Darstellungen aus der Sittengeschichte Roms in der Zeit von August bis zum Ausgang der Antonine;* 10th ed.; 4 vols. (Leipzig: Hirzel, 1922).

[7] Hugh Last, in *The Legacy of Rome,* ed. Cyril Bailey (Oxford: Clarendon, 1923) 231.

[8] Charles J. Bullock, "Dionysius of Syracuse—Financier," *CJ* 25 (1929) 260–76.

[9] Hook (1920) provides an exceptional example of historical criticism.

[10] Similarly, Greek New Comedy must be used with due caution as resources for economic information. The playwrights appealed to the upper 300 class, which could afford huge dowries; see Casson, 1976.

Skinner (1982) appends a bibliography relating to Greco-Roman ridicule of oral sex as a disgusting habit.[11] Many words have been written about temple prostitution in ancient Greece, but Leonard Woodbury (1978) claims that it was relatively rare.

With respect to charges of sexual excesses, it is important to note that it is difficult to establish for the Greco-Roman period anything approaching the scale of allegations of sexual atrocities committed in numerous cities and towns located in some of the more genteel areas of the United States. And, compared to Harlequin novels sold over the counter in the most respected emporia, Greco-Roman literature at its alleged steamiest and prurient worst is relatively Puritan in its depiction of intimacy. Near the end of 1984, Sydney Biddle Barrows, dubbed the "Mayflower Madam" because of her Social Register designation "Myf.," signifying direct lineage from a Mayflower passenger, joined Valeria Messalina in a decline from social prestige. But with a difference: Rome disapproved of Messalina; Barrows had a "Mayflower Defense Ball Party" thrown for her on May 2, 1985, by a "chic set" in New York. As for charges of immoderate luxury, it is probable that even Nero would have envied the casual manner with which a guest at Chicago's Ritz-Carlton Hotel washed down his $7.50 "Ritzburger" with an 1882 bottle of Chateau Lafite-Rothschild, which carried a price tag of $1125.00; not to speak of the woman who telephoned from her limousine with a request for a bottle of Remy Martin Louis XII Cognac, for which the same hotel charged her $930.00, not counting tax and tip.[12]

It was increasingly recognized in the twentieth century that Juvenal is not the most accurate guide to social realities. One of the scholars who helped redirect thinking was Albert Harkness (1896), who showed in his study, "Age at Marriage and at Death in the Roman Empire," that marriage was not so unstable as an author like Juvenal would lead us to believe.[13]

Rome must live with the notoriety thrust on her by some of her administrators, and Nero is the first to come to mind for most intepreters of St. Paul's era. Nevertheless, one is hard pressed to fix on two decades of Rome's ancient time that incorporated such prestigious infidelity to the public trust as was exhibited by Richard Nixon, a former president of the United States, and by seven members of her Congress, who were indicted in the course of a so-called Abscam operation: John Jenrette, Richard Kelly, Michael Myers, Raymond Lederer, John Murphy, Frank Thompson, and Harrison Williams. On the other hand, historians appear to be agreed that it would be a mistake

---

[11] Skinner; 1982:199–200 n. 5, with special reference to Roman authors. Attic comedy suggests a different atttitude, cf. Henderson, 1975. As Henderson points out, certain satire (see pp. 185–86) in Aristophanes is not to be construed as social protest (p. 52).

[12] *Chicago* 34,6 (June, 1985) 232–33.

[13] See also the warning against misuse of data from the ancient satirists in Tanzer, 1926; and for a protest against caricature of Juvenal as a dour writer, see Dunn, 1900.

to permit the scandal of "Watergate" to completely overshadow Richard Nixon's positive accomplishments, especially in foreign policy. And Mary Thornton (1971) thought along similar lines when she wrote about "Nero's New Deal." In an attempt to balance traditional caricatures, Thornton points out that by increasing the money supply through a public works program in a time of unemployment the Emperor brought Rome through a depression.

Not to grant antiquity its due is a species of mudwashing. Discussions of the question of racism in antiquity do well to include a study such as that of Frank Snowden's "The Negro in Ancient Greece," which showed that there is no evidence of racism in ancient Greece, and that Menander epitomizes the attitude, neither Ethiopian nor Scythian. Natural bent, not race, determines nobility (Snowden, 1948). Michael Ginsburg (1940) chastised Hendrik Bolkestein for concluding that Greco-Roman burial societies had not cleared the way for Christian community acts of love.[14] In his rebuke Ginsburg called attention to the social function of Roman military clubs.[15] And Harry Wedeck (1929) demonstrated that behind Roman *gravitas* lay very human feelings, especially in expression of affection for children.

Discrediting of Greco-Romans is especially evident in appraisal of their religious institutions and practices. A prime offender was Ernest Sihler, known especially for his autobiography, *From Maumee to Thames and Tiber* (1930),[16] which documents an era of impressive scholarship. In various studies, Sihler endeavored to strike a balance between Matthew Arnold's adulation of Hellenism and an appraisal that appeared to be required by commitment to Christian values. But his mode of presentation in *Testimonium Animae* (1908) and in the work entitled *From Augustus to Augustine* (1923) is similar to that of Johann Gerhard Wilhelm Uhlhorn, Abbot of Loccum, and permits no contest.[17]

The loftiest thoughts of Hellas and Rome intermingle with the effluvia that are characteristic of a major urban environment in any age, and Sihler forces the combination to stand up against the noblest expressions of the New Testament. In 1933 he stated, without an historian's blush: "I shall select the topics which most clearly and strikingly illumine the contrast" with the "faith, life and worship of the Christian church" (331). This approach was in keeping with the snide questions he asks in *Testimonium Animae*, about the

---

[14] Hendrik Bolkestein, *Wohltätigkeit und Armenpflege im vorchristlichen Altertum* (Utrecht: Oesthoek, 1939).

[15] See esp. *CIL* VI.10234 and 33885.

[16] Sihler's autobiography incorporates a captivating chapter on the beginnings of Johns Hopkins University (1930:95–115).

[17] (Johann) Gerhard Uhlhorn, *The Conflict of Christianity with Heathenism*, ed. and tr. from the 3d German ed. by Egbert C. Smyth and Charles Joseph Hardy Ropes; rev. ed. (New York: Scribner, 1879). Friedländer's *Darstellungen* (see n. 5 above) was the heifer for Uhlhorn's and many another's tillage.

Iobakchoi, a Dionysiac club located in Athens in the second century C.E. "Why did they call the meeting-place *mattress (stibas)?* Because many reclined in this drinking club after the ritual of poculation had progressed somewhat?" (307).[18] Ramsay MacMullen's answer restored honor to the historian's craft (1981:38). *Mutatis mutandis,* were one or two of the best minds of Greece given the floor and permitted, in the manner Sihler arbitrated antiquity, to evaluate institutionalized Christianity's performance during the "Constantinian Age," the Greece of Pericles would win the golden wreath. And non-Christian Romans would emerge as models of broadmindedness, at least to judge from Elmer Merrill's (1919) essay "The Church in the Fourth Century," which shows how Greco-Roman toleration was rewarded with intolerance.[19]

In the same year (1908) that Sihler was denigrating the quality of religious commitment in the Roman empire, George Hadzsits documented a high degree of personal piety among the Epicureans. Yet let one grant for the nonce that Roman religion was infected, for example, with a large ingredient of rote. The concession is trumped by Ernst von Dobschuetz (1914), who describes a development from simpler forms of Christian cult to the use of service books which urged sacred ceremony that looked very much like a Greco-Roman rite "aiming to produce an effect upon God" (259). Moving away from partisan debate, Herold Weiss (1967) demonstrated in "The *Pagani* among the Contemporaries of the First Christians" that there was a broad, strong current of religious fervor. And Eli Burriss's (1930) essay, "The Objects of a Roman's Prayers," carried the reminder that also gentile Romans prayed for spiritual blessings.[20] Burriss might have added a reference to Persius (*Satire* 2), whose condemnation of hypocritical piety might well have been included in the Bible. Frequently one reads of United States judges or juries, or both, exonerating drivers who under the influence of alcohol have killed or maimed others. Pittacus, tyrant of Mytilene, increased the penalty for offenses committed as a result of intoxication, on the assumption that the culprit could have refrained from getting drunk and was

---

[18] Compare the gratuitous inference expressed by Howard Clark Kee and Franklin W. Young, in *Understanding the New Testament* (Englewood Cliffs, New Jersey: Prentice-Hall, 1957), p. 442: "Some of the most moving epitaphs discovered from the period [presumably for the writing of 1 Peter] are those of husbands praising their wives' faithfulness—evidence, perhaps, of their rarity." The word "perhaps" does not excuse the slanderous slant. Similarly, the reputation of Corinth as a city of "profligacy and degradation" (p. 252) is used as grist for a generalization about morality in "the Graeco-Roman period" (p. 439), without recognition of the fact that the very attestation of Corinth's immorality by Greco-Roman writers was itself a testimonial to the better standards that prevailed in other parts of the Roman Empire.

[19] See also Moore, 1919; Pease, 1919; Laistner, 1951; Swift, 1965.

[20] In this connection MacMullen's advice (1981:52–53) on determining the reasons for worship in Greco-Roman society deserves to be heeded. His approach mirrors that of Clifford Moore, 1920.

therefore responsible.[21] As for off-color jests, Quintilian (6.3.29) pronounced them inappropriate for the scholar; and "there ought be no tolerance for obscenity in his speech," he lectured. Roman exposure of infants at least offered a chance, albeit remote, for survival, but there is no way of escape from saline solutions and other routes of legal annihilation for hundreds of thousands of embryos annually in a more technologically advanced society. And advocates of capital punishment in modern America cannot block out the fact that "an interesting feature of the later period of the Roman Republic is the practical discontinuance of the death penalty" (Green, 1929). "When the Green loses," says Juvenal, "Rome is struck aghast as after the defeat at Cannae," and the lines are echoed annually when a major city's sports franchise forecloses on the hopes of its devotees. St. Paul asks an orthodox defender of the faith, "Do you rob temples?" (Rom 2:22). And history will not permit one to forget that Pompey kept his hands off the gold in the temple at Jerusalem after his capture of the city in 63 B.C.E. (Josephus, *J.W.* 1.7.6). The systematic destruction of Greco-Roman shrines in the post-Constantinian era needs to be measured against the refusal of Seneca to endorse the plundering of sacred precincts in Asia Minor (Tacitus *Annals* 15.45).

Clifford Moore (192) bequeathed a model of sober evaluation of Greco-Roman life in the Christian era. And Levi Lind (1972), protesting against "decline and fall" thematic and the idea that antiquity is fair game for cheap defamation, tried to set the record straight in "Concept, Action, and Character: The Reasons for Rome's Greatness." Twelve years earlier, Frederick C. Grant summed the matter when he wrote in rejoinder to Erwin Goodenough upon publication of volumes 7–8 of the latter's *Jewish Symbols in the Greco-Roman Period:* "Religious symbolism, even pagan, needs to be taken at its highest and best, not a poor counterfoil to something else" (1960:62).

A deeper probe for the facts may in one case clear the ancients and in another instance show them to be fairly in balance with history's prevailing ethical and cultural standards. Lionel Casson (1966), expert on ancient naval matters, could find only one reference to galley slaves. "Leg irons, the whip, galleys that were floating concentration camps—all this" he emphasized, "belongs to the world of the sixteenth to the eighteenth century and to no earlier age" (44). In the course of centuries Lucretius has endured much negative criticism, but Cardinal Melchior de Polignac's accusation of hypocrisy drew the ire of Ernest Ament (1970), who charged the cleric with libeling the Roman author.[22] Had Morton Smith (1973a,b) taken energetic account of general Christian reluctance to collide with Rome's legal system,

---

[21] Aristotle *Rhetoric* 1402b.7; *Politics* 1274b.18–23.
[22] Ament, 1970; see esp. pp. 36–37.

which, as Smith correctly states, included interdiction of magical practices,[23] he would have rephrased his attribution of the use of magic to the Jesus of the Gospels. That some Greco-Roman auditors might have interpreted them so is of course indisputable.

Not even biblical writers escape the more subtle type of disparagement that has permeated biblical criticism. St. Luke, for example, is a target through the frequently expressed cliché that he is "not an historian in the modern sense." Of course he is not. But what historian of ancient times qualifies? Livy, with his patriotic fervor and anti-Carthage bias? Herodotos? He failed to impress Thukydides. And Dionysios of Halikarnassos took the latter to task. It would not be less a cliché were one to affirm that Aischylos is "not a playwright in the modern sense" of say a Tennessee Williams.[24]

The foregoing review of scholars' judgments suggests that, when dedication to factual precision rather than to the control of data by personal religious preference or philosophical presuppositions prevails, Canaanites and Babylonians, Greeks and Romans, and a host of other ancient peoples will appear to have been as earnest about their religious beliefs as have Jews and Christians, and not less practiced in the art of civilized and humane relationships.

Numerous apostolic injunctions admonish Christians against offending the sensibilities of their gentile neighbors, and there is no moral injunction in either the Old or the New Testament that has not been recited as well, and in some instances better, by gentile Greeks or Romans. And to judge from tales of atrocity and immorality attested of God's people in the writings of the Old Testament and in the deplorable history of ecclesiastical opposition against basic rights and principles, Greek and Roman history reveals at times a comparatively higher stage of moral and social sensitivity.

Whitewashing

Whitewashing is the objectionable counterpart of mudwashing.

Historical conscience calls for reassessment of humanity's most cherished heroes and inherited institutions, many of which have undergone well-meant distortion. High on the list for critique is William Tarn's Alexandolatry, which guided the brushstrokes for his idealized portrait of Alexander the Great. To offset the mesmerizing power of Tarn's presentation one can ponder the Macedonian commander's destruction of Thebes. It is a deed that needs to be viewed from the perspective of other wreckage. Cicero (De officiis 1.35, 3.46) and Velleius Paterculus (1.13.5) thought that the razing of Corinth by

---

[23] M. Smith, 1973b:220; cf. Pharr, 1932, not cited in Smith's indexes. For another perspective, with an apology for Smith, see Jonathan Smith, 1975:23–24.

[24] On ancient historians, see, e.g., Gudeman, 1903; Jerome, 1912; Ryberg, 1942; and Rogers, 1952. See also Hock, 1982; and Lateiner, 1977, who shows that Herodotos found fiction seviceable in the writing of history.

Lucius Mummius Achaicus in 146 B.C.E. brought dishonor on Rome. And if the devastation wrought on beautiful Dresden at the end of World War II is similarly adjudged by many to have been a senseless act and a blot forever on the British and American flags, it is certain that history can never forgive Alexander for his atrocious act. Yet his admission of the same, justified though it might be (as in the case of Dresden) by the canons ordinarily used in assigning responsibility for military carnage, dilutes some of the disgust invited by his savagery. But all his Hellenization of the world beyond Greece can never mitigate his brutal murder of Parmenio, inversely echoed in the reproach of Julius Caesar: *Et tu Brute?*

It is not sacrilege, wrote Ernst Badian (1960), to dispel romantic idealism.[25] And it would be sheer Romanophilism to flaunt, for example, the magnanimity of a Publius Scipio Africanus toward the Numidian Syphax (Diodorus Siculus 27, fragment 6), while ignoring the manner in which Rome treated Gaius Pontius, who had entrapped an entire Roman army during the Second Samnite War. After releasing thousands of Rome's finest warriors, Pontius provided them transport for the sick and enough provisions to see them on their way to the capital. His reward? Decapitation.

Livy burdened the future by tucking away some unsavory aspects of Rome's past under repeated allegations of "perfidy" and "cruelty" in his record of Hannibal's military career. But the Roman scholar's basic respect for Klio let Veritas slip through. After his dazzling victory at Lake Trasimene, the son of Hamilcar Barca searched diligently but vainly for the body of his brave antagonist, the consul Gaius Flaminius, to whom Hannibal wished to accord full military honors (Livy 22.7.5). The illustrious Carthaginian general was more successful at Cannae, where he rewarded the consul Aemilius Paulus's valor with a hero's funeral (Livy 22.52.6). Granted that awareness of war's pendulum may have evoked some of Hannibal's chivalry, it is certain that no such spirit of gallantry nor any thought of *tyche* encumbered the mind of Gaius Claudius Nero after the battle of the Metaurus in 207 B.C.E. On orders of this consul the head of Hasdrubal, who had fallen in the battle, was severed and flung in front of the Cathaginian outposts (Livy 27.51.11). Hannibal needed only a glimpse of Nero's grisly trophy, and his face flooded with fraternal grief. Years later, Publius Cornelius Scipio Aemilianus is reported to have shed tears when in 146 B.C.E. he gazed on his own handiwork, the ruins of Carthage.[26] The tears served as a libation on one of Scipio's alleged prophecies that found fulfillment six centuries later when Rome—sharing the fate of Ilium, Nineveh, Babylon, and Persepolis—was sacked in 410 by Alaric the Goth, and plundered in 455 by the Vandal Gaiseric.

In his study of Hellenistic impact on Christianity, von Dobschuetz

---

[25] Ernst Badian, "The Death of Parmenio," *TAPA* 91 (1960) 324–38.
[26] For further discussion of atrocities in Roman warfare, see Westington, 1938.

rebukes Eusebius for fulsome praise of Constantine (1914:259). Short of retching, he writes: "It comes near to apotheosis and neglects shamefully the demands of Christian sincerity" (263).

Periodically attempts are made to score extra marks for Rome by comparing her gradual amelioration of conditions under which slaves performed their service to legislation enacted in the Southern section of the United States prior to the Emancipation Proclamation. But slavery, like rape, is not entitled to benefit from comparative extenuation, and attitudes such as those expressed by Caius Cassius (Tacitus *Annales* 14. 42–45) cannot be expunged from history. More appropriate would be a comparison of the volume of protests that were made in antiquity and in the United States. Antiquity manifests little guilt about the system, and even St. Paul mounts no crusade, although he would not have shared the thinking of Leo I, who in 443 stated that slaves possessed neither the position nor character appropriate to the priesthood. On the other hand, Charles Hodge of Princeton, one of the contributors to a collection of essays entitled *Cotton is King*, pleads the Southern case in one of the most articulate exhibitions of apologetic to emanate from below the Mason and Dixon line; yet he labors under no censorship for exposing weaknesses in Southern law relating to the rights of slaves, and he is unambiguous about his own view that slavery has little to commend it as an institution. In the introduction to *Cotton is King*, editor Ebenezer Elliott (1860), president of Planters' College, Mississippi, asserts that the plight of slaves, as reflected in some ancient Jewish and Roman sources, is "not the labor system among us" (vi). In contrast to the Roman view of slaves as "chattel," Elliott argues that in the South "the person of the slave is not property, no matter what the fictions of the law may say; but the right to his labor is property, and may be transferred like any other property, or as the right to the services of a minor or an apprentice may be transferred." Under this system, which Henry Hughes termed "Warranteeism," slaves are in turn entitled to "the right of subsistence, the right of care and attention in sickness and old age" (vii). Unfortunately, some of the philological counterattack that was mounted in the North took its cue from the kind of lexical ignorance trumpeted in George Cheever's (1860) *The Guilt of Slavery* and merely nourished the South in its defensive position.

A subtle aspect of whitewashing is the practice of contemporizing an ancient document by interpreting some of its features in the light of one's particular interests. An exegete of the Classics may, for example, find the *Antigone* of Sophokles attractive because it seems to celebrate uncompromising individualism. But the question, as Levy (1963) points out, remains: What are the real motives that impel Antigone to bury and bewail her brother in the face of the danger that she invites? Similarly, it is tempting to seek support for modern liberationist thinking in St. Paul's writings, but the attempt to document emancipation of women in his writings is as futile as a search for chivalry and romance in Homeric epic. Frequently cited is

Gal 3:28, but this passage does not advocate emancipation for women any more than it does for slaves.

Faced with disconcerting data in Paul's writings, one is tempted to offer hypotheses of interpolation. But drawing on the source criticism of the older philology is much akin to Euripides's *deus-ex-machina* technique, and elimination of a passage such as 1 Cor 14:33b–36 merely delays the moment of reckoning. The fact remains that this text enjoys canonical status, and Jesus' own selection of twelve men remains the ultimate refuge of male clerical dominance. In lieu of resignation to traditional practice based on alleged normative and prescriptive authority of the biblical text, one is compelled to understand such textual embarrassment as one of the culture-bound features of the Bible. Interest in truth takes precedence over concern for apostolic perfection. One would, for example, like to know Peter's side of the affair that is discussed in Gal 2:11–21; and in the interest of improving Peter's reputation some one might want to hypothesize that anti-Petrinists interpolated the passage in whole or in part. But in such event the critic's credibility, not Peter's or Paul's, would be at stake.

Finally, mudwashing and whitewashing alternate when aesthetic considerations dispel criticism that lays claim to scientific ojectivity. John Addington Symonds put Theokritos's *Idyll* 16 among that poet's "worst poems." "Pinchbeck," he growled. Countered Norman Austin: "The poem has undeniable aesthetic merits" (1967:2).[27]

---

[27] Also see Belmont 1980:4 on Thomas Ethelbert Page's and Alfred Edward Housman's views of Horace *Odes* 4.7.

10

PHILOLOGICAL VOODOO OR PSEUDORTHODOXY

As published research reveals, philologists can readily lapse into hermeneutical sorcery of various species when they purchase values or perceptions of the present at the expense of an accurate view of antiquity. Morton Smith, who in view of his broad acquaintance with ancient sorcery might have denominated such vested-interest interpretive procedures as philological voodoo, used the less provocative term pseudorthodoxy, with insistence on the importance of the prefix *pseud*, when he administered a rebuke to Old Testament scholars. After itemizing a series of Old Testament data which he claimed "nobody" accepts or believes, he clarified definition by exposure of specific performance: "But everywhere there are persistent efforts to square the facts of the OT as far as possible with the traditional teachings of the institutions, and even more, to make them serviceable for homiletical presentation" (M. Smith, 1969:21). Variations of such methodology can be found even among the best scholars in ancient times, and in modern times among those also who have no theological turf to protect.

Rationalization

Model historian Thukydides could not overcome the temptation. Truesdell Brown (1962:262–63) argues that the Greek historian manipulated Homeric epic to show that the Trojan War was not really first-class, certainly not like the one Thukydides was describing. Thukydides's insistence on the historicity of the epic was like the stubborn rearguard action fought to preserve long-held conceptions of the historicity of Noah and his ark, or like theorizing about the juice of unfermented grapes "to win N. T. support for modern sumptuary legislation" (263). Similarly, Greek historians had a proclivity for rationalizing whatever data appeared to contradict established opinion. In the manner of some OT scholars' approaches to the "days" of Genesis 1, ancient historians were wont to call each season or even each month in Egyptian history a "year" (268). And in the first book of his History, Thukydides does not question the historicity of Hellen, the son of Deukalion, or of Minos and his thallasocracy, or of Achilles, Pelops, Tyndareus, Atreus,

Agamemnon, and others.[1] In an exposure of propensity for rationalization of history relative to the New Testament, Richard Hiers (1966) showed how New Testament scholarship struggled since 1900 against eschatology with a view to safeguarding the authority and validity of the scriptural message for the twentieth century.[2] Similarly, William Robinson (1965) interprets the dogmatic interest in A. J. B. Higgins, *Jesus and the Son of Man,* as an endeavor to cover up some of the loss sustained by historical inquiry.[3] Ventures into psychological analysis of ancient personages are hazardous, as Howard Kee (1958) observed when he queried John Knox for stating that Jesus would have been insane to claim Messiahship.[4]

The "principle of the Empty Head," as someone termed presuppositionless exegesis, is not to be advocated, but eisegesis is a subtle form of manipulation whereby the category of immutability transmutes the past into a shelter for the present. By reading one's own interests into an ancient text one can turn it, in the words of Henry Nash (1892), into a "portable fatherland."[5] In support, Joseph Thayer put under indictment a tendency to neutralize the remoteness of ancient texts through interpretations that the texts are *made to bear* (Thayer, 1895). Continental scholars were in Thayer's judgment especially prone to thetical exploration and attendant pre-judgment of data, and he reminded them "how much simpler history is than speculation" (Thayer, 1899:128). In *The Peril of Modernizing Jesus* (1937), Henry Cadbury declared anachronizing of documents a besetting temptation and reviewed the lesson in 1964 with a warning against seeing one's own forms of worship or catechetical instruction in early Christianity. "The words 'liturgical' and 'catechetical' are not very applicable to them," he wrote (1964:145). Hendrikus Boers (1970) criticized the Swiss theologian Oscar Cullmann for basing exegetical conclusions on systematic presuppositions and took Reginald Fuller to task for using assumptions relating to the "Historical Jesus" to validate the christology expressed in the New Testament.[6] A concern to invoke biblical authority in behalf of the enslaved and women's rights may result in under-exposure of those aspects of biblical

---

[1] See Walbank, 1960:221.

[2] Compare John Reumann's (1964) critique of a related approach in Solomon Zeitlin's *Who Crucified Jesus?*; Zeitlin argued for two Sanhedrins at the time of Jesus, one of puppets and another authentically religious.

[3] See also Minear's (1964) critique of Bo Reicke's "social" conservatism as evidenced in the latter's commentary on the Epistles of James, Peter, and Jude in the "Anchor Bible Series."

[4] On this type of hazard, see also Albright, 1949:373.

[5] Nash's essay remains a classic introduction to ancient Greco-Roman exegetical practice.

[6] Since the "historical Jesus" is presumably determined on the basis of standard historical methodology, such a figure is necessarily in conflict with the New Testament's christology, which transcends the categories within which historical methodology is competent to do its work. See also John O'Rourke's (1965) criticism of an "unreal world of scholarship" in a work by Pius Goicoechea; Teeple, 1960; and Dillon, 1972.

tradition that are not supportive, argues Wayne Meeks (1981) in a review of Leonard Swidler's *Biblical Affirmations of Woman*. "One may reasonably wonder," Meeks writes, "whether the problems exposed are not far too deep to be remedied by so facile a concept as 'affirmation.' "

It is readily apparent that practitioners of philological voodoo arrange matters in their own favor. Like Rozinante, they take the way that leads them to their own stable. Morton Enslin (1933:238) praised the authors of the *Beginnings of Christianity* for doing the opposite. They had, he wrote, "an incurable and wholesome fear of giving a specious clarity to what is really obscure." They did not cry "peace, peace, when there is no peace."[7] Scott, on the other hand, "produced the most decided alteration of scholarly opinion" on Homeric scholarship, yet it was said of his *Unity of Homer* (1920) that he found "little space to set forth evidence that ran counter to his thesis."[8] It is regrettable that Scott did not follow Susan Franklin's example. She waited for new inscriptions to throw light so as to "define the custom [of public appropriations] to exact limits of time or locality" (Franklin, 1901:82) On the positive side one can also register that the "Bungling Redactor" has all but disappeared from the vocabulary of scholars.

Noble Lie

Part of the banality of bad philology is the uniformity of its instruments; and unwillingness to face realities in a text has encouraged propagation of numerous varieties of Plato's "noble lie" during the history of classical and biblical exegesis.[9]

The lie may cloak itself in textual criticism that masks a moralistic alteration of an author's work. In a discussion of a fragment from Menander's poetic corpus, Leonard Woodbury (1979) shows that objection to homosexuality prompted alteration of the masculine *allon* to the feminine *allēn*, resulting in loss of point in the finely crafted poem.

Resort to "literary convention" is one of the routes taken to escape facing "the occurrence in ancient writers of ideas which" one "cannot accept," instructs Agnes Michels (1955) in a discussion of Propertius's references to ghosts. But the one "who did not believe in ghosts was," she says, "the exception in the ancient world."[10]

Alleged accuracy of St. Mark's Gospel has often been purchased through

---

[7] A related mistake is made, according to Morris Jastrow (1917:11), when a tradition is rejected "without satisfactorily accounting for its rise and growth." Such an error, he states, is "as fatal from the scientific point of view as to accept it in the face of insuperable difficulties."

[8] Dow, 1965:20 and 9.

[9] See Plato *Republic* 3.415b–c; *Laws* 663 d–e. Grammarians on occasion refer to "beneficial" lies, as in the standard description of the signs for the first aorist active; cf. Fobes, 1957, introductory remarks.

[10] Michels, 1955:174 n. 14.

appeal to his interest in detail. The protest proves too much. Ancient novelists even gave accurate mileage statistics.[11] But not all is top-flight scholarship. In the *Amphitruo,* Plautus ascribes a harbor to Thebes, even as William Shakespeare in the *Winter's Tale* not only gives Bohemia a sea coast but surrounds Delphi with water,[12] as Rudyard Kipling makes "the old Moulmein Pagoda" look "eastward to the sea," whereas it lies opposite Ragoon, which is on the western shore of the gulf of Martaban, with no China "crost the Bay." Yet poetic license is assured renewability if the *National Geographic Magazine* is to be forgiven for permitting barracudas to "prowl" off Portland, Oregon.[13]

Notorious is Jerome's contrived explanation of Paul's dispute with Peter, described in Galatians 2, as a pretense of disagreement over an issue of Christian observance. To save the reputation of John the Baptist, numerous commentators in earlier centuries argued that John's disciples, not John, had a problem about christology. This, despite the fact that Jesus explicitly says in Luke 7:22, "Go and tell John."[14] Also, as part of an endeavor to maintain the credibility of Jesus, historical judgments concerning Old Testament events and documents are still being readjusted in a few quarters to remain in accord with statements made in the New Testament.[15] Resort to the "noble lie" is especially evident in some discussions of the date for the crucifixion of Jesus. As someone put it, an early date makes the chronology of the gospels "run more smoothly." Those who maintain an early date of 30 C.E. ordinarily reckon John's ministry from Tiberius's co-regency with Augustus; but, as numerous commentators have pointed out, such mode of reckoning appears to be unprecedented.[16]

Nevertheless, while steering clear of the Scylla of credulity one must be wary of the Charybdis of undue skepticism. Pseudo-Kallisthenes 1.34 states that Alexander was officially enthroned as Pharaoh of the Egyptians in 332. Inscriptions have proved him right.[17] "Nothing ventured, nothing gained" lacked dogmatic finality for Russel Geer. "I shall not try," he said in a study

---

[11] See Mason, 1979.

[12] See Blackman, 1969.

[13] Thomas Y. Canby, "El Nino's Ill Wind," *National Geographic* 165, 2 (February, 1984) 154.

[14] Chrysostom, Luther, Calvin, Beza, Grotius, Bengel, and others sponsor the face-saving view; see Alfred Plummer's list in *A Critical and Exegetical Commentary on the Gospel According to S. Luke,* 4th ed. (Edinburgh: T. and T. Clark, 1901) 202.

[15] See, e.g., Horace Dwight Hummel, *The Word Becoming Flesh: An Introduction to the Origin, Purpose and Meaning of the Old Testament* (St. Louis: Concordia, 1979).

[16] For one of the most complete discussions, see Husband, 1915. Cf. Plummer, pp. 81–82, cited above in note 14; I. Howard Marshall, *The Gospel of Luke: A Commentary on the Greek Text* (Grand Rapids: Eerdmans, 1978) 133.

[17] See Fredricksmeyer, 1979:60–61 n. 58; for further information on Alexander's historian, see Prentice, 1923.

of Nero, "to interpret facts," but "merely to ascertain them" (Geer, 1931). By the time of the second centennial of SBL, Luke's alleged howler of associating Quirinius with the census cited in Luke 2 may be clarified. Granting for the present that he has confused some details, Lily Taylor (1933) thought the Evangelist might be right about the specification of return to one's residence.[18]

Less negative dogmatism does not necessarily spell capitulation to blind traditionalism. Henry Fowler (1930) reminds biblical scholars that Herodotos is "good authority for the great events of 490 and 480, for many participants in Marathon and Salamis were alive in his day." Similarly, he observes, some Hebrew historians who wrote even earlier than Herodotos are to be credited with relative accuracy from David on (213–14).

In fairness to biblical scholars who have displayed what appears in the judgment of some an excessive interest in charging biblical writers with errors, it is necessary to inquire into extenuating factors. Were it not for the special pleading that is amply documented in the history of both classical and biblical exegesis, it would not have been necessary to give what appears to be disproportionate emphasis to some of the problems. What Milton Humphreys (1915) said of Hephaistion the metrist's work bears axiomatic value: It is important "to prove the incompetence of" Hephaistion due to "the fact that the more incompetent he was, the more important it is to prove him so, now that great importance is attached to his statements" (33).[19]

Ex Silentio

Ex silentio argument permeates pages of learned discussion. Levi Post discovered that its use may involve a demand for repentance. After the recovery of Menander's *Dyskolos*, he discovered that Menander's thought is broader in range than he had imagined. In an article entitled "Virtue Promoted in Menander's *Dyscolus*," he recanted his injustice to the Greek playwright (Post, 1960). It was once thought that the deceptive slave in comedy was mainly a Roman creation, but then there came to light papyrus fragments that pointed to Greece.[20] Were there large imperial estates in Bithynia and Pontus, as Michael Rostovtzeff held? Thomas Broughton (1934) states that there is little evidence for the affirmative. The answer is important for one inquiring about the social conditions of the constituency to which 1 Peter is addressed.[21]

---

[18] For an outstanding review of the evidence, with detailed bibliography, see Fitzmyer, 1981:391–417; add Brewster, 1927 (see esp. p. 137 n. 27).

[19] The chief value of Hephaistion's work on Greek metric patterns is the collection of fragments of lost poems that it embodies.

[20] See Harsh, 1955.

[21] Among the earliest and most thorough applications of sociological methodology to the explication of 1 Pet is that of Elliott, 1981. In a discussion (*Int* 37:1983, 84–88) of Elliott's book,

Questions of authenticity offer "unlimited opportunity for unending disputation," cautioned George Calhoun (1934) in a discussion of Demosthenes *Oration* 29. He bemoaned the trend "to substitute hypothesis or hasty assumption for what after all must remain the primary data of philology," and "to envelope our text in a mist of pseudo-criticism." Such procedures, he said, are "easy stepping stones to professorial chairs." As though he were glossing the point, Elroy Bundy, campaigner against historicistic fantasy in Pindaric criticism, put the entire craft under discipline when he warned that idiosyncratic tastes may lead "us to prefer the irrelevancies we invent to the perfect tact of what is really there" in the text.[22] Quest for answers to questions of authenticity may narrow the data base to pre-ordained conclusions. This was the basic methodological weakness in the "Tübingen school" of Friedrich Baur, and it appears in discussions of genuineness of Pauline letters based on presence or lack of "feeling," "intensity," and "religious fervor." Fraenkel objected on such grounds to the genuineness of Horace *Odes* 3.16. Countering, R. Joseph Schork (1971) asked why all Horace's odes must be keyed to the same emotional pitch? Must we have one-track authors?

Antinomia and Laws of Inference

Violation of laws of inference can readily bring one into non-compliance with research requirements. For the unwary on the primrose path of literary criticism, such words as the following invite hearty approval at first reading: "It should be a basic principle in interpreting Aeschylus that when language and syntax are most difficult the poet has compressed the greatest number of meanings into the smallest possible space" (Lebeck, 1963:iii). It is also true that the poet can count on the background of the audience and so reduce the volume of diction. This would certainly be true of correspondence such as St. Paul's, in which density of texture can be ascribed to assumption of clarification by the dispatcher of the letter. Inferences of textual corruption or lack of documentary integrity would therefore come under careful review.[23] In the case of 1 Pet 3:3–4 it is by no means certain that the passage permits an inference of affluence about some of the addressees. The "not-this-but-that *topos*" in the passage may well incorporate imperatives as the equivalents of informative description, producing the following effect: "Our community does not have a primary interest in external adornment, but in

---

Danker failed to give sufficient indication of its broad range of contents.

[22] The quotation is from Miller, 1981:143, citing Bundy, 1962:35–36.

[23] On the question of integrity of documents, Ezra P. Gould (1892) argued that insistence on such might, in view of the complexity of factors of discontinuity, obscure the very sanity that was alleged for the documents.

the inner ornamentation."[24] Gildersleeve exposed the fallacy of attributing country orientation to one who speaks of trees, plants, birds, and tools, as does Aristophanes, and he questioned Maurice Croiset's view that Aristophanes must have been country bred because of his knowledge of country life. (1930:128–32).[25] Gildersleeve liquidates the process: "In my judgment all such argumentation, however seductive, is vain." In 1927 Morton Enslin thought that it was appropriate to question the probability of Paul's alleged rabbinic training. He concluded that it was an assumption and not a fact.

The subject of pseudonymity from time to time invites false inference. It is important to maintain a distinction between ethics and morality, not to speak of distinction between genres, when making documentary comparisons. Morton Smith fails to do the latter when he reprimands Josef Sint, author of *Pseudonymität im Altertum,* for stating that in the case of the *Sibylline Oracles* one cannot speak of deliberate falsification because the author was using an established literary form. Smith injects parenthetically: "This, of course, is nonsense; forgers regularly use established forms, e.g., the check and the will." (M. Smith, 1961:189) But Sint might well have replied that forging of checks and wills involves collision with explicit legal language and punitive procedures and that such is not ordinarily the case with pseudonymous publication in antiquity.

One of the most notorious instances of irrelevant inference has to do with the term *bidentes* in *Aeneid* 4.56–58. Vergil writes that Dido and Anna "visit the shrines of the Gods, and at every altar beg for peace; they sacrifice *bidentes* chosen in due fashion." Whether the term meant "two years old" or "with two teeth" was a hot topic in antiquity, as witness the research accorded the matter by Servius and, long before him, by Gellius, who lathered Vergil with much learned but irrelevant, that is, unscholarly opinion. Apparently not until the nineteenth century, so far as can be determined, did it occur to anyone to seek out the best possible source of information on the problem. In the presence of three farmers, who may never have read Vergil but would have had no trouble understanding him in the matter at hand, Knapp repeated an experiment carried out in 1853 by an Irish physician, James Henry—he looked into the mouth of a sheep. His on-site research confirmed Henry's detailed comment on the subject, to the effect that Vergil's *bidens* is not a synonym for *biennis* but refers to the two permanent teeth that at the age of one year replace two of the eight milk teeth, and these two teeth appear to be dominant until the end of the second year.

Occasionally an inference enrolls in the category of the bizarre. A member of the guild drolly argued that on the basis of a colleague's view of the means of transportation used by Ugaritic deities one might well conclude

---

[24] On the subject in general, see Watson, 1982:241.
[25] On Croiset, see Gildersleeve, 1930:145–46.

that donkey riding may have been beyond the technical competence of the Ugaritians (Pope 1964:74).

Pseudoproblemitis

From time to time scholars have cautioned their colleagues against merykia, more widely known as rumination syndrome, and sometimes called anathermia, a term suggested by its association in Mexico with beans. Stripped of technical jargon, these terms have in the main pseudoproblemitis as their referent, the need to recycle problems that require input of fresh data before any direction toward a genuine solution can be taken. Erwin Goodenough recommended resignation of membership from the guild that is most susceptible to the virus: "We cannot be alchemists endlessly repeating the same experiments" (1952:2). And if we do, we may not escape, as someone put it, the "danger of suffocation from our own exhaust fumes."

The basic cause has long been recognized. Except for groups dedicated to specific authors, such as Shakespeare, Bacon, and Browning, where the disease is as lethal as hemophilia, none are so susceptible to anathermia as are biblical and classical societies. This is due to the fact that these two scholarly classes deal with very small encompassments of literature. In biblical circles, for example, the discussion of "Son of man" has taken on the status of a cliché. And no matter how many "fresh" studies one reads on the year of the crucifixion of Jesus Christ, one has difficulty finding anything in them, except perhaps a reference to Sejanus's role in imperial politics, that has not been said better and more succinctly, and with full assemblage of data, than in the article, "The Year of the Crucifixion," by Richard Husband (1915), in which its author opts for 33 C.E.[26]

Since many recitals from antiquity do not satisfy the rigorous historical requirement for independent attestation, it is well to remember Paul Shorey's view of useless speculation on matters that do not admit of scientific verification. "Prof. Titchener," he said, "quotes the problem, 'Should a man be allowed to marry his widow's sister?' with the comment: 'I may be obtuse; but I confess that I can find in this question no food for thought'" (Shorey, 1916:208). One needs more than the eyes of Lynceus to see the things that are not there. Was Ovid ever *really* in love? Is Corinna real? In a discussion of Ovid's poems, John Sullivan (1961) reminded students of the futility of such engagement in pseudoproblematics. The approach taken by a contributor to *The Wycliffe Bible Commentary* injects a welcome tone of judicious modesty. Faced with the "problem" concerning the type of anesthesia used by God to induce such a deep sleep on Adam as would be in accord with the "divine mercy" in rendering the major surgery without pain, the commentator confessed: "That remains a mystery" (Enslin, 1963).

---

[26] See also Husband, 1916. There is also much valuable data to be had in Amadon, 1942, who dates the crucifixion in 31 C.E.

American scholars may appreciate the fact that pseudoproblemitis knows no ocean barrier. On the basis of alleged biblical data James Ussher put the creation of the world at 4004 B.C. Another British scholar, Philip Macdonnel, tackled problems in another bible and, on the basis of alleged astronomical data in books Pi and Rho of the *Iliad,* came up with 28 August 1185 B.C.E. as the date of Hector's death.[27]

Numerous explanations of origins of ancient matters are likely to be found as absurd as many of those proposed for the origin of ancient rites and customs at the banquets that inspired Plutarch's *Symposiacs.* As Benjamin Wheeler once said in another context, such speculative ventures only serve to "encumber would-be scholarship with vast accumulation of hopeless lumber" (Wheeler, 1900). James Frame echoed the thought in comment on 1 Thess 4:6 with an indictment of interpreters who "introduce an exegesis so frigid and unnatural as to make us wonder that such good names should be associated with an interpretation seemingly so improbable."

Humorist Josh Billings once made public confession concerning his speculations about intellectual activity: "Theze subjeks are tew much for a man ov mi learning tew lift. i kant prove any of them and i hav too mutch venerashun tew guess at them." Paul Shorey's spelling is the only improvement on the thought. There are "trifles or puzzles that will always remain matters of opinion," he tried to tell his colleagues (Shorey 1919:39). But not all had ears to hear. Not since its founding had *JBL* borne such an impressive assemblage of Greco-Roman material on a single problem of the New Testament as that which appeared in 1945 under the title "Barabbas." Author Horace Rigg (1945) offers a solution of the Barabbas "mixup" that would have made Menander envious but merited numerous rebukes for fantasy from a German expert on Zealots.[28] One is reminded of two noted surgeons, one English and one French. The Frenchman asked the Englishman how many times he had performed some feat of surgery requiring a rare combination of nerve and dexterity. "Thirteen times" came the answer. "Ah! but Monsieur, I have performed him 160 times. How many times did you save his life?" The Englishman replied, "I saved 11 out of 13. How many did you save out of 160?" "Ah! Monsieur, I lose 'em all, but the operation was very brilliant."

In his *Praise of Folly* Desiderius Erasmus sketched for all time the profile of grammarians who overlook no work in their provenance, no matter how barbarously or tediously written. To judge from critical rhetoric within the craft, preoccupation with puzzles has encouraged catena-like pedantry that

[27] Philip Macdonnel, "Who's Who in Homer," *CR* 55 (1941) 16.
[28] See Martin Hengel, *Die Zeloten* (Leiden: Brill, 1961). In the history of botched literary works the Bible does not take second place to Shakespeare, whose misfortune is lamented by Mark H. Liddell (1898). Many of the notes in commentaries, he observes, are "historic absurdities, are written mostly by scholars who look upon Shakespeare as modern English and are continually liable to misunderstandings just like those of the general readers" (466).

burdens numerous commentaries with collections of views that range from
philological improbabilities to monuments of perverted erudition whose
chief claim to fame is obscuration of the lucidity of the text. Many, for
example, are the alleged solutions to the "needle's eye" image (Luke 18:25).
But children who have not been misled by the textbooks know what is going
on and they laugh at the prospect of trying to get the hump through
grandma's needle.

Yet "some philological questions, although insoluble, are like old friends
and should not be neglected," challenges Walter Allen with a revisitation to
the phrase *fabam mimum* in one of Cicero's *Letters to Atticus* (Allen, 1951 and
1959).[29] And on occasion, review of evidence can enrich perception or
compound complexity. Sir William Ramsay thought that Iconium received
colonial status in the time of Hadrian, but Stephen Mitchell argues that "at
least from the reign of Claudius," Iconium "was ostensibly a double community," both polis and colony (Mitchell, 1979:415).

Improper Classification

Improper classification can be an abiding source of trouble, especially
for literary critics. Athenaeus 2.65a contains the only occurrence of the word
epyllion, cited by LSJM in the sense of "little epic." So-called pillars of
classical learning have used the term as though the "epyllion" existed as a
clearly defined form. Walter Allen suggested that the term be banned from
critical discourse or be used in a wider sense to mean "all poems in the new
narrative style as opposed to the Homeric epics" (Allen, 1940). New Testament scholars might well take the cue in discussions of "aretalogy," a term that
is similarly rare and not clearly defined in antiquity. In line with Allen's suggestion, it is advisable to take the term aretalogy out of its customary modern
association with the specialized miraculous activity of a deity and use it as
a generic term for all species of recitals of superior performance or character,
whether ascribed to deities or human beings, to high or low, and whether
biographical or autobiographical in form. Such classification would accord
with historical data respecting the use of the term *aretē.*[30]

Ideological Tenure

Ideas whose authority is measured by length of tenure die hard. As
Vincent Rosivach (1978) pointed out in connection with exposition of the
poet Catullus, commentaries can be a distressing source for perpetuation of
error.[31] The phrase *Morituri te salutamus* is, despite its inclusion in modern
descriptions of gladiatorial combat, not to be considered a standard salute.

---

[29] Despite the simplifications offered by emendation, Allen (1959) favors elucidation.

[30] See Danker, 1982:487; and above, pp. 9, 10, 13.

[31] Note the reference in Rosivach, 1978:213 to perpetuated error in LSJM, s.v. *skorpios.*

A study of the phrase by Harry Leon (1939) reveals that the only ancient references are to be had in Suetonius 21.6 and Dio Cassius 60.33.3–4, and both refer to the same episode, a naval battle under Claudius. It is of course possible that the use of the phrase in connection with one event may reflect more general usage, but possibility does not equal probability, and as the British scholar Alfred Housman once said, "Accuracy is a duty and not a virtue."[32] The fact is that we do not know and we ought to say so. *Mille verisimile non fauno un vero.* Freely rendered: "Repetition of a bad idea lends no more certainty to it. It only makes it an older bad idea."

Little Jack Horner

The converse of maintaining traditional error is the technique popularized in other connections in the Soviet Union and called the Little Jack Horner Syndrome. William Shakespeare immortalized the phenomenon in his fifty-ninth sonnet:

> If there be nothing new, but that which is
> Hath been before, how are our brains beguiled,
> Which, laboring for invention, bear amiss
> The second burden of a former child.

To judge from the notes appended to articles in learned journals in the closing decades of the twentieth century, it was a period burgeoning with new ideas, theories, and proper constructions for accommodation of the data from antiquity. But numerous footnotes record very little that was published more than ten years before the article went to press. The truth is, there was a trend toward neglect of scholarly ancestry by singers of Euphorion, who knew only their own day. Much of the flood of secondary literature is the direct result of the Jack Horner Syndrome but, if one is to believe reviewers, a comparison with what has been said before frequently reveals little that is genuinely fresh.

In 1969 Morton Smith invited biblical scholars to reevaluate a developing over-emphasis on novelty. "So long as I can remember," he said, "we have always had someone to inform us of the 'latest' publications, to assure us that his own and those of his students expressed the 'latest' views, and to dismiss the rest as 'superannuated'—as if scholarship were a matter of fashion" (M. Smith, 1969:19).

Few scholars appear to be aware of the fact that a collective interpretation of the term "Son of Humanity" was in vogue three decades before Thomas Manson of Great Britain advanced the corporate interpretation. In 1900, Nathaniel Schmidt reassessed the view as presented in his time and concluded that the figure in question is the angel Michael.

---

[32] Alfred Edward Housman, *Manilii, Astronomicon, Liber Quintus* (London: Richards, 1930). The quotation is from "Libro I Addenda," p. 105.

Several decades before the subject mushroomed in American biblical circles, *JBL* imported from Germany one of the finest summaries in the English language on the relation of Christianity to Hellenism[33] A close second is Selby McCasland's (1932) article, "Portents in Josephus and in the Gospels." Besides securing information from Josephus, McCasland pumps Suetonius and Dio Cassius. The two articles are tantamount to a poor scholar's Wendland or Wetstein, but little credit is accorded them, and students who limit their study to the literature of their own decade may never realize that they are dealing with tertiary and even more mathematically distanced productions. Along the same lines, Gildersleeve wrote in a wisdom-laden year: "In earlier days my righteous soul may have been vexed by the silent appropriation of the results of my work. The Greek *nemesan* is a legitimate feeling, but if I am not 'past feeling,' like the Scriptural reprobate, that feeling is chiefly one of amusement at the claims of discovery that are put forward from time to time, partly, perhaps largely, from the fact that in reviewing the course of my decades of study I have found that what I had thought was my own achievement, may have been little more than reminiscence. *t'ama d'ema* is often a vain boast" (Gildersleeve, 1915:482).

Preoccupation with novelty has demoralizing side-effects, and one of these is extemporized learning, a species of intellectual atrocity. Delivery of fresh sand, usually in the form of newly-discovered documents, into the arena of scholarly debate is almost certain to effect a rash. Gildersleeve describes a classic case. Upon the publication of hitherto unknown poems by Bakchylides, numerous scholars rushed into print. Because of the specialized knowledge required, very few, wrote Gildersleeve, could speak authoritatively about them. But he knows the weaknesses of the trade and can hear, even before the work of reconstruction of the mutilated passages is done, that Pindar was "a landlubber and Bacchylides a seasoned sailor" (Gildersleeve, 1930:47). Henry Cadbury (1960) had something similar to say about members of his own guild: "The ambition to say something new often outweighs the ambition to say something true" (197).

To recite portions of the dismal tale of unseasoned scholarship that greeted the discovery of the Qumran documents imposes such a drain on one's responsibility for reputations that it is best to follow the advice that Pindar (Olympian 1.35) gave himself in a different matter[34]

Interest in novelty begets fantasy, and one can repeat the experience of Don Quixote, whose distracted brain readily applied every object to his romantic ideas. The White Queen had no trouble, as every one knows, in believing six impossible things before breakfast. "We prefer to guess a lot than know so little," mourned Henry Cadbury in a presidential address (1937:12). One scholar's theoretical fog may, of course, years later be another's

---

[33] Dobschuetz, 1914.
[34] The curious will consult material in Sandmel, 1962.

assured instrument of illumination, for "when the new has been proved old we are satisfied that we understand it," wrote Frank Porter (1929:3). Nevertheless, proposals appear from time to time which lack the persuasiveness that attends conclusions based on sober consideration of the evidence. Very early in the history of SBL, T. W. Chambers (1887) replied to Samuel Cox, who had claimed that in Eph 2:3 "children of wrath" means "men who give way to wrath." His association of the term with Hellenistic *orgies* "makes a strong draft," says Chambers, "upon the confidence of his hearers or readers" (107). Similarly George Barton bombarded Prof. Wiener's catalog of what Barton viewed as philological monstrosities, criticizing its perpetrator for "improvised scholarship" and deflating Wiener's four principles of textual criticism by declaring that "what in them is true is not new and what is new is not true" (Barton, 1914:62). Despite the many valuable contributions in Erwin Goodenough's *Jewish Symbols*, Morton Smith charged the latter with the "fantasy" of "pandemic sacramental paganism" (1967:65).

Taking the easy way out in one's own favor is one of the bypaths to fantasyland, well-hawked by "cheap vendors of ruinous exegetical felicity," to paraphrase Italy's Il Duce. Before going through the gate of enchantment, synoptic buffs do well to heed Burton Easton's reminder (1910) that words used in Q and Mark and borrowed by Luke cannot be tabulated haphazardly as proof of Luke's fondness for the terms.[35]

Another side-effect of search for novelty is lapse out of basic scholarly morality and into plagiarism. In a paragraph on the evolution of certainty, Morton Enslin said that "ofttimes without a fresh reworking a judgment, originally expressed with caution, becomes the 'tested result of criticism.'" The "effort to avoid plagiarism consists too often merely in deleting the 'apparently's,' or 'possibly's,' or 'not improbably's.'" (Enslin, 1927:62). Similarly, Shorey had sharp words for those who "elude the responsibilities of accuracy by omitting quotation marks" (Shorey, 1906a:190).

A more refined type of plagiarism is related to the type of pseudorthodoxy that takes the gold and kills the goose. Such radical incivility is not practiced by seasoned researchers. They simply incorporate the fruits of the older philology, think Greek technology, and cry *eurēka*. Gildersleeve observed the process at work in connection with metrical theory. "The Fool's Paradise out of which you have been thrust is sure to become once more the land of Beulah, if you wait long enough" (Gildersleeve, 1930:166). As the song went, "Everything old is new again." Leonard Thompson (1981:343–44) suggests a route for repentance:

> Like other specialists, biblical critics thickly describe their data and interpretations from a controlling point of view which, in the course of time, passes through the organic rhythms of birth, maturation, exhaustion, and death. During times of transition from one controlling point of view to

---

[35] See also Easton, 1911.

another, a rather curious psychosocial effect occurs: the newer interpreters share a sense of being able to 'see through' an earlier approach and to lay bare its inadequacies. There may even be the sense that the data are appearing in their uninterpreted nakedness. Such, of course, is never the case. New critical concerns do not void earlier interpretations, nor do they unmask the text. Significant continuities can be traced through shifts in point of view, and the most recent interpreter always depends upon those millenia-long hermeneutical tangles to make the Bible accessible. New perspectives can, however, catch a glimpse of unnoticed elements in the text by relating it in fundamentally novel ways to human behavior and those sciences interpreting it.

Agnoia

Simple unawareness of developments within a discipline may stunt philological growth. Colwell noted an anarthrous noun in John 1:49 and published a study on the subject in 1933. Grammarians Archibald Robertson, Albert Debrunner, and Charles Moule promptly took account of it. Not so the contributors to *The Interpreter's Bible*. "But," sighed Colwell in 1960, "thirty to thirty-five years from the date of original publication, the commentators will be using fugitive material of this sort" (200).

Snobbery and its Antidote

Snobbery is a subtle ingredient of pseudorthodoxy, for it limits the vision. As Sanuel Angus (1909) noted, classicists as a tribe too often ignored the philological importance of the New Testament. But Henry Cadbury saw signs in 1938 of a breakdown of barriers between specialists in the "secular" and "sacred" areas (86). The words of Paul and those of others, wrote Moore in 1911, "must be interpreted with due regard to their Hellenistic as well as their Jewish environment." From the perspective of later decades this judgment is a truism, but at the same time a necessary reminder that the New Testament contains documents that reflect the thought and life of a subculture within Greco-Roman society. Much of the surviving Greek and Roman literature is written from a snobbish perspective. Even the bucolic literature is sanitized. Vergil writes about cows and bees, but his heart is with the grandeur that is Rome. We know much about imperial and senatorial matters, but little do we hear the tears of those who really bear the weight beneath the state.

The New Testament fills a major gap with its sectarian diction, much of which is vulgar to ears trained for Attic purity and requires upgrading at the stage of translation. Gildersleeve (1930), who considered periodic scything of snobbery a contribution to the philological landscape, pondered the relation of esthetic interest and the commanding weight of documentary content. In the course of a discussion of the theory and art of translation, and whether translations should improve on the original, he said that there was a serious side to the matter. "How much fewer fastidious souls," he declared, "would have been saved, if the Greek of the New Testament had not been transposed into the organ notes of the Authorized Version. Only the robuster sort can forgive *ean* with the indicative and associate with the riffraff of worse than plebeian names that figure in the last chapter of the Epistle to the Romans" (64). Gildersleeve's axiom, "if the style of the original is perverse or awkward, it falls outside of the artistic category" (63), cries for consideration from anyone who approaches biblical documents in terms of esthetic categories.

Lack of Integrity

Softness of tone in George Moore's (1905) prose is not to be construed as lack of earnestness.[36] Thinking of references made with minimum capital outlay, he wrote, "I have observed that a man who does not verify his references usually has a touching confidence that his predecessor was more honest" (Moore, 1905:170 n. 18).

A subtle violation of integrity was observed by Harry Orlinsky in connection with a critique he undertook of an early edition of Kittel's *Biblia Hebraica*. He found that textual difficulties were in some cases removed by the expedient of "interpretation" (Orlinsky, 1944:33).

From the preceding survey of scholarly approaches to data and their interpretation it is apparent that conscientious self-examination and a sense of responsibility for maintaining integrity within the craft left a positive stamp on biblical and classical spheres of inquiry. A prime target for criticism was the on-going temptation to force ancient data into a Procrustean thetical bed or to ignore the fact of an overly-constricted data base for certain avenues of inquiry. Akin to the foregoing temptation was the repeated exhibition of a zeal for novelty that frequently betrayed a lack of appreciation for the work of predecessors, if not clandestine plagiarism.

To conclude the matter, pseudo-science, especially when applied to the data of the Bible, deserves Matthew Arnold's verdict that it is "best called plainly what it is — utter blunder."

---

[36] Perhaps the second centennial observance of SBL will see the alternate spelling (Foote) of this scholar's name completely eradicated.

11

ASSORTED PHILOLOGICAL ABERRATIONS
AND AILMENTS

Philological voodoo performs in an environment of philological aberrations and ailments, of which there are varieties many. And, as biblical and classical studies amply attest, at the present level of competence for treatment many of them do not succumb to eradication as easily as did variola. At best, therefore, a centennial review of symptoms can hope that the future of the various guilds will see greater strides made toward purity of inquiry. Some may suggest that the clinical mode of discussion, despite the debt it owes to classical models, is inappropriate in a centennial volume, but the account merely reflects a rhetorical strain that runs through volume after volume of learned discussions and commentaries on the types of maladies here diagnosed. Moreover, a primary function of this chapter is not to pillory numerous scholars through a painfully detailed list of documented indiscretions. Rather, the lighter touch permits the scholarly community to share its wisdom and serve as Asklepiadai to the entire guild of interpreters without the pain of major surgery.

Logocheiropoiesia

Logocheiropoiesia, a strain of glossolalia, reached one of its most virulent stages in the scholastic period of theological studies. An outbreak of new strains in other areas of inquiry and for which there was no ready antidote took place in the centennial years. Those who developed this idiosyncratic phenomenon were unable, except for rapport with seven to twelve in their own circle, to expose themselves to recovery. To outsiders — in whose presence they display an extreme allergic reaction — they find it difficult to communicate in conventional prose and, according to René Wellek, use "a homemade terminology" that demands "a considerable effort of interpretation." Wellek cites Kenneth Burke as an "extreme" exhibit of such neological infliction and goes on to say: "They seem to feel the need of reformulating basic questions over and over again, to start *ab ovo* to think on aesthetic and critical problems which have a centuries-old history" (Wellek, 1953:123). Heavily injected with historical serum, biblical and classical philologists were once thought to be immune to the virus, but it was feared that increased demand for scholarly inquiry outside historical-critical and more traditional philological contexts would lead to unexpected outbreaks.

Less virulent strains of what is ordinarily known as jargon were noted from time to time. Classicists have periodically bemoaned the fact that students after four or six years in the gymnasial pattern in the United States could not read Greek or Latin. At least in this case the indigenous nature of the two languages had something to do with the lack of achievement. Contemporary production of material for linguistic torture is another matter, and Morton Enslin responded with reserved acerbity to Paul Schubert's *Form and Function of the Pauline Thanksgiving:* "It seems a pity that a scholar must sound as if he graduated from a school of education. When will jargon of this sort be put on the *index?*" (Enslin, 1940:78) Scholars who must increasingly deal with sheaves of bureaucratic prose will appreciate the fact that a decade later Albert Lynd lofted a similar lament about "pedagese" that passes for English in offices throughout the land" (1950:22–23). Not even Gallic scholars are immune. Taking account of Raymond Aron's description of historical writing as "the introspective calculation of possibilities," Benjamin Meritt commented that such diction was "a scholar's way of designating something non-scientific by a scientific name" (Meritt, 1962:9).

Occasionally scholars are caught in the crossfire of publishers' blurbs and scholars' efforts to bring rhetoric into harmony with reality. Michael Avi-Yonah and Emil Kraeling resigned themselves to the generous sentiments expressed in Erwin Goodenough's resumé of their enthusiastic contribution to the celebration of Israel's history, flora, and fauna: "I have given the review copy to my ten-year old grandson, who is delighted with its brightness and easy reading without critical misgivings" (Goodenough, 1963:141).

Pomposity keeps close company with jargon. But inspectors were on the trail. And even the editors of so prestigious an effort as the publication of the *Revised Standard Version* were not permitted to gaze enraptured at their egos. In 1947 W. Kendrick Grobel noted that in the phrasing of some of its notes *RSV* "retains the pompous language and the false premise of the *ARV* notes" with their references to "some (many, most) ancient authorities" and related expressions (Grobel, 1947, 362).

Tautologia

Tautologia is probably the most common, widely spread, and prevalent manifestation of philological disorders, and few in the craft possess the discipline exercised by Field Marshal von Moltke, who was said to be able to keep silent in six languages. In 1932, John Campbell exposed what must be the Guinness record for symptoms of the disease. Francisco Zorell, in connection with a discussion of the verb *koinōneō* in Heb 2:14, had informed his readers that the phrase in which the word occurs means: *mutuo inter se consortes sunt ejusdem communis naturae humanae.* Lest the magnitude of this achievement be lost on anyone for want of progress in Latin II, Zorell's reviewer wants it known that "here an idea which is scarcely in the Greek at all is expressed in no fewer than five different ways" (Campbell, 1932:32). Economically rendered: In a mutual relationship of interaffiliation with equippolence of shared humanity.

A closely related strain is the Pestalozzi virus, known on the street as the mountain-in-labor ailment. Rising to full academic height, Johann H. Pestalozzi (1746–1827) summarized his contribution to education: "If I look back and ask myself what I have really done toward the improvement of the methods of elementary education, I find that in recognizing observation as the absolute basis of all knowledge I have established the first and foremost important principle of instruction."[1] To combat the progeny of a Cambridge, England, dissertation, Abraham Malherbe (1977) called attention to the author's devotion of sixty pages to the use of the term *peithein* in literature up to the fourth century B.C.E. Malherbe observed that the net result was "the insight that the goal of persuasion, employing 'intellectual and existential arguments,' is to place the hearer in a position to make his own free decision" (149). The truth is, mathematics is against any scholar who thinks that an accumulation of data on a specific subject will necessarily spell conviction. In a rejection of a certain line of cumulative argument, Henry Cadbury (1926:209) quoted Lord Charnwood in support of his decision in the matter: " 'This is not one of those many instances in which indications separately slight collectively amount to an impressive or conclusive argument. Every one of these pieces of evidence by itself must be evaluated at nothing. And nothing may be added to nothing forever and ever, but the sum will still be nothing.' "

But history may after all be a poor teacher. In a presidential address before SBL in 1970 Harry Orlinsky informed the world that by the end of World War I, much biblical "talent and energy were spent in helping to demonstrate the law of diminishing returns" (Orlinsky 1971:3).

Parallelitis

Compounding of data may also compound error. Harry Orlinsky gave up an attempt to exorcise of its errors the third edition of Kittel's *Biblia Hebraica.* Peter Katz (Walters) informed the world that Orlinsky was not "very far from the truth when he says that not a single line in the apparatus of BH is free from mistakes regarding" the Septuagint.[2]

Indiscreet parallelizing may contribute to semantic paralysis. By appeal to parallels that span centuries, for example, the amount of *mythos* in a recital

---

[1] Quoted by Lynd, 1950:176.
[2] Cited by Orlinsky, 1971:7.

can be depreciated, with spurious increment for its *historia*. Polybios (34.2.9–10) followed this rationale when he likened the dolphin-ravening Scylla to natives in the Straits of Magellan catching swordfish. Polybios accepts much of Homer, and far less of Eratosthenes (Walbank, 1960:227). Similarly, Charles Chavel (1941) uses Mischna Pesachim 8.6 to validate the New Testament recital of amnesty for Barabbas (Mark 15:6–15 and parallels), despite the fact that there is no evidence from Greco-Roman documents for the practice.[3]

In *Paul and Palestinian Judaism*, Ed Sanders (1977) shows that much misunderstanding of ancient Jewish beliefs is traceable to indiscriminate use of alleged rabbinic parallels.[4] One of the most potent antidotes to misdirected parallelizing comes from the end of the nineteenth century.[5] Discussing the terms *theiotēs* and *theotēs*, Henry Nash insisted that bodies of thought behind the usage must be analyzed: "The ancient system of interpretation glorified God's Word by finding all possible meanings in it. Our system refuses to find in it anything that is not clearly there" (Nash, 1899:7).[6]

Basil Gildersleeve expressed himself repeatedly on the mania for heaping up parallel citations. Frequently, he said of the ramblers from Cecca to Mecca, "the appositeness of the citations is by no means in keeping with their number" (Gildersleeve, 1930:210). Across the street, Frank Porter said in a presidential address before SBL that "the question of new or old cannot be answered by finding of parallels, or not finding them" (Porter, 1929:5).

Of search for parallels in general, Samuel Sandmel (1962:7)[7] said: "It would seem to me to follow that, in dealing with similarities we can sometimes discover exact parallels, some with and some devoid of significance; seeming parallels which are so only imperfectly; and statements which can be called parallels only by taking them out of context. I must go

---

[3] See Winter, 1961:91–92, 198 nn. 2 and 6.

[4] It is difficult to understand why Sanders used Lloyd Gaston's review of a commentary on Luke (see *JBL* 94[1975]:140–41) as evidence for "continuation of the denigrating view of Judaism in English-speaking New Testament scholarship" (Sanders, 1977:55 n. 76), especially since the author of the book in question was zealous in protesting mudwashing of Jews. For example, an item on Pharisees: "Because of their notoriety in the New Testament they have as a class received a bad press, but their contribution to the continuity of the moral and religious life of Israel was enormous" (p. 68). Or, item on participation in the crucifixion: "Especially Luke is concerned to point out that it was not the Jewish people but their leaders who brought ruin to Jerusalem. . . . Anti-Semitism does display its ugly head when especially the Christian reader of the gospel thinks that 'the Jews' not he, are under the evangelist's scrutiny. Seven million Jews have known the pain of such evil application of the text" (p. 228).

[5] Sandmel (1962) preferred the term "parallelomania."

[6] The broad knowledge of the Greco-Roman world that Nash and a few of his contemporaries brought to NT interpretation was far less visible in *JBL*, apart from the work of Henry Cadbury, for at least five decades. On the use of Greco-Roman material in biblical study, see below.

[7] According to R. H. Charles, *Apocrypha and Pseudepigrapha* (1913) 1. 533, the term parallelomania was coined, as noted in Sandmel's discussion, by P. Menzel.

on to allege that I encounter from time to time scholarly writings which go astray in this last regard. It is the question of excerpt versus context, which I have touched on and now return to."

With fusillades directed especially against a stand-by known as "Strack-Billerbeck," which in his judgment was weighed in the critical balance and found wanting, Sandmel complained about scholars' uncritical use of Jewish sources in their comments on New Testament material. Others have cautioned the unwary that parallel lines never meet, and Eugene Nida's clear summaries of modern linguistic research, with special reference to semantic field, offered substantial antidote to parallelomania.[8]

False Prophecy

Given the nature of biblical subjects, it is not surprising that biblical scholars should from time to time don a prophet's mantle. But the readjustments that ancient prophets with revered credentials had to make on some of their psychic output suggests the need of caution. "Biblical science is doomed" in Germany because of "all-embracing totalitarian pragmatism . . .", prophesied Julius Morgenstern,[9] who ought to have known that Old Testament prophets were aware that tyrants had only times and times and a half. The totality was never theirs. And he could have said more about academicians who thought it was an insult to science to know what was going on in the world. In any event, such and related dire forecasts of a long dormancy of quality biblical scholarship in Germany after World War II simply failed of fulfillment, as had Paulsen's prediction that a third renaissance of the Classics would never come.

Psychedelic Scholarship

Periodically biblical and classical scholarship play host to the wondrous and the strange, often produced with Promethean ingenuity. In the privacy of hotel suites some may bemoan such productions as "perversities of scholarship." Others, echoing what one classicist termed "reckless proliferation of hypotheses," speak more elegantly about "truncation of truth." It must be granted that the Pan-Babylonian journalism and fantastic Jerahmeelite hypothesis at the turn of the nineteenth century extort, along with Gilbert Murray's interpretation of Homeric heroes as faded deities or "year spirits," a peculiar kind of admiration. And the vision of classicists hanging from Frazer's Golden Bough, with their Harrington-Cornford-Dionysiac fantasies gleaming in all their splendor, certainly challenges Ezekiel's wheel-in-wheels fantasy and evokes memory of George Hall's "Cardiff Giant," and of the "Moon Hoax" run by the New York Sun in August 1835. For protective

[8] See Nida, 1964 and 1969.
[9] See Morgenstern, 1942:4; and cf. Hyatt, 1948.

ointment Edgar Allan Poe's essay on Richard Adams Locke, editor of the *Sun*, ought to be read by all who venture to lay claim to another's credulity.

In 1936 Harold Stukey suggested a moratorium on procrusteanizing Greek religion within a framework of primitive religion. His caution suggests the necessity of recording Paul Achtemeier's (1974) reaction to a scholar's studies (M. Smith, 1973a,b) of an epistolary fragment ostensibly written by Clement of Alexandria to an otherwise unknown Theodore.[10] The fragment refers to a hitherto unknown "secret" version of Mark's Gospel that had allegedly fallen into the hands of Carpocrates. After acknowledging Smith's erudition — the heavily documented publication *Clement of Alexandria* (1973b) is a warehouse of information, especially on ancient magical practices, and Smith does not hesitate to incorporate views of some modern scholars that conflict with his own conclusions — Achtemeier proceeds to celebrate Smith's powers of imagination, punctuating with such phrases as: "arguments . . . awash in speculation"; "creative imagination . . . equal to the task"; "with such creativity all things are for the scholar, as for God, possible" (626); "a curiously facile, almost unreal, quality" (627); "vast amount of erudition, pressed into the service of a highly speculative 'field theory' of Christian origins" (628). Joseph Fitzmyer's (1973) shafts against such as "make crooked what was right and straight before" were more in number. Writing in *America*, he said: "For the contents of the majority" of the Cambridge volume, "Smith can justly be proud; he sought the advice and help of scores of scholars around the world and made excellent use of most of their counsel. Trouble is that Smith did not pay sufficient attention to the comments of some of them and did not allow the discipline of his scholarly profession to be his guide. And in this he turns out to be ridiculous." Going on with his demolition, Fitzmyer avers that Smith not only "published the Harvard technical discussion of Clement's letter, in which his scholarly skills are readily recognized, but . . . persuaded a second, otherwise reputable, publisher (Harper & Row) into putting out a popularization, entitled *The Secret Gospel: The Discovery and Interpretation of the Secret Gospel According to Mark*,"[11] whose title is "downright deceptive, for Smith has not discovered 'the Secret Gospel according to Mark. . . . In these days of Jesus-freaks, Jesus-people, Satanology, and the occult, all you have to tell a publisher is that you have discovered a 'secret gospel,' and Faust sells his soul!" (570) According to the *New York Times*, Smith expected lively controversy about his findings, less from documents than from people. He is quoted as saying: "I'm reconciled to the attacks. Thank God I have tenure."[12]

"Time was," wrote Bloomfield (1919), "when . . . a cock could not crow in the morning on his native dung-hill without being in the business of

---

[10] Achtemeier directs most of his critical attack against M. Smith, 1973b.

[11] See M. Smith, 1973a.

[12] *New York Times*, Tuesday, 29 May 1973, C 39. For a discussion of Paul and his world, see Smith, 1980.

staging a sun-myth" (77). The Oxford Solar Myth, sponsored in the nineteenth century by Frederick Paley for interpretation of the *Odyssey,* has long
been headstoned, but Francis M. Cornford still seduces adherents, and
usually to their embarrassment.[13] Bookseller Allen is said to have carried a
notation on Bohn's translation of Plato as "a fairly intelligible translation,
provided one use the Greek for a pony." John Crossan (1976b) made a similar
estimate of Cornford's conclusions about Aristophanes in a review of a study
by Dan Via on literary criticism.[14] Cornford's work, he commented,
"persuades completely, unless one reads Aristophanes to see if it is so." And
Crossan thought that Via should have done some critique of the secondary
source at the hand of the primary material.

Occasionally immigrants from the land of Nephelokokkygia are diagnosed in Everyperson's terms. Bruce Metzger says of certain scholars who
flourished at the beginning of the twentieth century that they caught
"Mandaic fever" (Metzger, 1964). In a SBL presidential address Ernest
Colwell eschewed medical diagnosis. He preferred to scorch "the followers
of Hort," who claimed to have espoused "objectivity," by incorporating
Housman's indictment of scholars who "use manuscripts as drunkards use
lamp-posts,—not to light them on their way but to dissimulate their
instability" (Colwell, 1948:3).

Senior Citizens Syndrome (SCS)

Difficult to avoid is the Senior Citizen's Syndrome. Old age elicits in
some scholars a feistiness or zest for bizarre adventures. The syndrome
respects no disciplines.

Not inclined to offer aid and comfort to certain higher critics, Gilbert
Murray argued in his last years for an early date for Daniel. Edgar
Goodspeed, who in his youth had deciphered mathematical papyri, joined
the SCS circle with an isagogical rhapsody on the theme: "The Greeks hated
anonymity." The reiterative nature of the presentation suggested that the
book was a prime exhibit of publishers' ability to test the expansiveness of
air. Goodspeed's study (1959), which assigns the First Gospel to the Apostle
Matthew, debunked a widely-held view of non-Matthean authorship for the
Gospel. Goodspeed took his cue from Isaiah 8:16–18 and argued that Jesus
searched for a secretary who would seal up his teaching for the future.
Publican Matthew appeared to be the perfect candidate. With all the
numerical combinations of sevens and tens in the First Gospel, who else but
someone like Matthew qualified as such a whiz at figures?

After having entered his name firmly into the history of Old Testament
research, William Albright (1971) ventured into a study of Matthew's

---

[13] One of the victims in the 1970s was Dan Via (1975).
[14] Francis M. Cornford, *The Origin of Attic Comedy* (London: Edward Arnold, 1914).

Gospel.[15] Fortunately Albright had already established his reputation beyond recall, and the First Gospel had retained canonical recognition under even less substantial treatment. Jack Kingsbury would help ensure its prestige.[16]

Sklerokardia

Sklerokardia is related to SCS. One of the formal symptoms is the use of the phrase, usually composed for a preface to a twenty-year-old work: "I see no need to modify positions advanced earlier."

Henry Cadbury, expert on things medical, quoted the German church historian Adolf Harnack's observation that despite refutation of a fashionable, long-held critical view, "particular fragments thereof still cling obstinately to men's minds, although they have no intellectual basis" (Cadbury, 1926:191).

Even more pitiful than scholars who display in print their loss, temporary or permanent, of critical acumen is the manifestation of morbidity in ministers who interpret their seminary diploma as an invitation to obsolescence. Decades after his mentors had given up views about the evolution of religion,[17] Harry Fosdick reshot scenes in *A Guide to Understanding of the Bible*.[18] Albright's indictment was mourning for the dead. "Besides his own," he wrote, Fosdick has "written the obituary of a whole scholarly approach" (1946:205).

Anyone wishing to ward off the onset of the SCS syndrome or associated maladies might profitably wear — as Pharisees were wont to wear phylacteries to remind themselves of the requirements of the Law — a copy of the following consolation that Paul Haupt used to extend to candidates for the doctorate at the time of their orals. He assured them that they had no need to fear the Faculty for "even if they gave the most ridiculous answers," there were "generally some distinguished OT scholars who have led the way" (1917:80).

It is apparent that, in contrast for example to popular conceptions of professional self-inventory in the legal and the medical professions, biblical and classical scholars can be viewed as vigorous in their corporate self-discipline. And one of the delights of membership in their associations is the realization that the truly great among them take their scholarly obligations seriously, but wear their crowns of office with delightful ease.

And like the Apostle Peter, who despite his failures remains an inspiration for the ages, even the greatest in the century that is past can afford to face their own missteps so that those who come after them may move with more certain tread.

[15] "Regrettably, a lost opportunity," writes Ralph Martin, about Albright's effort, in *New Testament Books for Pastor and Teacher* (Philadelphia: Westminster, 1984) 49.

[16] See, e.g., Jack Kingsbury, *Matthew, Structure, Christology, Kingdom* (Philadelphia: Fortress, 1975). Kingsbury was entrusted with the production of a commentary on Matthew in the commentary series, "Hermeneia."

[17] See early issues of *JBL*.

[18] Harry Emerson Fosdick, *A Guide to Understanding of the Bible: The Development of Ideas Within the Old and New Testaments* (New York: Harper, 1938).

12

RESEARCH WITH RESPONSIBILITY

To question the importance of maintaining academic integrity, free of restraints or pressures that inhibit fresh perception of the meaning of a given set of data, is inconceivable to many scholars. Yet even the most prestigious communities have not been reluctant to sacrifice avowed principle in the interest of preserving their vested interests against threatening change.

John D. Rockefeller could encourage mission work among the Chinese while the lives of workers at his Colorado Fuel & Iron Company were forfeited to the Moloch of industrial war. With tears in his eyes he could offer a widow $70,000 for an inherited oil property originally priced at $200,000. And, after he had driven numerous firms out of competition, he developed a reputation for philanthropy that rivalled the fame of Herodes Atticus and Opramoas. Those who recognized his genius for taking money in trust from God won chapels, libraries, and research laboratories, and retained positions. Standard Oil leaders, including John D. Archbold, found a champion in Chancellor James Roscoe Day of Syracuse University, who is said to have "invented the system of shaking down rich men for college endowments"[1] (Flynn 1932:441). The students at Syracuse sang:

> We have a Standard Oil pipe running up to John Crouse Hall
> And a gusher in the stadium will be flowing full next Fall.
> We need the money, Mr. Archbold,
> We need it right away.
> It's the biggest "ad" we've had
> Since the bull-dog ran away.

A young economist of great promise at Syracuse, John Commons, discovered that instructors could be shaken from their precarious academic perches for displaying what appeared too avid an interest in the rising labor movement, while a stadium "somewhat larger than the Colosseum at Rome" was in "blueprints."

Meanwhile, at the University of Chicago the students chanted to the tune of Daisy Bell:

---

[1] In his account of Syracuse University, W. Freeman Galpin (1960:469–83) endeavors to rescue Day from some charges of toadying.

John D. Rockefeller
Wonderful man is he.
Gives all his spare change
To the U. of C.
He keeps the ball a-rolling
In our great varsity.
He pays Dr. Harper
To help us grow sharper
For the glory of the U. of C.

The music was not sweet to Edward W. Bemis. He had been brought by President Harper from Vanderbilt University to serve in Chicago's Extension Department and as lecturer in the Department of Economics. But his economic views suggested that he had more of the spirit of an agitator than of an objective scholar, and for his indiscretions in questioning the role of heads of railroads in the Pullman strike of 1894 he was not reappointed, on grounds of "incompetence" (Flynn, 1932: 307–9). Flynn records an admonition that Harper addressed to Bemis: "Your speech at the First Presbyterian Church has caused me a great deal of annoyance. It is hardly safe for me to venture into any of the Chicago clubs. I am pounced upon from all sides. I propose that during the remainder of your connection with the university you exercise great care in public utterances about questions that are agitating the minds of people" (308–9).[2] Professor Oscar L. Triggs of the English Department did not make the mistake of the economist. He proclaimed George M. Pullman and John D. Rockefeller "superior in creative genius to Shakespeare, Homer and Dante."[3]

Because of his socialist writings and activities, Scott Nearing, a popular professor of economics at the University of Pennsylvania, received notice of termination in 1914, and later in the century, SBL found itself cowed.[4] And a professor at a large eastern Roman Catholic university reported that intimidation was being recycled at her institution: "I could announce" she

---

[2] Bemis is listed in the University of Chicago's *Annual Register* for 1 July 1892 to 1 July 1893, but not in the *Annual* for 1893–94. Capital's pressure on Labor at the time has periodically received documentation. For example, in February, 1886, Cyrus McCormick, owner of the Cyrus McCormick Reaper Works, ancestor of International Harvester, locked out 1400 of his employees "in reply to their demand that he reinstate some of their colleagues who had been discharged for strike and union activity"; Herbert Harris, *American Labor* (New Haven: Yale University, 1938) 85–86. The political-economic circumstances of Bemis's dismissal in the North suggest those experienced by a Southerner, Edward C. Boynton, whose contract at the University of Mississippi was not renewed because of his supposed disloyalty to the Confederacy at the time of the Civil War; see E. Merton Coulter, *The Confederate States of America 1861–1865* (Louisiana State University, 1950) 516.

[3] Jules Abels, *The Rockefeller Billions: The Story of the World's Most Stupendous Fortune* (N.Y.: Macmillan, 1965) 286.

[4] On SBL, see Saunders 1982:45–46; on harassment in the early decades of the twentieth century see Merle Curti, "The Setting and the Problems," in *American Scholarship* (1953) 1–32.

said, "that I had become a communist without causing a stir, but if I defended *Roe v. Wade* [the 1973 Supreme Court decisions legalizing abortion in the United States] I would not get tenure."[5]

Objectivity vs. Subjectivity

What one sees surfacing here is the problem of objectivity versus subjectivity and, even more profoundly, the conflict of detached inquiry and communal responsibility. Or, as Alvin M. Weinberg's classification of various approaches to the study of language suggests, a clash of discipline-orientation and mission-orientation. The very function of discipline-oriented research is to reduce subjectivity to a negligible factor while attempting to arrive at an accurate description of and interpretation of data, their relationships, and their interaction with other sets of data. What constitutes accuracy is, of course, a primary concern, and much of the methodological debate in both biblical and classical circles relates to this specific question. But the problem is compounded by virtue of the fact that the model of inquiry used in the physical sciences is not adequate for the understanding of texts whose primary feature is neither cerebral nor statistical.[6] Yet the history of interpretation reveals that attention to the meanings of words in their context and in the time of their usage — in brief, a data-oriented approach — was a standard antidote to mission-oriented-type exegesis. Thus, to some extent, the Antiochenes and the Victorines endeavored to balance the allegoristic approach inherited from Alexandria. And Erasmus summarized the remedy: "Some light will arrive for comprehension of the meaning of Scripture, if we attend not only to what is said, but also by whom it is said, to whom it is said, at what time, under what circumstances, what precedes, and what follows."[7] In an exposition of Erasmus's words, Richard Palmer (1981:26–27) writes:

> The process of interpretation increases the light of our understanding of the sense, then, in somewhat the way one increasingly knows an object better by seeing it from all sides, learning more and more about it as an object. One is not seeking a hermeneutical 'key' that will unlock a secret meaning hidden (often purposely) from the multitude; rather one is, through patient and unglamorous philological consideration of grammatical, etymological, lexical, and historical facts, arriving at what must have

[5] Daniel C. Maguire, "Abortion: A Question of Catholic Honesty," *The Christian Century* (14–21 September 1983) 803–7; see p. 804.

[6] Calhoun (1937) observes: "Objective interpretation is a difficult goal, but we can come very close to it by honestly exploring all possibilities without insisting upon one or another to the exclusion of the rest. At the same time, this very complexity precludes our dispensing with analysis altogether."

[7] The quotation is translated from the Latin text of Erasmus's *Ratio seu compendium verae theologiae*, in *Desiderius Erasmus Roterodamus Ausgewählte Werke*, ed. Annemarie Holborn and Hajo Holborn (Munich: Beck) 196.

been the originally intended meaning in the original context of the utterance. This may not necessarily be its literal meaning if one has reason to
believe that the author was speaking in figurative language. But the philological interpreter does not feel he has the license to assume that God is
the true author of the text and [that] He has inserted His meaning in some
kind of secret code.

Luther and Calvin share with Erasmus the basic understanding that the text
is not the lackey of its readers. Rather, readers must accommodate
themselves to the text (Palmer, 27).[8]

In the nineteenth and on into the twentieth century, numerous skir-
mishes would be fought over the validity of this and related philological
approaches. Many scholars have a great investment in the Bible not only as
a resource for knowledge about antiquity but as a reservoir of truth for faith
and life. Classicists, in turn, deal with documents that have been considered
the bible of Western culture and the authentic voice of the spirit of humanity
at its best. Both communities of scholars therefore have a substantial investment in a mission-oriented approach to linguistic study. Much of the philological debate therefore zeroes in on the problem: objective analysis versus
sensitivity to cultural or spiritual values. At the beginning of the century a
number of German scholars, in reaction to historical-critical methodology,
emphasized the role of great ideas in the history of culture. Martin Schuetze
(1933) scored the movement in his *Academic Illusions in the Field of Letters
and the Arts*. This thrust and counter-thrust mirrors much that came to pass.[9]
Ordinarily the debate was and is carried on in genteel fashion. But, as will
be seen below, when the cultural and spiritual values are interlocked with
dogmatic investment, the debate in some circles may terminate with departure of one or the other of the groups of debaters.

Paul Shorey was ardent in demonstrating how alleged objectivity can
lead to specialized atomization. In 1906 he ticked off some of the symptoms
in the ancient scholarship of Alexandria, Pergamos, and Rome. "The names
of their lucubrations read like a catalogue of German doctoral dissertations,"
he informed his public: "A Letter to a Friend on the Length of Syllables in
the (Lost) Epic Poets"; "Concerning an Obscure Quality of Hash Mentioned
in the New Comedy"; "On Aristophanes' Fit of Hiccoughs in the Platonic
Symposium"; "The Literature of Cookies"; "On Zeus Shoofly at Olympia"; and
"A Logarithmic Table of the Quantities of the Last Five Syllables of Every
Sentence in Plato's Dialogues" (1906a:176).

Dedication to philological principle can result in concentration on such
a narrow area that the very instrument for ostensibly avoiding distortion may

---

[8] Krentz (1975) interprets "the Reformation legacy of concern for the historical sense of the
Bible" as marking a "decisive turn that culminated in historical-critical methods of
interpretation" (87).

[9] See Wellek, 1967:119.

be responsible for its re-creation. Over-specialization was under intermittent indictment from the very beginning of both SBL and APA. In *Brief Mention* Basil Gildersleeve said that some scholars "watch the recession of the study of Greek and fix their eyes on Latin as the last hope of the continuity of culture, but it is a lesson to be taken to heart by Hellenists, who are prone to narrow their sphere as their domain becomes more specialized. If we of the Greek fold are to become Grecians as Sanskrit scholars become Sanskrit-ists, we shall lose our hold on the world" (Gildersleeve, 1930:117). This exercise in prescience is of a piece with his explanation of how he happened to write a dissertation on Porphyry under the Aristotelian scholar Jakob Bernays. Gildersleeve wondered what would have happened to him had he died between 1853 and 1867 with this sole contribution to the "literature" of the department. He also asked what might have happened had he been exposed to a theme of greater breadth for a "wide range of study" (Gildersleeve, 1930:155).[10]

Henry Nash similarly endeavored to impress biblical scholars with the importance of implementing philology with sensitivity to living circum-stances. "New Testament study," he wrote, "has sometimes suffered from an excess of academic atmosphere." All of us have lost to some extent the capacity for throwing ourselves "headlong into the arms of an emotion." Whereas we are individualists, he said, the people of the New Testament have a corporate consciousness (Nash, 1902:170). It was an insight that would find expression decades later from unanticipated quarters. With another topic in mind, Joseph Thayer indicted the "petrefaction of words throbbing with the most tender and sacred suggestions into hackneyed formalism" that paralyzes life "by routine" (1899:131). Morris Jastrow (1917) echoed Thayer's thought with a philological application. We dare not, he said, lose sight of the "human element in the documents." Linguistic criticism aimed at isolation of sources is frequently wooden, he cautioned, and cited John Peters, who showed that the Psalms are primarily the outcome of religious emotions experienced by worshippers. They are the expression of religious need of individuals, rather than prompted by military events.[11] Max L. Margolis said that atomization of texts was easier than enduring increment of difficulty in finding "relevance, continuity," and "coherence," and cited Heinrich Ewald as a model (Margolis, 1923:7).[12] And George Dahl (1938) warned that in atomistic study we face

---

[10] Also see Gildersleeve, 1890:120. On acceptance of responsibility for better teaching, see *Classical Investigation*, 1924.

[11] Peters, 1916:154. Similarly Montgomery (1937:35–41) calls attention to the poetic spirit beyond the mere intellectual concern in Hebrew expression.

[12] Margolis gives only the surname Ewald, apparently with Heinrich G. A. Ewald in mind. New Testament scholars will also think of Paul Ewald, a foe of unintegrated "archäologische Gelehrsamkeit." See Paul Ewald, *Die Briefe des Paulus an die Epheser, Kolosser und Philemon*, 2d ed. (Leipzig: Deichert, 1910) 136 n. 1 and passim. The advantages in citing given names, especially as inter-disciplinary work progresses, are apparent.

the hazard of sacrificing religious values. Loss of "messianic emphasis" in Psalms 2,22,45, and others would be a contributing factor to replacement of "order with chaos, and established values with near worthlessness." Therefore "it behooves us," he said, "to reexamine both our premises and our conclusions." All this was an invitation to listen to the heart of humanity, and existential literary criticism would later provide a different stethoscope.

Ambivalence still prevails respecting the responsibility of biblical and classical scholars in the face of basic threats to human values. While Earth was still smoldering from World War I, James Montgomery (1919) held up a flaming torch before the paradise of yesteryear and challenged his colleagues in SBL to recognize that the style of life espoused by Goethe, who studied Chinese during the battle of Jena, was not for his colleagues. His words might as well have been written in water, for during the Nazi era little attention was paid to the price that humanity might have to pay for totalitarian control. Many German scholars, as one can readily determine from prefaces in publications of that era, saluted Hitler without critique. But there were only sporadic manifestations of awareness in America's biblical and classical learned journals. Mission-oriented Werner Jaeger (1936) bemoaned the "rise of the doctrine that culture and knowledge are nationalistic possessions" and warned that narrow specialization could obscure "our main service to society . . . of keeping alive and developing the universal tradition of humanism." The editorial staff of the *Classical Bulletin* (17, no. 5 [1941] 36), cited *The Clergy Review* for November and December of 1939, which had warned that the "political and mental preparation for a revived Caesar-worship is nearing completion." "Modern history does not begin from scratch," postulated Mars Westington (1944) in a diagnosis of developments that preceded World War II Germany.

That contemporary application need not be prejudicial to scholarly dedication comes to clear expression in Robert Flynn's (1943) comments on Greek thoughts relative to war, and in B. L. Ullman's (1945) use of Vergil for a contemporary definition of peace. On the other hand, Kenneth Scott (1932) displayed questionable zeal for the Classics when he interpreted Benito Mussolini's work as an Augustan restoration and cited, without apparent rejoinder, Mussolini's program: "Italy has had enough of liberty for a while. What it needs now is law. The people want peace, work, bread, roads, and water." Had the Seven Sleepers of Ephesos awakened first in 1946, with only the *Harvard Theological Review* at their disposal for further bedtime reading, they could not have known that humanity had just passed through the most terrible war and the most incriminating exhibition of human potential for evil in all history. Among biblical scholars crying in the wilderness was Cadbury, who in 1937 called Heidelberg University to account for betrayal of its half-millennium avowed commitment to academic excellence in favor of partisan propaganda. In reaction to Johannes Hempel's *Das Ethos*, which criticized the Jewish pogrom described in the book of Esther, William Albright (1939) took some account of the savage events of November, 1938, but without apparent prescience of the apocalyptic dimension. After the hostilities were over, Morton Enslin (1946) called attention with unvarnished moral judgment to the "catastrophe" in German scholarship: "Many," he said, "have sold out to the demands of the hour, to the necessity of having their findings congenial to the outlook of those in political supremacy. That sort of prostitution ends scholarship." And in 1952 Albright called attention to one of the casualties of fascism in connection with Umberto Cassuto's explanation of an hapaxlegomenon in 2 Kings 4:42.

Along various routes, biblical scholars endeavored to avoid the smothering of their beloved documents under antiquarian clutter, and at each turn were met by flags raised in defense of philological objectivity by proponents of "pure" historical inquiry who interpreted such holistic concern as pragmatic pollution of territory that had been recaptured at great cost from vested interests. Some turned to a variety of compositional criticism and championed simple 'literary' reading of biblical documents. An extreme form of such approach is a study by a British contributor, John Gamble (1926), to the *Journal of Biblical Literature*. Entitled "Symbol and Reality in the Epistle to the Hebrews," it is practically a homily on spiritual aspiration. "In reading the books of the Bible, we often fail to see the wood for the trees," he wrote. We need to grasp the "carefully-planned structure" (162).[13]

In a presidential address before SBL in 1934, Frederick Grant took a more sophisticated approach and granted that dogma cannot be permitted to interfere with scholarly inquiry, but "we equally need to be encouraged to recognize the rights of constructive thought, if we are ever to get anywhere in the study of history and pass on from a consideration of the minutiae of exegesis, texts, and dates, to a full-range, clear-focussed picture of the past, and 'see life steadily and see it whole'" (Grant, 1935:12). In the Gospels he went on to say, we are not just dealing with great literature. They "are based upon, and record, a historical tradition." "The *Spirit* of Jesus, living on in the Church, was one with the historical Jesus, and was a genuinely creative force in the thought of men long after" (13). Morton Enslin sealed away these messages for a few years, and then in 1946, in the context of his reaction to German totalitarianism, and without apparent awareness of an element of contradiction in his judgment, issued a presidential warning against "the demand that our researches strengthen faith and provide blueprints for modern conduct."[14] Fleming Jones (1940) argued in a review of Albright's

[13] Similarly Nils W. Lund (1931) contended for the "artistic" dimension of 1 Corinthians 13. Kemper Fullerton (1930) combined compositional synthesis with detailed philological analysis. Beardslee (1920) sounded a call for appreciation of Isaiah through poetic appropriation.

[14] Methodologically considered, the concern of biblical and classical scholars for dogma-free transmission of the basic human values that find expression in both corpora of ancient

From the Stone Age to Christianity that "biblical scholarship derives its peculiar significance from wide-spread belief in the uniqueness and validity of the Bible revelation (189). The thought was echoed by Floyd V. Filson in 1950 with an invitation to consider faith as a medium for overcoming the atomization that was the result of so-called objectivity in research.

"One nail drives out another," wrote Maldonatus, and Robert Pfeiffer used his presidential podium to urge scholars not to mix religious faith with the works of research. "What was once philology," he said, "has become philosophy" (1951:12). This censure received lighthearted reinforcement a few years later at a Harvard Divinity School Christmas party. It was customary for students to present facetious gifts to faculty members, and at this particular celebration Paul Tillich received a box, which when opened was empty except for a card that read: "Pure Essence." To Father Georges Florovsky—with the beard of the Orthodox, but allegedly less often trimmed than most—went a long cigarette holder labelled: "For fire prevention." Finally came Pfeiffer's turn. Upon unwrapping a package the size of a shoebox, he drew out its contents, a mere two cards with words written in large letters: on the one, "Faith"; on the other, "Reason." Pfeiffer smiled broadly, held one in each hand, raised them over his head, and with his distinctive accent said proudly, "That's right. Never let them meet."[15]

In what sounded like the swan song of the old philology, S. Vernon McCasland (1954:4) proclaimed in a presidential address: "We want to know what the writers themselves meant and nothing more."[16] Harry Orlinsky thought the times demanded more planks in the platform, and in 1971 he mounted the podium and, in reinforcement of a plea put in a few years earlier by Robert Grant (1968), called for stronger historical consciousness and more exacting training in historical methodology. We do not merely want to know *what* happened but *why* it happened. We want to determine the economic, political, and social forces that determined the use and content of terms in documents. Five years later John Priest (1976) pleaded for movement beyond "time-honored attempts at setting the 'historical situation' " and called for new understanding of historicality, the insights of existentialism and structuralism, a fresh approach to socio-cultural factors, and a recognition of the values of psychoanalysis.[17] Yet there was no apparent interest in development of a theory that would account for such and other varieties of "scientific"

---

documents differs substantively from scholars' "prostitution" (the word is Enslin's, 1946:3) to institutional clout.

[15] Eldon Epp in personal correspondence vouches for this incident.

[16] Compare McCasland's (1953) blast against Austin Farrer's alleged allegorizing in *A Study in St. Mark*.

[17] Compare developments in the "Chicago School," Funk, 1976:18. On the hazard of psychologizing, see Albright, 1949:373.

expression and compel biblical scholars especially to face the question whether, and in what ways, they were involved in disciplined inquiry.

Basil Gildersleeve went through related trauma in an earlier day, but shrugged it off with typical Gildersleeveese. He had received *Les Formes littéraires de la pensée grecque,* by Henri Ouvre, which displayed a phenomenal philological ecumenicity, embracing, in Gildersleeve's terms, "the chefs-d'oeuvre of a Pindar, a Vergil, a Bossuet, newspapers, advertisements, shopsigns." "It is . . . a remarkable book," Gildersleeve wrote, "a barbed-wire trellis of metaphysical systematization, clothed with a tropical wealth of imagery. . . . Indeed, when I first opened the book I thought that my occupation was gone." But then he was comforted by the realization that its philological foundation could be shored by the products of his own researches (1930:111). Thus did Gildersleeve find the bridge between today and yesteryear.

Reaction

The periodic reaction that set in against calls for less cerebral emphasis was not without cause. Defenders of the older philology saw threats to objectivity from numerous directions of entrenched pre-judgment, whether of belief or unbelief. One of the primary objectives behind the founding of the Society of Biblical Literature was the creation of a climate in which inquiry could take place without the chilling effect of traditional controls. This did not mean that traditional views were unwelcome. In a determined effort at bridge-building Francis Brown (1882) helps readers distinguish the authority of the message from what later generations may discover about authorship of Old Testament books that find citation in the New Testament.[18]

From Brown's perspective it was only reasonable that any view could expect to run the risk of interrogation respecting its philological validity. Classicists were not exposed to the same problems as were their biblical colleagues, but like their colleagues in the biblical field they still had to contend with the fact that their ancient texts had been adulterated by interpreters' outgrown philosophical presuppositions and by hypotheses and theories that lacked the spacious warehousing facilities demanded by an enormous number of fresh data, many of which still await careful inventory. Basil Gildersleeve cleared the air with candid remarks about Homeric research. "Not that I did not start with a fine set of ready-made views of the separatist order, then the fashionable form of unbelief, and though in practice I am now little better than a Unitarian I have never lost my interest in the

---

[18] Volumes 1–6 of *JBL* suggest that the editors and contributors aim to be philological bridge-builders. There is a pervading tone of restraint in presentation of novelties, even though interpretations that are retained may pose problems.

syntactical stratification of the Homeric poems" (Gildersleeve, 1930:156). Pindaric symbolist through and through, he said that doctrine dies hard and in repentant tone he wrote: "If I were to edit Pindar again, even the ghost of the digamma would disappear" (157). Few scholars have found more ways to say, "I was wrong."

Yet Gildersleeve's invitation to change was less of a shock than that experienced by biblical interpreters. There is no set of books in the history of humanity that has endured such struggle over the meaning of its contents as has the Bible. Its scholars have been compelled to spend much of their time in clearing the battlefield of spent ammunition and of bivouacs that became permanent shelters for those who persist in fighting to the bitter end. Utterances of Isaiah and St. Paul, not to speak of words ascribed to Jesus, spark the adrenaline of all who have a vested interest in judgments made about their thoughts. At stake quite frequently is the stability of institutional structures that have developed out of specific interpretations of biblical documents. Those that have enjoyed the advantage of centuries of such control of the hermeneutical process have been able to be more magnanimous to the future, but the smaller sects that lack the capital of tradition, must needs be more parsimonious with what they grant to more liberated inquiry. There are no cults with Aischylus and Sophokles as objects of ultimate devotion; for in the context of the present inquiry it is necessary to discount those who give their academic all in philological devotion to these and other ancients. Battles still rage over the meaning of much that Plato wrote. But the fighting is done by elite troops. Indeed, for a century and more, and with the nostalgia of a Julian the Apostate, classicists have seen interest in the temples of Greco-Roman culture dwindling to the point of despair in the face of demolition of human values. And there appear to be no more Gildersleeves and Shoreys. On the other hand, especially the United States realized a resurgence of interest on the part of the church's non-clergy in the security of ancestral formulation of biblical faith.[19]

Classicists possessed advantage over biblical scholars in still another respect. They have not endured the need to make advance compensation for misappropriation of their research. Biblical researchers, on the other hand, face the problem of having their findings lauded by traditionalists when such findings concur with previously held opinions and condemned when they contravene cherished belief. A composite picture of such teeter-totter methodology is readily drawn from encounters described in the pages of the

[19] An attack, especially in St. Louis, Missouri, on the public production of *Sister Mary Ignatius* was a non-clerical reaction, for it challenged basic educational experiences; yet many who were indignant over its alleged blasphemies went to *Mass Appeal* without a word of protest, for this play dealt with bureaucracy and helped to balance the budget for the intimidated. Since ecclesiastical structures exist ostensibly for the benefit of the masses, it is understandable that investment in traditional communication would be all the more carefully protected.

learned journals. Its sponsors, like the monotheists mentioned by Paul in Rom 2:22, have been accused of pillaging the house of learning without proposing alternative approaches or theories, which are a base for advance in understanding. Nor do they offer resolutions of problems that might be uncongenial to their academic and ecclesiastical superiors. Archeologists are their favorite prey. They classify as arbitrary the judgments with which they disagree, and affirm as ultimate truth their own inherited theological constructions. They take but do not give and then have the ill grace to disparage tireless caretakers of history. "Higher critics!" "(Secular) humanists!" cry those who are fearful of facing the truth of history's data, and with a tonality reserved by Nazis in reference to Jews.

Should the preceding description of methodological piracy appear too mild the reader may prefer to imbibe in Pindaric style the rhetoric of Morton Smith on the importance of objectivity in the face of pseudorthodoxy (M. Smith, 1969) and wash it down with a review by Helmut Koester (1962) of a work on the Apostolic Fathers.

One expects universities to succumb to pressures exerted on them by their alumni. But from institutions dedicated to pursuit of what is alleged to be the ultimate in truth, namely the Bible, one anticipates appreciation of a critical stance that carefully examines the documents and scrutinizes the history of interpretation for distortion of the evidence, lest, as George Orwell put it, the very concept of objective truth fade out of the world and "lies pass into history."

Yet there is never lacking the suspicion that biblical scholars might be engaged in some nefarious plot to destroy the influence of the Bible and undermine ancestral faith. And in the spirit of the Second Council of Constantinople (553), which ordered books by Theodore of Mopsuestia to be burned, institutional leaders have from time to time permitted such anxiety to generate a chilling effect on progressive study at seminaries. Two of them, Southern Baptist Theological Seminary, Louisville, Kentucky; and the Lutheran Church-Missouri Synod's Concordia Seminary, St, Louis, Missouri, distinguished themselves by securing considerable news coverage for heresy hunting.

Controversy in Kentucky

As is the case with most church bodies, Baptists have weathered a number of controversies. About the time that Archibald Robertson was peacefully engrossed in comparative philology, many of his fellow Baptists were polemically engaged in comparative ecclesiology. Typical of such warfare is the difficulty at times to identify the specific allegiance of the combatants. In any event, in what came to be known as the Whitsitt Controversy, an anti-Roman Catholic faction caught the virus that they diagnosed in their opponents and developed what Baptists call a Bible-plus-history test of orthodoxy, a variation of the Bible-plus-tradition that some of them ascribe to Roman Catholicism. The Southern Baptist Theological Seminary, an academic Swiss belt in the war zone, soon found itself under siege; for the president of the Seminary, William Heth Whitsitt, who had distinguished himself in Baptist circles as a professor of church history, was under fire for daring to aver that Roger Williams probably received baptism by affusion and that English Baptists had their origin in the year 1641 (Gill, 1943:83). Scholarship versus orthodoxy! Unable to dispute facts of history, Whitsitt's opposition nailed him on tactics. They charged that he had claimed personal discovery of what had in fact been already in public domain. In his defense Whitsitt revealed that before others had written on the subject he had anonymously published his discovery in *The Independent*, a pedo-Baptist journal (Gill:84). This revelation meant appreciable loss of credibility and on 14 July 1898 Whitsitt resigned his post as president.

According to his biographer, Robertson not only remained loyal to his chief but recognized the basic issue of the controversy: "If the opponents won on the question of a date of history, all right of research on the part of the Seminary's Professors was destroyed." Using the media that were at his disposal, including the Louisville *Courier-Journal*, Robertson endeavored to speak words of reason to widely entrenched anxiety (Gill, 85).[20] His warning not to mix conscience and judgment was in harmony with his thoughts on evolution: "I am willing to believe in it, rather do, but not in atheistic evolution. . . . I say, write 'God' at the top, and what if he did use evolution? I can stand it if the monkeys can" (Gill:181).

Southern Baptist Theological Seminary throughout a long history continued to display little enthusiasm for satisfaction of self-sanctifying ignorance and has survived other challenges to academic responsibility for exploration of truth and the facts of history. But not one of its battles against a fundamentalist-type mindset can match in fury the hostilities that took place in the Lutheran Church-Missouri Synod, especially during the years 1969–74.

Controversy in Missouri

A centennial volume dealing with philological concerns cannot avoid recital of circumstances relating to the dismissal of more than forty faculty members who considered themselves committed in their various fields to accurate interpretation of biblical documents. Their story is the story of demise of untrammeled scholarly inquiry at the Lutheran Church-Missouri Synod's Concordia Seminary, at St. Louis, Missouri.[21]

---

[20] According to Gill (1943:85), Robertson's public relations effort was made on 31 August 1896.

[21] This centennial writer does not understand Ernest Saunder's statement that "heresy trials and teachers' oaths might be things of the past . . ." (Saunders, 1982:70), especially since he

One of the principals in the events that transpired was Martin Scharlemann, professor of New Testament. During the 1950s he had been instrumental in persuading students and clergy in the Lutheran Church-Missouri Synod to accept more responsibility for academic leadership in the Americas. To help bring about a change in theological climate, not only in his own denomination but throughout America, he read a paper before the New Testament section of the SBL, at its ninety-second annual meeting in December 1956, on the contributions of Origen to hermeneutical inquiry. At about the same time, Scharlemann was in conversation with Krister Stendahl and Otto Piper concerning a hermeneutics project.[22] He hoped to break the stranglehold with which dogmatic tradition and a fundamentalist-oriented approach threatened to throttle a spirit of lively exegetical inquiry in his own denomination and elsewhere. He had lived through a period during which William Arndt, professor at Concordia, a member of SBL, and co-editor with F. Wilbur Gingrich of the English version of Walter Bauer's lexicon of New Testament Greek (1957), had been humiliatingly grilled at conferences for questioning strains of overly-restrictive interpretation in some areas of his synod. Confronting members of his denomination with recent developments in exegetical inquiry, Scharlemann criticized those who in his judgment considered it fashionable to cart off the gold that biblical critics mined with much toil and then attacked the system that produced it.[23] After his declaration before a group of ministers in Illinois, to the effect that he was present to defend the proposition that the Bible contained errors, the rending of priestly garments could be heard throughout the synod.[24] Scharlemann was, in fact, gently reproving his fellow-clergy in the spirit of Morton Enslin, who used a presidential address on December 27, 1945, to admonish America's scholars "to keep their hands off the scales when weighing evidence" and thus avoid the kind of academic and cultic prostitution practiced during the years of the National Socialist regime (Enslin, 1946:8). Scharlemann's sin was to

---

makes no mention of the internationally known developments at Concordia Seminary. There is more involved here than local interest. As of 1985, Concordia Seminary was still on AAUP's list of institutions whose approach to honoring the rights of professors was in question (*Academe* 71, 3 [May-June, 1985] 4). Saunders also makes no mention of the action taken in 1962 by the trustees of Midwestern Baptist Theological Seminary to dismiss Ralph Elliott, Professor of Old Testament and Hebrew. Elliott in effect refused to repudiate his *The Message of Genesis*; see *The Maryland Baptist* (1 November 1962:1–2).

[22] Scharlemann's paper was later published under the title, "A Theology for Biblical Interpretation," *Concordia Theological Monthly* 29 (1958) 38–48. See also his essay, "Roman Catholic Interpretation," in *Festschrift Gingrich*, 1972:91–114.

[23] Cf. M. Smith, 1969:19–35.

[24] Scharlemann's paper, "The Bible as Record, Witness and Medium," was read in full on 3 April 1959 to the Missouri Synod's Council on Bible Study and then in part on April 7 and 8 to a District Pastors Conference in Northern Illinois (Danker, 1977:5).

think that clergy were not exempt from such ethics. Thus it came to pass that, pressured by constituents who had been accustomed to weigh Martin Chemnitz (seventeenth century champion of orthodoxy) in with St. Paul, the synod's officialdom ultimately compelled Scharlemann to make an apology before its highest tribunal, namely the synod in delegate assembly.[25] To the end, Scharlemann claimed that he had not recanted nor admitted any error.

Under the tutelage of Scharlemann and his colleagues in the exegetical department, approximately two thousand ministers had been introduced to the use of exegetical methods that were in general use for decades in America. Some of them became members of SBL and made significant contributions to biblical studies.

Together with the new freedom of inquiry went a direct challenge to traditional thinking on social, political, and economic issues in the Missouri Synod. All this meant waves, and the Missouri Synod was in the habit of seeing them controlled, not agitated. Scharlemann himself had hoped to be in the controlling seat. Besides reputedly having his eye on the presidency of Union Theological Seminary in New York City, he sought election as Concordia Seminary's president after the retirement of Alfred Fuerbringer, who had made valiant effort to bring the seminary into more responsible encounter with the American and international scene. After the election of John H. Tietjen as president of Concordia, Scharlemann could read only disaster for the Missouri Synod, for Tietjen represented Eastern seaboard thinking and would support some of Scharlemann's colleagues with whose social and political philosophies Scharlemann, as a highly placed chaplain in the Air Corps, was finding himself in vigorous disagreement. This opposition escalated under the mounting pressure of political and social dissent in the late 1960s. In company with a small number of colleagues, including Ralph Bohlmann who later became president of Concordia Seminary and then President of the Lutheran Church-Missouri,[26] Scharlemann joined forces with those who were anxious to bring the synod back to its traditional stance on inerrancy of the Scriptures and official isolation from other Christians with whom the denomination was not agreed in doctrines. Ultimately, he anticipated, his time would come to serve in some major leadership capacity, perhaps even as president of Concordia Seminary, and he would be able to hold in check any extreme directions taken by his associates on the right and at the same time move the synod in the direction of what he considered to be "radical" orthodoxy rather than the radical theology he attributed to some of his colleagues.

---

[25] See *Exodus from Concordia*, edited by the Board of Control of Concordia Seminary, St. Louis, Missouri (St. Louis: Concordia College, 1977).

[26] Ralph Bohlmann was instrumental in drawing up "A Statement of Confessional Principles" (hereafter cited as "Preus-Bohlmann document"), in which subscription to the "historicity of Jonah" was made a matter of theological obligation. Full text in Danker, 1977:76–86.

After the election of Jacob A. O. Preus to the presidency of the Lutheran Church-Missouri Synod in 1969, Scharlemann, supported by colleagues Ralph Bohlmann, Richard Klann, Robert Preus, and Lorenz Wunderlich, disclosed the nature of his campaign.[27] On 9 April 1970, Scharlemann wrote synodical President Jacob Preus, "requesting him to conduct an inquiry into the theological situation at the Seminary."[28] All of the alarmists received the hearty endorsement of Herman Otten, editor of what was then known as *The Christian News,* and were joined by those in the synod who were anxious to bring their denomination back to what they considered its traditional stance on inerrancy of the Scriptures.

During the Missouri Synod's convention at New Orleans, Louisiana, in 1973, official clearance was given for action to secure the suspension and ultimately the resignation of Concordia's president.[29] Tietjen refused "on the grounds of conscience," to resign.[30] He was also the last bureaucratic wall that protected the majority of faculty members against what he deemed an unjustified assault on their integrity as academicians and as subscribers to the principles of the Reformation. Certain confessional writings linked with the name of Martin Luther and associates provided the interpretive norm for evaluating biblical exposition. They had been expressly drawn up in protest against ecclesiastical manipulation of interpretive responsibility, and in the judgment of Tietjen and the majority of his colleagues invited no bondage to belief, for example, in "the Davidic authorship of Psalm 110" or "the historicity [sic!] of Jonah."[31] What did matter was fidelity to the Gospel and the right to free investigation of the Scriptures apart from prior ecclesiastical constraint. On the other hand, Tietjen and colleagues were compelled to face the fact that academia bears on-going responsibility for interpreting its noetic processes clearly to supporting constituencies.[32]

Tietjen's and the faculty majority's refusal to espouse what they considered pseudo-orthodoxy cost most of the faculty members their jobs. On 20 January 1974, after a series of attempts in 1973 to secure Tietjen's suspension, the seminary's Board of Control suspended Tietjen for alleged harboring of false doctrine, and late that same night Scharlemann became acting president of the seminary. One month later, 21 January 1974, two hundred and seventy-four students voted a moratorium of further education until such time as the seminary's board would identify their alleged false

---

[27] The five professors are listed on the dedicatory page of *Exodus,* 1977.

[28] *Exodus,* 1977:22.

[29] Details in Danker, 1977:135–46; *Exodus,* 1977:51–60.

[30] *Exodus,* 1977:59.

[31] See Preus-Bohlmann document in Danker, 1977:81; cf. Tietjen's endeavor to inculcate distinction between doctrinal content of the Scriptures and judgments as to "kind of narrative" in the Bible (*Exodus,* 1977:50).

[32] Danker, 1977:352–57; *Exodus* 1977:1–16.

teachers. Ninety-two voted no, preferring to side with Professors Scharlemann, Bohlmann, Klann, R. Preus, and Wunderlich. Forty-six faculty and staff members underwrote the moratorium. Like most of the students, they could not understand how their seminary president could be suspended, in part for harboring teaching that was alleged to be contrary to the Bible, and that they at the same time should be urged to reenter their classrooms.[33]

The Board of Control had worked late, and a minority of five of its members had endeavored valiantly to stem passage of the document, in support of which Scharlemann had said: "The way to handle rebellion is to crush it!"[34] It was a bit of rhetoric that sounded to some of its targets strikingly similar to John D. Rockefeller's response when he was told in the late 1800s that a number of Cleveland's refinery owners were reluctant to sell their holdings. John D. replied: "Those who refuse will be crushed" (Flynn, 1932:160). Did the faculty members intend to resume their teaching responsibilities on February 19, the Board asked. The penalty of non-compliance: No salary after February 18; no seminary-owned housing to be supplied after February 28; all offices to be vacated on or before February 28, 1974. No one signed, and at 12 noon it was all over. On Wednesday, February 20, St. Louis University and Eden Theological Seminary welcomed over four hundred students (including students on intern leave), faculty, and staff. Concordia Seminary was in Exile and became of the faculty internationally known as SEMINEX.[35] "Ninety percent of the faculty and eighty-five percent of the students were gone" (*Exodus* 1977:129.) On 20 May 1974 Bohlmann became acting president, after Scharlemann was unable to continue because of bad health. On 12 October 1974 Tietjen received his dismissal. Nine years later the self-styled "exiled" faculty of Seminex, which had changed its name to Christ Seminary-Seminex, were deployed in preparation for fresh ecumenical ventures, some of them to Lutheran School of Theology at Chicago; others to Pacific Lutheran School of Theology at Berkeley, California; and two, Lucille Hager and John Constable, along with Seminex's library, to Austin, Texas.

---

[33] On the Seminary Board's directive to the faculty "to return to their classes" or face dismissal, see *Exodus*, 1977:116–17. Members of the Biblical Department, most of them also members of SBL, who were subject to dismissal included Frederick W. Danker, Carl Graesser, Norman C. Habel, Holland H. Jones, Everett R. Kalin, Ralph W. Klein, Alfred von Rohr Sauer, and Robert H. Smith. Edgar Krentz was on sabbatical leave at the time and joined the group in their new quarters at a later date. For the full list, see Danker, 1977:216–17.

[34] Danker, 1977:304.

[35] The acronym was assumed by seminaries in other countries that found themselves in related oppressive circumstances. For details on the formation of Seminex, see Danker, 1977:302–23; *Exodus* 1977:105–28.

It is no joy to tell such tale of woe. Many who identify themselves as Christians do indeed believe that Easter encourages the celebration of opportunity to explore the horizons of a New Day. At the same time, they are convinced that the conduct of research along the lines of an Easter-egg hunt is contradictory to the principal message of Resurrection Morn. Yet if the recital of such experiences of academicians lends heart to others who feel the pressure of assault on responsibility to truth and to inquiry that is free of adjustment to what they consider improper institutional demands, it has been worth reopening some grief to tell it. And in a sense the story functions as hermeneutical medium for much of the discerning self-criticism that has found utterance in a century of philological history. Given the national and international political climate and the greater social problems that the future is certain to bring, the challenge to fidelity will indeed be more staggering than when Chester McCown (1956) gave forth, with all the vibrancy of classicists fighting a rearguard action in defence of Latin III, a lament on methodological divisions in the ranks of biblical scholars. "The vices and virtues of the past," he said, "should both warn and encourage. In post-Reformation times, both Catholic and Protestant seemed to care less what the Bible taught than to find in it what each already taught. Interrogated, the Bible had to say yes to their leading questions. Allegorical, symbolical, and typological interpretations ran riot. Exegesis had a long dogmatic period" (13).

After sketching major differences between ancient and modern world-views, McCown concluded:

> How the abyss between the ancient and the modern point of view shall be bridged is a question for the teacher of religion, the preacher, and the theologian (who may be also critical historians). Doubtless each will reach a solution on the basis of his own assumptions. Those who prefer an authoritarian or credal basis cannot be denied their choice. But if biblical scholarship is to retain a place of respectability among modern fields of research, it must maintain full freedom of investigation, thought, and expression, with no claim to a preferred status or special immunities, and with no theological presuppositions" (18).

Too often books on the Bible promise more than they deliver. As one reviewer put it, instead of challenging the theology of their authors, such books only reflect it.[36] If one agrees with Nathaniel Schmidt (1931) that the biblical student ought to recognize the "irresistible appeal of the important matters with which we are dealing" (xxii) one appears to be obligated to hear his conclusion, that the study be "carried on with all possible thoroughness and in a reverent spirit."

---

[36] Crossan, 1977:606–8.

Future with Excellence

After almost one hundred years, the words of T. K. Cheyne and J. Sutherland Black remain, with some discount of nineteenth century thought, a valid source of inspiration to those who come under the gun. We cannot conclude our preface, they state, "without a hearty attestation of the ever-increasing love for the Scriptures which critical and historical study, when pursued in a sufficiently comprehensive sense, appears to them to produce. The minutest details of biblical research assume a brightness not their own when viewed in the light of the great truths in which the movement of biblical religion culminates."[37] William Mackenzie (1911), President of Hartford Theological Seminary, endorsed the thought when he expressed satisfaction with nothing but the best in preparation for the ministry:

> The Christian religion cannot possibly retain moral and social leadership if its ministers lack an intellectual equipment which is equal to that required by any calling in the most highly civilized regions of the world. The idea that Christianity can conquer by means of men who do not know what mental discipline is, who hope to maintain their influence by a piety that is divorced from intelligence, or a message that is delivered by intellectual incompetents, is one of the most disastrous which any generation could inherit or cherish. The ministry must have its schools in which work must be as severe as in any other professional school in the land. The pulpits must be occupied by men who have given themselves to specific and technical preparation with as deep self-sacrifice, with as real diligence, as those who hope to occupy the front places in medicine or in law or in education (157).

An eminent dean of law spoke the definitive word when he said to his entering class: "Gentlemen, please realize that you have to work here; this is not a theological seminary."[38]

Attesting scholarly concern for excellence are numerous lamentations over the demise of interest in the primary languages for study of the Bible and the Classics. In 1919, James Montgomery mourned that Hebrew was passing from the seminaries and that exemption from Greek was "vigorously" being discussed. Sharing his sorrow, Max Margolis bemoaned students' lack of interest in Hebrew and Greek. Latin was added to the list by Morton Enslin in a presidential address before SBL in 1945.[39] Harry Orlinsky (1971) blamed part of the decline of interest in the study of Greek and Latin after World War I on archeology, which, he said in a presidential address, siphoned off excellent talent. Mars Westington (1944) feared for the future when he saw the Victory Corps effort during World War II divert students' interest

---

[37] T. K. Cheyne and J. Sutherland Black, eds. *Encyclopaedia Biblica*, 1 (London: Adam and Charles Black, 1899) xii. Cf. Clarence Craig (1943:294) who pleads for a "sound historical training" that accepts "the challenge to interpret the meaning of Christian faith."

[38] Quoted by Enslin, 1946:11.

[39] Enslin, 1946.

"from Latin to the lathe." But sorrow would be turned to joy at the end of SBL's first centennial when Hebrew regained a hold on seminarians at various points in America, and texts for students of Beginning Greek did not beg for purchasers. And things were not so bad for Latin, if an international symposium on Albius Tibullus could compete in 1984 with the Olympic Games for even a small bit of attention. There was indeed a passing hope that the United States might shed the dubious distinction of being, as someone quipped, the only major nation in the history of humanity "to move directly from" barbarism to decadence "without an interval of civilization."

Yet even the tears of Montgomery were scarcely the first to be shed. In Germany Heinrich Heine, certain that the Romans would never have found the time to conquer the world if they first had been compelled to master their grammar, bemoaned the time he had invested in learning irregular verbs. About the same time, Cornelius Conway Felton (1807–62), who was appointed professor at Harvard in 1834 and became its president in 1860, put in a plea for the greening of the Classics, which in his judgment were suffocating under academic sterility. His words and admonitions, recited in a review (Felton, 1836), put all that has been said above in a context of awareness, that humanity cannot be ignored in the process of diagnosing documents which are among the most significant that humanity has produced. In prophetic anticipation of sensitivity to the constitutive aspects of poetry, of the importance of broad literary appreciation, and the bearing of awareness of social contextuality on understanding of an ancient document no scholars before Gildersleeve outmatched Felton.[40] After giving a hearing to the customary Kassandra's dirge over the approaching demise of classical learning, Felton suggested in his review that classicists move out of strength, not weakness. The public, he pointed out, is fast learning that literary taste was not embalmed with the Greeks and Romans. "The endless field of modern literature is opened to the student of polite letters. . . ." As though he perceived the end of another century, he noted that the Classics are only part of a long history of classical production that extends through Dante, Tasso, Milton, Shakespeare, Alfieri, Schiller, and Goethe. Those who love these writers of a comparatively modern age will be delighted, he said, to compare their works to the products of Greece and Rome (370–71). For, he wrote, "a wide study of modern literature, which the opinions of the age favor daily more and more, will strengthen rather than weaken a discriminating love of the ancient classics. It will sharpen the judgment, and refine the taste; for both judgment and taste are more the result of many comparisons and of gradual approximation, than is apt to be supposed. The kind of taste for ancient literature thus acquired, a love of antique poetry for poetry's sake, is doubtless more common now than it has ever been before" (Felton, 1836:371).

---

[40] See Sihler, 1902, esp. 508–9.

After calling attention to the subtleties of tragic formulation, which require a broad knowledge of Greek history and mythology, Felton again programs the future as he explains the peculiar demands that Attic comedy puts on the reader. It is "idiomatic," he writes, "to the last degree. Expressions growing out of the manifold relations of cultivated life, mingled with forms of speech naturally springing to the lips of a people who were lovers of war and rulers of the sea, make it necessary to build up anew in our imaginations the structure of Athenian Society, if we would enter fully into the spirit of the raciest portion of their literature" (372).

Finely attuned to the human scene, but without giving quarter to low aim, Felton goes on to compliment Theodore Woolsey for his work on the *Alkestis* of Euripides (1834) and on the *Antigone* of Sophokles (1835). "In unravelling the most curious constructions, his precision and acuteness are admirable" (Felton:372). Besides precise handling of particles, Woolsey displays mastery of "many of the most peculiar, and, at first view, untranslateable words and turns of phrase," which "are given in the homely but expressive idioms of our own Saxon tongue" (373).

In bold contrast to Woolsey's philological and humanitarian breadth and depth is this mini-portrait of "many learned commentators" submitted by Felton:

> Spending their lives in the study of grammatical niceties, poring fourteen hours a day over manuscript readings, and conjectural emendations, and choral metres and allegorical interpretations, the fountains of sympathy with human feeling have been dried up in their bosoms, the majestic forms of nature have become lifeless in their eyes, and the myriad voices, uttered from every part of God's world have grown unmeaning to their souls. The friendly collision of mind with mind in the common intercourse of life, the genial glow of thought in conversation, the softening, refining, animating influence of cultivated society, touch no responsive chord in their hardened natures. For they,
>
>> "Bereft of light, their seeing have forgot,
>> Nor to their idle orbs doth sight appear
>> Of sun, or moon, or star, throughout the year,
>> Or man, or woman."
>
> They think every hour given to the calls of friendship, or the amenities of life, lost to the world because it is lost to their barren studies. They are stiff, dry, formal, pedantic; and they write over their study doors, such sage apothegms as "Temporis fures amici." How can such people feel the spirit of tragedy, or understand the inspiration of the lyric muse? (373).[41]

The theme echoed Horace's *quid brevi fortes iaculamur aevo multa* (Why waste brief strength on so much chase? *Odes* 2.16.17–18) and anticipated Matthew Arnold's sermonette in *A Southern Night:*

---

[41] With some amelioration of indictment, Felton writes: "There have been some learned commentators, to whom these remarks will not apply" (373).

> We who pursue
> Our business with unslackening stride,
> . . . .
> And see all sights from pole to pole,
> And glance, and nod, and bustle by,
> And never once possess our soul
> Before we die.

Apparently Felton had in mind the kind of pedantry that prompted Charles Francis Adams, Jr., great-grandson and grandson of two presidents of the United States, to charge the authorities of Harvard College on 28 June 1883 with sponsoring a "college fetich." In tones tuned to Milton's description of part of his education as an "asinine feast of sow thistles and brambles," Adams deplored the fact that his education had been top-heavy in the ancient classics and so poorly administrated that it was a "scandal to the intelligence of the age" and incapacitated him for mastery of a specialty in connection with the development of the railroad system.[42]

Cast in Felton's mold was Mortimer Lamson Earle (1864–1905), classicist at Columbia University and vice president of APA during the last three years of his life. Resolutions adopted by the Faculty of Philosophy at his university in November, 1905, characterize the esteem in which he was held by the international community of scholars and suggest the route along which both classical and biblical study can be found in the future.

> The most striking characteristics of Prof. Earle were his thoroughness of scholarship and fidelity to the duties he had undertaken, added to a singular acuteness of intellect and openmindedness, which made him accessible to a wide variety of interests. His teaching was thorough and exacting; he was a determined foe of superficiality, and the high standards which he set before his students were exemplified in his work. To advanced students his advice was invaluable, for the rich stores of his learning were unstintingly put at their disposal. . . . His independence of judgment was very great, but he was generally his own severest critic. His real and lasting contributions to a better understanding of Greek and Latin literature were very numerous. In his death not only Columbia University, but the whole world of scholarship has suffered a grievous loss.[43]

One of his nuggets recalled by students included this advice: "All is not gold that is written in German or in modern Latin" (Earle, 1912:xxii). It was also recollected that Earle had given the following words of encouragement to a student who was facing his dissertation task: "Please remember that my work as teacher does not end" with the seminar work in Greek authors, "and that I shall be constantly at your service for any advice or help in your studies that I can give you" (xxiii). So impressed was Earle with Lincoln's Gettysburg

---

[42] Charles Adams, "Editor's Table: The Dead-Language Superstition," *The Popular Science Monthly* 23 (September, 1883) 701–8.

[43] Earle, 1912:xix.

address that he translated it into Greek (287) and implemented Lincoln's vision by doing his share in the awakening of America to women's academic rights. "If the college education of women is to be what it should be, it must be broad without shallowness, minute without pettiness; it must be so conducted that the whole structure may be constantly regarded as well as the parts; it must be fitly framed together—vertebrate not invertebrate. We must have the star as well as the wagon."[44]

[44] Earle, xiv-xv. Quoted from an article by Earle that appeared in *Columbia University Quarterly* (June, 1900, 231–34).

13

ARTS AND HAZARDS OF REVIEWING

Under methodological considerations falls the topic of book reviewing. It is a subject that has yet to see satisfactory scientific treatment, but its necessity has been winsomely suggested by an admirer of a British scholar, William Ridgeway:

> 'Tis well to find what all acknowledge true:
> Yet *that* once stated, what remains to do?
> Grant Truth historic by the world received,
> Like Euclid proved, like Holy Writ believed,—
> Could sages drop their acrimonious pens
> To sport like children on each others' dens,
> No more each rival's theories destroy,
> Accept *one* doctrine for the tale of Troy,—
> What then remains, when everyone agrees,
> For learned men in Universities?[1]

Reviewers are the Aristarchoi of the philologians' guild, and dedication to rebuke, reproof, and exhortation is their way of adding zest to operations of the craft. Sometimes the passion for the task obscures the scholar's goal and the results are frequently not lacking in charming demonstration of basic humanity that calls to mind the spirit of Dr. John Campbell's rebuke of Samuel Johnson. The two were engaged in a conversation, and when Johnson was about to dispute a point, Campbell said: "Come, we do not want to get the better of one another. We want to increase each other's ideas."[2]

One of the more astute reviewers in ancient times was Dionysios of Halikarnassos. The fact that some of his strictures are considered unconvincing does not depreciate his stature. A close second is Plutarch, from whose review of Herodotos's work (*On the Malice of Herodotos*) one can extract the principal guidelines for the craft, despite his thesis, steeped in Platonic ethical theory, that the father of history was a literary crook, who

[1] Alfred Denis Godley, in *Essays and Studies Presented to William Ridgeway . . . On His Sixtieth Birthday, 6 August 1913*, ed. E. C. Quiggin (Cambridge, England: University Press, 1914), xxiii.

[2] Frederick A. Pottle and Charles H. Bennett, eds., *Boswell's Journal of a Tour to the Hebrides* (New York: Guild, 1936) 316.

189

lacked historical decency in heaping up libel upon libel over the heroes of Hellas. Athenaeus, journalistic gossip of the late second century, at one point in his *Scholars Banquet (Deipnosophistai)* (x. 428f.30) charges Aischylos with composing dramas when he was in his cups. As Francis Godolphin (1932) determines the matter, Athenaeus attributed to Aischylos the habits of the characters the playwright created in his dramas.

Included in the prolegomena to a work on the subject would certainly be the observation that there is a tendency to dismiss those views that cover territory of maximum ignorance on the part of the reviewer, who will not infrequently resort to the term "unconvincing" (code for "not so") and with little interest in refutation. Where lack of space precludes detailed refutation, fairness would suggest avoidance of this hit-and-run ploy.

Irrelevance

Related to the Senior Citizens Syndrome noted earlier is Dyskolia, popularly known in one of its more dominant strains as Irrelevancy Distemper, which is especially virulent in book reviewers. Irrelevant criticism is seldom absent from an annual periodical run.

Some of the manifestations must, in the spirit of 1 Pet 4:8, be cloaked in anonymity. Couched in all the sublimity of a creation account, we are assured that a certain conjectural emendation was "without manuscript evidence." One is reminded of the answer Fulvius Propinquas gave when asked by an imperial official whether the documents that he had produced were autographs: "Yes! And so is the handwriting."

Another reviewer proclaimed that BAGD was in error in referencing two volumes for the Liddell-Scott-Jones-McKenzie *Greek-English Lexicon*. The colleague appears to have had a reprinted one-volume edition and assumed that this was all that ever was.[3] Someone else objected to an author's use of the expression double entente instead of double entendre. Fact is, the author wished to express simple ambiguity without suggestion of indelicacy.

Besides being apparently unsympathetic to some aspects of the new criticism, James Kallas (1970), in the course of comment on Paul Minear's *I Saw a New Earth*, missed discussion of topics that the author expressly disclaimed as secondary to his interest in the semasiological structure of the Apocalypse. Samuel Sandmel (1958) noted in a review of Erwin Goodenough's *Jewish Symbols in the Greco-Roman Period* that the cost of each of Goodenough's volumes came to about $7.50. He was not complaining, but observing that the price might inhibit broad circulation. Yet it would have been more to the point to note that less than four cents per page for

---

[3] Some facts of publication on LSJM: The revised edition was published in ten parts between 1925 and 1940. Vol. 1 is clearly marked on the title page as containing *alpha* to *kōps;* vol. 2, *lambda* to *ōiōdēs*.

elaborately illustrated text of the quality described by Sandmel was well worth the price. Two decades later, students were to pay ten or more cents per page, sans pictures. In a where-have-all-the-flowers-gone tone Morton Enslin (1956) registered annoyance over the entry of end-notes in a book on St. Augustine. One cannot have it both ways. Publishers keep the price down by simplifying production procedures.

The treasurer of SBL was ever diligent in noting the fiscal responsibility with which Enslin's editorship of *JBL* was conducted. Whether Enslin (1967) ever heard from the publisher to whom he suggested that the elimination of "so-called modern art" in a certain scholar's work could have lessened the cost "even a few pennies" must be left to the judgment of one whose favorite genre is societal epistolography. In any case, faced with the evidence of the astronomical price of $7.50 printed on the jacket, Enslin wrote in a depth-structural tone of cosmic sorrow, "It is a pity that was not done."

Occasionally a reviewer notes what appears to be an irrelevancy in a book under review. Robert Grant during preparation of a review of volume four of *Die Religion in Geschichte und Gegenwart* (Grant, 1961) concluded that the article "New Deal" did "not seem closely related to the theme of the encyclopedia." But in publications of this type editorial forewords ought to be taken into careful account. Discussion of social developments is an important feature of this reference work, and "New Deal" includes a number of cross references to related articles. Had Grant wished to finger a really irrelevant article, he would have had his chance when volume five came out, in 1961, with an article entitled "San Francisco." Discerning users noted that there was no article on Philadelphia, Pennsylvania in this volume; none on New York in the one that preceded; and none on Chicago, Illinois, in the first. A major church convention happened to have been held in San Francisco in 1959, and the editors had read and heard the phrase "San Francisco declared so and so" in connection with matters Lutheran. Arthur Carl Piepkorn, expert on the history of Lutheranism and a good many other subjects, was asked to write an entry "San Francisco" and obliged with an article in which he offered principally ecclesiastical and academic institutional statistics.

Self-diagnosis is the surest cure for dyskolia, and on another occasion Grant cleared his name with the admission that what he *misses* is not after all "fully relevant" to the author's purpose (Grant, 1971:228). Another did penance on this wise: "It would, however, be picayune to continue such a criticism of this book since it was obviously not intended for such scrutiny" (Fitzmyer, 1972:439).

One of the few scholars to develop resistance to all strains of dyskolia was Arthur Nock, who seemed to hear from each author these lines from Horace:

> Si quid novisti rectius istis,
> Candidus imperti, si nil, his utere mecum.
> *(Epistles* 1.6.68–69)

"If you have better advice, please tell me; otherwise follow me in mine." Zeph Stewart (1972) said of Nock that he "once defended his gentle reviews by saying that young scholars should not be discouraged, older scholars should be honored for the good work they had done." Nock, he wrote, "was always willing to see the good or useful features even of work that he considered disappointing or unconvincing." Much as he "disliked the errors of fact and approach," for example in Erwin Goodenough's *Jewish Symbols,* "he still valued the labor of amassing the evidence and he also maintained cordial personal ties with the author" (3–4).

Those who have not known the type of mercies featured by Nock can take comfort in the anecdote recorded in Boccalini's *Advertisements from Parnassus* and recited by Edgar Poe in *The Poetic Principle:* "Zoilus once presented Apollo a very caustic criticism upon a very admirable book; whereupon the god asked him for the beauties of the work. He replied that he only busied himself about the errors. On hearing this, Apollo, handing him a sack of unwinnowed wheat, bade him pick out *all the chaff* for his reward."

Good manners is another matter and need not be construed as incompatible with devotion to truth. The curate responsible for censuring Don Quixote's library protested the "irregular proceedings" of indiscriminate tossing from the windows and himself resolved first to read at least the title-page of every book. In these latter days a serious effort to digest the "prelims" is a fair expectation. And *ira,* whether *classica* or *theologica,* ought to be run through the sieve of the sage who said, "I do well to be angry, but I have mistaken the times." The admonition issued by Casper Kraemer, Jr. (1930) has become part of scholars' Ten Commandments. "The need for polemics has passed," he wrote as he took Deissmann to task for his "rather pugnacious attitude toward the old-school theologians who resented the newer interpretation of the papyri" (141). One is reminded of Arnold Jones, who wrote in the preface to *The Cities of the Eastern Roman Provinces* that he was grateful for the suggestions and corrections offered by epigraphist Louis Robert, but he could not thank him for the manner in which he had presented them.[4]

Some victims of poor manners have enriched literature with their own responses. Pindar expressed his resolve to soar through the heavens and outchant the "cawking daws." Jerome classified the critics of his Bible translation as "two-legged asses" and "barking dogs." And Erasmus, borrowing powder from Plutarch, discharged the ultimate salvo in *The Praise of Folly:* "There is an old saying, 'I hate a pot-companion with a memory.' Here is a new one: 'I hate a hearer that remembers anything.'"

Near the beginning of the twentieth century, L. B. Mitchell (1908), who had no interest in picking fly specks out of pepper, expressed doubts about the value of reviewers' lists of errata. "I wonder," he wrote, "if anyone ever

---

[4] See Arnold H. M. Jones, *The Cities of the Eastern Roman Provinces* (1937), 2d ed. (Oxford: Clarendon, 1971) v.

reads or profits much by the list of misspelled words and other errata compiled from the book being reviewed. I shall not complain, however, on this score. This feature in a review is perfectly harmless and helps to fill up space. Nay more, it must have a place here, for it certainly belongs to no other department of a periodical. Perhaps some candidate for an advanced degree will some time collect for a thesis a list of errata, in some of our text or reference books. I confess that I always jump over the accounts of these deplorable errata, always with the promise, however, that when I shall own the book, the corrections will be embodied in it forthwith — which thing has never been done." Thorough lists of errors and corrections in the review of a reference work may, of course, prove a boon to the student. Such, for example, is the detailed list supplied by Richard Bruère (1941) in his review of a concordance of Lucan.

Perusal of reviews suggests that in the estimation of some scholars one of the most serious crimes is to make a book readable. The ultimate in the preferred scholarly look can be judged from any page in Ernst Käsemann's commentary on Romans; German or English, it makes no difference. In earlier decades many church-goers appeared to evaluate the reliability of their Bibles in direct proportion to their unreadability. Edgar Goodspeed received criticism both from learned and unlearned circles for daring to paragraph the Bible and allotting dialogue to separate lines.[5] The criticism is akin to that of a reviewer who denigrated a learned work because it contained too many clarifying captions. The reviewer felt insulted. Likewise, dour scholars have from time to time frowned on a publication whose ponderous tone is relieved by occasional flashes of wit. A British reviewer accused Gildersleeve of lacking "humour and charm" when he adopted the "lighter style." And a German "summarist" accused him of engaging in cutesy style and wit, both of which were alleged to be foreign to their author. Countered Gildersleeve, "Here, to be sure, the summary is longer than the original, but that need not surprise us in a German" (Gildersleeve, 1930:112).

All scholars who are confident that posterity will offer them their just due will find further solace in the criticisms that were levelled at Homer and compiled by Henrietta Apfel (1938). Rebuke ranges from bad grammar to the use of impossible themes. And certainly no one in the craft will ever be exposed to something so astringent as a letter written by Philostratos — in a genre made famous nineteen centuries later by Walter Savage Landor — and addressed to Chariton, perpetrator of one of the earliest soap operas, whose heroin Callirhoe finds her name misspelled even by such as claim to know her intimately (Reardon, 1982). Taunts Philostratos: "You don't really think, do you, that people who know any Greek at all are going to recall your story when you're gone? Even alive you're just a nobody. How much less when

---

[5] Goodspeed, 1953:159: "One theologian declared he had never before seen a book so paragraphed."

you're dead!"[6] And should the merits of a treatise not be appreciated by Yahoos in the publishing industry, or if published, should a reviewer suggest that its sale be stopped, the reviewee is reminded that Cremutius Cordus was forced to commit suicide in 25 C.E., when Sejanus controlled the pens of Rome. But his daughter Marcia had hidden some of the copies of his work and published them when Gaius renewed Rome's reputation for freedom of inquiry.[7]

On the other hand, some books are better left untouched. Posterity is in debt to Nero for reconsidering his ill-conceived ban on the *Notebooks* of Fabricius Veiento (Tacitus *Annales* 14.50.1–2).[8] Freedom from censorship ensured merciful oblivion. And many a true lover of literature will most certainly join von Gutschmid in thanks to Apollo and the Muses for allowing Diogenes Laertius' *Pammetros* (Poems in all Meters) to vanish.

In retrospect, few victims of negative reviews have the opportunity for redress that even remotely approaches the action of Dionysios of Syracuse, and few reviewers have both the courage and the good manners of an ancient poet from Cythera. The Syracusan tyrant loved to recite his own poems. Philoxenos was not enchanted and said so. Whereupon, Dionysios ordered him to the quarries. After his release he went to a feast, in the course of which Dionysios recited his poetry. Philoxenos was asked for an opinion. Not having developed an ear for the royal lyrics, Philoxenos respectfully pleaded: "Send me back to the quarries."

In modern times probably no one manifested more resiliency than did James Frazer, who perdured incineration of his provocative work, *The Golden Bough*. Writing in the third edition of *Balder the Beautiful* (1935), he took a jaunty view of science: "It is the fate of theories to be washed away like children's castles of sand by the rising tide of knowledge, and I am not so presumptuous as to expect or desire for mine an exemption from the common lot. I hold them all very lightly and have used them chiefly as convenient pegs on which to hang my collections of facts." Cicero put it more succinctly in the *Tusculan Disputations* (3.19.46): "I invite refutation, for truth is my only concern in any and every inquiry."

Lest an impression of lopsided approach to reviewing be here conveyed the reader is encouraged to consult Sterling Dow's (1946) examination of the index to volumes 1 and 10 and Supplements 1–6 of *Hesperia*, including critique of indexes in other publications that feature epigraphic material. His review article covers 17 pages and is a model of such constructive appreciation that it would only expose one's ignorance to ask why so much effort was expended on what appears at first sight to be mere lists. Through Dow's

[6] Translation based on text in Boisonade, 1842, no. 8 = Teubner, Kayser, 1871, no. 66.

[7] Dio Cassius 57.24.2–4; Geer, 1930.

[8] Tacitus *Annals* 14.50.1–2, cited by H. J. Rose, *A Handbook of Greek Literature*; 4th ed, reprinted (London: Methuen, 1956) 11.

careful scrutiny there surfaces a wealth of history, and one actually feels the vibrancy of Athenian democracy. All this in an index!

As the dates accompanying the comments made by reviewers in *JBL* indicate, the *Journal of Biblical Literature* did not include a section for reviews until more than half a century had passed. Some of the earliest volumes of the journal do indeed contain articles with informed comment on various publications—see, for example, Isaac Hall (1885), E. C. Bissell (1886), and S. M. Jackson (1887)—but in SBL's infancy no provision was made for a special book review section. Part of the need was met, beginning in 1925, with a section entitled "Books Received." Two years later, SBL's corresponding secretary, George Dahl, informed members that the question of publishing book reviews had been broached, but that it might be well to discuss such a question of policy at an annual meeting (*JBL* 46[1927] v). Finally, in 1936, the first issue of vol. 55 carried the caption, "Book Reviews: New Testament and Early Christian Section," with discussion of twelve books (pp. 87–100), six of which were discussed in one article. The comment, most of it by Robert Casey and Kirsopp Lake, ranges from eleven lines to two pages. The second issue of the same volume carries the caption, "Book Reviews: Old Testament Section," includes eight discussions (pp. 159–74), three of them major, ranging from three to five pages in length, and five in the form of brief notes by William Albright. Alternating with discussions relating to New Testament publications in the third issue (pp. 235–46, under a revised caption, "Book Reviews: New Testament Section"), the Old Testament section in the fourth issue (pp. 308–26) contains sixteen reviews, which range in length from five lines to three pages.

Beginning with vol. 27 of *PAPA* (1896), under the caption "Biographical Record" (pp. lxvii-lxxviii), APA listed some of its members' philological contributions. For volume 28 (1897) the caption was altered to read, "Bibliographical Record," and the section continued through vol. 80 (1949). The demise of the feature was perhaps partially due to the escalation of trivial items submitted for listing. Nor was the annual appearance of *TAPA*, with its inclusion of *APA Proceedings* (*PAPA*), conducive to the inclusion of a book review section. Specialized journals which appeared at least quarterly were in a better position to satisfy the need for timely information.

In contrast to the slow pace at which *JBL* moved in supplying its readers with knowledge about other publications is the rapidity with which, for example, the editors of the *American Journal of Theology* processed such information. Ranging in length from one to eleven pages, a total of 139 books came under review in *AJT* 1 (1897). The first volume (1906) of *Classical Philology* similarly made deep probes of scholarly production, with fifty reviews ranging from seven lines to five pages in length. Its associate publication, the *Classical Journal,* carried forty-two reviews in the first volume (1905–6). The difference in initial impact may well be due to the fact that SBL took a long period of time to define itself, whereas *AJT, CP,* and *CJ* were products of carefully designed incubation and part of a comprehensive academic strategy, which did not provide for the type of penury that for decades bedeviled the editors of *JBL*.

Whatever the shortcomings in SBL's earlier policies relative to display of other scholarly production, the second half of the Society's first century offered evidence of more than sufficient atonement. The ever-broadening body of literature recognized in *JBL's* book review sections offers SBL's membership ample opportunity to remain abreast of the many developments taking place in biblical and related studies.

Part IV
Literary Philology

Language cannot be unlocked by logic;
It can be unlocked only by sympathy.

Benjamin Wheeler

LITERARY PHILOLOGY

Biblical and classical scholars repeatedly face the challenge of refining their methodologies in the face of fresh developments in other areas of inquiry. But they also require indulgence for failure at times to exhibit the sense of history that protects one from transmuting exposure to a methodology into discovery of a new phenomenon.

The error is not without hazard, for the temptation is strong to translate a species of inquiry into theory itself. The danger was especially acute in the latter half of the twentieth century, when citation of secondary literature that was more than ten years old was considered academically suicidal. It is not surprising, then, that some biblical and classical undergraduate students thought that comparative literary study, structuralism, or close reading of a text were among the latest fruits of time. The fact is that literary philology, in the more comprehensive sense of approaching documents as totalities and as part of the larger structure of human existence, had been in ferment in the Western World for more than a century, along with a complex cross-fertilization of methodologies.

In a centennial volume, therefore, one has the responsibility of at least cultivating a profounder sense of gratitude for those who dared to take ship out of safe harbors of tradition. Increment in the present ought not to be celebrated at the expense of appropriate attribution for scholars' legacies.

Comparative Literature

About the year 1893, Charles Gayley pleaded for the organization of a society of comparative literature so that literary criticism might proceed on a more scientific basis. A decade later (1903) two issues of *The Journal of Comparative Literature* appeared, edited by George E. Woodberry, J. B. Fletcher, and Joel Spingarn.[1] Even though no society had taken shape, Gayley expressed his pleasure over developments, and, in a presidential address

[1] Students were able to keep abreast of developments in comparative literature through the journal *Comparative Literature* (1949–), not to be confused with *The Journal of Comparative Literature*, which was discontinued. Also of service was the quarterly published at the University of Maryland: *Comparative Literature Studies.*

before the Pacific Coast Division of the American Philological Association, 29 December 1902, he discussed the question, "What is Comparative Literature?" (Gayley 1903). Gayley was not happy with the term comparative literature, which is traceable in its non-Teutonic form to Hutcheson Posnett, in 1886.[2] "To speak of a comparative object is absurd," said Gayley (57). But the term was here to stay, and Gayley was concerned with substantive issues.[3] One cannot "adopt, as universal, canons of criticism constructed upon particular premises," whether they be those of a Lessing or an Aristotle, Gayley informed his audience. "The principles of the drama," he exemplified, "cannot be derived from a consideration of the Greek drama alone, nor of European drama, but of all drama, wherever found. . . . From such comparative formulation of results proceed the only trustworthy canons for that kind of composition; some of them general, some dependent upon conditions historically differenced" (56–57). In the course of his remarks, Gayley observed that for some time German, French, and especially Italian scholars had been engaged in the pursuit of comparative literary study. Drawing on their contributions, he outlined the various directions taken by practitioners of comparative methodology. Breadth of perspective is fundamental, he counseled, for "students nowadays increasingly recognize that the cradle of literary science is anthropology. The comparative method therefore sets civilized literatures side by side with the popular, traces folklore to folklore, and these so far as possible to the matrix in the undifferentiated art of human expression" (61).[4]

Less than a decade earlier and at a different podium, Joseph Thayer, president of the Society of Biblical Literature, lamented the lack of comparative literature courses, Jewish, Christian, and others (Thayer, 1895:13). He was addressing himself, of course, to the provincialism that characterized so much of biblical scholarship. Gayley, on the other hand, could point to numerous localities where comparative literature had gained a foothold. It was his understanding that the University of Michigan offered something in that line already in 1887, and he pointed to California for 1889. Columbia studied "literature at large" in 1892, but a Department of Comparative Literature was not formally established until 1899. Such was the progress that Gayley could say in his presidential address, "At the present day courses

[2] Hutcheson Macaulay Posnett, *Comparative Literature* (New York: Appleton, 1886). In the *Contemporary Review,* June 1901, Posnett states how he founded the new "science." From the same period, see *Zeitschrift für Vergleichende Litteratur-Geschichte* and Louis Paul Betz, *La Litterature comparée essai bibliographique* (1886–1910), 2d ed. (Strasbourg, 1904).

[3] See also Shorey, 1906:376–77.

[4] On the application of folklore to the study of literature in the twentieth century, see below, especially Dundes, 1965, editor of a series of studies by folklore specialists: see also Archer Taylor's essay in the same volume (Taylor, 1965). For application to the study of Herodotos, see Lang, 1984. Watson Heston (1892a,b) anticipates much use of folklore for interpretation of the Bible.

of comparative study are pursued in all larger universities," with emphasis on the study of international borrowings, or source-hunting, and exploration of the larger influence or movements involving various literatures (Gayley, 1903:63).[5]

The early issues of *JBL* and *TAPA* boldly reflect confidence in detailed historical-critical philology to solve problems in biblical and classical texts. Desire for an antidote to traditionalist-literalist dogmatic mentality accompanied a brisk belief in the evolution of religious ideas in the early years of the Society of Biblical Literature.

Benjamin Bacon (1903) put the case for the defense in "Ultimate Problems of Biblical Science." Our method is historical, "imbued with the doctrine of evolution," he affirmed. "Biblical thought is a segment of the spiritual evolutionary process" (Bacon 1903:3). Bacon failed to note the contradiction in trying to escape from a dogmatic traditionalism and at the same time endeavoring to weld an alleged "scientific" methodology to a "doctrine" of evolution.[6]

Before biblical scholars overcame the attraction of the Darwinian model,[7] they questioned the validity of applying to literary production the methods used in Darwin's biological investigations. "Literature, like its material, language," said Gayley, "is not an organism, but a resultant medium" (63). Since it is a social phenomenon, advances in experimental psychology, anthropology, ethnology, and the history of art in general will contribute, Gayley insisted, to our understanding of its various manifestations. As a science, Comparative Literature is philology in its own right, he said, and the narrower linguistic philology of glottology as sponsored by Whitney must relinquish some of its claim to the term. Thus Gayley ultimately enunciated something akin to what biblical scholars would debate for decades: Does the historical-descriptive aspect of literary expression take precedence over the literary side of language as an expression of the human spirit? And Gayley's view of literature "as a solidarity and as a product of the social individual" (68) was prophetic of approaches from other perspectives by students of a linguistic bent different from that of Whitney's. Gayley further captured the

---

[5] Already in the late 1870s Americans were alerted to such developments. See the anonymous review of Eduard Grisebach's *Die treulose Witwe, eine Chinesische Novelle, und ihre Wanderung durch die Weltliteratur,* 3d ed. rev. (Stuttgart: A. Kroener, 1877) in *North American Review* 125 (1877) 159–61.

[6] In view of the lack of agreement on so many issues of New Testament criticism, the term scientific as used in the early issues of *JBL* appears in retrospect as triumphalistic as the traditionalism that opposed it. On Bacon's place in American criticism, see Harrisville, 1976.

[7] A contrasting methodology, bluntly stated a hundred years later, marks a "shift away from an historicist and evolutionary model toward a communications model" (Barr, 1979:600). Barr's observation fails to take account of the very discernible change in approach to the evolutionary model that appeared in the pages of *JBL* about a decade after Bacon's article.

beat of the future with his term Literary Philology, which he preferred to Comparative Literature, and which can be used to embrace the various directions taken in literary studies by classicists and biblical scholars.[8]

While biblical scholars were in the main engrossing themselves in the continental type of biblical philology, with emphasis on dissection of biblical literature and discussion of sources,[9] classicists displayed increasing interest in documents as totalities, and some recognized the values of pilgrimage into other cultures.

Four articles in *TAPA* in the 1920s offered a foretaste of things to come. In "The Plot of the *Miles Gloriosus*" Blanche Brotherton (1924) used oriental tales to demonstrate coherence in Plautus's drama about a swaggering poltroon. Two years later Cornelia Coulter and Marbury Ogle did chores for their biblical colleagues. Coulter (1926) tracked the "Great Fish" in ancient and medieval story. Ogle (1928) made the discovery of the "Wonder Child" (1928) and found traces of Herodotos's story of Demaratos in the apocryphal gospels and beyond, down to the Middle Ages. Ben Perry (1926) used the comparative method in "An Interpretation of Apuleius' *Metamorphoses*."

Members of SBL had been staying closer to their own hearth, but were invited to peer farther when Paul Laubenstein (1932) associated apocalyptic literature and negro spirituals in "An Apocalyptic Reincarnation." Laubenstein calls attention to the prevailing perceptuality: visual, auditory, kinesthetic, and affective. He shows that the literature of the southern slaves was pervaded by a sense of affliction; marked by a sense of electedness; permeated with optimistic attitudes; characterized by love of peace; emphatic about the Day of Judgment, with description of natural cataclysms; expressed in concrete imagery; and conveyed in anonymity and cryptic use of words. Almost two decades elapsed before anything comparable found expression in *JBL*. Without making a reference to Laubenstein, Amos Wilder (1956) noted in a presidential address the use of encoded language in negro spirituals, as, for example, in the phrase "crossing over Jordan" (= "entry into free territory"). Laubenstein had pointed out, along with a number of other examples of ambiguities, that in the apocalyptic imagery of the spirituals the Messiah saves with a "ticket," of course only for the ransomed.

One of the earliest applications of the comparative literary method to appear in *JBL* with reference to a specific biblical pericope is Kemper

[8] Gayley, 1903:67, complimented George E. Woodberry, one of the editors of *The Journal of Comparative Literature*, for the vision he expressed in the first editorial, but disagrees with one of Woodberry's narrower limitations of comparative inquiry to such accidental features as "alliteration and rhyme."

[9] Crossan, 1976:xiii, sums the matter: "Literary criticism in the full sense of the term sat with Cinderella in the biblical ashes." But Crossan does not point to earlier efforts made before Amos Wilder, Robert Funk, and Dan Via to escape the older orbit. For Paul Shorey's defense of classical studies against "hoary fallacies and irrelevancies" that were being used by hostile critics of a classical education, see his address, "The Case for the Classics" (1910).

Fullerton's (1934) study entitled "On Job, Chapters 9 and 10."[10] Fullerton uses literary analysis to eliminate unjustifiable excisions and draws on Aischylos's *Agamemnon* and *Prometheus* for finer perception of the literary art expressed in the Book of Job. Luitpold Wallach (1943) looked at Indian, Greek, and Hebrew variations of the theme of the Blind and the Lame man engaged in mutual assistance, with special reference to the *Ezekiel Apocryphon*. An intra-biblical study by J. Merle Rife (1941), "The Literary Background of Revelation II-III," with Amos 1–2 seen as the model for Revelation 2–3, appeared in the same decade. In 1950 Theodore Gaster concentrated on the mythological texts of Ugarit, but in keeping with the title of his book, *Thespis*, took ample account of Greek dramatic forms in his discussion of cultural-anthropological and history-of-religion features.

In the 1960s and 1970s interest in comparative literary study blossomed afresh. Homer provided an attractive take-off point. Albert Lord (1951) emphasized oral recitation of epic poetry and endeavored to show the formative aspects of formula and theme in the composer's art. Calvin Brown (1966), in "Odysseus and Polyphemus: The Name and the Curse," invokes numerous tales from various cultures relating to power through name recognition. Odysseus, in a moment of hybris, gives away his name to Polyphemos, who then pronounces a terrible curse on his tormenter. Like a ring that betrays in some tales a hero's whereabouts and threatens to put the person back into the giant's power, the name makes possible the curse. The blinding of Polyphemos by Odysseus is not, as ordinarily assumed, the dramatic cause of Odysseus's subsequent misfortunes, argues Brown. Aigistheus brought misery on himself by his own folly, but so did Odysseus.

An impressive demonstration of the hermeneutical value of folklore was made by Gerald Gresseth, who compared the *Odyssey* and the *Nalopākhyāna* (1979). In the corresponding Latin sector, L. A. Mackay cantilevered his way from Vergil to Al Capp (1963).[11] Mackay was convinced that "Aeneas reappears with remarkable precision in the Li'l Abner of Al Capp." Also, Greek and Hebrew literature render comparative service in a study of Hebrew and Phoenician cosmology by John Brown (1968). As is apparent from the references cited above, and as Gayley pointed out at the beginning of the twentieth century, comparative literary analysis and study of folklore are intimately associated. But even before Gayley broached the subject of comparative literature, Basil Gildersleeve (1930) ranged from Eastern dancers to Uncle Remus and Galsworthy to demonstrate how light can shine upon things long hidden in the night (189–190). In a study of bastardy thematic in 1 Sam 20:30, Joshua Finkel (1936) commented on his use of folklore material:

---

[10] See also Fullerton's earlier essay, "The Original Conclusion of Job," ZAW 42 (1924) 116–36. Cf. Hyde, 1924, on Hellenistic orientation of the Song of Songs.

[11] MacKay, 1963:164; see bibl. p. 157 n. 1.

"It is thus evident that folklore no less than archaeology may sometimes confirm the authenticity of a text" (143).

New Literary Criticism

Efforts exerted by biblical scholars and classicists to bridge the chasm between historical-critical philology and concern for sensitivity to documents as creations of the mind and spirit exhibit dependence on a variety of developents in literary criticism and other disciplines.

A common feature in many of these developments is their lack of integrity as scientifically identifiable disciplines. This deficiency is manifested, for example, by the looseness of the term New Criticism, an expression that can be mistakenly associated exclusively with the work of, among others, Ivor Richards, Thomas Eliot, and associates.

One of the earliest critics to use the terminology is Noah Porter in an essay entitled, "The New Criticism" (1870). Porter states that the old criticism was basically snobbish and confined itself to form, such as choice of words, rhythm of verse, proportion of parts, order of development, effectiveness of the introduction, the argument, and the peroration. The "New Criticism," claimed Porter, is more hospitable to a variety of literary expression and concerns itself with the "matter," such as weightiness and truth of thought, energy and nobility of sentiments, splendor and power of imagery, heroic manhood, or the refined womanhood of the heroine. In brief, the literary work is not primarily an object for dissection, but a welcome partner in the exploration of a larger shared humanity (296). In Porter's judgment, the features of the "New Criticism" largely reflect an historical-critical emphasis. As such, they are in the main antithetical to Joel Spingarn's doctrine expressed in a lecture delivered at Columbia University, 9 March 1910, and with the same title as that of Porter's (Spingarn, 1940). Reflecting the aesthetic orthodoxy of Benedetto Croce, Spingarn declares that of primary interest is what poets try to do and how they bring their intention to expression. His exposition is tantamount to a review of the major tenets reflected in most of the literary criticism that focuses on the literary object as a self-contained world, displaying:

1. The primacy of language as the basic paradigm for critical activity.
2. The primacy of language over history.
3. The primacy of what is universally human over that which is narrowly historical.
4. The primacy of linguistic depth over a superficial interest in didactic or moral profit.
5. The primacy of expression over Aristotelian dogma.
6. The primacy of organic expression over traditional genres of literature.
7. The free and original movement of the work as opposed to its place in an alleged evolution of literature.

With this emphasis on the liberation of an artistic literary work from traditional confinement, Spingarn reflects what Edgar Allan Poe had expressed a half century earlier. Few critics have declared so passionately as did Poe the right of a poem to exist for its own sake, free of prior judgment as to what it ought to be:

In *The Poetic Principle*, first published in 1850 (Philadelphia: John Sartain), Poe has this to say about the transcendent rights of the poem (1940:6–7):

> While the epic mania—while the idea that, to merit in poetry, prolixity is indispensable—has, for some years past, been gradually dying out of the public mind, by mere dint of its own absurdity—we find it succeeded by a heresy too palpably false to be long tolerated, but one which, in the brief period it has already endured, may be said to have accomplished more in the corruption of our Poetical Literature than all its other enemies combined. I allude to the heresy of *The Didactic*. It has been assumed, tacitly and avowedly, directly and indirectly, that the ultimate object of all Poetry is Truth. Every poem, it is said, should inculcate a moral; and by this moral is the poetical merit of the work to be adjudged. We Americans especially have patronized this happy idea; and we Bostonians, very especially, have seen it developed in full. We have taken it into our heads that to write a poem simply for the poem's sake, and to acknowledge such to have been our design, would be to confess ourselves radically wanting in the true Poetic dignity and force:—but the simple fact is, that, would we but permit ourselves to look into our own souls, we should immediately there discover that under the sun there neither exists nor can exist any work more thoroughly dignified—more supremely noble than this very poem—this poem *per se*—this poem which is a poem and nothing more—this poem written solely for the poem's sake.

In 1909, W. C. Brownell issued a blistering attack against Poe's basic position, calling him an expert in "domestication of the exotic" (Brownell, 1940:236). Poe "was an artist," wrote Brownell, "with a controlling bent toward artifice, exaggeratedly theoretic, convinced that the beautiful is the strange and the sad the poetic, and exercising his imagination through every expedient of ingenious invention, to the end of producing effects of strangeness to the point of abnormality and of sadness to the point of horror" (273).

Brownell's criticism bears all the marks of an exposition of an earlier reviewer's estimate of Poe's works. Writing in *North American Review* (1856), an anonymous critic grants Poe's mastery of technique, but complains that his work "lacks the *vis vitae* which alone can make of words living things" (428). In only a few efforts, the writer goes on to say, does Poe enlist "the sympathy of his readers"; for his work is "destitute of moral sentiment" (445).

The moment of truth in the reviewer's criticism is the precision with which the reviewer penetrates the core of Poe's critical theory, that perfection of expression constitutes its being. In Poe's judgment, moral and intellectual concerns are better satisfied in prose than in poetry. Sensation is preeminent, and beauty is everything. And "of all the poetical tones," wrote Poe, "melancholy . . . is the most legitimate," for it is the tone of the "highest manifestation" of beauty.[12] Through detailed analysis of "The Raven," Poe explains how he achieved what he considered the ultimate expression of beauty.[13] Nevertheless Poe still suffers in America from the kind of criticism expressed by Ralph Waldo Emerson, who exhibited his own tone-deafness when he referred to Poe as "that jingle-man." Similarly, James Russell Lowell wrote in "Fable for Critics":

> Here comes Poe with his Raven, like Barnaby Rudge—
> Three-fifths of him genius and two fifths sheer fudge.

Poe's ultimate vision is that of a "novel universe swelling into existence, and then subsiding into nothingness, at every throb of the Heart Divine. And this heart, what is it? *It is our own.* In man, the sense of individual identity will be gradually merged in the general consciousness. . . . The general sum of the separate sensations of created things is precisely the amount of happiness which appertains by right to the Divine Being, when concentrated within Himself."[14] For Poe the world of the poem becomes the very universe, and poets themselves give way to the poem as the expression of the ultimate in ultimacies. Whatever one may say about the limitations in Poe's critical views, there is a point at which he probes deeply the very core of human existence, and existentialists and structuralists would write bewildering variations of the theme on which Poe had made magisterial pronouncements.

Biblical and classical scholars do not appear to have given much thought to specific aspects of Poe's poetical theory, but they could not escape the increasing demand of a literary work for recognition on its own terms, divorced from laws of interpretation that threatened to throttle the life of the text. Among the voices that could not totally be ignored were those of the "newer" New Criticism, including Ivor Richards, Thomas Eliot, Yvor Winters, John Ransom,[15] Allen Tate, Robert Warren, Cleanth Brooks, Kenneth Burke, Edmund Wilson, and Richard Blackmur. If one may speak of a critical position in the absence of what is commonly understood as a "school," Wellek's depiction is to the point (1967:120–21):

> . . . in a general history of American criticism we can see that the new critics all react against a common preceding situation. They were all

---

[12] The quotation is from Poe, "The Philosophy of Composition," *The Works of Edgar Allan Poe,* 1 (New York: Scribner, 1927) 36. Through detailed analysis of "The Raven" Poe explains how he achieved what he considered the ultimate expression of beauty. On Poe's classical interests and probable origins of his critical theory, see Alterton, 1923.

[13] Ibid., 33–46.

[14] Anonymous reviewer (1856), citing Poe's *Works,* 2 (1856) 214.

[15] Ransom authored *The New Criticism* (Norfolk, CT: New Directions, 1941). For a general introduction to the "New Critics" see *Critiques,* 1949. Richard McKeon (1936, 1941, 1982) bridges ancient and modern developments in criticism.

dissatisfied with the impressionistic, vaguely romantic, and sentimental "appreciation" prevalent inside and outside of the universities; and they disapproved of the purely journalistic criticism associated with Mencken and his praise of the naturalistic novel; they felt uncomfortable with the New Humanist movement because of its hostility to contemporary writing and its rigidly moralistic view of literature. . . . In reaction . . . they turned largely, at first at least, to a study of poetry, especially modern poetry, concentrating on the actual texts of the works under inspection and stressing the peculiarity of a work of art which they conceived of as comparatively independent of its background in history, biography, and literary tradition. In this turn to the text, this stress on the unity of a work of art, this refusal to reduce literature to its causes can be found what may be described as the common denominator of the new critics.

This emphasis on the liberation of the poem from exploitation of vested critical interests is the nucleus of the approach described by Spingarn (1910). What is important, he writes in echo of Goethe, is the answer to the question: "What has the writer proposed to himself to do? and how far has he succeeded in carrying out his own plan?" (435).

And so it came to pass that shortly after World War I a fresh breeze began to quicken the Society of Biblical Literature. Raymond Beardslee (1920) helped open the windows of SBL to its caress with a call for appreciation of Isaiah through poetic appropriation. James Montgomery (1926) also thought it was time for a change and complimented Christina Rossetti, who, he said, "knew nothing of Literarkritik, whose function is that of dissection and detection of sources, . . ." yet had discovered that the Seer was a poet.

Drama in John

Now that Beardslee had cleared the path, a few New Testament scholars saw fresh avenues for research, and for a decade it was "drama in John."

A classicist had hinted at what might be done. In 1912, J. Elmore discussed dramatic elements in Martial. Among them are the "robber robbed," "surprise," and "antithesis." Whatever were the roots of influence, the year 1925 focused attention on the literary character of the Fourth Gospel. Of three important productions, Robert Strachan's was most explicit: *The Fourth Evangelist: Dramatist or Historian?*[16] Clayton Bowen thought the entire SBL ought to know about these developments, so he wrote "The Fourth Gospel as Dramatic Material" (1930). In this essay Bowen affirmed the

---

[16] Robert Harvey Strachan, *The Fourth Evangelist: Dramatist or Historian* (London: Hodder and Stoughton, 1925); Carl Everett Purinton, *Literature of the New Testament* (New York: Scribner, 1925); Benjamin Willard Robinson, *The Gospel of John* (New York: Macmillan, 1925). It is not certain whether Norman Petersen was aware of such productions when he stated that "biblical critics have until recently lacked an understanding of literature like that found among literary critics."

right of biblical documents to be approached as literary works with beginning and end and some evidence of "plot." With a thrust toward "redaction"
criticism, he informed biblical scholars that the Fourth Gospel was not "*a
narrative at all*," but "a story written or composed straight ahead, in some sort
of purposed sequences" (293), namely as "a series of dramatic scenes" (296),
something like a "pageant" (305). In 1950 Theodor Gaster traced dramatic
features in ritual form from Canaanite texts down to an English Mummer's
Play. A decade later, John Bowman (1962) applied the interpretive tactic to
the Book of Revelation.

James Muilenberg was so impressed with Bowen's breakthrough that in
1932 he made use of further developments that were taking place outside
biblical circles and endeavored to show the importance of taking relationships of form and content into consideration. A year earlier, Ernest Burch
(1931) applied the same type of criticism to St. Mark's record: "Tragic Action
in the Second Gospel." And the thirteenth chapter of 1 Corinthians received
from Nils Lund the verdict: "an artistic piece of literature."

In the classical sector Cornelia Coulter (1931) pursued the matter with
a study of Plato's *Apology*. Homer came in for examination by Levi Post
(1939), with emphasis on moral agonistic. "Drama is action," wrote Post, "and
action is composed of aspiration, futility, decision, indecision, struggle, circumstance, suspense, and achievement or failure" (159).[17]

Ancient authors in general appear to have earned from classicists greater
respect in the early decades of the twentieth century for their creative
contributions than did biblical writers from either Old or New Testament
scholars, for whom source analysis was the door to knowledge and dictionaries the key to reading texts. To some extent this circumstance was due to
German influence. In their work on the classics, German scholars had shown
a bifurcated critical interest: detailed historical-philological inquiry and a
grasp of documents as literary wholes. In the case of the Bible, on the other
hand, dissection had been paramount. What is noteworthy, then, in connection with classical studies, beginning with the 1920s, is not the fact that
certain studies were attentive to literary productions for their own sake, but
that there was a sudden surge of such interest at the time, beyond doubt
attributable to acquaintance with developments in the New Criticism.[18]

Samuel Bassett is among those who overcame the mesmerizing power
of the old philology and in 1927 called the attention of both biblical and
classical scholars to the Greek habit of presenting "truth hidden in the
language of imagery." In 1 Cor 13:12, the phrase "through a glass darkly"
carries, he said, both a positive and a negative connotation.[19]

---

[17] Rowe (1967) followed a similar line of thought in a study of Caesar's *Bellum Civile*. Cf.
Walbank, 1960:234.

[18] Cf. Segal, 1968:3–4.

[19] Bassett (1927) compares Num 12:8 LXX. His interpretation antedates a similar solution

Milman Parry (1928) argued for *sense* as a third level of meaning in the standardized poetic diction in Homeric epic. Besides *signification* (a denotative function) and *meaning* (contextual factor) there is the level of *sense*, that is, a semantic delimitation brought about by repeated use. A decade later Ben Perry (1937) observed that Homeric preference for paratactic as opposed to hypotactic ordering of thoughts is a feature of oral expression.

In the 1950s, and thereafter, currents that flowed through the New Criticism ran swiftly in classical studies. Protests against historicization mounted. It is a "felony," cries Frank Copley (1958), in a discussion of a poem by Catullus, to try to make the world of the poem square with *our* world. The poet's world as depicted in a poem is "for that poem" a real world (9–13). Similarly, in a discussion of Lucretius, Erling Holtsmark (1967) states that his aim is to avoid "the quicksands of biographical bias and deal with the poetic text on its own merit" (193). He then proceeds to explore the structure and language of Lucretius 2:1–19. In 1955, L. MacKay warned monotheists and atheists not to ascribe to a polytheist all their own doubts and scruples. Instead of looking for allegory in Book Six of the Aeneid, we are to take note of the *symbolism* that permeates the simultaneous handling of several levels of meaning. Vergil exalts Augustus, indulges in legendary narrative, and evokes salient values of Roman history.[20]

Exploration of Euripides's use of imagery in the *Medea* rewards Stewart Flory (1978) and his readers with renewed appreciation for the artistic genius of this playwright. Lines 895–903 of the drama contrast Medea's own trusting hand with Jason's deceitful hand, and her own hand must finally grasp the sword.

A study of imagery in Propertius 1.2.23–26, in which the Roman elegiast views Cynthia's *cultus* as a sign of infidelity (Watson, 1982:238), prompts one to be sensitive to what may be comparable imagery in 1 Peter 3:2–7, which appears to suggest luxurious living, but with infidelity projected at another level of meaning.

Christine Perkell (1981) is appreciative of the critical work done on the passage dealing with the Corycian gardener in Vergil's fourth *Georgic* (4.116–48), but aims to probe in greater depth the symbolic value of the gardener and the relation of the passage to the poem's major themes. She concludes that the gardener is, "in his harmony with nature and in his

---

offered by Norbert Hugede, *La métaphore du miroir* . . . (Delachaux: Neuchâtel, 1957). David H. Gill, in *CBQ* 25 (1963) 427–29, proposed a variation of the solution offered by Basset and by a German scholar, J. Behm.

[20] Augustus capitalized on the power of symbol, as signalled by his description of the recovery of the standards in the *Res Gestae* and by his pictorial emphasis on the statue from Prima Porta, designed "especially for the oriental mind, accustomed to symbolic actions." C. S. Walton, "Oriental Senators in the Service of Rome," *JRS* 19 (1929) 39 n. 7.

freedom to pursue an entirely esthetic ideal, . . . the creation of Vergil's imagination . . . and longing" (Perkell:177).[21]

Allied with absorption in imagery and symbolism is the search for patterns in literary works. Within the realm of biblical studies such investigation ranges from the mathematical computations of an Ivan Panin[22] to the intricate chiastic structures claimed by Charles Talbert for Luke-Acts. Talbert claims that classicists have set the pace for the architectural analysis that he undertakes (Talbert, 1947:5–8). But it is one thing to look across the fence and another to turn one's ear to the critical debate that goes on beyond the fence.[23] What was once avant garde may be totally passé, as is the case in some respects with the "New Criticism."[24]

In an essay entitled "The *Telemachy* and Structural Symmetry," Stephen Bertman (1966) cites J. T. Sheppard, of Great Britain,[25] and an American, Cedric Whitman (1958), as exemplars of pattern research. With an ecstasy that matched the enthusiasm of Panin, George Duckworth (1960) exulted in connection with his study of Vergil: "The subject is a technical one, but it has the excitement of a journey into new and uncharted territory. If the presence of exact or approximate Golden Mean ratios everywhere in the Aeneid seems improbable or even fantastic, I can assure the reader that it seemed so likewise to me when I first discovered their existence. Each step in my investigation led to new and equally surprising results."[26] Patricia Johnston (1977) explores chiastic structures in Vergil's *Georgics* and suggests that such awareness helps clarify Vergil's unusual versions of the myths relating to Proserpina and Eurydice. Past disasters cannot be reversed, but the loss of Proserpina leads to learning of the art of cultivating grain, and the loss of Eurydice to instruction in the art of acquiring a new hive of bees. In the same issue of *TAPA*, David Claus shows how Hesiod uses structural devices to "develop his ideas and enlarge the capacity of his language."

To ward off overzealousness in the search for patterns, Charles Segal hoisted Otto Schroeder's warning, via Gildersleeve: *Cave furorem arithmeticum* (Segal, 1968:13–14). Herbert Benario declared disinterest in

---

[21] On shortcomings in symbolist interpretation, see Segal, 1968, esp. pp. 14–18.

[22] Ivan Panin, *The New Testament from the Greek Text as Established by Bible Numerics* (Toronto: Book Society of Canada, 1914; 2d ed. 1935). Panin expressed his enthusiasm for the work in these words from the preface to the second edition: "Every item therein, howe'er trifling to the eye of mere man, dealt out as it is by the Divine Artificer with the same weight and measure recently discovered in the new stellar atomic world with its electrons, neutrons, nuclei, and the rest, imposes upon the translator an entirely new standard: wholly different from those hitherto followed in the merely mundane doings of men." For Basil Gildersleeve's view of statistical analysis, see his *Brief Mention* (1930) 114.

[23] Cf. critique by Fitzmyer, 1981:96–97.

[24] See Segal, 1968:11.

[25] J. T. Sheppard, *The Pattern of the Iliad* (London, 1922).

[26] See also Murley (1937) on structure and proportion in the forty-fourth ode of Catullus.

the structure and architectures of *Aeneid* Book 10—"it has been done before" (Benario, 1967:23 n. 3)—and concentrated instead on the poet's allusions with emphasis on what he "*says.*"

Images and symbols may open doors to archetypal reality through a "new critical" probing of mythopoeic levels, with frequent reference to double meanings. In a study of sacrificial imagery in the *Oresteia,* Froma Zeitlin lets us see Klytemnestra as a "paradigm of creative destructiveness" and "of nihilistic generation" (1966:650). A year earlier, John Clark and Anna Motto (1965) argued that Juvenal's Third Satire is not of the "You are there" variety. For Daniel Harmon (1974), who learned about the use of ambiguity in poetry from the New Critics, Propertius offers opportunity to document an exploration of reality through fantasy.

Similar to the experience of the author of the Third Gospel and Acts at the hands of critics is the critical fate suffered by Nero's spiritual advisor, Seneca. For a long time scholars did not take Seneca seriously as a creative writer. This was partially due to narrow exploration of the influence of rhetoric and Stoic philosophy on his tragic poetry. To assist in his rehabilitation, William Owen (1968) calls attention to Seneca's revitalization of metaphor and fresh interpretation of myths. Similarly, Petronius's apparently anarchic presentation is, according to Zeitlin (1971), esthetically significant and manifests artistic integrity.[27]

Precisely to what extent the "New Critics" directly influenced the biblical scholars who were mentioned earlier cannot be determined, but concerning the indebtedness of Amos N. Wilder to the New Criticism there is no doubt, and it is evident that he hoped to turn the Society of Biblical Literature away from preoccupation with source criticism and other approaches that dispensed with attention to creative features in texts. In an essay, "The Nature of Jewish Eschatology," Wilder (1931) pointed to the "largely imaginative" elements in Jewish apocalyptic, which can be "properly understood when appraisal of the literary and poetic mind is added to that of the scholar" (201). And in the same essay he wrote of "myth" in a manner that anticipated his remarks almost a quarter century later, when he called attention to the literary stature of Eliot and Richards, with emphasis on the importance of the role of myth in poetic statement (Wilder, 1956). Variations and expansions of the thoughts expressed in this presidential address appeared over a period of years and climaxed in a brief study entitled *Theopoetic* (1976). In sum, Wilder protests against the dominance of intellectual or moral dogmatism and pleads for recognition of "the role of the symbolic and the prerational in the way we deal with experience" (1976:2).

On balance, this protest is a variation of one made by another member of the Society, Henry Nash, a half-century earlier. Nash observed that the

---

[27] Compare Gilbert Highet (1941), and see Graham Anderson's strictures (1982:95–96) against Zeitlin's interpretation.

New Testament, "considered as a whole," had two main characteristics. "In the first place, it is the product of a consuming religious passion. Of course, there is reflection in it. There is some speculation. But the bulk of it is the work of men who were, above all things, zealots in religion. This we are not. We are religious, yet the critical element is strong in us." Besides giving expression to the perennial problem of mind versus spirit and heart, Nash noted that standard methods of criticism tend to exalt individualism and ignore the fact that New Testament people have a corporate consciousness (1902:170–71).

Without explicit attribution, Wilder echoed Nash's observation and pointed to the corporate consciousness of humanity as opposed to experiences within limited cultural structures. *Mutatis mutandis,* Wilder (1976) distinguishes two "levels of human mentality and imagery which change relatively rapidly. But there are," he goes on to say, "deeper levels of consciousness and culture and language associated with momentous revelations in the earlier history of mankind in which continuity remains unbroken" (93). This depth structure of reality is the realm of myth that finds expression, precisely because of humanity's many-sided grasp of experience, with varying formulation in the course of history.

Structuralism

How to maintain a balance between truth and form was the challenge confronting critics. Both biblical scholars and classicists had a stake in the matter. Biblical students were committed to their canonical classics on the assumption that these documents met the world's need for basic spiritual resources. And, if Gildersleeve and Shorey were correct, classicists were in fealty bound to transmit the heritage of Greece and Rome to a world that was committing spiritual and cultural suicide.

The movement toward the exaltation of the poem as a universe of rhythm and tonality had reached in Poe's rhetoric a plateau of definition for which there remained primarily the task of modification. Poe had a firm theoretical grasp of his assignment as a poet, and he was able to articulate the mode of executing that responsibility: the use of words in the creation of Beauty. But he had not dealt systematically with the question of "meaning." It remained for linguistic research to open fresh opportunities for dialog at the beginning of the twentieth century. And among the most seminal developments was the emergence of structuralist theory.

Structuralism itself is not a new phenomenon. Isolation of the general structures of human enterprise, whether in history, literature, linguistics, anthropology, psychology, or socio-economics, has been an ongoing feature of the human quest for understanding, especially since the time of the ancient Greek philosophers. Recognition of structure makes scientific theory possible. And structuralist theory, as generally understood in linguistic-literary discussion, basically denotes the view that a system, configuration, or network of interrelationships, common to humanity, is responsible for the generation of any and all speech and documentary expression. The system or set of inter-relationships underlying any utterance or text constitutes the primary meaning of that utterance or text.[28] Whereas historical-critical study and traditional philology are diachronically oriented, the new linguistic approach functions synchronically. This means that, when dealing with a literary document, the structuralist thinks in terms of the document as a world in itself, whose meaning in the primary sense is independent of any historical circumstantiality that relates to the author, the original recipients, or specific interests of the contemporary reader.

Application of structuralist theory may take a number of routes. Among the earliest structuralists committed to study of phonology are the Russian Formalists and the associated Prague School. Five years before Ferdinand de Saussure had written *Cours de linguistique générale* (Lausanne: Payot, 1916) the Czech scholar Vilem Mathesius appealed for a synchronistic approach to language phenomena. His presentation, made on 6 February 1911, at a meeting of the Royal Czech Society of Sciences, bears the title *On the Potentiality of the Phenomena of Language.* According to Roman Jakobson, had Mathesius delivered his lecture in Moscow instead of in Prague, "it would have caused a veritable revolution in linguistics."[29] Saussure gained a reputation while Mathesius quietly encouraged investigation of the possibilities latent in synchronic linguistics for application to the study of phonology. On 6 October 1926, the first meeting of the Prague Linguistic Circle was convened by Mathesius, in company with three other Czechs, B. Havranek, Jan Rypka, Bohumil Trnka; Henrik Becker, a German, and a Russian, Roman Jakobson. In contrast to the New Critics and their followers, who engaged in associative analysis and study of patternism and other surface organizational features, the formalists explored the possibilities of synchronic linguistics, yet not without due diachronic awareness, in the development of a linguistically oriented theory of poetry.[30]

Formalist influence eventually made itself felt in classical circles. James Notopoulos (1949) entered Homeric debate and questioned the validity of

[28] Popularization of such approach and application to the teaching of Latin and Greek is a feature of *CJ* 52 (1957) 265–78. For the terminology of structuralists and the use of structuralism in biblical interpretation, see Patte 1976.

[29] Cited by Vachek, 1966:5.

[30] See Vachek, 1966, "Appendix I. Basic Information on Some Members of the Prague Group," 122–36. For the early history of "The Prague School" see Mathesius, "Appendix II. Ten Years of the Prague School," ibid. 137–51; selected bibliography, ibid. 166–78. In general, the Prague Group is more interested in extra-lingual reality than are the Russian Formalists; see Vachek: 7. On Russian formalism, see Victor Erlich, *Russian Formalism,* 3d ed. (The Hague/Paris, 1969), and L. Matejka and K. Pomorska, *Readings in Russian Poetics: Formalist and Structuralist Views* (Cambridge: M.I.T., 1971).

applying the same principles of literary criticism to both written and oral productions. Certainly with respect to the latter, he said, one cannot invoke Aristotelian views of organic unity. He therefore proposed the application of formalist principles to a recurring phenomenon of Homeric grammar, under the title, "Parataxis in Homer: A New Approach to Homeric Literary Criticism."

Philodemos (*On Poems*) and Dionysios of Halikarnassos (*On Composition*) had ingeniously inverted the critical process by experimenting as to what might happen if a given literary phrase underwent a transference of wording. Dionysios, for example, rearranged *Iliad* 12.433–35 and 13.392–93 and drew certain conclusions from this procedure. Nathan Greenberg (1958) tried the technique in a study of metathesis as a critical instrument for the study of poetry.

Insights avowedly derived from Russian formalism and Prague structuralism are used by Jerrold Brown (1981) in a study of Horace's use of "a complex pattern of repeated and alternating structures on various grammatical levels" in *Ode to Pyrrha* 1.5.

Among the most well known applications of structuralism by Russian Formalists to narrative material is the work of Vladimir Jakovlevic Propp (1958), who described in *Morphology of the Folktale* the narrative codes of the Russian fairy tale.[31] For his analysis, first published in Russian in 1928, Propp begins with the motifs that he isolated. These he defines in terms of their functions, which in turn follow a strict sequence. For example, the receipt of a magical agent is one function, but it always precedes transference to a designated place. Propp isolated seven character types: villain, donor, helper, princess, dispatcher, hero, and false hero. The network of functions in their relationships constitutes a large part of the structure of the tale, which is an immanent system that exists apart from socio-cultural data and historical information. Although associated with the Russian Formalists, Propp is not to be considered mainstream,[32] and credit for isolation of the basic laws of the narrative is to be assigned, as Hendricks (1970) reminded the scholarly community, to Axel Olrick,[33] who recorded his discoveries two decades before Propp published.

As indicated, Russian Formalists and the Prague School represent one phase, with varying emphases, of the new developments that took place in linguistics at the turn of the century. Under the influence of Martin

---

[31] Jakolevic Propp, *Morphology of the Folktale*, pt. 3 of *International Journal of American Linguistics*, 24, no. 4 (October, 1958) = Publication 10 of the Indiana University Research Center in Anthropology, Folklore, and Linguistics; the work is also vol. 9 of the Bibliographical and Special Series of the American Folklore Society.

[32] See Tzevatan Todorov, *L'Héritage méthodologique de formalisme*, *L'Homme*, 1 (1965) 65; cited in Hendricks, 1970:95.

[33] Axel Olrick, "Epic Laws of Folk Narrative" (= "Epische Geschichte der Volksdichtung," *Zeitschrift für Deutsche Altertum* 51 [1909] 1–12) in Dundes, 1965.

Heidegger, a philosophical-hermeneutical dimension, which was far more abstract than the phonological, entered into linguistic studies and especially in biblical circles in the second half of the twentieth century. This understanding of structuralism owes much to Martin Heidegger's basing of the hermeneutical task not on a *method* but "on a permanent structure of human existence." Also in the debit ledger are Sigmund Freud's exploration of the deep recesses of the mind and Saussure's *Cours de linguistique générale*.

Dissection of a text in terms of the old philology leads, in the minds of structuralists, to loss of meaning. To avoid such disaster, it is necessary first to respect the text as a totality. One then has the option of decoding the deep structures of human experience that have been encoded in the text.[34] All stories, for example, have one or more of the following ingredients: characters who do things or have things done to them; objects that are transferred, lost, or found; conditions that are experienced, met, achieved, or that exercise influence; feelings, such as joy, pain, sorrow, anger, with the many possibilities of effecting conditions, motivating characters, or moving objects. All such and other functions, called actants, make possible the generation of a story. They are the basic grammar or universal language, the Esperanto of the depths, which underlies the verbalizations that may take place in any particular language and assume an infinite variety of expression. In Jesus' parables, for example, two roles appear with some frequency: superior (master-king-parent) and inferior (servant-subject-child). The specific characters or activities connected with these basic roles are limited only by the desires of the narrator, but the basic "structure," which is characteristic of narrative in numerous cultures, makes the stories possible. In "Parable and Example Story: A Literary-Structuralist Approach," Dan Via (1974) presented the basic outline of his work on parables from a structuralist perspective, and acknowledged his debt to Erhardt Güttgemann's earlier studies.[35] At the same time he enters into dialogue with John Crossan, "Parable and Example in the Teaching of Jesus" (1974), and questions Crossan's relatively low estimate of Jesus' creativity in parabolic details (Via, 1974:126).

In several essays published in *Semeia*, which began to be published in 1974 as part of SBL's program of research and publication,[36] Güttgemanns (1976) warns biblical scholars, with words directed especially to those who are responsible for preparing ministers of the Gospel, that the future will

---

[34] The principle finds inchoate expression in an anonymous reviewer's comment in *North American Review* 102 (1866) 553: "In all real poetry the form is not a garment, but a body. Our very passion has become metaphysical and speculates upon itself. Their [Greek tragedians'] simple and downright way of thinking loses all its savor when we assume it to ourselves by an effort of thought." On the importance of grasping the larger totality, see Louw, 1982.

[35] For the basic articles, see Güttgemanns, 1976. For an earlier summary of the subject, see the articles in *Interpretation* 28 (April, 1974).

[36] Almost a century earlier, *AJA* and *CJ* made a related type of move toward specialized publication.

display a glaring contrast between the preparation of those who have been disciplined in old philological methodology and those who have been exposed to new linguistic theory. It is quite probable that specific phases or emphases in structuralist interpretation, including the six-actant model of Algirdas Julien Greimas[37] will pass, but the more thoughtful among those who were limited to the learning of the old philology will certainly not think kindly of mentors who short-changed them in their education. On the other hand, the old philology will have its renaissance, and it may well be along the lines of the type of literary criticism that is practiced by Charles Segal and others, who have made use of insights developed by A. G. Gadamer, who, according to Stephen Kresic (1981:10), "affirms that understanding is not a repetition, duplication or reproduction of a past intention (the *mens auctoris*) but rather a genuinely productive procedure that involves the interpreter's own hermeneutical situation in communication with the author. For Gadamer, understanding is not reconstruction of the past but mediation, transmission, and translation of past meaning into the present situation, the so-called 'fusion of horizons.' "[38]

The New Hermeneuticians emphasize the importance of dialoging with the text, and encourage especially classicists to help "establish a fusion of horizons between contemporary literary hermeneutics and traditional philological hermeneutics." To do this, says Kresic, they "ought to be conscious of the contemporary theoretical principles of understanding and interpretation of literary texts . . ." (10). In what amounts to a revision of Poe's theory, Kresic states that the function of literature can be reduced basically to one: "Through its significantly patterned language, in an organic and dramatic way, literature tells us the truth about ourselves and about the world in which we live" (1).

The proper sphere of philology, Segal writes in the same volume, is not interpretation, which develops out of the interpreter's conditioned sense of values and contextual responsibility, but provision of the resources basic for interpretation. Such resources include linguistic, historical, and cultural factors. "Hermeneutics, in a sense, stands," affirms Segal, "on the other side of interpretation: its concern is the problems, assumptions, mental processes through which one enters into relation with the work of literature." Hermeneutical conception of a work "exists at the point of crossing between self and other, the world implied in the poem and the world of the reader" (1981:287). From such perspective hermeneutics is contemporary domestication of the text, and Segal's view is largely in line with that of structuralists. If the world of the text participates in the basic structure of the human mind, it not only interprets the reader and the reader's context, but the reader is

[37] A. J. Greimas, *Sémantique structurale recherche de méthode* (Paris: Larousse, 1966) 172–91.
[38] Kresic's reference is to Gadamer's *Wahrheit und Methoden*, 2d ed. (Tübingen: Mohr [Siebeck], 1965).

able to bring illuminating power to the text.

Charles Segal's (1967) exploration of the poetic terrain of Pindar *Nemean* 7 is a model commentary on his own dictum and demonstrates that the constitutive elements of poetic *meaning* are essentially contextual, imagistic, and associative. An overly-formalistic approach can destroy in-depth access to this meaning of the poem. Poetry is basically connotative, but this connotative meaning is not the "denotative meaning of prose" (435). Alongside the formal unity of the ode, there is a "pervasive symbolic unity which consists in the inter-relation of certain themes and images throughout the poem." These images "recur throughout the ode, delineate certain patterns, follow certain rhythms, suggest certain analogies."[39] Taken together, says Segal, they "form the meaning of the ode" (434). He then goes on to point out that the meaning does not depend on a topic sentence or central thought, but on "the total movement and the interweaving of narrative, imagery, factual utterance, and gnomic generalization into a single whole. Such meaning, as always in poetry, is sensuous and concrete rather than abstract. It inheres in the sounds of words, the beat of the verse, the sensuous texture of imagery, the involving vividness of narrative detail, rather than in moral generalization" (434). Pindar's poetry is indeed "concrete," but through his particular symbolism Pindar arrives at that which is universal. Such an approach to the problem of meaning offers access to the "poetic" aspects in some prose writers, such as Herodotos, Plato, Livy, Tacitus, and Apuleius (435).

Once the reader of the Seventh *Nemean* comes to it in the proper hermeneutical frame of mind, this ode, which has baffled numerous interpreters, can be entered through any of three portals. First, the imagery of *ponos,* labor. We see Pindar, the poet, who labors as an athlete to be worthy of the Muse; Sogenes, victorious toiler in the Nemean competition; Odysseus, model of suffering; Ajax, "most valiant, save Achilles, in the strife"; Neoptolemos, sacker of Troy and legendary president of the Games; and Herakles (who is mentioned with effective economy). A second point of entry is the interplay of the poem's imagery of birth, light, and water. Birth is an escape from darkness, and life is only an interval. But poetry, the rivulet of song from the rills of the Muses, flows with streams of glory in praise of a victor, whose deeds will not be wrapt in darkness: through Pindar's poetry Sogenes finds immortality. A third port of entry is the pendulum-like oscillation between contrasting worlds.[40]

Segal does indeed engage in a dialogue with the text. A vast amount of

---

[39] Cf. David H. Porter, who finds that Aischylos and Sophokles have the movement of smaller components imitating a larger over-all rhythm in a play: "Structural Parallelism in Greek Tragedy: A Preliminary Study," *TAPA* 102 (1971) 465–96. One of Porter's observations especially deserves further consideration: ". . . an audience does not need to be consciously aware of the parallelism of movement within a play in order to respond to it" (495).

[40] Compare Zeitlin, 1965; Mack, 1978.

philological quarrying has entered into this study, which is in its own right a "poetic" production, for it recreates the majesty and the communicative power of the ancient song in such a way that one cannot avoid its contemporaneity. Much of this accomplishment is due to the fact that Segal does not here engage in philological moralizing, but permits depth to speak to depth. Like Pindar, he has accounted for the depth traditions of humanity, for the contingencies of history, including biographical details, but above all for beauty *and* truth. Philology and the New Criticism here enjoy a symbiosis that is baptized by the new developments in linguistics and philosophical hermeneutics.[41]

In the absence of generally accepted literary theory, itself apparently an apocalyptic vision, Segal's approach offers an exemplar—not a paradigm—that bridges the atomistic interests of the old philology and the systemic interest of newer approaches to text,[42] without exposing one to Adolf Harnack's indictment of Origen for engaging in hermeneutical alchemy.

Philology has come a long path since Gayley's time. And Literary Philology is assured of a long life. For biblical students it points a way out of the cul de sac of source criticism and antiquarian inquiry to exposition that touches the common humanity represented in the depth structure of the biblical texts.

Summary

In retrospect, it may be affirmed that positivistic philology interposed itself between the text and its pre-text period, with emphasis on source criticism and historical considerations, whereas newer critical approaches placed themselves this side of the text. At the same time, these newer approaches assumed a pre-contemporary stance so as to maintain critical purity of motive, with minimum static from the critic's contemporary environment.

This clinically sanitary approach was, in respect to motivation, closely related to the old philology, which had sought objectivity and relief from dogmatic presuppositions. Yet this sanitary approach in effect alienated the text, for the ghost of Poe came back to haunt. Poe's reduction of poetic art to the production of beauty, as opposed to Keat's beauty-truth creed, must constitute the ultimate termination of supremacy for such cathartic literary

---

[41] For a comparable study and penetrating awareness of mythopoeic values, see Segal, 1977.

[42] For similar appreciation of the older philology at the service of the newer criticism see, for example, Benario (1960), who demonstrates the importance of historical background for apprehension of poetic impact in the Horatian celebration of what Pliny termed *immensa Romanae pacis maiestas*. In a study of autobiographical features in the fourth book of Ovid's *Tristia*, B. R. Fredericks (1976) shows how exploration of historical data aids in appreciation of an aesthetically unified entity. Marilyn Skinner (1982) uses facts established by prosopography to "arrive at a much fuller understanding of the poetic meaning of the Lesbia affair."

theory. For in the end one encounters a situation akin to what was deplored under the tyranny of philological positivism—a text that is purely of anti-quarian interest, a dissected cadaver. Only knowledge of the anatomy has increased. A criticism that is limited to such technical features as mathematically oriented symmetry, phonemic and grammatical patterns, and textured imagery will in the end monopolize the conversation and engulf the text in silence.

Poe had the poet's intuitive appreciation of the basic problem, and he brought to inchoate expression the critic's need to function on the frontiers of what is intrinsically human above and beyond the momentary verbal exposition of what constitutes the poetic. Linguistic science, socio-political philosophy, Freudian psychology, anthropology, and philosophical hermeneutics offered literary critical intuition the opportunity to move in the direction of more pervasive theoretical statement. Saussure, Lévi-Strauss, Chomsky, Greimas, Propp, and others have helped propel the study of texts to a point where the underlying universal aspects of a given text can be discerned with a minimum of interference from the reader-auditor's limited cultural experience. Implicit in such approaches is the prospect of genuine dialog.

At the same time, Poe's concern that the literary creator retain identity needs to be taken seriously. Poe could not resolve the problem, for he had excluded precisely the point at which the reader-auditor functions, not as an inventory clerk but as a critic, for whom assumptions respecting moral, aesthetic, psychological, and social values do exist. The classics themselves, both biblical and Greco-Roman, derive in part from the exercise of related values and assumptions. Aischylos, Sophokles, and Euripides are not viewed as great dramatists simply because they wrote in Greek. There is a vast difference between their works and the Zenon Papyri. As numerous literary documents from antiquity attest, their works formed a recognized canon before the Alexandrians performed acts of criticism on them. Yet despite the fact that there throbs beneath the lines of the three Greek tragedians and the tragedies of Seneca the common beat of humanity's heart, or granted that both Greeks and Romans share the basic structure of the mind, there are, in the judgment of generations of scholars and non-academicians, qualitative differences, and this commonality of judgment, which reaches back beyond the transmission of sanctioned appraisal, lays claim to consideration as a part of the depth-structure that needs to be decoded.

Anything that survives from antiquity will at some time hold value for someone. Economic, intellectual, and social data are of varying interest to students of the past, but many of the data happen to be contained in documents whose literary quality is adjudged to be inferior relative to other documents. In the same breath it must be asserted that it remains for literary theory to establish the criteria whereby such value judgments can reach for scientific validation. But before literary investigation can lay claim to theory, it is obliged to work through the basic epistemological issue.[43] It may well be that there is no subject matter.

Obligation for the struggle rests especially heavy on biblical students, some of whom are inclined to borrow developments from this or that sector of inquiry, despite cautions expressed by their mentors. To satisfy pragmatic interests, or out of sheer lassitude, they are tempted at times to transmute a species into a genus, and to confuse multiplication of jargon with establishment of a "discipline," and frequently without awareness of the distinction between discipline-oriented and mission-oriented fields.[44] Out of paint-by-number or hunt-and-peck hermeneutics there emerges such an unscientific genre of inquiry as "Structural Exegesis" and related progeny. Students are led to think that the use of what is properly one approach to some aspects of an interpretive problem is itself the implementation of exegetical-hermeneutical theory.

Gildersleeve once admonished interpreters that they ought to "know what the letter means before they let themselves be carried away by the spirit" (1930:114). On the other hand, according to T. S. Eliot, humanity "cannot stand too much reality." Engagement in a literary philology that takes seriously the concerns of positivistic philology and the social dimension implicit in structuralism appears to offer a way out of a dilemma that has plagued the history of interpretation for two millennia and points to a promising route for exegetical-hermeneutical inquiry.

Such an approach envisages a hierarchy of specialization, but does not lose sight of the creative factors that give to a generally recognized "great" text its distinctive quality. This means recognition of the social, political, and cultural factors that provided the original hermeneutical context for appreciating the "value" of the work with all its words. In brief, an apprehension of the world that was humanized by beings such as we are. In a sense no one can ever enter the world of the past, but acquaintance with some of its furniture and awareness of the commonality of human experience, hopes, and aspirations will improve the understanding. Yet one's call on the words dare not be casual. As Wheeler put it, one must "summer" and "winter" with them. And sympathy best turns the key that unlocks language.

There is an ultimate fitness to the conjunction of classical study with biblical study, and the fear that humanism will triumph over the claims of God is a tawdry intrusion that deserves exorcism. At the beginning of SBL's century, Benjamin Bacon (1887) asked, "Is Theology Scientific?" In 1946 Claude Lévi-Strauss, no mean student of language, served on a panel at a

---

[43] Malina (1978) echoes a century of concern about the relation of scientific inquiry and allegiance to human values.
[44] Cf. Garvin, 1974:2905.

meeting of educators in Colorado, and when his turn came to critique, he gave the substance of an answer:[45]

> I heard somebody telling somebody that the purpose of education was to improve the lot of mankind, and I was reminded of another definition which was given several centuries ago by the most materialistic and down-to-earth philosopher, Francis Bacon. He said that education was to glorify God *and* to improve the lot of mankind. If, while improving the lot of mankind, we forget to glorify God, then we are lost and our children are lost.

[45] Claude Lévi Strauss, "France's View," *Humanistic Values for a Free Society: Proceedings of the Third Regional Conference on the Humanities, Estes Park, Colorado, June 1946* (Denver: University of Denver, 1947) 166–67.

ABBREVIATIONS

AJP	*American Journal of Philology*
AJT	*American Journal of Theology*
ANRW	*Aufstieg und Niedergang der römischen Welt: Geschichte und Kultur Roms im Spiegel der neueren Forschung,* ed. by Hildegard Temporini and Wolfgang Haase (Berlin: De Gruyter, 1972 –).
APA	American Philological Association
ASCSA	American School of Classical Studies at Athens
ASOR	American Schools of Oriental Research
ASP	American Society of Papyrology
ASP	*American Studies in Papyrology*
BAG	Bauer-Arndt-Gingrich (see Bibliography)
BAGD	Bauer-Arndt-Gingrich-Danker (see Bibliography)
BASP	*Bulletin of the American Society of Papyrologists*
BZW	Beihefte zur ZAW
BZNW	Beihefte zur ZNW
CBQ	*Catholic Biblical Ouarterly*
DAB	*Dictionary of American Biography*
DNB	*Dictionary of National Biography*
CHNT	*Corpus Hellenisticum Novi Testamenti*
CIL	*Corpus Inscriptionum Latinorum*
CJ	*Classical Journal*
CP	*Classical Philology*
CR	Classical Review
CW	Classical World
CSCP	Cornell Studies in Classical Philology
CPJ	Corpus Papyrorum Judaicarum
fl.	floruit
HSCP	Harvard Studies in Classical Philology
HTR	Harvard Theological Review

IDB	G. A. Buttrick (ed.), *Interpreter's Dictionary of the Bible* (Nashville: Abingdon, 1962).
IDBSup	Supplementary volume to *IDB* (1976).
JAOS	*Journal of the American Oriental Society*
JBL	*Journal of Biblical Literature*
JJP	*Journal of Juristic Papyrology*
JNES	*Journal of Near Eastern Studies*
JR	*Journal of Religion*
JRS	*Journal of Roman Studies*
LSJM	Liddell-Scott-Jones-McKenzie, *Greek-English Lexicon,* 2 vols. (Oxford: Oxford University, 1925–1940). (A supplement, edited by E. A. Barber with the assistance of P. Maas, M. Scheller, and M. L. West, was published in 1968.)
MTBS	F.W. Danker, *Multipurpose Tools for Bible Study,* 3d ed. (St. Louis: Concordia, 1970).
n.	note
n.s.	new series
No.	Number
OCT	Oxford Classical Texts
PAPA	*Proceedings of the American Philological Association.*
PASCSA	*Papers of the American School of Classical Studies at Athens*
pt.	part
RB	*Revue Biblique*
SBLMS	Society of Biblical Literature Monograph Series
SBLDS	SBL Dissertation Series
SBLSCS	SBL Septuagint and Cognate Studies
TAPA	*Transactions of the American Philological Association*
TLG	*Thesaurus Linguae Graecae.* See Berkowitz, 1977.
TLL	*Thesaurus Linguae Latinae* (Leipzig: Teubner, 1900 –).
YCS	*Yale Classical Studies*
ZAW	*Zeitschrift für die altestamentliche Wissenschaft*
ZNW	*Zeitschrift für die neutestamentliche Wissenschaft*

BIBLIOGRAPHY

Abbott, Frank Frost
1908   Review of *Thesaurus linguae Latinae-epigraphicae: A Dictionary of the Latin Inscriptions,* 1, fascicles 5–10 (Adit-Alig), by George N. Olcott. *CJ* 3:292–93.

Abbott, Frank Frost, and Allan Chester Johnson
1926   *Municipal Administration in the Roman Empire.* Princeton: Princeton University.

Abbott, Thomas Kingsmill
1890   "Has *POIEIN* in the New Testament a Sacrificial Meaning?" *JBL* 9:137–52.

Abbot, Ezra, ed.
1870   *A Critical Greek and English Concordance of the New Testament,* by Charles Frederick Hudson and Horace L. Hastings. Boston: Scriptural Tract Repository.

Abel, D. Herbert
1943   "Genealogies of Ethical Concepts from Hesiod to Bacchylides." *TAPA* 74:92–101.

Achtemeier, Paul John
1972   "The Origin and Function of the Pre-Marcan Miracle Catenae." *JBL* 91:198–221.

1974   Review of *The Secret Gospel* and *Clement of Alexandria and a Secret Gospel of Mark,* both by Morton Smith (1973a,b). *JBL* 93:625–28.

1975   "The Lucan Perspective on the Miracles of Jesus: A Preliminary Sketch." *JBL* 94:547–62.

Agard, Walter Raymond
[1953] 1967 "Classical Scholarship." In *American Scholarship,* 1967:146–67.

Albright, William Foxwell
1939   Review of *Das Ethos des Alten Testaments* (BZAW 67), by Johannes Hempel. *JBL* 58: 392–94.

1946   Review of *A Guide to Understanding of the Bible*, by Harry E. Fosdick. *JBL* 65:205–8.

1949   Review of *History of the Persian Empire (Achaemenid Period)*, by A. T. Olmstead. *JBL* 68:371–77.

1952   Review of *A Critical and Exegetical Commentary on the Books of Kings*, by James A. Montgomery. *JBL* 71:245–53.

Albright, W. F., and Christopher S. Mann
1971   *Matthew: Introduction, Translation and Notes*. Anchor Bible. Garden City, N.Y.: Doubleday.

Allen, Frederic DeForest
1888   "On Greek Versification in Inscriptions." *PASCSA* 4:35–204. Boston: Damrell and Upham.

Allen, James Turney, and Gabriel Italie
1954   *A Concordance to Euripides*. Berkeley: University of California Press.

Allen, Joseph Henry, and James Bradstreet Greenough
1872   *A Latin Grammar for Schools and Colleges, Founded on Comparative Grammar*. Boston: Ginn.

Allen, Walter
1940   "The Epyllion: A Chapter in the History of Literary Criticism." *TAPA* 71:1–26.

1951   "The Lucii Afranii of Cic. *Att.* 1.16.13." *TAPA* 82:127–35.

1959   "Stage Money (*fabam mimum.* Cic. *Att.* 1.16.13)." *TAPA* 90:1–8.

Alterton, Margaret
1925   *Origins of Poe's Critical Theory*. University of Iowa Humanistic Studies 2, no. 3. Iowa City: University of Iowa.

Amadon, Grace
1942   "Ancient Jewish Calendation." *JBL* 61:227–80.

Ament, Ernest J.
1970   "The *Anti-Lucretius* of Cardinal Polignac." *TAPA* 101:29–49.

American Scholarship
1953   *American Scholarship in the Twentieth Century*, ed. by Merle Curti. New York: Russell and Russell.

Ancient Roman Statutes
1961   *Ancient Roman Statutes: A Translation with Introduction, Commentary, Glossary, and Index*, by Allan Chester Johnson, Paul Robinson Coleman-Norton, and Frank Card Bourne. In *The Corpus of Roman Law (Corpus Juris Romani)*, 2. Austin, Texas: University of Texas.

Anderson, Graham
1982   *Eros Sophistes: Ancient Novelists at Play.* Chico: Scholars
              Press.

Angus, Samuel
1909   "Modern Methods in New Testament Philology." *HTR*
              2:446–64.

Anonymous
1856   Review of *The Works of the Late Edgar Allan Poe with a
              Memoir by Rufus Wilmot Griswold, and Notices of his Life
              and Genius, by N. P. Willis and J. R. Lowell,* 4 vols. *North
              American Review* 83:427–55.

1871   Review of *An Elementary Greek Grammar,* by William
              Watson Goodwin. *North American Review* 112:427.

Antioch On-the-Orontes
1941   *Antioch On-the-Orontes.* III. *The Excavations 1937–1939,* ed.
              Richard Stillwell. "Greek and Latin Inscriptions," pp. 83–115.
              Princeton: Princeton University.

Apfel, Henrietta Veit
1938   "Homeric Criticism in the Fourth Century B.C." *TAPA*
              69:245–58.

Armayor, O. Kimball
1978   "Herodotus' Catalogues of the Persian Empire in the Light of
              the Monuments and the Greek Literary Tradition." *TAPA*
              108:1–9.

Attridge, Harold William
1976   *The Interpretation of Biblical History in the "Antiquitates
              Judaicae" of Flavius Josephus.* Missoula: Scholars Press.

1979   " 'Heard Because of His Reverence' (Heb 5:7)." *JBL* 98:90–93.

Aune, David Edward
1983   *Prophecy in Early Christianity and the Ancient Mediterranean
              World.* Grand Rapids: Eerdmans.

Austin, John Norman
1967   "Idyll 16: Theocritus and Simonides." *TAPA* 98:1–21.

Bacon, Benjamin Wisner
1887   "Is Theology Scientific?" *New Englander and Yale Review*
              46:57–66.

1903   "Ultimate Problems of Biblical Science." *JBL* 22:1–14.

1923   "Notes on the Gospel of Mark." *JBL* 42:137–49.

Badian, Ernst
1960   "The Death of Parmenio." *TAPA* 91:324–338.

1972   *Publicans and Sinners: Private Enterprise in the Service of the Roman Republic.* Ithaca, N.Y.: Cornell University.

Bagnall, Roger S., ed.
1980   *Research Tools for the Classics.* Chico: Scholars Press.

Baird, Joseph Arthur
1969a   *A Critical Concordance to the Synoptic Gospels.* Wooster: Biblical Research Associates.
1969b   *Audience Criticism and the Historical Jesus.* Philadelphia: Westminster.

Ball, Allan Perley
1909   "The Theological Utility of the Caesar Cult." *CJ* 5:304–9.
Barr, David Lawrence
1979   Review of *Literary Criticism for New Testament Critics,* by Norman R. Petersen. *JBL* 98:600–1.

Barry, Phillips
1904   "On Luke XV. 25, *Symphonia:* Bagpipe." *JBL* 23:180–90.
1908   "Daniel 3:5, *Symponyah.*" *JBL*:99–127.
1913   "The Apocalypse of Ezra." *JBL* 32:261–72.

Bartchy, S. Scott
1973   *"Mallon Chresai": First-Century Slavery and the Interpretation of 1 Corinthians 7:21.* SBLDS, 11. Missoula: Scholars Press.

Barton, George Aaron
1914   "The Hermeneutic Canon 'Interpret Historically' in the Light of Modern Research." *JBL* 33:56–77.
1924   Some Influences of Apollos in the New Testament. *JBL* 43:207–23.

Bassett, Samuel Eliot
1928   "1 Cor. 13, 12. *blepomen gar arti di' esoptrou en ainigmati.*" *JBL* 47:232–36. (Abstract in *PAPA* 58 (1927) xvi.)

Bauer-Arndt-Gingrich (BAG)
1957   *A Greek-English Lexicon of the New Testament and Other Early Christian Literature: A translation and adaptation of the fourth revised and augmented edition of Walter Bauer's Griechisch-Deutsches Wörterbuch zu den Schriften des Neuen Testaments und der übrigen urchristlichen Literatur,* by William F. Arndt and F. Wilbur Gingrich. Chicago: University of Chicago.

Bauer-Arndt-Gingrich-Danker (BAGD)
1979   *A Greek-English Lexicon . . . urchristlichen Literatur,* by
        William F. Arndt and F. Wilbur Gingrich. Second Edition
        Revised and Augmented by F. Wilbur Gingrich and
        Frederick W. Danker from Walter Bauer's Fifth Edition
        (1958). Chicago: University of Chicago.

Beardslee, Raymond A.
1920   "Hebrew Poetry: A Criticism." *JBL* 39:118–30.

Beginnings
1920–33   *The Beginnings of Christianity.* Pt. 1. *The Acts of the Apostles,*
           ed. by Frederick Foakes Jackson and Kirsopp Lake. 5 vols.
           London: Macmillan.

Belkin, Samuel
1940   *Philo and the Oral Law: The Philonic Interpretation of Biblical
        Law in Relation to the Palestinian Halakah.* Cambridge:
        Harvard University.

Belmont, David Eugene
1980   "The Vergilius of Horace, *Ode* 4. 12." *TAPA* 110:1–20.

Benario, Herbert William
1967   "The Tenth Book of the Aeneid." *TAPA* 98:23–36.

Benario, Janice Martin
1960   "Book 4 of Horace's *Odes:* Augustan Propaganda." *TAPA*
        91:339–52.

Benko, Stephen
1980   "Pagan Criticism of Christianity during the First Two Cen-
        turies A.D." In *ANRW* 23:2:1055–1118.

Benko, Stephen, and John J. O'Rourke, eds.
1971   *The Catacombs and the Colosseum: The Roman Empire as the
        Setting of Primitive Christianity.* Valley Forge: Judson.

Benner, Allen Rogers, and Herbert Weir Smyth
1906   *Beginner's Greek Book.* New York: American Book Co.

Bennett, Charles Edwin
1910–14   *Syntax of Early Latin.* Part 1, on the verb (1910): part 2, on the
           cases (1914). Boston: Allyn and Bacon.

Bennett, Charles Wesley
1888   *Christian Archaeology.* New York: Phillips and Hunt. (2d ed.
        rev. by Amos Williams Patten; New York: Eaton and Mains,
        1898).

Berkowitz, Luci
  1977   *Thesaurus Linguae Graecae Canon of Greek Authors and Works from Homer to A.D. 200.* Costa Mesa, California: TLG Publications.

Berry, George Ricker
  1897   *A New Greek-English Lexicon to the New Testament, Supplemented by a Chapter Elucidating the Synonyms of the New Testament with a Complete Index to the Synonyms.* Chicago: Wilcox and Follett.

Bertman, Stephen
  1966   "The *Telemachy* and Structural Symmetry." *TAPA* 97:15–27.

Betz, Hans Dieter
  1969   "On the Problem of the Religio-Historical Understanding of Apocalypticism." *Journal of Theology and the Church* 6:134–56.
  1985   *Essays on the Sermon on the Mount.* Philadelphia: Fortress.

Betz, Otto
  1972   "The Concept of the So-called 'Divine Man' in Mark's Christology." In *Studies in New Testament and Early Christian Literature: Essays in Honor of Allen P. Wikgren,* ed. by David E. Aune, pp. 229–240. Leiden: Brill.

Bewer, Julias A.
  1926   "The Hellenistic Mystery Religion and the Old Testament." *JBL* 45:1–13.

Bible in Modern Scholarship, The
  1965   *The Bible in Modern Scholarship: Papers read at the 100th meeting of the Society of Biblical Literature, December 28–30, 1964,* ed. by J. Philip Hyatt. Nashville: Abingdon.

Bissell, F. C.
  1886   "Strack's Hebrew Grammar." *JBL* 6:110–12.

Blackman, David John
  1969   "Plautus and Greek Topography." *TAPA* 100:11–22.

Blass-Debrunner-Funk (BDF)
  1961   *A Greek Grammar of the New Testament,* by Friedrich Blass and rev. by Adolf Debrunner. A translation and revision of the ninth-tenth German edition by Robert Funk, incorporating Debrunner's supplementary notes. Chicago: University of Chicago.

Bloomfield, Maurice
  1888   "The Origin of the Recessive Accent in Greek." *AJP* 9:1–41.

1919   "Fifty Years of Comparative Philology in America." *TAPA* 50:62–83.

Boak, Arthur Edward Romilly, and Campbell Bonner
1931   "The Papyrological Work at the University of Michigan." *Chronique d'Égypte* 6, no. 12 (July):392–395.

Boers, Hendrikus Wouterus
1970   "Jesus and the Christian Faith: New Testament Christology Since Bousset's *Kyrios Christos*." *JBL* 89:450–56.

Bonner, Campbell
1934   *A Papyrus Codex of the Shepherd of Hermas (Similitudes 2–9, with a Fragment of the Mandates)*. Nos. 129–130. University of Michigan Studies, Humanistic Series, 22. Ann Arbor: University of Michigan.

1940   *The Homily on the Passion, by Melito Bishop of Sardis, with Some Fragments of the Apocryphal Ezekiel*. Studies and Documents, 12. Philadelphia: University of Pennsylvania.

1943   "The Techniques of Exorcism." *HTR* 36:41–47.

Bonner, C., and Herbert Chayyim Youtie
1937   *The Last Chapters of Enoch in Greek* (97,6–104, 106–107). *Studies and Documents*, 8. London: Christophers.

Bonner, Robert Johnson
1934   "Paul Shorey." *CJ* 29:641–43.

Bowen, Clayton R.
1930   "The Fourth Gospel as Dramatic Material." *JBL* 49:292–305.

Bowman, Alan K.
1971   *The Town Councils of Roman Egypt. ASP*, 11. Toronto:Hakkert.

Bowman, John Wick
1962   "Revelation, Book of." In *IDB* 4:58–71.

Bradeen, Donald William, and Malcolm Francis McGregor, eds.
1974   *"PHOROS": Tribute to Benjamin D. Meritt*. Locust Valley, NY: J. J. Augustin.

Bradley, Charles Frederick, and Charles Horswell
1889   *New Testament Word Lists, Greek-English, Containing all Words Occurring Ten Times or More*. Kenilworth, IL: C. Horswell.

Bradley, David G.
1953   "The *TOPOS* as a Form in the Pauline Paraenesis." *JBL* 72:238–46.

Brewster, Ethel H.
1927   "A Weaver of Oxyrhynchus: Sketch of a Humble Life in Roman Egypt." *TAPA* 58:132–54.

Brotherton, Blanche
1924   "The Plot of the *Miles Gloriosus.*" *TAPA* 55:128–36.

Broughton, Thomas Robert Shannon
1934   "Roman Landholding in Asia Minor." *TAPA* 65:207–39.

Brown, Calvin S.
1966   "Odysseus and Polyphemus." *Comparative Literature* 18:193–202.

Brown, Francis
1882   "The New Testament Witness to the Authorship of Old Testament Books." *JBL* 2:95–121.

Brown, Jerrold C.
1981   "The Verbal Art of Horace's Ode to Pyrrha." *TAPA* 111:17–22.

Brown, John Pairman
1968   "Cosmological Myth and the Tuna of Gibralter." *TAPA* 99:37–62.

Brown, Truesdell Sparhawk
1962   "The Greek Sense of Time in History as Suggested by Their Accounts of Egypt." *Historia* 11:257–270.

Brownell, William Crary
[1909] 1940 "Poe." *In* Foerster, 1940:235–92.

Bruère, Richard Treat
1941   Review of *A Concordance of Lucan,* by R. Deferarri, M. Fanning, and A. Sullivan. *CP* 36:304–6.

Buck, Carl Darling
[1904] 1928 *A Grammar of Oscan and Umbrian.* Boston: Ginn.

1910   *Introduction to the Study of the Greek Dialects: Grammar, Selected Inscriptions, Glossary.* Boston: Ginn. (Rev. ed. 1928.)

1913   "The Interstate Use of the Greek Dialects." *CP* 8:133–59.

1933   *Comparative Grammar of Greek and Latin.* Chicago: University of Chicago.

1955   *The Greek Dialects: Grammar, Selected Inscriptions, Glossary.* Chicago: The University of Chicago.

Buck, Carl Darling, and Walter Petersen
1944   *A Reverse Index of the Greek Nouns and Adjectives Arranged by Terminations with Brief Historical Introductions.* Chicago: University of Chicago.

Budesheim, Thomas L.
1976   "Paul's *Abschiedsrede* in the Acts of the Apostles." *HTR*
            69:9–30.

Bullock, Charles J.
1929   "Dionysius of Syracuse—Financier." *CJ* 25:260–76.

Bundy, Elroy Lorraine
1962   *Studia Pindarica*. Berkeley: University of California.

Burch, Ernest Ward
1931   "Tragic Action in the Second Gospel: A Study in the Narrative
            of Mark." *Journal of Religion* 11:346–58.

Burgess, Theodore Chalon, and Robert Johnson Bonner
1907   *Elementary Greek: An Introduction to the Study of Attic
            Greek*. Chicago: Scott, Foresman.

Burnett, Anne Pippin
1985   *The Art of Bacchylides*. Cambridge: Harvard University.

Burriss, Eli Edward
1930   "The Objects of a Roman's Prayers." *CW* 23:105–108.

Burton, Dolores M.
1981a   "Computers and the Humanities: Automated Concordances
            and Word Indexes, The Fifties." *Computers and the
            Humanities* 15:1–14.

1981b   "Automated Concordances and Word Indexes: The Early
            Sixties and the Early Centers." *Computers and the Humanities*
            15:83–100.

1981c   "Automated Concordances and Word Indexes: The Process,
            the Programs, and the Products." *Computers and the
            Humanities* 15:139–54.

Burton, Ernest DeWitt
[1888] 1898 *Syntax of the Moods and Tenses in New Testament Greek*. 3d
            ed. Chicago: The University of Chicago.

1918   *Spirit, soul, and flesh; the usage of "pneuma," "psyche," and
            "sarx" in Greek writings and translated works from the earliest
            period to 225 A.D.; and of their equivalents . . . in the Hebrew
            Old Testament*. Reprinted with additions and revision from
            AJT 1913–1916. Chicago: University of Chicago.

Burton, Harry Edwin
1911   *A Latin Grammar*. New York: Silver, Burdett and Company.

Buttmann, Alexander, and Joseph Henry Thayer
1873   *A Grammar of New Testament Greek*, by Alexander
            Buttmann, ed. by J. H. Thayer. Andover: Draper.

Cadbury, Henry Joel
 1918   "The Basis of Early Christian Antimilitarism." *JBL* 37:66–94.

 1923   "Between Jesus and the Gospels." *HTR* 17:303–6.

 1926   "Lexical Notes on Luke-Acts." II. "Recent Arguments for Medical Language." *JBL* 45:190–209.

 1930   "*Theatrizo* No Longer a NT Hapax Legomenon." *ZNW* 29:60–63.

 1931   "Erastus of Corinth." *JBL* 50:42–58.

 1934   "The Macellum of Corinth." *JBL* 53:134–41.

 1937a   "Motives of Biblical Scholarship." *JBL* 56:1–16.

 1937b   *The Peril of Modernizing Jesus.* New York: Macmillan.

 1938   "The Present State of New Testament Studies." In *Haverford Symposium,* 79–110.

 1939   Review of *Gerasa, City of the Decapolis,* by Carl H. Kraeling. *JBL* 58:299–302.

 1960   "New Testament Scholarship: Fifty Years in Retrospect." *The Journal of Bible and Religion* 28:194–198.

 1964   "Gospel Study and Our Image of Early Christianity." *JBL* 83:139–45.

Calhoun, George Miller
 1934   "A Problem of Authenticity (Demosthenes 29)." *TAPA* 65:80–102.

 1937   "Homer's Gods: Prolegomena." *TAPA* 68:11–25.

Callaway, Joseph Sevier
 1948   "Paul's Letter to the Galatians and Plato's *Lysis.*" *JBL* 67 (1948) 353–55.

Cameron, Howard Donald
 1970   "The Power of Words in the *Seven Against Thebes.*" *TAPA* 101:95–118.

Campbell, John Young
 1932   "*KOINŌNIA* and its Cognates in the New Testament." *JBL* 51:352–80.

Capart, Jean, ed.
 1936   *Travels in Egypt (December 1880 to May 1891): Letters of Charles Edwin Wilbour.* Brooklyn: Brooklyn Museum, 1936.

Carlston, Charles E.
 1980   "Proverbs, Maxims, and the Historical Jesus." *JBL* 99:87–105.

Case, Shirley Jackson
1914   *The Evolution of Early Christianity: A Genetic Study of First-Century Christianity in Relation to its Religious Environment.* Chicago: University of Chicago.

1923   *The Social Origins of Christianity.* Chicago: University of Chicago.

1927   "The Life of Jesus." In *Religious Thought in the Last Quarter Century,* ed. Gerald Birney Smith, pp. 26–41. Chicago: University of Chicago.

1929   *Experience with the Supernatural in Early Christian Times.* New York: Century.

Casey, Robert P.
1945   "Professor Goodenough and the Fourth Gospel." *JBL* 64:535–42.

Casson, Lionel
1950   "The Isis and Her Voyage." *TAPA* 81:43–56.

1951   "Speed Under Sail of Ancient Ships." *TAPA* 82:136–48.

1966   "Galley Slaves." *TAPA* 97:35–44.

1976   "The Athenian Upper Class and New Comedy." *TAPA* 106:29–59.

Catacombs and the Colosseum
1971   *The Catacombs and the Colosseum: The Roman Empire as the Setting of Primitive Christianity,* ed. Stephen Benko and John J. O'Rourke. Valley Forge: Judson.

Chambers, Talbot Wilson
1886   "The Phrase 'Children of Wrath.'" *JBL* 6:105–8.

Charlesworth, James Hamilton
1983   *The Old Testament Pseudepigrapha. 1. Apocalyptic Literature and Testaments.* Garden City, New York: Doubleday.

Chase, Alston Hurd
1941   *A New Introduction to Greek.* Ann Arbor: Edwards Brothers. (Rev. ed., 1944; 3d rev. ed., 1961.)

Chavel, Charles B.
1941   "The Releasing of a Prisoner on the Eve of Passover in Ancient Jerusalem." *JBL* 60:273–78.

Cheadle, John Raymond
1939   *Basic Greek Vocabulary.* New York: Macmillan.

Cheever, George Barrell
    1860   *The Guilt of Slavery and the Crime of Slaveholding Demonstrated from the Hebrew and Greek Scriptures.* New York: Cheever.

Claflin, Edith Francis
    1905   *The Syntax of the Boeotian Dialect Inscriptions.* Baltimore: Lord Baltimore.

Clark, Mark Edward
    1983   " 'SPES' in the Imperial Cult." In *Society of Biblical Literature 1983 Seminar Papers,* ed. Kent Harold Richards, pp. 315–19. Chico:Scholars Press.

Clark, John R., and Anna Lydia Motto
    1965   "*Per iter tenebricosum:* The Mythos of Juvenal 3." *TAPA* 96:267–76.

Classical Investigation.
    1924   *The Classical Investigation Conducted by the Advisory Committee of the American Classical League.* Pt. 1. *General Report: A Summary of Results with Recommendations for the Organization of the Course in Secondary Latin and for Improvement in Methods of Teaching.* Princeton: Princeton University.

Claus, David B.
    1977   "Defining Moral Terms in *Works and Days." TAPA* 107:73–84.

Clay, Dorothy Madsen
    1958–60   *A Formal Analysis of the Vocabularies of Aeschylus, Sophocles, and Euripides.* Pt. 1 (Minneapolis, 1960); pt. 2 (Athens, Greece, 1958). (A dissertation, completed in 1957.)

Cobern, Camden McCormick
    1917   *The New Archeological Discoveries and Their Bearing upon the New Testament and upon the Life and Times of the Primitive Church.* New York: Funk and Wagnalls.

Cohen, Martin A.
    1965   "The First Christian Century As Jewish History." In *Bible in Modern Scholarship:*227–51.

Coleman-Norton, Paul Robinson
    1951   "The Apostle Paul and the Roman Law of Slavery." In *Johnson Festschrift:*155–77.

Coleman-Norton, P. R., Frank Card Bourne, and John van Antwerp Fine, eds.
    1951   *Studies in Roman Economic and Social History in Honor of Allan Chester Johnson.* Princeton: Princeton University.

Colwell, Ernest Cadman
1933   "A Definite Rule for the Use of the Article in the Greek New Testament." *JBL* 52:12–21.

1948   "Biblical Criticism: Lower and Higher." *JBL* 67:1–12.

1960   "New Testament Scholarship in Prospect." *Journal of Bible and Religion* 28:199–203.

Colwell, E. C., and Julius Robert Mantey
1939   *A Hellenistic Greek Reader: Selections from the Koine of the New Testament Period.* Chicago: University of Chicago.

Colwell, E. C., and Ernest W. Tune
1965   *A Beginner's Reader-Grammar for New Testament Greek.* New York: Harper.

Contemporary Literary Hermeneutics
1981   *Contemporary Literary Hermeneutics and Interpretation of Classical Texts,* ed. by Stephan Kresic. Ottawa: Ottawa University.

Cook, James I.
1981   *Edgar Johnson Goodspeed, Articulate Scholar.* Chico: Scholars Press.

Cook, William Burt, Jr., ed.
1924   *Catalogue of the Egyptological Library and Other Books from the Collection of the Late Charles Edwin Wilbour.* Brooklyn: Brooklyn Museum.

Cooper, Lane
1916   *A Concordance to the Works of Horace.* Washington, DC: Carnegie Institution of Washington.

Copley, Frank Olin
1957   "Catullus, *c.* 1." *TAPA* 82:200–6.

1958   "Catullus *c.* 4: The World of the Poem." *TAPA* 89:9–13.

Coulter, Cornelia Catlin
1926   "The 'Great Fish' in Ancient and Medieval Story." *TAPA* 57:32–50.

1931   "The Tragic Structure of Plato's Apology." *PAPA* 62:xxv-xxvi.

Coy, Edward Gustin
1890   *Greek for Beginners, A Companion Book to the Hadley-Allen Greek Grammar: An Introduction to Either Coy's First Reader, or the Anabasis of Xenophon.* New York: American Book Co.

Corpus Papyrorum Judaicarum
1957–64   *Corpus Papyrorum Judaicarum*, ed. by Victor Avigdor
            Tcherikover, Alexander Fuks, and Menahem Stern, with an
            epigraphic contribution by David M. Lewis. 3 vols.
            Cambridge: Harvard University, for the Magnes Press of the
            Hebrew University.

Craig, Clarence Tucker
1938   "Current Trends in New Testament Study." *JBL* 57:359–75.

1943   "Biblical Theology and the Rise of Historicism." *JBL*
            62:281–94.

Critiques
1949   *Critiques and Essays in Criticism, 1920–1948, Representing
            the Achievements of Modern British and American Critics,*
            selected by Robert Wooster Stallman. New York: Ronald.

Crosby, Alphaeus
1844   *A Grammar of the Greek Language.* Boston: J. Munroe. (38th
            ed., London: Woolworth, 1870.)

Crosby, Howard
1880   "The Coming Revision of the Bible." *North American Review*
            131:439–56.

Crossan, John Dominic
1974   "Parable and Example in the Teaching of Jesus." *Semeia*
            1:63–104.

1976a   *Raid on the Articulate: Comic Eschatology in Jesus and Borges.*
            New York: Harper.

1976b   Review of *Kerygma and Comedy in the New Testament: A
            Structuralist Approach to Hermeneutics,* by Dan O. Via, Jr.
            JBL 95:486–87.

1977   Review of *Poet and Peasant,* by Kenneth E. Bailey. *JBL*
            96:606–8.

Curti, Merle, ed.
1953   *American Scholarship in the Twentieth Century.* New York:
            Russell and Russell.

Dahl, George
1938   "The Messianic Expectation in the Psalter." *JBL* 57:1–12.

Dana, Harvey Eugene, and Julius R. Mantey
1927   *A Manual Grammar of the Greek New Testament.* New York:
            Macmillan.

Daniel, Jerry L.
1979		"Anti-Semitism in the Hellenistic-Roman Period." *JBL* 98:45–65.

Danker, Frederick William
1972		"Under Contract: A Form-Critical Study of Linguistic Adaptation in Romans." In *Festschrift Gingrich,* 1972:91–114.

1982		*Benefactor: An Epigraphic Study of a Greco-Roman and New Testament Semantic Field.* St. Louis: Clayton.

Danker, F. W., assisted by Jan Schambach
1977		*No Room in the Brotherhood: The Preus-Otten Purge of Missouri.* St. Louis: Clayton.

Davies, Stevan L.
1980		*The Revolt of the Widows: The Social World of the Apocryphal Acts.* Carbondale: Southern Illinois University Press.

Davis, Ozora Stearns
1893		*Vocabulary of New Testament Words Classified According to Roots with Statistics of Usage by Authors.* Hartford: Hartford Seminary.

Davis, Philip W.
1973		*Modern Theories of Language.* Englewood Cliffs, NJ: Prentice Hall.

Dee, James H.
1974		"Arethusa to Lycotas: Propertius 4.3." *TAPA* 104:81–96.

Deferrari, Roy Joseph, and James Marshall Campbell
1932		*A Concordance of Prudentius.* Cambridge: Medieval Academy of America.

Deferrari, R. J., Maria Inviolata Barry, and Martin R. P. McGuire
1939		*A Concordance of Ovid.* Washington, DC: Catholic University of America.

Deferarri, R. J., Maria Walburg Fanning, and Anne Stanislaus Sullivan
1940		*A Concordance of Lucan.* Washington, DC: Catholic University of America.

Deferrari, R. J., and Maria Clement Eagan
1943		*A Concordance of Statius.* Brookland, DC: R. J. Deferrari.

Dillon, Richard J.
1972		Review of *Auferstehung und Offenbarung,* by Adriaan Geense. *JBL* 91:558–63.

Dinsmoor, William Bell
1931		*The Archons of Athens in the Hellenistic Age.* Cambridge: Harvard University.

1939   *The Athenian Archon List in the Light of Recent Discoveries.* Morningside Heights, New York: Columbia University.

Dobschuetz, Ernst von
1914   "Christianity and Hellenism." *JBL* 33:245–65.

Dow, Sterling
1937   *Prytaneis: A Study of the Inscriptions Honoring the Athenian Councillors. Hesperia,* Supplement 1. Athens: American School of Classical Studies.

1950   "Archaeological Indexes: A Review Article. Principally a review of *Hesperia, Index to Volume I-X and Supplements I-VI* (Athens, 1946)." *AJA* 54:41–57.

1951   "Illustrations in Textbooks." *Journal of General Education* 5:101–15.

1965   *Fifty Years of Sathers: The Sather Professorship of Classical Literature in the University of California.* Berkeley: University of California.

Dow, Sterling, and Robert F. Healey
1965   *A Sacred Calendar of Eleusis.* Harvard Theological Studies, 21. Cambridge: Harvard University.

Drisler, Henry, ed.
1870   *An English-Greek Lexicon. With Many New Articles, an Appendix of Proper Names, and Pillon's Greek Synonyms, by Charles Duke Yonge.* New York: Harper.

Duckworth, George E.
1960   "Mathematical Symmetry in Vergil's *Aeneid.*" *TAPA* 91:184–220.

Dundes, Alan, ed.
1965   *The Study of Folklore.* Englewood Cliffs, NJ: Prentice-Hall.

Dunn, Frederic Stanley
1900   "Juvenal as a Humorist." *PAPA* 31:xlix.

Dura Europos
1929   *The Excavations at Dura-Europos Conducted by Yale University and the French Academy of Inscriptions and Letters: Preliminary Report of the First Season of Work, Spring 1928,* ed. by Paul Victor Christopher Baur and Mikhail Ivanovich Rostovtzeff. New Haven: Yale University.

1931   *The Excavations . . . Letters: Preliminary Report of Second Season of Work October 1928–April 1929,* ed. by P. Bauer and M. Rostovtzeff. New Haven: Yale University.

1933   *The Excavations . . . Letters: Preliminary Report of Fourth Season of Work, October 1930 to March 1931*, ed. by P. Baur, M. Rostovtzeff, and Alfred R. Bellinger. New Haven: Yale University.

1936   *The Excavations . . . Letters: Preliminary Report of Sixth Season of Work, October 1930 to March 1931*, ed. by M. Rostovtzeff, A. Bellinger, C. Hopkins, and Charles Bradford Welles. New Haven: Yale University.

1939   *The Excavations . . . Letters: Preliminary Report of the Seventh and Eighth Seasons of Work 1933–1934 and 1934–1935*, ed. by M. Rostovtzeff. Frank Edward Brown, and C. Welles. New Haven: Yale University.

1952   *The Excavations . . . Letters: Preliminary Report of the Ninth Season of Work, 1935–1936. Pt. 3. The Palace of the Dux Ripae and the Dolicheneum*, ed. by M. Rostovtzeff, A. Bellinger, F. Brown, and C. Welles. New Haven: Yale University.

Earle, Mortimer Lamson
1912   *The Classical Papers of Mortimer Lamson Earle with a Memoir*, ed. by Gertrude M. Hirst, Fred A. Knapp, Gonzales Lodge, Edward D. Perry. New York: Columbia University. (An edition "printed from type, 1911" is paginated differently.)

Easton, Burton Scott
1910   "Linguistic Evidence for the Lucan Source L." *JBL* 29:139–80.

1911   "The Special Source of the Third Gospel." *JBL* 30:78–103.

1932   "New Testament Ethical Lists." *JBL* 51:1–12.

Edwards, Richard Alan
1975   *A Concordance to "Q".* Sources for Biblical Study, 7. Missoula: Scholars Press.

Egbert, James Chidester
[1896] 1906 *Introduction to the Study of Latin Inscriptions*. Rev. ed. with supplement. New York: American Book Co.

Elliott, Ebenezer Newton, ed.
1860   *Cotton is King, and Pro-Slavery Arguments: Comprising the Writings of Hammond, Harper, Christy, Stringfellow, Hodge, Bledsoe, and Cartwright, on this Important Subject*. Augusta: Pritchard, Abbott and Loomis.

Elliott, John Hall
1966   *The Elect and the Holy: An Exegetical Examination of I Peter 2:4–10 and the Phrase "basileion hierateuma."* Leiden: Brill.

1981   *A Home for the Homeless: A Sociological Exegesis of I Peter, its Situation and Strategy.* Philadelphia: Fortress.

Elliott, Leslie Robinson
1945   *A Comparative Lexicon of New Testament Greek.* Kansas City: Central Seminary.

Ellison, John W., ed.
1957   *Nelson's Complete Concordance of the Revised Standard Version Bible.* New York: Nelson.

Elmer, Herbert Charles
1928   *Latin Grammar.* New York: Macmillan.

English, J. M.
1898   "Elements of Persuasion in Paul's Address on Mar's Hill, at Athens." *AJT* 2:97–109.

Enslin, Morton Scott
1927a   *"Ephobounto gar,* Mark 16:8." *JBL* 46:62–68.

1927b   "Paul and Gamaliel." *Journal of Religion* 7:360–75.

1933   "A Notable Contribution to Acts." *JBL* 52:230–8.

1940   Review of *Form and Function of the Pauline Thanksgiving,* by Paul Schubert. *JBL* 59:76–78.

1946   "Is There a Future for Biblical Studies?" *JBL* 65:1–12.

1956   Review of *A Companion to the Study of St. Augustine,* ed. Roy W. Battenhouse. *JBL* 75:241–3.

1963   Review of *The Wycliffe Biblical Commentary,* ed. by Charles F. Pfeiffer (OT) and Everett Harrison (NT). *JBL* 82:129–30.

1967   Review of *Jesus in the Gospels,* by Ernest W. Saunders. *JBL* 86:470–1.

Erlich, Victor
1955   *Russian Formalism: History, Doctrine.* Leiden:Mouton. (3d edition, The Hague: Mouton, 1969).

Exler, Francis Xavier J.
1923   *The Form of the Ancient Greek Letter: A Study in Greek Epistolography.* Washington, DC: Catholic University of America.

Exodus from Concordia
1977   *Exodus From Concordia,* ed. by the Board of Control of Concordia Seminary (St. Louis, Missouri). St. Louis: Concordia College.

Farmer, William Reuben
1956   *Maccabees, Zealots, and Josephus: An Inquiry into Jewish Nationalism in the Greco-Roman Period.* New York: Columbia University.

Fears, Jesse Rufus
1976   "The Solar Monarchy of Nero and the Imperial Panegyric of Q. Curtius Rufus." *Historia* 25:494–6.

1977   *Princeps A Diis Electus: The Divine Election of the Emperor as a Political Concept at Rome.* Papers and Monographs of the American Academy in Rome, 26. Rome: American Academy.

Feldman, Louis H.
1950   Jewish "Sympathizers" in Classical Literature and Inscriptions. *TAPA* 81:200–8.

1968   "Abraham the Greek Philosopher in Josephus." *TAPA* 99:143–56.

1970   "Hellenizations in Josephus' Version of Esther." *TAPA* 101:143–70.

1984   *Josephus and Modern Scholarship (1937–1980).* Berlin: de Gruyter.

Felton, Conway
1836   Review of *Alkestis* of Euripides and *Antigone* of Sophokles, ed. by Theodore Dwight Woolsey. *North American Review* 42:370–88.

Ferguson, William Duncan
1913   *The Legal and Governmental Terms Common to the Macedonian Greek Inscriptions and the New Testament, with a Complete Index of the Macedonian Inscriptions.* The University of Chicago Historical and Linguistic Studies, 2d series, vol. 11, pt. 3. Chicago: University of Chicago.

Ferguson, William Scott
1899   *The Athenian Archons of the Third and Second Centuries Before Christ.* CSCP, 10. New York: Macmillan.

1907   *The Priests of Asklepios: A New Method of Dating Athenian Archons.* University of California Publications in Classical Philology 1, no. 5. Berkeley: University of California.

1932   *Athenian Tribal Cycles in the Hellenistic Age.* Harvard Historical Monographs, 1. Cambridge: Harvard University.

1944   "The Attic Orgeones." *HTR* 37:61–130. (Appendixes 1–4, pp. 131–40; Appendix 3, by Sterling Dow.)

Festschrift Gingrich
1972   *Festschrift to Honor F. Wilbur Gingrich, Lexicographer, Scholar, Teacher and Committed Christian Layman,* ed. by Eugene Howard Barth and Ronald Edwin Cocroft. Leiden: Brill.

Filson, Floyd Vivian
1939   "The Significance of the Early House Church." *JBL* 58:109–12.

1950   "Method in Studying Biblical History." *JBL* 69:1–18.

Fine, John van Antwerp
1951   *Horoi: Studies in Mortgage, Real Security and Land Tenure in Ancient Athens. Hesperia,* Supplement 9. Baltimore: ASCSA.

Finkel, Joshua
1936   "Filial Loyalty as a Testimony of Legitimacy: A Study in Folklore." *JBL* 55:133–43.

Fiorenza, Elisabeth Schüssler
1984   *In Memory of Her: A Feminist Theological Reconstruction of Christian Origins.* New York: Crossroad.

Fischer, Gustavus
1876   *Latin Grammar, Together with a Systematic Treatment of Latin Composition.* Vol 1: Etymology and an Introduction to Syntax. Vol. 2: Details of Syntax. New York: Schermerhorn.

Fishwick, Duncan
1972   "The Institution of the Provincial Cult in Roman Mauretania." *Historia* 21:698–711.

Fisk, Benjamin
1831   *A Grammar of the Greek Language.* Boston: Hilliar, Gray, Little, and Wilkens.

Fiske, George Converse
1900   "Notes on the Worship of the Roman Emperors in Spain." *HSCP* 11:101–39.

Fitzmyer, Joseph Augustine
1973   "How to Exploit a Secret Gospel." (Review of M. Smith 1973a,b.) *America* (June 23):570–72.

1981   *The Gospel According to Luke I-IX.* Vol. 1. Garden City, New York: Doubleday.

1972   Review of *Who's Who in the New Testament,* by Ronald Browning. *JBL* 91:438–9.

Flory, Stewart
1978   "Medea's Right Hand: Promise and Revenge." *TAPA* 108:69–74.

Flynn, John T.
1932   *God's Gold: John D. Rockefeller and His Times.* Harcourt, Brace and Company.

Flynn, Robert P.
1943   "Greek Thought on Culture as a Casualty of War." *The Classical Bulletin* 20:10–11.

Foakes-Jackson. *See* Jackson, Frederick Foakes.

Fobes, Francis Howard
1957   *Philosophical Greek, an Introduction.* Chicago: University of Chicago.

Foerster, Norman, ed.
[1930] 1940 *American Critical Essays XIXth and XXth Centuries.* Reprint. London: Oxford University.

Forbes, Clarence Allen
1933   *Neoi: A Contribution to the Study of Greek Associations.* Philological Monographs, 2. Middletown, CT: APA.

1936   "Books for the Burning." *TAPA* 67:114–25.

Fowler, Harold North
1932   *Corinth: Results of Excavations Conducted by the American School of Classical Studies at Athens.* Vol. 1, pt. 1. *Introduction, Topography, Architecture,* with contributions by Carl William Blegen, Benjamin Powell, and Charles Alexander Robinson, Jr. Cambridge: Harvard University.

Fowler, Henry Thatcher
1930   "Herodotus and the Early Hebrew Historians." *JBL* 49:207–17.

Fraenkel, Hermann
1975   "Three Talks on Grammar." In *California Studies in Classical Antiquity,* 7:113–53. Berkeley: University of California.

Frank, Tenney
1930   *Life and Literature in the Roman Republic.* Sather Classical Lecture, 6. Berkeley: University of California.

Frank, Tenney, et al., eds.
1933–40   *An Economic Survey of Ancient Rome.* 5 vols. and General Index. Baltimore: Johns Hopkins.

Frankfort, Henri
1948   *Kingship and the Gods: A Study of Ancient Near Eastern Religion as the Integration of Society and Nature.* Chicago: The University of Chicago.

Franklin, Susan Braley
1901   "Public Appropriation for Individual Offerings and Sacrifices in Greece." *TAPA* 32:72–82.

Fredericks, B. R.
1976   "*Tristia* 4. 10: Poet's Autobiography and Poetic Autobiography." *TAPA* 106:139–54.

Fredricksmeyer, Ernst A.
1979   Divine Honors for Philip II. *TAPA* 109:39–61.

Freyne, Sean
1980   *Galilee from Alexander the Great to Hadrian, 323 B.C.E. to 135 C.E.: A Study of Second Temple Judaism.* South Bend: University of Notre Dame.

Friberg, Barbara, and Timothy Friberg
1981a   "A Computer-Assisted Analysis of the Greek New Testament Text." In *Computing in the Humanities,* ed. by P. C. Patton and R. Holoien, 15–51. Lexington: Heath.

1981b   *Analytical Greek Testament: Greek-Text Analysis.* Grand Rapids: Baker.

Friedlander, Paul, and Herbert B. Hoffleit
1948   *Epigrammata: Greek Inscriptions in Verse from the Beginnings to the Persian Wars.* Berkeley: University of California.

Fullerton, Kemper
1930   "Double Entendre in the First Speech of Eliphaz." *JBL* 49:320–74.
1934   "On Job, Chapters 9 and 10." *JBL* 53:321–49.

Funk, Robert Walter
1961   *See* Blass-Debrunner-Funk (BDF), 1961.

1966   *Language, Hermeneutic, and Word of God: The Problem of Language in the New Testament and Contemporary Theology.* New York: Harper.

1973   *A Beginning-Intermediate Grammar of Hellenistic Greek.* 2d ed. 3 vols. Missoula: Scholars Press.

1976   "The Watershed of the American Biblical Tradition: The Chicago School, First Phase, 1892–1920." *JBL* 95:4–22.

Gager, John G.
1972   *Moses in Greco-Roman Paganism.* SBLMS, 16. Nashville: Abingdon.

1975   *Kingdom and Community: the Social World of Early Christianity.* Englewood Cliffs, NJ: Prentice-Hall.

Gallivan, Paul A.
1973   "The False Neros: A Re-Examination." *Historia* 22:364–65.

Galpin, William Freeman
1960   *Syracuse University.* Vol. 2. *The Growing Years.* Syracuse: Syracuse University.

Gamble, John
1926   "Symbol and Reality in the Epistle to the Hebrews." *JBL* 45:162–70.

Garbrah, Kweku Arku
1977   *A Grammar of the Ionic Inscriptions from Erythrae: Phonology and Morphology.* Meisenheim am Glan: Anton Hain.

Garvin, Paul L.
1974   "Specialty Trends in the Language Sciences." *Current Trends in Linguistics,* ed. Thomas A. Sebeok. Vol. 12. *Linguistics and Adjacent Arts and Sciences,* 2889–2909. The Hague: Mouton. (The article was originally published in 1969 by the Center for Applied Linguistics Information and Clearinghouse System.)

Gaster, Theodore H.
1950   *Thespis: Ritual, Myth and Drama in the Ancient Near East.* New York: Henry Schuman.

Gaston, Lloyd
1973   *Horae Synopticae Electronicae: Word Studies of the Synoptic Gospels.* Sources for Biblical Study, 3. Missoula: Society of Biblical Literature.

Gates, John Edward
1972   *Lexicographic Resources Used by Biblical Scholars.* SBLDS 8. Missoula: Scholars Press.

Gayley, Charles Mills
1903   "What is Comparative Literature?" *Atlantic Monthly* 92:56–68. (Digest in *PAPA* 34[1903]:lxxiv-lxxx.)

Geer, Russel Mortimer
1931   "Notes on the Early Life of Nero." *TAPA* 62:57–67.

1930   "One Ancient Attempt at Censorship." *CW* 23:144.

Gentili, Bruno
1981   "The Interpreting of the Greek Lyric Poets in our Time: Synchronism and Diachronism in the Study of an Oral Culture." In *Contemporary Literary Hermeneutics,* 109–120.

Georgacas, Demetrius John
1971   *The Names for the Asia Minor Peninsula and a Register of Surviving Anatolian Pre-Turkisch Placenames.* "Beiträge zur Namenforschung," n.s., 8. Heidelberg: Carl Winter.

1976   "The Present State of Lexicography and Zagustas' *Manual of Lexicography." Orbis* 25:359–400.

Gibson, Elsa
1978   *The "Christians for Christians" Inscriptions of Phrygia.* Harvard Theological Studies, 32. Missoula: Scholars Press.

Gignac, Francis Thomas
1970   "The Language of the Non-Literary Greek Papyri." *Proceedings of the International Congress of Papyrology. Michigan,* 1970:139–72.

1976–81   *A Grammar of the Greek Papyri of the Roman and Byzantine Periods.* Vol. 1, *Phonology* (1976); vol. 2, *Morphology* (1981). Milan: Istituto Editoriae Cisalpino-La Golliardica.

Gildersleeve, Basil Lanneau
1876   "On *ei* with the Future Indicative, and *ean* with the Subjunctive in the Tragic Poets." *TAPA* 7:5–23.

1877   *The Apologies of Justin, Martyr. To Which is Appended The Epistle to Diognetus. With an Introduction and Notes.* New York: Harper.

1878   "Contributions to the History of the Articular Infinitive in Greek." *TAPA* 9:24–26.

[1885]
1890a   *Pindar: The Olympian and Pythian Odes,* rev. ed. New York: American Book Co.

1890b   *Essays and Studies: Educational and Literary.* Baltimore: N. Murray. (See evaluation by Lawton, 1891.)

1902   "Problems in Greek Syntax." *AJP* 23:1–2.

1909   "The Range and Character of the Philological Activity of America." *PAPA* 40:xxxviii-xxxix.

1915   "Indiculus Syntacticus." *AJP* 36:481–87.

1916   "*Hopos* and *Hopos An.*" *AJP* 37:210.

1930   *Selections from the "Brief Mention" of Basil Lanneau Gildersleeve*, ed., with a biographical sketch and an index, by Charles William Emil Miller. Baltimore: Johns Hopkins.

Gildersleeve, B. L., and Gonzales Lodge
1894   *Gildersleeve's Latin Grammar*. 3d ed. New York: University Publishing Co.

Gildersleeve, B. L., and Charles Emil William Miller
1900–11   *Syntax of Classical Greek from Homer to Demosthenes*. Pt. 1. *The Syntax of the Simple Sentence Embracing the Doctrine of the Moods and Tenses* (1900). Pt. 2 (1911, a continuation of pt. 1; the work was not completed). New York: American Book Co.

Gilliam, James Frank
1979   "Introduction" to the session, "Epigraphie et armées." In *Actes du VII congres international d'epigraphie grecque et latine, Constantza, 9–15 septembre 1977*, ed. D. M. Pippidi. Bucharest: Editura Academie.

Gill, Everett
1943   *A. T. Robertson: A Biography*. New York: Macmillan.

Gingrich, F. Wilbur
1933   "New Testament Lexical Notes." *JBL* 52:262–3.

1945   "New Testament Lexicography and the Future." *Journal of Religion* 25:179–182.

1954   "The Greek New Testament as a Landmark in the Course of Semantic Change." *JBL* 73:189–96.

1965   *Shorter Lexicon of the Greek New Testament*. Chicago: University of Chicago. Revised ed. by Frederick Danker, 1983.

Ginsburg, Michael
1940   "Roman Military Clubs and Their Social Functions." *TAPA* 71:149–56.

Godolphin, Francis Richard Boroum
1932   "A Note on the Technique of Ancient Biography." *CP* 27:275–80.

Goell, Theresa, and Friedrich Karl Dorner
1963   *Arsameia Am Nymphaios: Die Ausgrabungen im Hierothesion des Mithradates Kallinikos von 1953–1956*. Berlin: Mann.

Goetchius, Eugene van Ness
1965   *The Language of the New Testament*. New York: Scribner.

1968   Review of *A Practical List of Greek Word Roots,* by Thomas Rogers. *JBL* 87:490–1.

Goodenough, Erwin Ramsdell

1928   "The Political Philosophy of Hellenistic Kingship." *YCS* 1:55–102.

1935   *By Light, Light: The Mystic Gospel of Hellenistic Judaism.* New Haven: Yale University.

1937a   "Symbolism in Hellenistic Jewish Art: The Problem of Method." *JBL* 56:103–14.

1937b   "New Light on Hellenistic Judaism." *Journal of Bible and Religion* 5:18–28.

1938   *The Politics of Philo Judaeus: Practice and Theory.* New Haven: Yale University.

1939   "Problems of Method in Studying Philo Judaeus." *JBL* 58:51–58.

1940   *An Introduction to Philo Judaeus.* New Haven: Yale University.

1943   "Report to the Editor." *JBL* 62:x-xI.

1945   "John, a Primitive Gospel." *JBL* 64:145–82.

1946   "Philo on Immortality." *HTR* 39:85–108.

1948   Review of *Philo,* by Harry A. Wolfson. *JBL* 67:87–109.

1952   "The Inspiration of New Testament Research." *JBL* 71:1–9.

1953–68   *Jewish Symbols in the Greco-Roman Period.* 13 vols. Princeton NJ: Princeton University, for Bollingen Foundation, New York.

1963   Review of *Our Living Bible,* by Michael Avi-Yonah and Emil Kraeling. *JBL* 82:140–41.

Goodspeed, Edgar Johnson

1898   "The Ayer Papyrus: A Mathematical Fragment." *AJP* 19:25–39. Reprint: "The Ayer Papyrus: Geometrical Processes," in *Chicago Literary Papyri* (Chicago: University of Chicago,, 1908:19–27.

1903   "The Ayer Papyrus." The American Mathematical Monthly (May issue).

1907   *Index Patristicus.* Leipzig: Hinrichs. (Rev. ed., Naperville: Allenson, 1960.)

1912   *Index apologeticus sive clavis Iustini Martyris operum aliorumque apologetarum pristinorum.* Leipzig: Hinrichs.

1930   "New Manuscript Acquisitions for Chicago. III. One Year's
            Progress on New Testament Manuscripts." *The University of
            Chicago Magazine.* January:137–42.

1933   *The Meaning of Ephesians.* Chicago: University of Chicago.

1942   "The Possible Aramaic Gospel." *JNES* 1:315–40.

1945   *Problems of New Testament Translation.* Chicago: University
            of Chicago.

1953   *As I Remember.* New York: Harper.

1959   *Matthew, Apostle and Evangelist.* Philadelphia: Winston.

Goodspeed, Edgar Johnson, and Ernest Cadman Colwell
1935   *A Greek Papyrus Reader.* Chicago: University of Chicago.

Goodspeed, Thomas Wakefield
1916   *A History of the University of Chicago, Founded by John D.
            Rockefeller. The First Quarter-Century.* Chicago: University of
            Chicago.

1925   *The Story of the University of Chicago 1890–1925.* Chicago:
            University of Chicago.

1926   *Ernest DeWitt Burton, A Biographical Sketch.* Chicago:
            University of Chicago.

1928   *William Rainey Harper: First President of the University of
            Chicago.* Chicago: University of Chicago.

Goodwin, William Watson
1860   *Syntax of the Moods and Tenses of the Greek Verb.* Cambridge:
            Sever and Francis.

1870   *An Elementary Greek Grammar.* Boston: Ginn.

1930   *Greek Grammar.* Revised by Charles Burton Gulick. Boston:
            Ginn.

Gordon, Arthur Ernest, and Joyce Stiefbold Gordon
1957   *Contributions to the Palaeography of Latin Inscriptions.*
            Publications in Classical Archaeology 3, no. 3:i-ix, 65–241.
            Berkeley: University of California.

1958–65   *Album of Dated Latin Inscriptions, Rome and the
            Neighborhood, Augustus to Nerva.* 4 vols. Berkeley: University
            of California.

Gottwald, Norman Karol, ed.
1983   *The Bible and Liberation: Political and Social Hermeneutics.*
            Maryknoll, New York: Orbis.

Gould, Ezra P.
1892   "Anomalies of the New Testament Literature." *JBL* 11:61–67.

Grady, Eleanor Hunsdon
1931   *Epigraphic Sources of the Delphic Amphictyony.* Dissertation, Columbia University. Walton, New York: Reporter Company.

Grant, Frederick Clifton
1935   "The Spiritual Christ." *JBL* 54:1–15.

1953   Editor of *Hellenistic Religions, The Age of Syncretism.* New York: Liberal Arts.

1957   Editor of *Ancient Roman Religion.* New York: Liberal Arts.

1960   Review of *Jewish Symbols in the Greco-Roman Period,* vols. 7–8, by Erwin Goodenough. *JBL* 79:61–64.

1969   Review of *Jewish Symbols in the Greco-Roman Period,* vol. 13, by Erwin R. Goodenough. *JBL* 88:370.

Grant, Robert McQueen
1952   *Miracle and Natural Law in Graeco-Roman and Early Christian Thought.* Amsterdam: North-Holland.

1961a   *Gnosticism: A Sourcebook of Heretical Writings from the Early Christian Period.* New York: Harper.

1961b   Review of *Die Religion in Geschichte und Gegenwart,* vol. 4. *JBL* 80:306.

1968   "American New Testament Study 1926–1956." *JBL* 87:42–50.

1970   *Augustus to Constantine: The Threat of the Christian Movement into the Roman World.* New York: Harper.

1971   Review of *Hellenistic Influences on the Book of Wisdom and Its Consequences,* by James M. Reese. *JBL* 90:227–28.

Green, William McAllen
1929   "An Ancient Debate on Capital Punishment." *CJ* 24:267–75.

Greenberg, Nathan A.
1958   "Metathesis as an Instrument in the Criticism of Poetry." *TAPA* 89:262–70.

Greene, William Chase
1944   *Moira.* Cambridge: Harvard University.

Grese, William C.
1979   *Corpus Hermeticum XIII and Early Christian Literature.* CHNT, 5. Leiden: Brill.

Gresseth, Gerald K.
1979   "The *Odyssey* and the *Nalopākhyāna.*" *TAPA* 109:63–85.

Grobel, W. Kendrick
1947   "The Revision of the English New Testament." *JBL* 66:361–84.

Gudeman, Alfred
   1903   "The Incongruities in the Speeches of Ancient Historians, from Herodotus to Ammianus Marcellinus." *PAPA* 34:xliii-xlvi.

Güttgemanns, Erhardt
   1976   *"Generative Poetics.* 1. What is Generative Poetics? Theses and Reflections Concerning a New Exegetical Method," pp. 1–22; "Introductory Remarks Concerning the Structural Study of Narrative," pp. 23–125; "Narrative Analysis of Synoptic Texts," pp. 127–179; "Linguistic-Literary Critical Foundation of a New Testament Theology," pp. 181–213. *Semeia,* 6. Missoula: SBL.

Hadas, Moses
   1931   "Gaderenes in Pagan Literature." *CW* 25:25–30.

   1959   *Hellenistic Culture: Fusion and Diffusion.* New York: Columbia University.

Hadley, James
   1860   *A Greek Grammar for Schools and Colleges.* New York: Appleton.

   1869   *Elements of the Greek Language Taken from the Greek Grammar.* New York: Appleton. (Hadley's Grammar was largely rewritten and published by Frederic Allen in 1884.)

   1873   "Ross on Italicans and Greeks." In *Essays: Philological and Critical, Selected from the Papers of James Hadley,* 141–67. Paper delivered at a meeting of the American Oriental Society, November 1858. New York: Holt and Williams.

Hadley, James, and Frederic de Forest Allen
   1884   *A Greek Grammar for Schools and Colleges.* Rev. ed. New York: Appleton.

Hadzsits, George Depue
   1908   "Significance of Worship and Prayer Among the Epicureans." *TAPA* 39:73–88.

Hahn, Emma Adelaide
   1953   *Subjunctive and Optative: Their Origin as Futures.* Philological Monographs, 16. New York: APA.

Hahn, E. A., and Edgar Howard Sturtevant
   1951   *A Comparative Grammar of the Hittite Language.* New Haven: Yale University.

Hale, William Gardner
   1893   " 'Extended' and 'Remote' Deliberatives in Greek." *TAPA* 24:156–205.

1901   "The Origin of Subjunctive and Optative Conditions in Greek and Latin." *HSCP* 12:109–23.

1906   "A Century of Metaphysical Syntax." In *Congress of Arts and Science at St. Louis, Universal Exposition, St. Louis, 1904*, ed. by Howard J. Rogers, 3:191–202. Boston: Houghton, Mifflin.

1907   *A First Latin Book*. Chicago: Atkinson, Mentzer and Grover.

Hale, W. G., and Carl Darling Buck
1903   *A Latin Grammar*. Boston: Ginn.

Hall, Isaac H.
1885   "A New Arabic-French Dictionary." *JBL* 5:108.

Hanfmann, George Maxim Anossov, and William E. Mierse, eds.
1983   *Sardis from Prehistoric to Roman Times: Results of the Archaeological Exploration of Sardis*. Cambridge: Harvard University.

Harkness, Albert
1861   *First Greek Book; Comprising an Outline of the Forms and Inflections of the Language, a Complete Analytical Syntax, and an Introductory Reader with Notes and Vocabulary*. New York: Appleton.

1864   *Latin Grammar for Schools and Colleges*. New York: Appleton

Harkness, Albert Granger
1896   "Age at Marriage and at Death in the Roman Empire." *TAPA* 27:35–72.

Harmon, Daniel P.
1974   "Myth and Fantasy in Propertius 1:3." *TAPA* 104:151–65.

Harner, Philip Balch
1973   "Qualitative Anarthrous Predicate Nouns: Mark 15:39 and John 1:1." *JBL* 92:75–87.

Harper, William Rainey, and William Everett Waters
1888   *An Inductive Greek Method*. New York: Ivison, Blakeman.

Harper, W. R., and Clarence Fassett Castle
1893   *An Inductive Greek Primer*. New York: American Book Co.

Harrisville, Roy A.
1976   *Benjamin Wisner Bacon: Pioneer in American Biblical Criticism*. Missoula: Scholars Press.

Harry, Joseph Edward
1898   "The Omission of the Article with Substantives after *houtos, hode, ekeinos* in Prose." *TAPA* 29:48–64.

1901   "A Misunderstood Passage in Aeschylus." *TAPA* 32:64–71.

1905   "The Perfect, Subjunctive, Optative, and Imperative in Greek." *CR* 19:347–54.

Harsh, Philip Whaley
1955   The Intriguing Slave in Greek Comedy." *TAPA* 86:135–42.

Hastings, Harold Ripley
1912   *On the Relation Between Inscriptions and Sculptured Representations on Attic Tombstones.* Bulletin of the University of Wisconsin, 485. Madison: University of Wisconsin.

Hatch, William Henry Paine
1908   "Some Illustrations of New Testament Usage from Greek Inscriptions of Asia Minor." *JBL* 27:134–46.

1939   "The Primitive Christian Message." *JBL* 58:1–13.

Haupt, Paul
1917   "Alcohol in the Bible." *JBL* 36:75–83.

Haverford Symposium
1938   *The Haverford Symposium on Archaeology and the Bible,* ed. by Elihu Grant. New Haven: ASOR.

Heidel, William Arthur
1900   "On Plato's *Euthyphro.*" *TAPA* 31:163–81.

Heisserer, Andrew Jackson
1980   *Alexander the Great and the Greeks: The Epigraphic Evidence.* Norman: University of Oklahoma.

Henderson, Jeffrey
1975   *The Maculate Muse: Obscene Language in Attic Comedy.* New Haven: Yale University.

Henderson, Virginia Helene
1930   *Index Verborum Terentianus.* Iowa City: University of Iowa.

Hendricks, William O.
1970   "Folklore and the Structural Analysis of Literary Texts." *Language and Style* 3:83–121.

Herbert, Kevin
1972   *Greek and Latin Inscriptions in the Brooklyn Museum.* Wilbour Monographs, 14. Brooklyn: Brooklyn Museum.

Heston, Watson
1892   *Old Testament Stories, Comically Illustrated.* New York: Truth Seeker Company.

Heston, Watson, and George E. Macdonald
1892   *New Testament Stories Comically Illustrated.* New York: Truth Seeker Company.

Hewitt, Joseph William
1927   "The Terminology of 'Gratitude' in Greek." *CP* 22:142–61.

Hiers, Richard H.
1966   "Eschatology and Methodology." *JBL* 85:170–84.

Highet, Gilbert
1941   "Petronius the Moralist." *TAPA* 72:176–94.

Hilgert, Earle
1984   *Bibliographia Philoniana 1935–1981.* In *ANRW,* Pt. II, *Principat* 21/1:47–97.

Hill, Andrew Elmer
1980   "The Temple of Asclepius: An Alternative Source for Paul's Body Theology?" *JBL* 99:437–39.

Hock, Roland F.
1978   "Paul's Tentmaking and the Problem of his Social Class." *JBL* 97:555–64.

1980   *The Social Context of Paul's Ministry. Tentmaking and Apostleship.* Philadelphia: Fortress.

Hock, Rudolph Paul
1982   "Puns, Aelius Maurus, and the Composition of the *Historia Augusta.*" *TAPA* 112:107–13.

Hockey, Susan
1980   *A Guide to Computer Applications in the Humanities.* Baltimore: Johns Hopkins University.

Holladay, Carl H.
1977   *"Theios Aner" in Hellenistic-Judaism: A Critique of the Use of this Category in NT Christology.* Missoula: Scholars Press.

Holly, David
1983   *Comparative Studies in Recent Greek New Testament Texts.* Subsidia Biblica, 7. Rome: Biblical Institute.

Holtsmark, Erling Bent
1967   "On Lucretius 2. 1–19." *TAPA* 98:193–204.

Hooper, Finley A.
1956   "Data from Kom Abou Billou on the Length of Life in Graeco-Roman-Egypt." *Chronique d'Egypte* 31, no. 62 (July):332–40.

1961   *Funerary Stelae from Kom Abou Billou.* The University of Michigan Kelsey Museum of Archaeology Studies, 1. Ann Arbor: Kelsey Museum of Archaeology.

Horn, Robert Chisolm
  1926   *The Use of the Subjunctive and Optative Moods in the Non-
               literary Papyri.* Dissertation, University of Pennsylvania.

Horning, Estella B.
  1983   *Hymns in Hebrews: A Formal and Christological Analysis.*
               Evanston: Northwestern University.

Householder, Fred W., Jr.
  1940   "The Mock Decrees in Lucian." *TAPA* 71:199–216.

Hullinger, Robert N.
  1980   *Mormon Answer to Skepticism: Why Joseph Smith Wrote the
               Book of Mormon.* St. Louis: Clayton.

Humphreys, Milton W.
  1915   "Hephaestion and Irrationality." *TAPA* 46:29–33.

Husband, Richard Wellington
  1915   "The Year of the Crucifixion." *TAPA* 46:5–27.

  1916   *The Prosecution of Jesus, its Date, History, and Legality.*
               Princeton: Princeton University.

Hussey, George B.
  1892   "Greek Sculptured Crowns and Crown Inscriptions." *PASCSA*
               5 (1886–1890):135–61.

Hyatt, J. Philip
  1948   Review of *The Study of the Bible Today and Tomorrow,* ed. by
               H. R. Willoughby. *JBL* 67:180.

  1965   Edition of *The Bible in Modern Scholarship: Papers read at the
               100th meeting of the Society of Biblical Literature, December
               28–30, 1964.* Nashville: Abingdon.

Hyde, Walter Woodburn
  1924   "Greek Analogies to the Song of Songs." In *The Song of Songs,
               A Symposium,* ed. by Wilfred H. Schoff, pp. 31–42.
               Philadelphia: Commercial Museum.

Hynes, William J.
  1981   *Shirley Jackson Case and the Chicago School.* Chico: Scholars
               Press.

Inez, Mary
  1946   "Ancient Ruler-Cult and the Early Christian Apologists."
               Classical Bulletin 22, 5 (February):33–35.

Ingalls, Wayne B.
  1979   "Formular Density in the Similes of the *Iliad.*" *TAPA*
               109:87–109.

Isserlin, B. S. J.
  1955   "The Isis and Her Voyage: Some Additional Remarks." *TAPA*
              86:319-20.

Jackson, Frederick J. Foakes
  1930   *Josephus and the Jews: The Religion and History of the Jews as
              Explained by Flavius Josephus.* London: SPCK.

Jackson, S. M.
  1887   "Eberhard Vischer's Theory of the Composition of Revela-
              tion." *JBL* 7:93-95.

Jaeger, Werner
  1936   "Classical Philology and Humanism." *TAPA* 67:363-74.

Jastrow, Morris
  1917   "Constructive Elements in the Critical Study of the Old
              Testament." *JBL* 36:1-30.

Jayne, Walter
  1925   *The Healing Gods of Ancient Civilizations.* New Haven: Yale
              University.

Jenkins, Edgar Bryan
  1932   *Index verborum Terentianus.* Chapel Hill: University of North
              Carolina.

Jerome, Thomas Spencer
  1912   "The Tacitean Tiberius, a Study in Historiographic Method."
              CP 7:265-92.

Jewish People
  1974-76   *The Jewish People in the First Century: Historical Geography,
              Political History, Social, Cultural and Religious Life and
              Institutions,* ed. by Samuel Safrai and Menahem Stern, in co-
              operation with D. Flusser and Willem Cornelis van Unnik.
              "Compendia Rerum Iudaicarum ad Novum Testamentum,"
              Section 1. Vol. 1, 1974; vol. 2, 1976. Philadelphia: Fortress.

Jewish Writings
  1984   *Jewish Writings of the Second Temple Period: Apocrypha,
              Pseudepigrapha, Qumran Sectarian Writings, Philo, Josephus,*
              ed. by Michael E. Stone. 1984. Compendia Rerum
              Iudaicarum ad Novum Testamentum, Section 2, vol. 2.
              Philadelphia: Fortress.

Johnson Festschrift
  1951   *Studies in Roman Economic and Social History in Honor of
              Allan Chester Johnson,* ed. by Paul Robinson Coleman-
              Norton, Frank Card Bourne, and John van Antwerp Fine.
              Princeton: Princeton University.

Johnson, Allan Chester
1936   *Roman Egypt to the Reign of Diocletian.* Vol. 2 of Frank, 1933–1940.

Johnson, A. C., and Henry Bartlett van Hoesen
1931   *Papyri in the Princeton University Collections.* Nos. 1–14. Baltimore: Johns Hopkins.

Johnson, A. C., and Louis C. West
1949   *Byzantine Egypt: Economic Studies.* Princeton University Studies in Papyrology, 6. Princeton: Princeton University.

Johnson, Sherman Elbridge
1958   "Early Christianity in Asia Minor." *JBL* 77:1–17.

Johnson, Norman Burrows
1948   *Prayer in the Apocrypha and Pseudepigrapha: A Study of the Jewish Concept of God. JBL* Monograph, 2. Philadelphia: SBL.

Johnston, Patricia A.
1977   "Eurydice and Proserpina in the *Georgics." TAPA* 107:161–72.

Jones, Fleming
1940   Review of *From the Stone Age to Christianity,* by William F. Albright. *JBL* 60:189.

Kadletz, Edward
1978   "The Cult of Apollo Deiradiotes." *TAPA* 108:93–101.

Kallas, James
1970   Review of *I Saw a New Earth: An Introduction to the Visions of the Apocalypse,* by Paul S. Minear. *JBL* 89:510–11.

Karris, Robert J.
1973   "The Background and Significance of the Polemic of the Pastoral Epistles." *JBL* 92:549–64.

Kee, Howard Clark
1958   Review of *The Death of Christ,* by John Knox. *JBL* 77:165–68.

Kennedy, George A.
1980   *Classical Rhetoric and Its Christian and Secular Tradition from Ancient to Modern Times.* Chapel Hill: University of North Carolina.

Kelsey, Francis Willey
1908   "Is there a Science of Classical Philology?" *CP* 3:369–85.

1911   Edition of *Latin and Greek in American Education with Symposia on the Value of Humanistic Studies.* New York: Macmillan.

Kent, John Harvey
1966   *Corinth: Results of Excavations Conducted by the American School of Classical Studies at Athens.* Vol. 8, pt. 3. *The Inscriptions 1926–1950.* Princeton, NJ: ASCSA.

Kent, Roland G.
1932   Review of *Greek Grammar,* by William Watson Goodwin, rev. ed. by Charles Burton Gulick. *CJ* 27:381–84.

Keyes, Clinton W.
1935   "The Greek Letter of Introduction." *AJP* 56:18–44.

Kim, Chan-Hie
1972   *Form and Structure of the Familiar Greek Letter of Recommendation.* SBLDS, 4. Missoula: Scholars Press.

Kingsbury, Jack Dean
1983   *The Christology of Mark's Gospel.* Philadelphia: Fortress.

Kittredge, George Lyman
1903   "James Bradstreet Greenough." *HSCP* 14:1–16.

Klein, Ralph Walter
1974   *Textual Criticism of the Old Testament. The Septuagint after Qumran.* Philadelphia: Fortress.

Kleist, James Aloysius
1902   *A Short Grammar of Classical Greek, With Tables for Repetition, an Authorized English Edition for High Schools, Academies, and Colleges.* St. Louis: B. Herder.

1936   *The Gospel of Saint Mark, Presented in Greek Thought-units and Sense Lines, with a Commentary.* Milwaukee: Bruce.

Knapp, Charles
1928   "Scholarship." *CW* 21 (Monday, January 9):81–84.

Koester, Helmut
1962   Review of *A Theological and Historical Introduction to the Apostolic Fathers,* by John Lawson. *JBL* 81:416–19.

1965   "Paul and Hellenism." In *Bible in Modern Scholarship*:187–95.

Kolenkow, Anitra Bingham
1980   "Relationships between Miracle and Prophecy in the Graeco-Roman World and Early Christianity." *ANRW* 11, 23/2:1470–1506.

Kraeling, Carl Herman, ed.
1938   *Gerasa, City of the Decapolis: An Account Embodying the Record of a Joint Excavation Conducted by Yale University and the British School of Archaeology in Jerusalem (1928–1930), and Yale University and the American Schools of Oriental Research (1930–1931, 1933–1934).* New Haven: ASOR.

Kraemer, Casper John, Jr.
1930   Review of *Light from the Ancient East,* by Adolf Deissmann. *CW* 23:140–42.

Kraft, Robert Alan, ed.
1972   *Septuagintal Lexicography.* Septuagint and Cognate Studies, 1. Missoula: SBL.

Krentz, Edgar Martin
1975   *The Historical-Critical Method.* Philadelphia: Fortress.

Kresic, Stephan
1981   "Editor's Introduction." In *Contemporary Literary Hermeneutics,* ed. by Stephan Kresic, 1–11. Ottawa: Ottawa University.

Krodel, Gerhard
1971   "Persecution and Toleration of Christianity Until Hadrian." In *Catacombs and the Colosseum:*255–67.

Kubo, Sakae
1975   *A Reader's Greek-English Lexicon of the New Testament and a Beginner's Guide for the Translation of New Testament Greek.* Andrews University Monographs, 4. Grand Rapids: Zondervan.

1979   *A Beginner's New Testament Greek Grammar.* Washington DC: Washington University Press of America.

Laistner, Max Ludwig Wolfram
1951   *Christianity and Pagan Culture in the Later Roman Empire, together with an English Translation of John Chrysostom's "Address on Vainglory and the Right Way for Parents to Bring up Their Children."* Ithaca: Cornell University.

Lake, Kirsopp, and Henry Joel Cadbury, eds.
1933   "Additional Notes to the Commentary." In *The Beginnings of Christianity.* Pt. 1 vol. 5, *The Acts of the Apostles.* London: Macmillan.

Lane, George Martin
1859   "Latin Lexicography." *Bibliotheca Sacra* 16:139–67.

Lane, G. M., and Morris Hicky Morgan
1898   *A Latin Grammar for Schools and Colleges*. New York: Harper.

Lang, Mabel Louise
1977   *Cure and Cult in Ancient Corinth, A Guide to the Asklepieion*. Princeton: ASCSA.

1984   *Herodotean Narrative and Discourse*. Cambridge: Harvard University.

Lange, Stella
1936   "The Wisdom of Solomon and Plato." *JBL* 55:293–302.

Larsen, Jakob Aall Ottesen
1938   "Roman Greece." *In* Frank, 1933–40, 4:259–498.

1957   "Lycia and Greek Federal Citizenship." *Symbolae Osloenses* 33:5–26.

Larson, Curtis W.
1946   "Prayer of Petition in Philo." *JBL* 65:185–203.

La Sor, Sanford, Peter Hintzoglou, and Eric H. Jacobsen
1973   *Handbook of New Testament Greek: An Inductive Approach Based on the Greek Text of Acts*. 2 vols. Grand Rapids: Eerdmans.

Lateiner, Donald
1977   "No Laughing Matter: A Literary Tactic in Herodotus." *TAPA* 107:173–82.

Latin and Greek in American Education
1911   *Latin and Greek in American Education, With Symposia on the Value of Humanistic Studies*, ed. by Francis W. Kelsey. New York: Macmillan.

Lattimore, Richmond
[1942] 1962   *Themes in Greek and Latin Epitaphs*. Illinois Studies in Language and Literature, 28/1–2. Urbana: University of Illinois. Reprinted by the same press, 1962.

Laubenstein, Paul F.
1932   "An Apocalyptic Reincarnation." *JBL* 51:238–52.

Lawton, William Cranston
1891   "Gildersleeve's Essays and Studies." *Atlantic Monthly* 67 (May):700–6.

Lebeck, Anne
1965   *Image and Idea in "Agamemnon" of Aeschylus,* Dissertation,
            Columbia University, 1963. (Published in 1971 under the title
            The Oresteia: A Study in Language and Structure [Washington
            DC: The Center for Hellenic Studies].)

Lee, J. A. L.
1983   *A Lexical Study of the Septuagint Version of the Pentateuch.*
            SBLSCS, 14. Chico: Scholars Press.

Lefkowitz, Mary R., and Maureen B. Fant
1977   *Women in Greece and Rome.* Toronto: Samuel-Stevens.

1982   *Women's Life in Greece and Rome.* Baltimore: John Hopkins
            University.

Leon, Harry Joshua
1939   "Morituri te Salutamus." *TAPA* 70:46–50.

1960   *The Jews of Ancient Rome.* Philadelphia: Jewish Publication
            Society of America.

Levien, Roger Eli
1972   *The Emerging Technology: Instructional Uses of the Computer
            in Higher Education.* New York: McGraw-Hill.

Levy, Charles S.
1963   "Antigone's Motives: A Suggested Interpretation." *TAPA*
            94:137–44.

Levy, Felix A.
1947   "Contemporary Trends in Jewish Bible Study." In *Study of the
            Bible Today and Tomorrow,* ed. by Harold R. Willoughby,
            98–115. Chicago: University of Chicago.

Lewis, Charlton Thomas
1888   *A Latin Dictionary for Schools.* New York: American Book Co.

Lewis, Charlton Thomas, and Charles Lancaster Short, eds.
1879   *Harper's Latin Dictionary, A New Latin Dictionary.* Founded
            on the translation of Freund's Latin-German Lexicon, ed. by
            Ethan Allen Andrews. "Revised, enlarged, and in great part
            rewritten." New York: American Book Co.

Lewis, Naphtali
1968   *Inventory of Compulsory Services in Ptolemaic and Roman
            Egypt. ASP,* 3. New Haven: ASP.

Liddell, Mark H.
1898   "Botching   Shakespeare."   *Atlantic   Monthly   82*
            (October):461–72.

Lieberman, Saul
1942   *Greek in Jewish Palestine: Studies in the Life and Manners of Jewish Palestine in the II-IV Centuries C. E.* New York: Jewish Theological Seminary of America.

1950   *Hellenism in Jewish Palestine: Studies in the Literary Transmission, Beliefs and Manners of Palestine in the I Century B.C.E.-IV Century C.E.* Texts and Studies of the Jewish Theological Seminary of America, 18. New York: Jewish Theological Seminary of America.

Lindsay, Wallace Martin
1897   *Handbook of Latin Inscriptions Illustrating the History of the Language.* Boston: Allyn and Bacon.

Lind, Levi Robert
1972   "Concept, Action, and Character: The Reasons for Rome's Greatness." *TAPA* 103:235–83.

Loeb, *Philo*
1929–62 *Philo: Greek Text with Translation,* ed. by Francis Henry Colson, George Herbert Whitaker, and Ralph Marcus. 12 vols. "Loeb Classical Library." London: Heinemann.

Longfellow, William Pitt Preble
1885   Review of *Papers of the American School of Classical Studies at Athens,* 1 (1885). *AJA* 1:202–6.

Lord, Albert Bates
1951   "Composition by Theme in Homer and Southslavic Epos." *TAPA* 82:71–80.

Lord, Louis Eleazar
1947   *A History of the American School of Classical Studies at Athens, 1882–1942, An Intercollegiate Project.* Cambridge: Harvard University.

Louw, J. P.
1982   *Semantics of New Testament Greek.* Chico: Scholars Press. (Originally written in Afrikaans, in 1973, and first published in 1976 in an Afrikaans edition.)

Lund, Nils W.
1931   "The Literary Structure of Paul's Hymn to Love." *JBL* 50:266–76.

Lyman, Mary Ely
1930   "Hermetic Religion and the Religion of the Fourth Gospel." *JBL* 49:265–76.

Lynd, Albert
    1950   *Quackery in the Public Schools.* Boston: Little, Brown.

Machen, John Gresham
    1923   *New Testament Greek for Beginners.* New York: Macmillan.

MacKay, Louis Alexander
    1955   "Three Levels of Meaning in *Aeneid* VI." *TAPA* 86:180–89.

    1963   "Hero and Theme in the *Aeneid.*" *TAPA* 94:157–66.

Mackenzie, William Douglas
    1911   "The Place of Greek and Latin in the Preparation for the
                Ministry." In Kelsey, 1911:Symposium 4, no. 1, pp. 154–70.
                New York: Macmillan.

Mack, Sara
    1978   *Patterns of Time in Vergil.* Hamden, CT: Archon Books.

MacMullen, Ramsay
    1981   *Paganism in the Roman Empire.* New Haven: Yale University.

Macurdy, Grace Harriet
    1910   "Traces of the Influence of Plato's Eschatological Myths in
                Parts of the Book of Revelation and the Book of Enoch." *TAPA*
                41:65–70.

Magie, David
    1905   *De Romanorum iuris publici sacrique vocabulis sollemnibus in
                Graecum sermonem conversis.* Teubner: Leipzig.

    1950   *Roman Rule in Asia Minor to the End of the Third Century
                after Christ.* 2 vols. Princeton: Princeton University.

Malherbe, Abraham Johannes
    1968   "The Beasts at Ephesus." *JBL* 87:71–80.

    1977a   Review of *Faith and Human Reason,* by Dieter W. Kemmler.
                JBL 96:149–50.

    1977b   *Social Aspects of Early Christianity.* Rockwell Lectures at
                Rice University, April, 1975. Baton Rouge: Louisiana State
                University.
    1978   Review of *Teles (The Cynic Teacher),* by Edward O'Neil. *JBL*
                97:599–600.

Malina, Bruce J.
    1978   "What are the Humanities: A Perspective for the Scientific
                American." In *The Humanities and the Public Life,* ed. by
                William L. Blizek, 33–47. Lincoln, NE: Pied Publications.

    1981   *The New Testament World: Insights from Cultural Anthro-
                pology.* Atlanta: John Knox.

1982   "The Social Sciences and Biblical Interpretation." *Interpretation* 36:229–42.

Mantey, Julius Robert
1951   "The Causal Use of *eis* in the New Testament." *JBL* 70:45–48.

Marcus, Ralph
1946–47   "Selected Bibliography (1920–1945) of the Jews in the Hellenistic-Roman Period." In *Proceedings of the American Academy for Jewish Research,* 16:97–181.

1951   "On Causal *eis.*" *JBL* 70:129–30.

Marcus, Ralph, and Henry St. John Thackeray
1930–55   *A Lexicon to Flavius Josephus.* Parts 1–4. Paris: P. Geuthner.

Margolis, Max Leopold
1923   "Our Own Future: A Forecast and a Programme." *JBL* 42:1–8.

Mason, Hugh John
1974   *Greek Terms for Roman Institutions: A Lexicon and Analysis.* American Studies in Papyrology, 13. Toronto: Hakkert.

1979   "Longus and the Topography of Lesbos." *TAPA* 109:149–63.

Mathisen, Ralph W.
1981   "Epistolography, Literary Circles and Family Ties in Late Roman Gaul." *TAPA* 111:95–109.

Mayer, Herbert T.
1979   *Pastoral Care: Its Roots and Renewal.* Atlanta: John Knox.

McCarren, Vincent Paul, and William Tajibnapis
1977   *A Critical Concordance to Catullus.* Leiden: Brill.

McCasland, Selby Vernon
1932   "Portents in Josephus and in the Gospels." *JBL* 51:323–35.

1939   "The Asklepios Cult in Palestine." *JBL* 58:221–27.

1951   *By the Finger of God: Demon Possession and Exorcism in Early Christianity in the Light of Modern Views of Mental Illness.* New York: Macmillan.

1953   Review of *A Study in St. Mark,* by Austin Farrer. *JBL* 72:200–2.

1954   "The Unity of the Scriptures." *JBL* 73:1–10.

1957   "Signs and Wonders." *JBL* 76:149–52.

McClees, Helen
1920   *A Study of Women in Attic Inscriptions.* New York: Columbia University.

McCown, Chester Charlton
1956   "The Current Plight of Biblical Scholarship." *JBL* 75:12–18.

McDonough, James T., Jr.
1967   "Computers and the Classics." *Computers and the Humanities*
            2:37–40.

McGaughy, Lane C.
1972   *Toward a Descriptive Analysis of "Einai" as a Linking Verb in*
            New Testament Greek. SBLDS, 6. Missoula: Scholars Press.

McGiffert, Arthur Cushman
1909   "The Influence of Christianity upon the Roman Empire."
            HTR 2:28–49.

McKeon, Richard Peter
1936   "Literary Criticism and the Concept of Imitation in Antiq-
            uity." *Modern Philology* 34:1–35.

1943–44   "The Philosophic Bases of Art and Criticism." *Modern*
            Philology 41:65–87, 129–71.

1982   "Criticism and the Liberal Arts: The Chicago School of
            Criticism." *Profession 82* (Modern Language Association of
            America), 1–18. (A briefer form of this paper was presented
            in 1982 at the Association of Departments of English
            Seminar at Northern Illinois University.)

McKinlay, Arthur Patch
1939   "The 'Indulgent' Dionysius." *TAPA* 70:51–61.

McNamee, Kathleen
1981   *Abbreviations in Greek Literary Papyri and Ostraca.* Bulletin
            of the Society of Papyrologists; Supplements, 3. Chico:
            Scholars Press.

Meeks, Wayne Atherton
1981   Review of *Biblical Affirmations of Woman,* by Leonard
            Swidler. *JBL* 100:466–67.

1983   *The First Urban Christians: The Social World of the Apostle*
            Paul. New Haven: Yale University.

Meritt, Benjamin Dean
1931   *Corinth: Results of Excavations Conducted by the American*
            School of Classical Studies at Athens. Vol. 8, pt. 1. *Greek*
            Inscriptions 1896–1927. Cambridge: Harvard University.

1932   *Athenian Financial Documents of the Fifth Century.* Univer-
            sity of Michigan Studies, Humanistic Series, 27. Ann Arbor:
            University of Michigan.

1933   "The Inscriptions." *Hesperia* 2:149–69.

1937   *Documents on Athenian Tribute.* Cambridge: Harvard
            University.

1940   *Epigraphica Attica*. Martin Classical Lectures, 9. Cambridge: Harvard University.

1962   *Greek Historical Studies, Lectures in Memory of Louise Semple Taft*. Cincinnati: University of Cincinnati.

1964   "Athenian Calendar Problems." *TAPA* 95:200–60.

Meritt, B. D., and Allen Brown West
1934   *The Athenian Assessment of 425 B.C.* Michigan Humanistic Series, 33. Ann Arbor: University of Michigan.

Meritt, B. D., Henry Theodore Wade-Gery, and Malcolm Francis McGregor
1939–53   *The Athenian Tribute Lists*. Vol. 1, Cambridge: Harvard University, 1939; vol. 2, Princeton: American School of Classical Studies, 1949; vol. 3, Princeton: Princeton University, 1950; vol. 4, Princeton: ASCSA, 1953.

Meritt, B. D., and William Kendrick Pritchett
1940   *The Chronology of Hellenistic Athens*. Cambridge: Harvard University.

Meritt, Lucy Shoe
1984   *A History of the American School of Classical Studies at Athens*. Vol. 2. *1939–1980*. Princeton: ASCSA.

Merriam, Augustus C.
1883   "The Caesareum and the Worship of Augustus at Alexandria." *TAPA* 14:5–35.

Merrill, Elmer Truesdell
1919   "The Church in the Fourth Century." *TAPA* 50:101–21.

Metzger, Bruce M.
1946   *Lexical Aids for Students of New Testament Greek*. Princeton: B. M. Metzger.

1964   Review of *A Mandaic Dictionary*, by Ethel S. Drower, and Rudolf Macuch. *JBL* 83:330–31.

Michels, Agnes Kirsopp Lake
1955   "Death and Two Poets." *TAPA* 86:160–79.

Miller, Andrew M.
1981   "Pindar, Archilochus and Hieron in *P.* 2.52–56." *TAPA* 111:135–43.

Miller, Charles William Emil
1925   "Addresses in Memory of Professor Gildersleeve." *PAPA* 56:xxviii-xxxii.

Minear, Paul Sevier
1941   *And Great Shall be Your Reward: The Origins of Christian Views of Salvation.* Yale Studies in Religion, 12. New Haven: Yale University.

1942   "The Needle's Eye: A Study in Form Criticism." *JBL* 61:157–69.

1965   Review of *The Anchor Bible: The Epistles of James, Peter, and Jude,* by Bo Reicke. *JBL* 84:181–84.

1968   *I Saw a New Earth: An Introduction to the Visions of the Apocalypse.* Washington, DC: Corpus Books.

Mitchell, Lynn Boal
1908   "On Book Reviews." *CJ* 3:230–31.

Mitchell, Stephen
1979   "Iconium and Ninica: Two Double Communities in Roman Asia Minor." *Historia* 28:409–35. Appendix, 435–38.

Moir, John S.
1982   *A History of Biblical Studies in Canada: A Sense of Proportion.* SBL, Biblical Scholarship in North America, 7. Chico: Scholars Press.

Montgomery, James Alan
1919   "Present Tasks of American Biblical Scholarship." *JBL* 38:1–14.

1926   "The Education of the Seer of the Apocalypse." *JBL* 45:70–80.

1937   "Aesthetic in Hebrew Religion." *JBL* 56:35–41.

Moore, Clifford Herschel
1911   Review of *Die hellenistische Mysterienreligionen,* by R. Reitzenstein. *CP* 6:509–511.

1912   "Editorial: William Watson Goodwin." *CJ* 8:1–4.

1919   "The Pagan Reaction in the Late Fourth Century." *TAPA* 50:122–34.

1920   "Life in the Roman Empire at the Beginning of the Christian Era." In *Beginnings* 1:218–62.

Moore, Frank Gardner
1919   "A History of the American Philological Association." *TAPA* 50:5–32.

Moore, George Foot
1905   "*Symphonia* not a Bagpipe." *JBL* 24:166–78.

1927–30   *Judaism in the First Centuries of the Christian Era: The Age of the Tannaim.* 3 vols. Cambridge: Harvard University.

Morgenstern, Julian
1942 "The Society of Biblical Literature and Exegesis." *JBL* 61:1–10.

Mosley, Derek J.
1965 "The Size of Embassies in Ancient Greek Diplomacy." *TAPA* 96:255–66.

Mott Charles
1971 *The Greek Benefactor and Deliverance from Moral Distress.* Dissertation, Harvard University.

Moulton, Warren J.
1903 "Inscriptions from Bir es-Seba." *JBL* 22:195–200.

Mountford, James Frederick, and Joseph Theodore Schultz
1930 *Index Rerum et nominum in scholiis Servii et Aelii Donati tractatorum.* Ithaca: Cornell University.

Mowry, Lucetta
1952 "Revelation 4–5 and Early Christian Liturgical Usage." *JBL* 71:75–84.

Muilenberg, James
1932 "Literary Form in the Fourth Gospel." *JBL* 51:40–53.

Mullins, Terence Y.
1968 "Greeting as a New Testament Form." *JBL* 87:418–26.

1980 "Topos as a New Testament Form." *JBL* 99:541–47.

Murley, Joseph Clyde
1930 "Plato and the New Testament: Parallels." *Anglican Theological Review* 12:438–42.

1937 "The Structure and Proportion of Catullus LXIV." *TAPA* 68:305–17.

Murphy-O'Connor, Jerome
1983 *St. Paul's Corinth: Texts and Archaeology.* Wilmington, DE: Michael Glazier.

Murray, Michael
1981 "The New Hermeneutic and the Interpretation of Poetry." In *Contemporary Literary Hermeneutics,* 1981:53–73.

Mussies, G.
1976 "Greek in Palestine and the Diaspora." In *Jewish People* 1976, 2:1040–64.

Muss-Arnolt, William
1892 "On Semitic Words in Greek and Latin." *TAPA* 23:35–156. (Indexes of Greek and Latin words, pp. 151–56.)

Nash, Henry S.
1892   "The Exegesis of the School of Antioch: A Criticism of the
            Hypothesis that Aristotelianism was a Main Cause in its
            Genesis." *JBL* 11:22–37.

1899   *"Theiotēs-Theotēs,* Rom. 1:20; Col. 2:9." *JBL* 18:1–34.

1902   "The Idea of the Logos in Relation to the Need of Law in the
            Apostolic Age." *JBL* 21:170–87.

Nassen, Paula J.
1975   "A Literary Study of Pindar's *Olympian* 10." *TAPA* 105:219–40.

Nelson, Carroll A.
1979   *Status Declarations in Roman Egypt. ASP,* 19. Amsterdam:
            Hakkert.

Neusner, Jacob, ed.
1968   *Religions in Antiquity: Essays in Memory of Erwin Ramsdell
            Goodenough.* Leiden: Brill.

Neyrey, Jerome H.
1980   "The Form and Background of the Polemic in 2 Peter." *JBL*
            99:407–31.

Nickelsburg, George, Jr.
1972   *Resurrection, Immortality, and Eternal Life in Intertestamen-
            tal Judaism.* Harvard Theological Studies, 26. Cambridge:
            Harvard University.

1984   "Stories of Biblical and Early Post-Biblical Times," pp. 33–88;
            "The Bible Rewritten and Expanded," pp. 89–156. In *Jewish
            Writings,* 1984.

Nida, Eugene Albert
1964   *Toward a Science of Translating.* Leiden: Brill.

1969   *The Theory and Practice of Translating.* Leiden: Brill, for the
            United Bible Societies.

1972   "Implications of Contemporary Linguistics for Biblical
            Scholarship." *JBL* 91:73–89.

1974   *On Language, Culture, and Religion: In Honor of Eugene A.
            Nida,* ed. by Matthew Black and William A. Smalley.
            Approaches to Semiotics, 56. The Hague: Mouton. (List of
            Nida's publications, xxi-xxvii).

1975   *Language Structure and Translation: Essays by Eugene A.
            Nida.* Stanford: Stanford University.

Nock, Arthur Darby
1925   "Diatribe Form in the Hermetica." *The Journal of Egyptian
            Archaeology* 11:126–37.

1933a   "The Vocabulary of the New Testament." *JBL* 52:131–39.

1933b   *Conversion: The Old and the New in Religion from Alexander the Great to Augustine of Hippo.* Oxford: Oxford University.

1938   *St. Paul.* New York: Harper.

1941   Review of *Maledictions et Violations de Tombes,* by Andre Parrot. *JBL* 60:88–95.

1944   "The Cult of Heroes." *HTR* 37:141–74.

1955   Review of *Jewish Symbols in the Graeco-Roman Period,* vols. 1–4, by Erwin R Goodenough. *Gnomon* 27:558–72.

1957   Review of *Jewish Symbols in the Graeco-Roman Period,* vols. 5–6. by Erwin R. Goodenough. *Gnomon* 29:524–33.

1960   Review of *Jewish Symbols in the Graeco-Roman Period,* vols. 7–8, by Erwin R. Goodenough. *Gnomon* 32:728–36.

1964   *Early Gentile Christianity and its Hellenistic Background.* New York: Harper.

Nock, A. D., and Andre Marie Jean Festugiere eds.
1946–54   *Corpus Hermeticum.* 4 vols. Paris: Societe d'Edition.

Norlin, George
1934   "Paul Shorey—the Teacher." *CP* 29:188–91.

Nortwick, Thomas van
1979   "Penelope and Nausicaa." *TAPA* 109:63–85.

Notopoulos, James A.
1949   "Parataxis in Homer: A New Approach to Homeric Literary Criticism." *TAPA* 80:1–23.

Nott, J. W.
1888   "Egēgertai in 1 Cor. XV." *JBL* 8:41–42.

O'Brien, Peter Thomas
1979   *Introductory Thanksgivings in the Letters of Paul.* Novum Testamentum Supplements, 49. Leiden: Brill.

Ogle, Marbury Bladen
1928   "The Discovery of the Wonder Child." *TAPA* 59:179–204.

Olcott, George N.
1904–12   *Thesaurus linguae latinae epigraphicae: A Dictionary of the Latin Inscriptions.* Fascicles 1–22. "A-Asturia." Rome: Loescher.

1935   *Thesaurus Linguae Latinae Epigraphicae: The Olcott Dictionary of the Latin Inscriptions.* Vol. 2 ed. by Leslie F. Smith and John H. McLean. New York: Columbia University.

Oldfather, William Abbott
  1937   "Suggestions for Guidance in the Preparation of a Critical
              Index verborum for Latin and Greek Authors." *TAPA* 68:1–10.

Oldfather, W. A., Arthur Stanley Pease, and Howard Vernon Canter
  1918   *Index verborum quae in Senecae Fabulis necnon in Octavia
              praetexta reperiuntur.* University of Illinois Studies in
              Language and Literature 4, no. 2. Urbana: University of
              Illinois.

Oldfather, W. A., and Lloyd William Daly
  1932   "A Quotation from Menander in the Pastoral Epistles?" *CP*
              38:202–4.

Oldfather, W. A., and Kenneth Morgan Abbott, with the assistance of "other
friends and former students."
  1934   *Index Apuleianus.* Philological Monographs, 3. Middletown:
              APA. (Howard Vernon Canter and Ben Edwin Perry joined
              Oldfather in the task of editing the assemblage of data).

Oldfather, W. A., K. M. Abbott, and H. V. Canter
  1938   *Index verborum Ciceronis Epistularum.* Urbana: University of
              Illinois.

Oldfather, W. A., K. M. Abbott, and H. V. Canter
  1964   *Index verborum in Ciceronis Rhetorica necnon incerti auctoris
              libros ad Herennium.* Urbana: University of Illinois.

Oliver, James Henry
  1933   Selected Greek Inscriptions." *Hesperia* 2:480–513.

  1936   "The Monument with the Marathon Epigrams." *Hesperia*
              5:225–34.

Omeltchenko, Stephen William
  1977   *A Quantitative and Comparative Study of the Vocalism of the
              Latin Inscriptions of North Africa, Britain, Dalmatia, and the
              Balkans.* North Carolina Studies in the Romance Languages
              and Literatures, 180. Chapel Hill: University of North
              Carolina.

O'Neil, Edward Noon
  1963   *A Critical Concordance of the Tibullan Corpus.* APA
              Philological Monograph, 21. New York: APA.

  1977   *Teles (The Cynic Teacher).* Missoula: Scholars Press.

Orlinsky, Harry
  1944   "The Hebrew Root *SKB*." *JBL* 63:19–44.

  1971   "Whither Biblical Research?" *JBL* 90:1–14.

O'Rourke, John D.
1965   Review of *De conceptu "HYPOMONE" apud S. Paulum,* by Pius Goicoechea. *JBL* 84:469–70.

Owen, William Bishop and Edgar Johnson Goodspeed
1906   *Homeric Vocabularies: Greek and English Word-Lists for the Study of Homer.* Chicago: University of Chicago.

Owen, William H.
1968   "Commonplace and Dramatic Symbol in Seneca's Tragedies." *TAPA* 99:291–313.

Pack, Roger Ambrose
1955   "Artemidorus and His Waking World." *TAPA* 86:280–90.

Packard, David W.
1968–69   *A Concordance to Livy.* 4 vols. Cambridge: Harvard University.

Palmer, Richard
1981   "Allegorical, Philological, and Philosophical Hermeneutics: Three Modes in a Complex Heritage." In *Contemporary Literary Hermeneutics* 1981:15–37.

Panin, Ivan
1914   *The New Testament from the Greek Text as Established by Bible Numerics.* 2d ed. 1935. Toronto: Book Society of Canada.

Parassoglou, George M.
1978   *Imperial Estates in Roman Egypt.* ASP 18. Amsterdam: Hakkert.

Parker, S. Thomas
1975   "The Decapolis Reviewed." *JBL* 94:437–41.

Parry, Milman
1928   "The Homeric Gloss: A Study in Word-Sense." *TAPA* 5:233–47.

Paton, James Morton, ed.
1927   *The Erechtheum.* Measured, Drawn, and Restored by Gorham Philip Stevens. Text by Lacey Davis Caskey, Harold North Fowler, Paton, and Stevens. Cambridge: Harvard University.

Patte, Daniel
1976   *What is Structural Exegesis?* Philadelphia: Fortress.

Patton, Peter C., and Renee A. Holoien, eds.
1981   *Computing in the Humanities.* Lexington: Heath.

PCair.Isid.
1960   *The Archive of Aurelius Isidorus in the Egyptian Museum, Cairo, and the University of Michigan (PCair Isidor.),* ed. by Arthur Edward Romilly Boak and Herbert Chayyim Youtie. Ann Arbor: University of Michigan.

P.Col.I (= PCol. Inv. 480). *See* Westermann, 1929.

PCol.II (1R)
1932   *Tax Lists and Transportation Receipts from Theadelphia,* No. 1 recto a and b, ed. by William Linn Westermann and Clinton Walker Keyes. Columbia Papyri, Greek Series, 2. New York: Columbia University.

PCol.III (= Zen.I)
1934   *Zenon Papyri, Business Papers of the Third Century B.C. Dealing with Palestine and Egypt,* ed. by William Linn Westermann and Elizabeth Sayre Hasenoehrl. Vol. 1. Columbia Papyri, Greek Series, 3. New York: Columbia University.

PCol.V (IV)
1956   *Tax Documents from Theadelphia: Papyri of the Second Century A.D.,* No. 1, verso b and a; ed. by John Day and Clinton Walker Keyes. Columbia Papyri, Greek Series, 5. New York: Columbia University.

PCol.VI (= PCol.123)
1954   See Westermann, 1954,

PCol.VII
1979   *Columbia Papyri VII: Fourth Century Documents from Karanis,* transcribed by Roger S. Bagnall and Naphtali Lewis; ed. with translation and commentary by Bagnall. *ASP,* 20. Missoula: Scholars Press.

PCorn.
1926   *Greek Papyri in the Library of Cornell University,* ed. by William Linn Westermann, and Casper J. Kraemer, Jr. New York: Columbia University.

Pearson, Lionel
1954   "The Diary and the Letters of Alexander the Great." *Historia* 3:429–55.

Pease, Arthur Stanley
1919   "The Attitude of Jerome Towards Pagan Literature." *TAPA* 50:150–67.
1945   "William Abbott Oldfather." *PAPA* 76:xxiv-xxvi.

Perkell, Christine Godfrey
1981   "On the Corycian Gardener of Vergil's Fourth *Georgic*." *TAPA* 111:167–77.

Perrin, Bernadotte
1895   "Genesis and Growth of an Alexander-Myth." *TAPA* 26:56–68.

Perry, Ben Edwin
1926   "An Interpretation of Apuleius' *Metamorphoses*." *TAPA* 57:238–60.

1937   "The Early Greek Capacity for Viewing Things Separately." *TAPA* 68:403–27.

1940   "The Origin of Epimythium." *TAPA* 71:391–419.

Peters, John P.
1916   "Ritual in the Psalms." *JBL* 35:143–54.

Petersen, Norman Richard
1978   *Literary Criticism for New Testament Critics*. Philadelphia: Fortress.

Pfeiffer, Robert Henry
1937   "Hebrews and Greeks before Alexander." *JBL* 56:91–101.

1949   *History of New Testament Times, With an Introduction to the Apocrypha*. New York: Harper.

1951   "Facts and Faith in Biblical History." *JBL* 70:1–14.

Pharr, Clyde
1932   "The Interdiction of Magic in Roman Law." *TAPA* 63:269–95.

Pietersma, Albert
1977   *Chester Beatty Biblical Papyri IV and V: A New Edition with Text-Critical Analysis*. ASP, 16. Toronto: Hakkert.

Pleket, H. W.
1965   "An Aspect of the Emperor Cult: Imperial Mysteries." *HTR* 58:331–47.

PMich.I. See *PMich.Zen*. 1931.

PMich.II.
1933   *Papyri from Tebtunis*. Michigan Papyri II, Nos. 121–128, Pt. 1, ed. by Arthur Edward Romilly Boak. University of Michigan Studies, Humanistic Series, 28. Ann Arbor: University of Michigan.

PMich.III.
1936   *Papyri in the University of Michigan Collection: Miscellaneous Papyri*. Michigan Papyri III, Nos. 131–221, ed. by John Garrett Winter et al. University of Michigan Studies, Humanistic Series, 40. Ann Arbor: University of Michigan.

PMich.V.
1944   *Papyri from Tebtunis,* Nos. 226–356, Pt. 2, ed. by Elinor M. Husselman, Arthur Boak, and William F. Edgerton. University of Michigan Studies, Humanistic Series, 29. Ann Arbor: University of Michigan.

PMich.VII.
1947   *Latin Papyri in the University of Michigan Collection,* Nos. 167–168, 429–463, ed. by Henry A. Sanders, with contributions by James F. Dunlap. University of Michigan Studies, Humanistic Series 48. Ann Arbor: University of Michigan.

PMich.VIII.
1951   *Papyri and Ostraca from Karanis,* Nos. 464–521; ostraca, Nos. 972–1111, ed. by Herbert Chayyim Youtie and John Garrett Winter. Second Series. Michigan Papyri VIII. University of Michigan Studies, Humanistic Series, 50. Ann Arbor: University of Michigan.

PMich.IX.
1971   *Papyri From Karanis,* Nos. 522–576, ed. by Elinor Mullett Husselman. Third Series. APA Monograph, 29. Cleveland: Case Western Reserve University, for APA.

PMich.XIV
1980   *Michigan Papyri XIV,* Nos. 675–684 ed. by Vincent P. McCarren. *ASP,* 22. Chico: Scholars Press.

PMich.Zen.
1931   *Zenon Papyri in the University of Michigan Collection.* Michigan Papyri I, Nos. 1–120, ed. by Campbell Cowan Edgar. University of Michigan Studies, Humanistic Series, 24. Ann Arbor: University of Michigan.

P.NYU.
1967   *Greek Papyri in the Collection of New York University. I. Fourth Century Documents from Karanis,* ed. by Naphtali Lewis. Leiden: Brill.

Poe, Edgar Allan
[1850] 1940 "The Poetic Principle." *In* Foerster, 1940:1–28.

Polacek, Adalbert
1981   "Holocaust, Two Millennia Ago." In *Proceedings of the XVI International Congress of Papyrology, New York, 24–31 July 1980,* 699–706 = *ASP,* 23. Chico: Scholars Press.

Pomeroy, Sarah B.
1975   *Goddesses, Whores, Wives, and Slaves: Women in Classical Antiquity.* New York: Schocken.

Pope, Marvin
  1963   Review of *The Wycliffe Bible Commentary*, ed. by Charles F. Pfeiffer (OT) and Everett F. Harrison (NT). *JBL* 82:129–30.

Pope, Marvin
  1964   Review of *Before the Bible*, by Cyrus H. Gordon. *JBL* 83:72–76.

Porter, Frank Chamberlin
  1908   "The Pre-existence of the Soul in the Book of Wisdom and in the Rabbinical Writings." In *Old Testament and Semitic Studies in Memory of W. R. Harper*, 1:207–69. Chicago: University of Chicago.

  1929   "The Problem of Things New and Old in the Beginnings of Christianity." *JBL* 48:1–23.

Porter, Noah
  1870   "The New Criticism." *The New Englander* 29:195–316.

Post, Levi Arnold
  1939   "The Moral Pattern in Homer." *TAPA* 70:158–90.

  1960   "Virtue Promoted in Menander's Dyscolus." *TAPA* 91:152–61.

Poultney, James Wilson
  1959   *The Bronze Tables of Iguvium*. Philological Monographs, 18. Baltimore: APA.

PPrinc.I.
  1931   *Papyri in the Princeton University Collections*. Vol. 1, Nos. 1–14, ed. by Allan Chester Johnson and Henry Bartlett van Hoesen. Johns Hopkins University Studies in Archaeology, 10. Baltimore: Johns Hopkins.

PPrinc.II.
  1936   *Papyri in the Princeton University Collection*. Vol. 2, Nos. 15–107, ed. by Edmund Harris Kase. Princeton University Studies in Papyrology 1. Princeton: Princeton University.

PPrinc.III
  1942   *Papyri in the Princeton University Collections*. Vol. 3, Nos. 108–191, ed. by Allan Chester Johnson and Sidney Pullman Goodrich. Princeton University Studies in Papyrology, 4. Princeton: Princeton University.

PPrinc.Scheide
  1938   *The John H. Scheide Biblical Papyri: Ezekiel*, ed. Allan Chester Johnson, Henry Snyder Gehman, and Edmund Harris Kase. Princeton University Studies in Papyrology, 3. Princeton: Princeton University.

Prentice, William Kelley
    1923   "Callisthenes, the Original Historian of Alexander." *TAPA*
                54:74–85.

Priest, John
    1976   Review of *Psychoanalysis and the Bible,* by Dorothy F. Zeligs;
                and of *The Choicemaker,* by Elizabeth B. Howes and Sheila
                Moon. *JBL* 95:661–63.

Princeton Encyclopedia of Classical Sites
    1976   *Princeton Encyclopedia of Classical Sites,* ed. Richard
                Stillwell, William L. MacDonald, Marian Holland McAllister.
                Princeton: Princeton University.

Purinton, Carl Everett
    1928   *Translation Greek in the Wisdom of Solomon.* Dissertation,
                Yale University. New Haven. See also same title in *JBL*
                47:276–304.

PYale
    1967   *Yale Papyri in the Beinecke Rare Book and Manuscript
                Library,* ed. by John F. Oates, Alan E. Samuel, and Charles
                Bradford Welles. *ASP,* 2. New Haven: ASP.

Raubitschek, Antony Erich and Lilian H. Jeffery
    1949   *Dedications from the Athenian Akropolis: A Catalogue of the
                Inscriptions of the Sixth and Fifth Centuries B.C.* Cambridge:
                Archaeological Institute of America.

Rawson, Beryl
    1974   "Roman Concubinage and Other *De Facto* Marriages." *TAPA*
                104:279–305.

Reardon, B. P.
    1982   "Theme, structure, and narrative in Chariton." *YCS* 27:1–27.

Reckford, Kenneth J.
    1977   "Catharsis and Dream-Interpretation in Aristophanes'
                Wasps." TAPA 107:283–312.

Reese, James M.
    1970   *Hellenistic Influence on the Book of Wisdom and its Conse-
                quences.* Analecta Biblica, 41. Rome: Pontifical Biblical
                Institute.

Reinhold, Meyer
    1971   "Usurpation of Status and Status Symbols in the Roman
                Empire." *Historia* 20:275–302.

Remus, Harold
  1982   "Does Terminology Distinguish Early Christian from Pagan
            Miracles?" *JBL* 101:531–51.

Renehan, Robert
  1982   *Greek Lexicographical Notes: A Critical Supplement to the
            Greek-English Lexicon of Liddell-Scott-Jones.* Hypomnemata,
            2d series. Untersuchungen zur Antike und zu ihrem
            Nachleben, 74/2. Göttingen: Vandenhoeck & Ruprecht.

Research Tools for the Classics
  1980   *Research Tools for the Classics,* ed. by Roger S. Bagnall. Chico:
            Scholars Press.

Reumann, John
  1964   Review of *Who Crucified Jesus?,* by Solomon Zeitlin. *JBL*
            84:84–86.

Richard, Earl
  1979   "The Polemical Character of the Joseph Episode in Acts 7."
            JBL 98:255–67.

Richardson, Bessie Ellen
  1933   *Old Age Among the Greeks: The Greek Portrayal of Old Age
            in Literature, Art, and Inscriptions, with a Study of the
            Duration of Life among the Ancient Greeks on the Basis of
            Inscriptional Evidence.* The Johns Hopkins Studies in
            Archeology 16. Baltimore: Johns Hopkins.

Riddle, Donald W.
  1947   "Reassessing the Religious Importance of Paul." In
            Willoughby 1947:314–28.

Rife, John Merle
  1933   "The Mechanics of Translation Greek." *JBL* 52:244–52.

  1941   "The Literary Background of Revelation II-III." *JBL*
            60:179–82.

Rigg, Horace Abram, Jr.
  1945   "Barabbas." *JBL* 64:417–56.

Rigsby, Kent
  1966   "Bibliography of the Works of C. Bradford Welles." In *Essays
            in Honor of C. Bradford Welles,* ix-xxii. *ASP,* 1. New Haven:
            ASP.

Ringwood, Irene Cecilia
  1927   *Agonistic Features of Local Greek Festivals Chiefly from
            Inscriptional Evidence.* Poughkeepsie, NY.

Robbins, Vernon K.
1978   "By Land and by Sea: The We-Passages and Ancient Sea
        Voyages." In *Perspectives on Luke-Acts* ed. by Charles H.
        Talbert, 215–242. Danville, VA: Association of Baptist
        Professors of Religion.

Robertson Festschrift
1933   *Greek Papyri of the First Century, Presented to Archibald
        Thomas Robertson on the Occasion of his Seventieth Birthday,*
        by William Hersey Davis. New York: Harper.

Robertson, Archibald Thomas
1908   *A Short Grammar of the Greek New Testament.* New York:
        Armstrong and Son.

1914   *A Grammar of the Greek New Testament in the Light of
        Historical Research.* New York: Hodder and Stoughton,
        Doran.

[1914] 1931 *A Grammar of the Greek New Testament in the Light of
        Historical Research.* 4th ed. New York: Hodder and
        Stoughton, Doran.

Robertson, A. T., and William Hersey Davis
1931   *A New Short Grammar of the Greek Testament.* New York:
        Harper.

Roberts, Louis
1968   *A Concordance of Lucretius.* Supplement to *AGON.* Berkeley:
        University of California.

Robinson, Benjamin W.
1904   "Some Elements of Forcefulness in Jesus' Comparisons." *JBL*
        23:106–79.

Robinson, Charles Alexander, Jr.
1943   "Alexander's Deification." *AJP* 64:286–301.

Robinson, David Moore
1924   "A New Latin Economic Edict from Pisidian Antioch." *TAPA*
        55:5–20.

1926   "Greek and Latin Inscriptions from Asia Minor." *TAPA*
        57:195–238.

Robinson, David Moore and Edward J. Fluck
1937   *A Study of the Greek Love-Names Including a Discussion of
        Paederasty and a Prosopographia.* Baltimore: Johns Hopkins.

Robinson, Edward
1836   *A Greek and English Lexicon of the New Testament.* Boston:
        Crocker and Brewster.

Robinson, William Childs
1965   Review of *Jesus and the Son of Man,* by A. J. B. Higgins. *JBL* 84:460–61.

Roebuck, Carl Angus
1951   *Corinth: Results of Excavations Conducted by ASCSA: The Asklepieion and Lerna,* Based on the Excavations and Preliminary Studies of F. J. de Waele. Princeton: ASCSA.

Rogers, Robert Samuel
1952   "A Tacitean Pattern in Narrating Treason-Trials." *TAPA* 83:279–311.

1959   "The Emperor's Displeasure—*amicitiam renuntiare.*" *TAPA* 90:224–37.

Rogers, Thomas
1968   *A Practical List of Greek Word Roots with Greek and English Derivatives.* Nashville: Abingdon.

Roper, Theresa K.
1979   "Nero, Seneca and Tigellinus." *Historia* 28:346–57.

Ropes, Charles Joseph Hardy
1902   "The Literary Work of Joseph Henry Thayer." *AJT* 6:285–93.

Rose, Herbert Jennings
1938   "A Colloquialism in Plato, *Rep.* 621b8." *HTR* 31:91–92.

Rosivach, Vincent J.
1978   "Sources of Some Errors in Catullan Commentaries." *TAPA* 108:203–16.

Rostovtzeff, Mikhail Ivanovitsch
1926   *The Social and Economic History of the Roman Empire.* (2d ed. rev. by Peter Marshall Fraser; Oxford: Oxford University [1957].)
1941   *The Social and Economic History of the Hellenistic World.* 3 vols. Oxford: Oxford University.

Rowe, Galen O.
1967   "Dramatic Structure in Caesar's *Bellum Civile.*" *TAPA* 98:399–414.

Rowell, Henry Thompson
1954   "Seventy-Five Years of the *American Journal of Philology.*" *AJP* 75:33–358.

Russell, Elbert
1932   "Possible Influence of the Mysteries on the Form and Inter-relation of the Johannine Writings." *JBL* 51:336–51.

Ryberg, Inez Scott
  1942   "Tacitus' Art of Innuendo." *TAPA* 73:383–404.

Safrai, Samuel
  1974–76   See *Jewish People.*

Sage, Evan T.
  1919   "The Publication of Martial's Poems." *TAPA* 50:168–76.

Sampley, J. Paul
  1980   *Pauline Partnership in Christ: Christian Community and Commitment in Light of Roman Law.* Philadelphia: Fortress.

Samuel, Alan E.
  1965   "The Role of *Paramone* Clauses in Ancient Documents." *JJP* 15:221–311.

  1972   *Greek and Roman Chronology: Calendars and Years in Classical Antiquity.* Handbuch der Altertumswissenschaft, 1/7. Munich: Beck.

Sanders, Ed Parish
  1977   *Paul and Palestinian Judaism, A Comparison of Patterns of Religion.* Philadelphia: Fortress.

Sanders, Henry Arthur
  1927   "Francis Willey Kelsey." *CP* 22:308–10.

  1935   Edition of *A Third-Century Papyrus Codex of the Epistles of Paul.* University of Michigan Studies, Humanistic Series, 38. Ann Arbor: University of Michigan.

Sanders, Jack T.
  1962   "The Transition from Opening Epistolary Thanksgiving to Body in the Letters of the Pauline Corpus." *JBL* 81:348–62.

  1971   *The New Testament Christological Hymns: Their Historical Religious Background.* Society of New Testament Studies Monograph Series, 15. Cambridge, England: Cambridge University.

Sandmel, Samuel
  1958   Review of *Jewish Symbols in the Greco-Roman Period*, vols. 4–6, by E. R. Goodenough. *JBL* 77:380–83.

  1962   "Parallelomania." *JBL* 81:1–13.

  1979   *Philo of Alexandria: An Introduction.* New York: Oxford University.

Sandys, John Edwin
  1908   *A History of Classical Scholarship.* Vol. 3, esp. pp. 450–470. Cambridge, England: Cambridge University.

Sandy, Gerald N.
1970   "Petronius and the Tradition of the Interpolated Narrative."
             TAPA 101:463–76.

Sanford, Eva Matthews
1935   "Propaganda and Censorship in the Transmission of
             Josephus." *TAPA* 66:127–45.

Sardis
1916   *Sardis.* Vol. 6. Part 1. *Lydian Inscriptions,* ed. by Enno
             Littmann. Leiden: Brill.

1932   *Sardis.* Vol. 7. *Greek and Latin Inscriptions,* ed. by William
             Hepburn Buckler and David Moore Robinson. Publications
             of the American Society for the Excavation of Sardis. Leiden:
             Brill.

Saunders, Ernest W.
1982   *Searching the Scriptures. A History of the Society of Biblical
             Literature, 1880–1980.* Chico: Scholars Press.

Schmidt, Nathaniel
1900   "The 'Son of Man' in the Book of Daniel." *JBL* 19:22–28.

1931   "Memoir on the History of the Society: The Society of
             Biblical Literature and Exegesis, 1880–1930." *JBL* 50:xiv–xxiii.

Schork, R. Joseph
1971   "*Aemulos Reges:* Allusion and Theme in Horace 3.16." *TAPA*
             102:515–39.

Schroyer, Montgomery J.
1936   "Alexandrian Jewish Literalists." *JBL* 55:261–84.

Schubert, Paul
1935   *The Form and Function of the Pauline Thanksgiving.* Disserta-
             tion, University of Chicago. Chicago: University of Chicago
             Libraries. Also published as BZNW, 20 (1939).

Schuetze, Martin
1933   *Academic Illusions in the Field of Letters and the Arts. A
             Survey, a Criticism, a New Approach, and a Comprehensive
             Plan for Reorganizing the Study of Letters and Arts.* Chicago:
             University of Chicago.

Schulte, William Henry
[1931] 1935   *Index verborum Valerianus.* Iowa Studies in Classical
             Philology, 3.

1937   "The Making and Use of an *Index Verborum.*" *Classical
             Bulletin,* 13 (March):46–47.

Scott, John Adam
  1921   *The Unity of Homer.* Berkeley: University of California.

  1925   "Addresses in Memory of Professor Gildersleeve." *PAPA* 56:xix-xxviii.

  1930   Review of *Latin Grammar,* by Charles Elmer. *CJ* 25:549–54.

Scott, Kenneth
  1928   "The Deification of Demetrius Poliorcetes." *AJP* 49:137–66; 217–39.

  1929   "Plutarch and the Ruler Cult." *TAPA* 60:117–35.

  1930   "Emperor Worship in Ovid." *TAPA* 61:43–69.

  1931   "The Significance of Statues in Precious Metals in Emperor Worship." *TAPA* 62:101–23.

  1932   "Mussolini and the Roman Empire." *CJ* 27:645–57.

Searles, Helen McGaffey
  1898   *A Lexicographical Study of the Greek Inscriptions.* Studies in Classical Philology, 2. Chicago: University of Chicago.

Sebeok, Thomas A., ed.
  1963–76   *Current Trends in Linguistics.* 14 vols. The Hague: Mouton.

Segal, Charles
  1967   "Pindar's Seventh *Nemean*." *TAPA* 98:431–80.

  1968   "Ancient Texts and Modern Criticism: Some Recent Trends in Classical Literary Studies." *Arethusa* 1:1–25.

  1977   "Sophocles *Trachiniae:* myth, poetry, and heroic values." *YCS* 25:99–158.

  1981   "Horace's Soracte Ode (1,9): Of Interpretation, Philogic and Hermeneutic." In *Contemporary Literary Hermeneutics* 1981:287–92.

Shanahan, Ellen
  1982   "Is There an Hermetic Hermeneutic?" In *Society of Biblical Literature 1982 Seminar Papers,* ed. by Kent Harold Richards, 515–19. Chico: Scholars Press.

Sherk, Robert K.
  1962   "The Charles E. Wilbour Inscriptions from Egypt." *TAPA* 93:443–48.

  1969   *Roman Documents From the Greek East: "Senatus Consulta" and "Epistulae" to the Age of Augustus.* Baltimore: Johns Hopkins.

Shero, Lucius Rogers
1963 "The American Philological Association: An Historical Sketch." *PAPA* 94:x-l.

Shorey, Paul
1906a "Philology and Classical Philology." *CJ* 1:169–96.

1906b "Relations of Classical Literature to Other Branches of Learning." In *Congress of Arts and Science, Universal Exposition St. Louis, 1904*, 3:370–385. Boston: Houghton, Mifflin.

1910 "The Case for the Classics." *The School Review* 18:585–617. Reprinted in *University Bulletin*, n.s. ll(no. 17):38–70.

1916 "Illogical Idiom." *TAPA* 47:205–34.

1917 "The Assault on Humanism, II." *The Atlantic Monthly* 120 (July):94–105.

1919 "Fifty Years of Classical Studies in America." *TAPA* 50:33–61.

1921 "Cultural vs. Materialistic Education." (Address at the First Cornell Convention, Cleveland, 13 May 1921.) *Cornell Alumni News* 23:437–40.

1925a "Henry Arthur Jones." *The Trend*. N. s. 1 (May 30):88–89 and 92.

1925b "The Deathless Classics." *The Saturday Review of Literature* 1 (July 25):925–26.

1926 "Literature and Pseudo-Science in the College." *The Smith Alumnae Quarterly* 17:405–18.

1927 "Democracy and Scholarship." *School and Society* 26(Saturday, December 24):792–98.

1933 *What Plato Said*. Chicago: University of Chicago.

Sihler, Ernest Gottlieb
1902 "Klassisiche Studien und Klassischer Unterricht in den Vereinigten Staaten, II." *Neue Jahrbucher für Pädagogik* 15:503–16.

1908 *Testimonium Animae, or Greek and Roman Before Jesus Christ: A Series of Essays and Sketches Dealing with the Spiritual Elements in Classical Civilization*. New York: Stechert.

1923 *From Augustus to Augustine: Essays and Studies Dealing with the Contact and Conflict of Classic Paganism and Christianity*. Cambridge, England: Cambridge University.

1930 *From Maumee to Thames and Tiber: The Life Story of an American Classical Scholar*. Washington Square East, New York: New York University.

1933   "The First Twelve Roman Emperors, Their Morals and Characters: A Complement to the *Testimonium Animae.*" *Bibliotheca Sacra* 90:159–74; 331–42; 438–48.

Silberschlag, Eisig
1933   "The Earliest Record of Jews in Asia Minor." *JBL* 52:66–77.

Silva, Moises
1983   *Biblical Words and Their Meaning: An Introduction to Lexical Semantics.* Grand Rapids: Zondervan.

Sinclair, John McH.
1968   "A Technique of Stylistics Description." *Language and Style* 1:215–42.

Skinner, Marilyn B.
1982   "Pretty Lesbius." *TAPA* 112:197–208.

Smith, Gerald Birney, ed.
1927   *Religious Thought in the Last Quarter Century.* Chicago: University of Chicago.

Smith, Jacob Brubaker
1955   *Greek-English Concordance to the New Testament: A Tabular and Statistical Greek-English Concordance Based on the King James Version, with an English-to-Greek Index.* Scottdale, PA: Herald.

Smith, Jonathan Z.
1975   "Good News is No News: Aretalogy and Gospel." In *Christianity, Judaism, and other Greco-Roman Cults. Studies for Morton Smith at Sixty.* Studies in Judaism and Late Antiquity 12, 21–38. Leiden: Brill.

Smith, Morton
1961   Review of *Pseudonymität im Altertum, Ihre Formen und Ihre Gründe*, by Josef A. Sint. *JBL* 80:188–89.

1967   "Goodenough's Jewish Symbols in Retrospect." *JBL* 86:53–68.

1969   "The Present State of Old Testament Studies." *JBL* 88:19–35.

1971   "Prolegomena to a Discussion of Aretalogies, Divine Men, the Gospels and Jesus." *JBL* 90:174–99.

1973a   *The Secret Gospel: The Discovery and Interpretation of the Secret Gospel According to Mark.* New York: Harper.

1973b   *Clement of Alexandria and a Secret Gospel of Mark.* Cambridge: Harvard University.

1980   "Pauline Worship as Seen by Pagans." *HTR* 73:241–49.

Smith, Wesley D.
1965   "So-called Possession in Pre-Christian Greece." *TAPA* 96:403–26.

Smutny, Robert Jaroslav
1966   *Greek and Latin Inscriptions at Berkeley.* Berkeley: University of California.

Smyth, Herbert Weir
1894   *The Sounds and Inflections of the Greek Dialects: Ionic.* Oxford: Oxford University.

1900   *The Greek Melic Poets.* New York: Macmillan.

1906   "The Greek Language in its Relation to the Psychology of the Ancient Greeks." In *Congress of Arts and Science, Universal Exposition, St. Louis, 1904,* ed. by Howard J. Rogers, 3:131–161. Boston: Houghton, Mifflin.

1920   *A Greek Grammar for Colleges.* New York: American Book Co.

1956   *Greek Grammar,* rev. ed. by Gordon Messing. Cambridge: Harvard University.

Snowden, Frank M.
1948   "The Negro in Ancient Greece." *American Anthropologist* 50:31–44. (Abstract in *TAPA* 77 [1946]:322–23.)

Snyder, Graydon Fisher
1985   *Ante Pacem: Archeological Evidence of Church Life Before Constantine.* Atlanta: Mercer University.

Sophocles, Evangelinus Apostolides
1842   *A Romaic Grammar, Accompanied by a Chrestomathy with a Vocabulary.* Hartford: H. Huntington.

1847   *A Greek Grammar, for the Use of Schools and Colleges.* Hartford: H. Huntington, and Belkamp and Hamersly.

1857   *Romaic or, Modern Greek Grammar.* Boston: Hickling, Swan, and Brewer.

1870   *Greek Lexicon of the Roman and Byzantine Periods from B.C. 146 to A.D. 1100.* Boston: Little, Brown.

Sowers, Sidney G.
1965   *The Hermeneutics of Philo and Hebrews.* Richmond, Virginia: Knox.

Spingarn, Joel Elias
[1910] 1940   "The New Criticism." In Foerster [1930], 1940:426–50. Also reprinted in *Criticism in America: Its Function and Status,* 9–45 (New York: Harcourt, Brace [1924]).

Spivak, Gayatri Chakravorty
  1976   "Preface" in *Of Grammatology,* by Jacques Derrida.
              Baltimore: Johns Hopkins.

Sprague, Rosamond Kent
  1967   "Parmenides, Plato, and 1 Corinthians 12." *JBL* 86:211–13.

Standerwick, Henry Fischer
  1932   *Etymological Studies in the Greek Dialect-inscriptions.*
              Columbia University Language Dissertations, 10. Baltimore:
              Waverly.

Stearns, Wallace N.
  1896   "Supplement" to a *Greek-English Lexicon to the New Testa-
              ment, Revised and Enlarged by Thomas Sheldon Green.*
              Boston: H. L. Hastings.

Stegenga, John
  1963   *The Greek-English Analytical Concordance of the Greek-
              English New Testament.* Jackson, MS: Hellenes-English
              Biblical Foundation.

Stern, Menahem
  1974   "The Jewish Diaspora." In *Jewish People,* 1974–76, 1:117–83.

  1976   "The Jews in Greek and Latin Literature." In *Jewish People,*
              1974–76, 2:1101–59.

Sterrett, John Robert Sitlington
  1885   *Preliminary Report of an Archaeological Journey Made in Asia
              Minor During the Summer of 1884.* Boston: Cupples, Upham.

Stewart, Zeph, ed.
  1972   *Arthur Darby Nock: Essays on Religion and the Ancient
              World.* 2 vols. Cambridge: Harvard University.

Stillwell, Richard
  1941   *Antioch on the Orontes.* III. Princeton: Princeton University.

Stinespring, William Franklin
  1939   "The Critical Faculty of Edward Robinson." *JBL* 58:379–87.

Stirewalt, Martin Luther, Jr.
  1974   Review of *Form and Structure of the Familiar Greek Letter of
              Recommendation,* by Chan-Hie Kim. *JBL* 93:479–80.

Stone, Michael E.
  1984   See *Jewish Writings.*

Stowers, Stanley Kent
  1981   *The Diatribe and Paul's Letter to the Romans.* SBLDS, 57.
              Chico: Scholars Press.

1984   "Social Status, Public Speaking and Private Teaching: The Circumstances of Paul's Preaching Activity." *Novum Testamentum* 26:59–82.

Strong, James
1894   *The Exhaustive Concordance of the Bible.* New York: Hunt and Eaton.

Strugnell, John
1958   "Flavius Josephus and the Essenes: Antiquities XVIII. 18–22." *JBL* 77:106–15.

Study of the Bible Today and Tomorrow
1947   *See* Willoughby, 1947.

Stukey, Harold J.
1936   "Purity in Fifth and Fourth Century Religion." *TAPA* 67:286–95.

Sturtevant, Edgar Howard
1920   *The Pronunciation of Greek and Latin, The Sounds and Accents.* Chicago: University of Chicago.

1933   *A Comparative Grammar of the Hittite Language.* Philadelphia: Linguistic Society of America.

Sturtevant, Edgar Howard and Emma Adelaide Hahn
1951   *A Comparative Grammar of the Hittite Language.* New Haven: Yale University.

Sullivan, John P.
1961   "Two Problems in Roman Love Elegy." *TAPA* 92:522–36.

1981   "Synchronic and Diachronic Aspects of Some Related Poems of Martial." In *Contemporary Literary Hermeneutics,* 1981:215–25.

Swarney, Paul R.
1970   *The Ptolemaic and Roman Idios Logos. ASP,* 8. Toronto: Hakkert.

Swift, Louis J.
1965   "Arnobius and Lactantius: Two Views of the Pagan Poets." *TAPA* 96:439–48.

Talbert, Charles Harold
1974   *Literary Patterns, Theological Themes and the Genre of Luke-Acts. SBLMS,* 20. Missoula: SBL, Scholars Press.

1975   Review of *Die Abschiedsrede des Paulus an die Kirche Apg 20, 17–38,* by Hans-Joachim Michel. *JBL* 94:145.

1977   *What is a Gospel? The Genre of the Canonical Gospels.*
        Philadelphia: Fortress.

1978   "Biographies of Philosophers and Rulers as Instruments of
        Religious Propaganda in Mediterranean Antiquity." In *ANRW,*
        11, *Principat* 16/2:1619–51.

1980   "Prophecies of Future Greatness: The Contribution of
        Greco-Roman Biographies to an Understanding of Luke
        1:5–4:15." In *The Divine Helmsman: Studies on God's Control
        of Human Events, Presented to Lou H. Silberman,* ed. James L.
        Crenshaw and Samuel Sandmel, 129–41. New York: KTAV.

Tarán, Leonardo, ed.
1980   *Paul Shorey, Selected Papers.* New York: Garland.

Tanzer, Helen H.
1926   "The Humanity of the Romans." *PAPA* 57:xxiii–xxiv.

Taylor, Archer
1965   "Folklore and the Student of Literature." In *The Study of
        Folklore,* ed. Alan Dundes, 25–33. Englewood Cliffs, NJ:
        Prentice Hall.

Taylor, Greer M.
1966   "The Function of *PISTIS CHRISTOU* in Galatians." *JBL*
        85:58–76.

Taylor, Hugh Scott
1947   "A Community of Scholars." In *The Modern Princeton,* ed.
        Charles G. Osgood, et al. Princeton: Princeton University.

Taylor, Lily Ross
1912   *The Cults of Ostia.* Bryn Mawr Monograph, 11. Bryn Mawr:
        Bryn Mawr College.

1920   "The Worship of Augustus in Italy During His Lifetime." *TAPA*
        51:116–33.

1931   *The Divinity of the Roman Emperor.* Philological Monograph,
        1. Middletown, Connecticut: APA.

1933   "Quirinius and the Census of Judaea." *AJP* 54:120–33.

Teeple, Howard M.
1960   "Notes on Theologians' Approach to the Bible." *JBL*
        79:164–66.

Terry, Milton S.
1894   "Scope and Plan of the Apocalypse of John." *JBL* 13:91–100.

Thayer, Joseph Henry
1886   *A Greek-English Lexicon of the New Testament, being Grimm's Wilke's Clavis Novi Testamenti.* Translated, revised, and enlarged by J. H. Thayer. New York: American Book Co.

1895   "The Historical Element in the New Testament." *JBL* 14:1–18.

1899   "Recent Discoveries Respecting the Lord's Supper." *JBL* 18:110–31.

Thompson, James W.
1975   " 'That Which Cannot be Shaken': Some Metaphysical Assumptions in Heb 12:27." *JBL* 94:580–87.

1979   "Hebrews 9 and Hellenistic Concepts of Sacrifice." *JBL* 98:567–78.

Thompson, Leonard L.
1981   "The Jordan Crossing: *SIDQOT* Yahweh and World Building." *JBL* 100:343–58.

Thornton, Mary Elizabeth Kelly
1971   "Nero's New Deal." *TAPA* 102:621–29.

Threatte, Leslie
1980   *The Grammar of Attic Inscriptions.* Vol. 1. *Phonology.* Berlin: de Gruyter.

Torrey, Charles Cutler
1892   "Maccabees (Family)," and "Maccabees (Books)." In *Encyclopedia Biblica*, 3, cols. 2850–2858 and 2858–2886. London: Adam & Black.

1942   "Notes on the Greek Text of Enoch." *JAOS* 62:52–60.

1945   *The Apocryphal Literature: A Brief Introduction.* New Haven: Yale University.

Tracy, Sterling
1928   "III Maccabees and Pseudo-Aristeas: A Study." *YCS* 1:239–52.

Ullman, Berthold Louis
1945   "We want a Vergilian Peace." *CJ* 41:1–3.

Vachek, Josef, ed.
1966   *The Linguistic School of Prague: An Introduction to Its Theory and Practice.* Bloomington IN: Indiana University.

Value of the Classics
1917   *Value of the Classics* (A record of the Addresses delivered at the Conference on Classical Studies in Liberal Education held at Princeton University, 2 June 1917, together with an introduction and a collection of statements and statistics), ed. by Andrew F. West, et al. Princeton: Princeton University.

Van Cleef, Frank Louis
1895   *Index Antiphonteus.* Cornell Studies in Classical Philology, 5. Boston: Ginn.

Van Hook, La Rue
1920   "The Exposure of Infants at Athens." *TAPA* 51:134–45.

Van Nostrand, John James
1925   *The Imperial Domains of Africa Proconsularis: An Epigraphical Study.* University of California Publications in History 14, no. 1:1–88.

Van Nortwick, Thomas
1979   "Penelope and Nausicaa." *TAPA* 109:63–85.

Vardaman, Jerry
1962   "A New Inscription which Mentions Pilate as 'Prefect' " *JBL* 81:70–71.

Via, Dan Otto
1974   "Parable and Example Story: A Literary-Structuralist Approach." *Semeia* 1:105–33.

1975   *Kerygma and Comedy in the New Testament: A Structuralist Approach to Hermeneutic.* Philadelphia: Fortress.

Vincent, Marvin Richardson
1887–1900   *Word Studies in the New Testament.* 4 vols. New York: Scribner.

Vlastos, Gregory
1948   Review of *Asclepius,* by Emma J. Edelstein and Ludwig Edelstein. *Review of Religions* 13:269–90.

Wacholder, Ben Zion
1974   *Eupolemus: A Study of Judaeo-Greek Literature.* Cincinnati: Hebrew Union College.

Waite, Stephen V. F.
1970   "Computers and the Classics." *Computers and the Humanities* 5:47–51.

1972   "Computers and Classical Literature: 1971–1972." *Computers and the Humanities* 7:99–104.

Walbank, Frank William
1960   "History and Tragedy." *Historia* 9:216–34.

Walbank, Michael B.
1978   *Athenian Proxenies of the Fifth Century B.C.* Toronto: Samuel Stevens.

Wallach, Luitpold
    1943   "The Parable of the Blind and the Lame: A Study in Com-
                parative Literature." *JBL* 62:333–39.

Walther, James Arthur
    1966   *New Testament Greek Workbook: An Inductive Study of the
                Complete Text of the Gospel of John.* Chicago: University of
                Chicago.

Walton, Alice
    1894   *The Cult of Asklepios.* Cornell Studies in Classical Philology,
                3.

Warwick, Henrietta Holm
    1975   *A Vergil Concordance.* Minneapolis: University of Minnesota.

Watson, Patricia
    1982   "Ovid and *Cultus: Ars Amatoria* 3. 113–28." *TAPA* 112:237–44.

Wedek, Harry E.
    1929   "Affection for Children Among the Romans." *CW* 22:193–95.

Weiss, Herold
    1967   "The *Pagani* Among the Contemporaries of the First Chris-
                tians." *JBL* 86:42–52.

Wellek, René
    [1953] 1967 "Literary Scholarship." In *American Scholarship* 1953:111–45.

Welles, Charles Bradford
    1934   *Royal Correspondence in the Hellenistic Period.* New Haven:
                Yale University. Reprint, by Ares. 1974.

West, Allen Brown
    1931   *Corinth. Results of Excavations Conducted by the American
                School of Classical Studies at Athens.* Vol. 8, pt. 2. *Latin
                Inscriptions 1896–1926.* Cambridge: Harvard University.

West, Andrew F., et al., eds.
    1917   See *Value of the Classics,* 1917.

Westermann William Linn
    1929   *Upon Slavery in Ptolemaic Egypt.* (= *PCol.I* [PCol.Inv. 480].)
                New York: Columbia University.

    1948   "The Paramone as General Service Contract." *JJP* 2:9–50.

    1954   *Apokrimata: Decisions of Septimius Severus on Legal Matters.
                Text, Translation, and Historical Analysis.* Legal Commentary
                by A. Arthur Schiller. New York: Columbia University. (The
                text is re-edited in Youtie-Schiller, 1955.)

Westington, Mars McClelland
  1938   *Atrocities in Roman Warfare to 133 B.C.* Chicago: University of Chicago.

  1944   "War Hits the Classics." *Classical Outlook* 21(January):37.

  1944–45 "Nazi Germany and Ancient Sparta." *Education* 65:152–64.

Wetmore, Monroe Nichols
  1911   *Index Verborum Vergilianus.* New Haven: Yale University. (The second printing, 1930, displays a two-page list of "Errata et Corrigenda.")

  1912   *Index Verborum Catullianus.* New Haven: Yale University.

Whatmough, Joshua
  1963   *The Dialects of Ancient Gaul: Grammar.* Pt. 1. *Alpine Regions Narbonensis, Aquitania, Germania Inferior.* Ann Arbor: Edwards Brothers.

  1970   *The Dialects of Ancient Gaul: Prolegomena and Records of the Dialects.* Cambridge: Harvard University.

Wheeler, Benjamin Ide
  1899   *Dionysus and Immortality: The Greek Faith in Immortality as Affected by the Rise of Individualism.* Ingersoll Lecture 1898–1899. Boston: Houghton, Mifflin.

  1899   "Language as Interpreter of Life." *Atlantic Monthly* 84 (October):459–66.

  1900   "The Place of Philology." *PAPA* 31:li-lvii.

White, John Lee
  1971   "Introductory Formulae in the Body of the Pauline Letter." *JBL* 90:91–97.

  1972a   *The Form and Function of the Official Petition: A Study in Greek Epistolography.* SBLDS, 5. Missoula: SBL.

  1972b   *The Form and Function of the Body of the Greek Letter: A Study of the Letter-Body in the Non-Literary Papyri and in Paul the Apostle.* SBLDS, 2. Missoula: SBL.

White, John Williams
  1896   *The First Greek Book.* Boston: Ginn.

White, J. W., and Morris H. Morgan
  1892   *An Illustrated Dictionary to Xenophon's Anabasis, with Groups of Words Etymologically Related.* Boston: Ginn.

Whitman, Cedric Hubbell
  1958   *Homer and the Heroic Tradition.* Cambridge: Harvard University.

Whitney, J. Ernest
1888   "The 'Continued Allegory' in the First Book of the *Faery Queene.*" *TAPA* 19:40–69.

Wikgren, Allen, Ernest Colwell, and Ralph Marcus
1947   *Hellenistic Greek Texts.* Chicago: University of Chicago.

Wilder, Amos Niven
1931   "The Nature of Jewish Eschatology." *JBL* 50:201–6.

1956   "Scholars, Theologians, and Ancient Rhetoric." *JBL* 75:1–11.

1976   *Theopoetic: Theology and the Religious Imagination.* Philadelphia: Fortress.

Williams, Charles Kaufman, II
1981   "The City of Corinth and its Domestic Religion." *Hesperia* 50:408–421.

Willoughby, Harold Rideout
1922   "The Next Step in New Testament Study." *Journal of Religion* 2:159–78.

1927   "The Study of Early Christianity." In *Religious Thought in the Last Quarter Century,* ed. George Birney Smith, 42–69. Chicago: University of Chicago.

1929   *Pagan Regeneration. A Study of Mystery Initiation in the Graeco-Roman World.* Chicago: University of Chicago.

1947   Edition of *The Study of the Bible Today and Tomorrow.* Chicago: University of Chicago.

1954   Review of *Hellenistic Religions,* by Frederick C. Grant. *JBL* 73:171–72.

Winer and Thayer
1869   *A Grammar of the Idiom of the New Testament, Prepared as a Solid Basis for the Interpretation of the New Testament,* by George Benedict Winer. Translation and revision by Joseph Henry Thayer of the 7th ed. "enlarged and improved" by Gottlieb Lünemann. Andover: Draper. (New impression with alterations, 1874.)

Winsbey, Carlton L.
1979   *Syntax of New Testament Greek.* Washington, DC: University Press of America.

Winslow, Donald
1971   "Religion and the Early Roman Empire." In *Catacombs and the Colosseum,* 1971:237–54.

Winter, John Garrett
  1933   *Life and Letters in the Papyri*. The Jerome Lectures. Ann
              Arbor: University of Michigan.

Winter, Paul
  [1961] 1974 *On the Trial of Jesus*. 2d ed. Berlin: de Gruyter.

Wolfson, Harry Austryn
  1947   *Philo: Foundations of Religious Philosophy in Judaism, Chris-
              tianity and Islam*. Cambridge: Harvard University.

Woodbury, George E.
  1903   "Editorial." *Journal of Comparative Literature* 1:3–9.

Woodbury, Leonard
  1978   "The Gratitude of the Locrian Maiden: Pindar *Pyth.* 2.18–20."
              TAPA 108:285–99.

  1979   "Gold Hair and Grey, Or the Game of Love: Anacreon Fr.
              13:358 *PMG*, 13 Gentili." *TAPA* 109:277–87.

Yerkes, Royden Keith
  1952   *Sacrifice in Greek and Roman Religions and Early Judaism*.
              New York: Scribner.

Yoder, James
  1961   *Concordance to the Distinctive Greek Text of Codex Bezae*.
              Grand Rapids: Eerdmans.

Young, Norma D.
  1939   *Index verborum Silianus*. Iowa City: Athens Press.

Youtie, Herbert Chayyim
  1936   "Publicans and Sinners." *Michigan Alumnus Quarterly Review*
              43:650–62.

  1944a   "Sambathis." *HTR* 37:209–18.

  1944b   Review of *PPrinc.III*, 1942. *CP* 39:119–23.

  1951   The Heidelberg Festival Papyrus: A Reinterpretation. In
              Johnson Festschrift, 1951:178–208.

  1958   *The Textual Criticism of Documentary Papyri: Prolegomena*,
              ed. by E. G. Turner. University of London, Institute of
              Classical Studies Bulletin, Supplement 6.

  1973–75   *Scriptiunculae*. 3 vols. Amsterdam: Hakkert. (The third
              volume contains concordances of Youtie's articles, reviews,
              and books, and various indexes.)

Youtie, H. C., and A. Arthur Schiller
  1955   "Second Thoughts on the Columbia Apokrimata (P.Col.123)."
              Chronique d' Egypte 30,60 (July):327–45.

Zeitlin, Froma I.

1965   "The Motif of the Corrupted Sacrifice in Aeschylus' *Oresteia*." *TAPA* 96:463–508.

1966   "Postscript to Sacrificial Imagery in the *Oresteia* (*Ag.* 1235–37)." *TAPA* 97:645–53.

1971   "Petronius as Paradox: Anarchy and Artistic Integrity." *TAPA* 102:631–84.

Zeitlin, Solomon

1931   *Josephus on Jesus, with Particular Reference to the Slavonic Josephus and the Hebrew Josippon.* Philadelphia: Dropsie College.

Zuntz, Gunther

1942   "Notes on the Greek Enoch." *JBL* 61:193–204.

1943   "The Greek Text of Enoch 102:1–3." *JBL* 63:53–54.

EPILOGUE

The debt of Western civilization to Greece and Rome is inestimable, and even Rome had to give way to Byzantine supremacy. And so it came to pass that Athens, the heart of classical Greece and the site of one of St. Paul's most memorable sermons, abides to this day a living symbol of humanity engaged in quests for truth and beauty.

On 13 October 1944, Sir Henry Maitland Wilson, Allied Commander in the Mediterranean, broadcast to the Greek people: "Your day of liberation is at hand." In less than twenty-four hours the Greek flag was flying over the Athenian Acropolis.

The German troops, many of whom had read Xenophon and Plato in the original, had treated Athens with some of the care that an invader with a cultural conscience ought to bestow, and some shared their bread with the populace, whose rations were severely limited because of Allied pressure on the ports. Certainly some thoughts must have reached back 2,424 years to another autumn day when the hordes of Xerxes heard a signal for retreat.

In observance of the occasion, the American Friends of Greece ran a special issue of the *Philhellene*, which included the following sonnet by Emma Adelaide Hahn, and which was reprinted in the *New York Herald Tribune*, "Week of Verse" for 3 December 1944 (section 2, p. 4):

The Liberation of Athens

Athens, who mother-city e'er shall be
For men not of a single race or age,
But all such as love beauty, or engage
In wisdom's quest, through all eternity—
Athens, where none to tyrants bend the knee;
Buskin and sock trod an untrammeled stage;
Laws ruled, not men; and one undaunted Sage
Drained hemlock that his spirit might go free—
Athens, who launched the ships that swept the foe
From Salamis' blue bay, and trained the voice
Whose eloquence against the invading force
Earned well the Crown—Athens still keeps her course!
As went the old, the new barbarians go;
And once again Greeks conquering rejoice.

DATE DUE

	261-2500		Printed in USA